The
New Basel
Capital Accord

Benton E. Gup

Culverhouse College of Commerce

University of Alabama

Australia · Canada · Mexico · Singapore · Spain · United Kingdom · United States

THOMSON

TM

The New Basel Capital Accord
Benton E. Gup

ISBN: 0-324-20298-9

Printed and bound in the United States by Phoenix
1 2 3 4 5 6 7 8 9 07 06 05 04

For more information, contact Texere, 622 Third Avenue, 10th Floor, New York, NY 10017, or find us on the Web at www.etexere.com.

Permission to reprint the contributed articles has been provided to TEXERE by the copyright holders.

This publication is designed to provide accurate and authoritative information in regard to the subject matter covered. It is sold with the understanding that the publisher is not engaged in rendering legal, accounting or other professional services. If legal advice or other expert assistance is required, the services of a competent professional person should be sought.

Composed by: Gex Publishing Services

Library of Congress Cataloging in Publication Data has been applied for.

The names of all companies or products mentioned herein are used for identification purposes only and may be trademarks or registered trademarks of their respective owners. Texere disclaims any affiliation, association, connection with, sponsorship, or endorsements by such owners.

PREFACE

The new Basel Capital Accord (Basel II) is scheduled to be implemented in December 2006 in those countries that are willing to adopt the new rules. More than 100 countries adopted the rules of the 1988 Basel Capital Accord (Basel I), which requires banks to have an 8% capital standard. It is not likely that as many countries will participate in Basel II because it is complex, costly, and contentious.

Basel II is *complex* because there are hundreds of pages of documentation describing the three methods that can be used to compute risk-based capital. The advanced method for computing capital requires vast amounts of data and computer models to predict losses and other factors. In addition, using different methods and models to compute the capital required for a given loan can result in different amounts of capital for that same loan. Thus, the complexity provides ample opportunities for regulatory and pricing arbitrage.

The *cost* for implementing Basel II is high. The costs range from an estimated $10 million for small banks to $150 million or more for large banks. In addition, there will be ongoing costs for maintaining the systems.

Basel II is *contentious*. It was created to deal with internationally active, large, complex financial organizations, and that does not describe most banks. Only 10 banking organizations in the United States will be required to implement the advanced internal ratings-based (A-IRB) approach, and the remaining 7,800-plus banks can opt in to the A-IRB approach, use the foundation internal ratings-based (IRB) approach, or continue to use a modified version of Basel I. In the European Union, all financial institutions are required to implement the Basel II approaches. The debate is still going on within other countries on whether to apply Basel II.

Against this background, this book presents the views about Basel II by authors who are academics and regulators from around the world. One common thread that runs through the chapters is that Basel II is not a finished product—a lot more work needs to be done before it can be implemented.

Benton E. Gup

DEDICATION

To Jean, Lincoln, Andrew, Carol, and Jeremy.

CHAPTER OUTLINE

An International Perspective

TABLE OF CONTENTS

Introduction to the Basel Capital Accords

Benton E. Gup

Basel, Switzerland, is the home of the Bank for International Settlements (BIS), an international organization that fosters cooperation toward monetary and financial stability. It serves as a bank for central banks, and it is the principal center for international cooperation among central banks.[1] Within the framework of international cooperation, the BIS formulates *recommendations* to the financial community aimed at strengthening the international financial system. For example, the 1988 Basle Capital Accord became an international standard. The New Basel Capital Accord is expected to replace it at the end of 2006.

Basle is located on the northern border of Switzerland, next to France and Germany. Notice the different spelling of Basle/Basel in the two accords. Basle is the French version of the city name, and Basel is the German version and the official name used in Switzerland. About 19% of the population in Switzerland speaks French, while 64% speaks German.[2] The BIS officially changed the spelling from Basle to Basel in May 1999 for its own uses. For simplicity, "Basel" is used in the rest of this book to refer to both accords.

THE BASEL COMMITTEE ON BANKING SUPERVISION

The Basel Committee on Banking Supervision was established by the central-bank Governors of the Group of Ten (G 10) countries in 1974, following the failure of Bankhus I. D. Herstatt in Cologne, Germany. The closure of this bank had a global impact because of

---

1. This brief description of the BIS is based on information from its Web site, *http://www. bis.org.*
2. **Merriam-Webster–Map of Switzerland,** (visited 11/6/02).

incomplete foreign exchange transactions. It disrupted the foreign exchange settlement operations of the Clearing House International Payments System (CHIPS) and resulted in losses for Herstatt's counterparties that had irrevocably paid out Deutsche mark to Herstatt that day.[3]

The Basel Committee is a committee of central bankers and regulators from Belgium, Canada, France, Germany, Italy, Japan, Luxembourg, the Netherlands, Spain, Sweden, Switzerland, United Kingdom, and the United States, who meet at the BIS. Although only 13 countries serve on the Basel Committee, more than 100 countries apply the Basel framework in their banking systems.[4] The Basel Committee originally focused on sharing information among its members. Over time, the focus shifted to international harmonization through the issuance of "best practices" papers, and the development of common supervisory standards among its members, although its standards are not legally binding.[5]

1988 CAPITAL ACCORD (BASEL I)

In 1988, the Basel Committee on Banking Supervision, acting under the BIS, endorsed the Basel Capital Accord. Subsequently, central bankers in other countries endorsed similar accords. The purposes of the 1988 Basel Capital Accord (Basel I) are to 1) harmonize international bank capital standards in order to strengthen the soundness and stability of the international banking system, and 2) to diminish a source of competitive inequality among international banks. It provided only one measure of risk and capital for internationally active banks. The single capital standard did not take into account that risks vary from bank to bank.

A cornerstone of the Basel I framework is that it provided for a minimum capital requirement of 8% for internationally active banks in order to 1) ensure an adequate level of capital, and 2) ensure competitive equality.

In the United States, the capital requirements apply to all FDIC-insured banks, and similar rules were applied to savings associations. Under the Federal Deposit Insurance Corporation

---

3. For further information about Bankhus Herstatt, see Gup (1998), Chapter 2.
4. "The New Basel Capital Accord: An Explanatory Note," 2001; also see: The Basel Committee on Banking Supervision, *http://www.bis.org/bcbs/aboutbcbs.htm.*
5. Hawke (February 27, 2003).

Improvement Act of 1991 (FDICIA), banks with total risk-based capital ratio of 8%–9.9% are considered "adequately capitalized," while a ratio of 10% or more is "well-capitalized." Banks with lower risk-based capital ratios are considered undercapitalized and may be subject to "prompt corrective action." Thus, the capital requirements in the United States are more stringent than in most other countries.

Under Basel I, bank capital has two tiers. Tier 1 includes shareholders equity and retained earnings, and it is 4%. Tier 2 includes additional internal and external funds available to the bank and also is 4%.[6] Basel I is a simple "one-size-fits-all" standard, and it focused primarily on credit risk. Basel I has four risk weights for the following assets:

1. 0% weight for cash and claims on Organization for Economic Cooperation and Development (OECD) central banks and national governments.[7]
2. 20% weight for claims on private sector OECD banks, OECD subnational government entities, and cash items in the process of collection.
3. 50% weight for first mortgages on 1–4 family real estate, and local government project finance in OECD countries.
4. 100% weight for commercial and consumer loans, and loans to non-OECD governments.

Unfortunately, from the regulators point of view, the simple structure encouraged transactions whose principal benefit was to arbitrage bank capital. These transactions included the use of securitization and off-balance sheet exposures. Also, banks took large credit risks in the least creditworthy borrowers who had the highest expected returns in a risk-weight class (Kupiec, 2001). As John Hawke, Jr., Comptroller of the Currency (2002) stated, the Basel rules encouraged some banks to move high-quality assets off their balance sheets, thereby reducing the average quality of bank loan portfolios.

The risk-weight classes did not match realized losses. Flood (2001) examined loan charge-offs and delinquency rates for banks and thrifts during the 1984–1999 period. Flood found that the 1998 Capital Accord risk weights did not accurately track the credit experience in the U.S. Collateralized loans had the least risk. Commercial loans appear to be under-burdened by the Basel I weights, and mortgages were overburdened.

---

6. Tier 2 capital is limited to no more than 100% of Tier 1 capital.
7. Flood (March 9, 2001).

The leverage ratio of Basel I is no longer an appropriate measure of a bank's capital adequacy because it is not related to risks that vary from bank to bank. In addition, regulatory capital arbitrage undermined that approach.

In the years that followed the 1988 Basel I Capital Accord, the United States experienced massive bank failures in the late 1980s and early 1990s. During the 1980–1996 period, 133 of the International Monetary Fund's 181 member countries experienced significant banking sector problems, including those countries that signed on to the Basle Accord.[8] Large banks in Japan began having problems beginning in 1990, and their problems had not been resolved by 2003. In the late 1990s and early 2000s, there were financial crises in Southeast Asia, Russia, Turkey, and Latin America, where bank capital requirements may have had some impact.

The problems of regulating large, complex financial organizations that have global operations is another issue driving the New Basel Capital Accord. Some institutions are so large and so complex that bank regulators have difficulty assessing how effectively these organizations manage their risks.

All of these factors suggest that changes in the capital requirements were needed, and they are forthcoming.

THE NEW BASEL CAPITAL ACCORD (BASEL II)

The New Basel Capital Accord (hereafter called Basel II), proposed in January 2001, will replace the 1988 Basel I Capital Accord when it is expected to be implemented by year-end 2006. Basel II applies to holding companies (on a consolidated basis) that are parents of banking groups; but insurance subsidiaries are excluded in some G 10 countries.[9] Because capital adequacy measured only at the highest consolidated level is not sufficient to ensure that capital is immediately available to absorb losses and protect depositors at each bank, the accord will also apply on a sub-consolidated basis to all internationally active banks at every tier below the top banking group level.

Basel II is complex, containing 674 numbered paragraphs/ sections with definitions and explanations, many of which are subject to various interpretations. By way of illustration, Basel II has a reference definition of "default" (paragraphs 272 and 466).

---

8. Lindgren, et al. (1996). Also see Gup (1998; 1999).
9. "The New Basel Capital Accord," Consultative Document, January 2001, 2–3; "Overview of the New Basel Accord, January 2001, # 56, page 11.

In comments about Basel II that were sent to the BIS,[10] MBNA America Bank N. A., a major U.S. credit card bank, points out that the U.S. Federal Financial Institutions Examination Council (FFIEC) definition of default risk is better suited for retail exposures. The International Swaps and Derivatives Assoc., Inc. (ISDA) stated that the reference definition of default for corporate exposures (where it is defined at the obligor level) is only partially applicable for retail exposures (where they argue that it should be defined at the transaction level). Finally, Japanese Bankers Association pointed out that every country has its own definition of default.

Basel II also has more than 500 pages of supporting documents providing details for banks participating in the Quantitative Impact Studies (QIS) that are used to test various models.

The major difference between the two capital accords is that Basel II provides for more flexibility and risk sensitivity than Basel I. Basel II consists of three mutually reinforcing pillars: Pillar 1—minimum capital requirements, Pillar 2—supervisory review process, and Pillar 3—market discipline.

As shown in equation 1, Pillar 1 retains the current definition of capital and the minimum 8% requirement in the numerator. In the denominator, the measures for credit risk are more complex than Basel I, market risk is the same, and operational risk is new. In the United States, banks that do not adopt the Advanced IRB (A-IRB) approach will continue to use Basel I standards. U.S. bank regulators will require about ten large, internationally active banking organizations to use the A-IRB approach.

$$\frac{\text{Total capital (definition unchanged)}}{\text{Credit risk } + \text{ Market risk } + \text{ Operational risk}} \geq 8\% \text{ minimum capital ratio} \qquad \text{(eq. 1)}$$

Where
Credit risk can be measured by:

1. Standardized approach—a modified version of the existing method, based on external credit ratings when available.
2. Foundation Internal Rating-Based (IRB) approach.
3. Advanced IRB approach (A-IRB).

Market risk can be measured by:

1. Standardized approach
2. Internal models approach

---

10. The comments are listed in the references.

Operational risk can be measured by:

1. Basic indicator approach
2. Standardized approach
3. Internal measurement approach

Credit Risk

Credit risk is the risk of default by a creditor or counterparty. Banks must allocate risk weights to on- and off-balance sheet items that produce a sum of risk-weighted asset values.[11] A risk weight of 100% means that the item is included in the calculation at its full value—e.g., 8% of the value. Similarly, a risk weight of 50% means that it is included at 4% of its value. The use of internal and external credit ratings and their associated probabilities of default are used to determine the risk weights. This is a major change from Basel I.

The credit risk weights apply to banking-book exposures in six categories: corporate, banks, equity, retail, project finance, and sovereigns; and they depend, in part, on credit ratings. For countries that are members of the Organization for Economic Cooperation and Development (OECD), the risk weight is zero.[12] For other countries, it can be as high as 150% depending on their credit rating. Similarly, the risk categories for corporate lending range from 20% to 150%.[13] For corporations that do not have credit ratings, their risk weighting is only 100%. Since this is lower than the maximum risk weighting of 150% for firms with a credit rating below BB-, it provides an incentive for corporations with potentially low ratings to not be rated. Needless to say, many countries, including those in EUROCONTROL, that are not part of the OECD would like a zero risk weight.[14]

---

11. The off-balance sheet items include, but are not limited to, collateral, guarantees, and credit derivatives that credit risk mitigants. "Credit risk mitigation" is used to reduce credit losses.

12. The sovereign members of the OECD are considered part of a "club." The zero weight for sovereign OECD members is referred to as the "club rule." See Overview Paper for the Impact Study, October 2002, 4–5. Certain multilateral development banks (MDBs), such as the World Bank, also have zero risk weights.

13. "The New Basel Capital Accord," Consultative Document, January 2001.

14. EUROCONTROL, 2002, represents Austria, Belgium, Bulgaria, Cyprus, Croatia, Denmark, France, Germany, Spain, Greece, Hungary, Ireland, Italy, the former Yugoslavia Republic of Macedonia, Luxembourg, Malta, Moldova, Monaco, Norway, Netherlands, Portugal, Slovak Republic, Czech Republic, Romania, U.K., Slovenia, Sweden, Switzerland, and Turkey.

The retail class includes residential mortgages, credit card loans, installment loans, revolving credits, and small business loans.

The standardized approach is appropriate for smaller banks, and the *internal rating based* (IRB) approach for larger ones. Under the IRB approach, banks use their own models to assess borrowers' credit risk and the credit risk in their portfolios. The IRB approaches are subject to the approval of bank supervisors and the Basel Committee. Capital is based on the estimated one-year default rate for assets.

In the *foundation method,* the banks estimate the probability of default for each borrower, and the supervisors provide the other inputs. In the *advanced method,* the bank provides all of the inputs. Under both the foundation and A-IRB methods, the range of risk weights is greater than is available in the *standardized method.*

Market Risk

The definition of market risk is unchanged from Basel I. Market risks arise from on- and off-balance sheet positions due to changes in market prices. They are most commonly associated with risks in the trading books for debt and equity securities, foreign exchange, and commodity risks.[15] Market risk is typically measured by value-at-risk (VAR).

Operational Risk

Operational risk refers to losses resulting from inadequate or failed internal processes, people and systems, or from external events. It includes, but is not limited to, the risk of inadequate or failed internal systems, such as computer failures or fraud, compliance issues, as well as external events, including lawsuits. For example, the failure due to fraud at the National Bank of Keystone (West Virginia) in September 1999 was the largest loss to the FDIC's Bank Insurance Fund since the savings-and-loan crises. Fraud also contributed to eight of the eleven banks that failed in 2002. The failure of Barings Bank in the United Kingdom was due to fraud. Thus, fraud is a major component of operational risk.

---

15. "Overview of the Amendment to the Capital Accord to Incorporate Market Risks," (1996).

The disruptions to the U.S. financial markets caused by the terrorist attacks on September 11, 2001 also represent operational risks for banks involved in securities trading and settlements.[16]

The *basic indicator method* uses one indicator to represent the operational risk for the entire bank, and it ties capital to a single measure of business activity, such as Gross Income. The *standardized method* utilizes different indicators for different lines of business. The *internal measurement method*/advanced measurement approach (AMA) uses internal loss data and the bank's own methodology to estimate the amount of capital required. It is estimated that it will be less than 20% of the total capital.[17] In the United States, banks that are required to use the A-IRB approach will also be required to use the AMA for operational risk.

Following field-testing of the proposals in several Quantitative Impact Studies (QIS), the Basel Committee addressed some of the concerns.[18] For example, credit exposures to small- and medium-sized enterprises (SMEs) will not be treated the same as large enterprises in terms of maturities.[19] Cyclicality of bank lending/risk is being taken into account. The IRB risk weights will be more sensitive to revolving retail exposures, including credit cards. There will be increased flexibility in measuring operational risk.

CONCLUSION

Basel II will replace Basel I at the end of 2006, when it is expected to be implemented. However, in the United States, only about 10 of the largest internationally active banks will be required to use the A-IRB and AMA approaches. Other banks may "opt-in" to use the new Basel II standards or continue to use Basel I. It is expected that only a small number of large banks will opt-in.

The New Basel Capital Accord places emphasis on banks' internal controls, increased flexibility in risk management, and more risk sensitivity. It explicitly recognizes credit risk, market risk, and operational risk. It will be a major change from the way that banks and regulators operate now. Consequently, there are many questions and issues concerning the New Basel Accord that need to be addressed. For example, will it work any better than the 1988

---

16. See "Potential Terrorist Attacks," GAO-03-251; GAO-03-414, 2003.
17. "Update on New Basel Capital Accord," June 25, 2001.
18. "Overview Paper for the Impact Study," October 2002.
19. SMEs are those firms with consolidated annual sales of less than Euro 50 mn.

Accord? What risk measures should be used? Does market discipline work? How will it affect developing countries? This book examines these and other issues that are of importance to academics, regulators, and practitioners.

REFERENCES

Comments on Basel II: Comments on Basel II were sent by interested parties to the Basel Committee on Banking Supervision, Bank for International Settlements in 2001, and in March 2003 for the Comments on QIS3 Technical Guidance and Second Working Paper on Securitization. The comments were found on the following web sites: *http://www.bis.org*; *http://www.bis.org/bcbs/cacomments.htm*; and *http://www.bis.org/bcbs/qis/qis3.htm#resp*.

BIS web site, *http://www.bis.org*.

Flood, Mark, (2001), Comments on Basel II, "Basel Buckets and Loan Losses: Absolute and Relative Loan Underperformance at Banks and Thrifts," March 9.

Gup, Benton E., (1998), *Bank Failures in the Major Trading Countries of the World: Causes and Remedies*, Westport, CT, Quorum Books.

Gup, Benton E., (1999), *International Banking Crises: Large-Scale Failures, Massive Government Interventions*, Westport, CT, Quorum Books.

Hawke, John D., Jr., (2002), Comptroller of the Currency, "The Road to Basel II: Good Intentions and Imposing Challenges," Press Release NR 2002-49, Office of the Comptroller of the Currency, Washington, D.C., June 6.

Hawke, John D., Jr., (2003), Testimony before the Subcommittee on Domestic and International Monetary Policy, Trade and Technology of the Committee on Financial Services, U.S. House of Representatives, February 27.

International Swaps and Derivatives Assoc., Inc. (ISDA), (2001), Comments on Basel II, May.

Japanese Bankers Association, (2001), Comments on Basel II, May 31.

Kupiec, Paul H., (2001), Comments on Basel II, "The New Basle Accord: The Devil is in the (Calibration) Details," International Monetary Fund, May 23.

Lindgren, Carl-Johan, Gillian Garcia, and Matthew I. Saal, (1996), *Bank Soundness and Macroeconomic Policy*, Washington, D.C., International Monetary Fund.

MBNA America Bank N. A., (2001), Comments on Basel II, May 31.

Merriam-Webster–Map of Switzerland; *http://www.m-w.com/maps/ switzerland.html* (visited 11/6/02).

"Overview of the New Basel Accord," (2001), Consultative Document, Basel Committee on Banking Supervision, Bank for International Settlements, Basel, Switzerland, January.

"Overview of the Amendment to the Capital Accord to Incorporate Market Risks," (1996), Basel Committee on Banking Supervision, Bank for International Settlements, Basel, Switzerland.

"Overview Paper for the Impact Study," (2002), Basel Committee on Banking Supervision, Bank for International Settlements, Basel, Switzerland, October.

"Potential Terrorist Attacks: Additional Actions Needed to Better Prepare Critical Financial Market Participants," (2003), U.S. Government Accounting Office, GAO-03-251, February 12.

"Potential Terrorist Attacks: Additional Actions Needed to Better Prepare Critical Financial Market Participants," (2003), U.S. Government Accounting Office, GAO-03-414, February 12.

"The New Basel Capital Accord," (2001), Consultative Document, Basel Committee on Banking Supervision, Bank for International Settlements, Basel, Switzerland, January.

"The New Basel Capital Accord: An Explanatory Note," (2001), Secretariat of the Basel Committee on Banking Supervision, Bank for International Settlements, Basel, Switzerland, January.

"Update on New Basel Capital Accord," (2001), BIS Press Release, Bank for International Settlements, Basel, Switzerland, June 25.

2

The New Basel Capital Accord: Is 8% Adequate?

Benton E. Gup

The new Basel Capital Accord will replace the 1988 Basel Capital Accord when it is implemented in 2006. The 1988 accord provided only one measure of risk and capital for internationally active banks. The single-capital standard did not take into account that banks can have varying degrees of risk. The impetus for the new accord is to deal with this problem by placing more emphasis on a bank's internal controls, increasing the flexibility in risk management, and increasing risk sensitivity. It explicitly recognizes credit risk, market risk, and operational risk.

The new accord maintains both the current definition of capital and the minimum requirement of 8% of capital to risk-weighted assets.[1] Therein lies the problem. For U.S. banks, the minimum capital requirement is too low. This article explains why. According to the Basel Committee on Banking Supervision's "Core Principles for Effective Supervision" (1997), "Banking supervisors must set minimum capital requirements for banks that reflect the risks that banks undertake." It goes on to point out that the 1988 accord addressed credit risk and off-balance-sheet risks.

In the *Report on International Developments in Banking Supervision* (1998), the Basel Committee on Banking Supervision states, "A central mission of the Committee is to ensure that the Basel Capital Accord keeps pace with the rapid evolution in the marketplace and remains an effective and relevant international standard." Since 1988, banks' on- and off-balance-sheet risks have increased, but the minimum 8% capital requirement has not changed. Changing

---

1. For details, see the Bank for International Settlements, Consultive Document, "The New Basel Capital Accord," January 2001, and "The New Basel Capital Accord: An Explanatory Note," January 2001.

the way banks compute the 8% capital requirement is not the same as raising it. In fact, the capital requirement will be lower than 8% for some banks.

The remainder of this chapter is divided into three parts. Part 1 examines the decline in U.S. bank capital ratios. Part 2 shows that bank risk has increased since 1988. Particular attention is paid to off-balance-sheet derivatives, real estate loans, subprime loans, and equities. Part 3 is the conclusion.

I. THE DECLINE IN U.S. BANK EQUITY CAPITAL/ASSET RATIOS

Table 1 reveals the decline in the ratio of U.S. bank equity capital to total assets that occurred during the 1896–2002 period. The ratio was computed by dividing equity capital by total assets. No adjustments were made to take into account minority interests, goodwill, or intangibles. Accordingly, the equity capital/asset ratio is higher than the FDIC's "core capital (leverage)" ratio that makes such adjustments.[2]

The ratios in 1896 and 1900 reflect a time when many banks were still operating under the real bills doctrine—borrowing short-term and lending short-term. Today, banks borrow short-term and lend long-term—a riskier strategy. As shown in Table 1, bank equity capital/asset ratio declined from 23.5% in 1896 to a low of 5.8% in 1980. Then the ratio began to increase.

During the 1985–1992 period, the FDIC had 1,373 insured banks fail.[3] These failures accounted for 76.3% of the total disbursements made by the FDIC during the 1934–2001 period. This dark period in our history is generally associated with bad commercial real estate loans, leveraged buyouts, and loans to developing nations. There is no doubt that the 1988 Accord, the large number of bank failures and payouts by the FDIC, and the Prompt Corrective Action (PCA) rules directed by the Federal Deposit Insurance Corporation Improvement Act of 1991 (FDICIA) influenced the increased bank equity capital/asset ratio in the subsequent years.

---

2. The core capital (leverage) ratio was first reported in *The FDIC Quarterly Banking Profile*, Third Quarter, 1993, and the data went back to 1987. The core capital ratio is measured against "adjusted average assets." The adjustments involve exclusions of disallowed intangible assets, unrealized losses on equity securities, and unrealized gains or losses on available-for-sale securities. The asset amount that is subject to these adjustments is the quarterly average assets figure reported on Schedule RC-K of the Call report. The data reporting requirements for regulatory capital can be viewed on the FDIC web site at *http://www.fdic.gov/regulations/resources/call/index.html*.

3. *FDIC Annual Report, 2001*.

In 2002, 4th Quarter, it was 9.2%, while the FDIC core capital ratio was 8.0%.[4] Most banks hold more than the minimum capital requirement in order to support future growth.

To put the 8% capital requirement for banks in perspective with respect to other industries, Table 1 shows that the average capital/asset ratio for all corporations that filed U.S. income taxes was 35% in 1998. Bank capital/asset ratios are *significantly* lower.

Bank capital/asset ratios were lower than that of all corporations long before the 1988 Capital Accord that established the 8% capital/risk asset ratio. This raises the question of what is the optimal capital structure for banks? One can argue that because banks are regulated financial intermediaries, they have higher debt ratios (lower capital/asset ratios) than most other types of firms. On the other hand, a high capital/asset ratio may put banks at a competitive disadvantage to unregulated financial firms. And a capital/asset ratio that is too low may contribute to systemic risk. But should the minimum ratio be 8%, 12%, or perhaps 18% as it was in 1900 before modern bank regulations existed? The answer to that question is beyond the scope of this article.

Table I. Capital/Asset Ratios

DATE	BANK EQUITY CAPITAL/ASSET RATIO	FDIC CORE CAPITAL (LEVERAGE) RATIO	ALL CORP. CAPITAL/ASSET RATIO
1896 (June 30)	23.5%		
1900 (June 30)	17.9		
1950 (June 30)	7.6		
1980 (December 30)	5.8		25.5%
1988 (December 30)	6.2	5.89	
2000 (December 30)	8.5	7.70	35.1 (1998)*
2002 (December 30)	9.2	7.87	

* Latest available data.
Sources: *All-Bank Statistics, United States, 1896–1955; Statistical Abstract of the United States, 1989, 1993, 2001; The FDIC Quarterly Banking Profile,* Fourth Quarter, 2002.

---

4. Under FDICIA, "well capitalized" institutions have at least 10% total risk-based capital, 6% Tier 1 capital, and 5% Tier 1 leverage capital, all expressed as a percentage of risk-weighted assets. Institutions with less capital have lower ratings. The PCA requirements are unique to the U.S.

2. CHANGING RISK PROFILE OF BANKS

The risk profile of U.S. banks has changed dramatically since the 1998 Accord. The increased risks presented here are associated with off-balance-sheet derivatives, real estate, and subprime lending. To some extent, the increased risk is reflected in rising loan losses. Net charge-offs as a percent of average loans and leases increased from 0.99% in 1988 to 1.12% in 2002 (3rd Qtr).[5] This section also discusses how some foreign banks compute their regulatory capital.

Derivatives

The biggest dollar changes occurred in off-balance-sheet derivatives and real estate loans. In the 4th Quarter of 1993, off-balance-sheet derivatives were $11.8 trillion, or 3.2 times greater than bank assets.[6] By the 4th Quarter of 2002, they amounted to $56.3 trillion, or 6.7 times total bank assets.[7] JPMorgan Chase Bank, the largest dealer in derivatives, accounted to half of the notional amount of total derivatives contracts. The top seven banks account for 96% of the notional amount of derivative contracts, and 99% are held by the top 25 banks.[8] The largest banks hold about 96% of their derivatives in trading accounts. In contrast, smaller banks tend to use derivatives for risk management. A total of 408 banks held derivative contracts in 2002.

In the 3rd Quarter of 2002, 86% of the notional amount of derivatives contracts were interest rate contracts, 11% were foreign exchange contracts, and equity, commodity, and credit contracts accounted for the remaining 3%. As early as 1995, banks accounted for 5–10% of the energy (oil and gas) trading markets, and in July 2002, Bank of America began trading electricity derivatives.[9]

---

5. *The FDIC Quarterly Banking Profile*, First Quarter, 1989, Third Quarter 2002.

6. *The FDIC Quarterly Banking Profile, Fourth Quarter, 1993*. The FDIC first reported the derivative data in 1993.

7. *FDIC Quarterly Banking Profile, Fourth Quarter, 2002;* "OCC Bank Derivatives Report, Third Quarter 2002," December 2002. The OCC reported total derivatives to be $53.2 trillion. The $509 billion difference between the FDIC and OCC totals are because the OCC excludes spot foreign exchange contracts in their notional amount of derivatives.

8. "OCC Bank Derivatives Report, Third Quarter 2002," December 2002.

9. "OCC Bank Derivatives Report, Third Quarter 2002," December 2002; *Energy Derivatives* (1995); Brannigan and Kranhold (2002).

According to Puwalski (2003), equity and commodity derivatives are the most risky type of derivative contracts, followed by foreign exchange, and interest rate contracts, which have the least risk. The risk also depends on whether the bank is hedging, dealing (matched trading, market making, and positioning), or speculating in the contracts. Hedging interest rate risk with interest rate contracts is the most prevalent use of derivatives among banks.

As the market for derivatives has grown, so have the participants. Banks accounted for 47% of the market in 2002. Other participants included reinsures (14%), insurers (9%), hedge funds (8%), asset managers (5%), and others (17%).[10]

As shown in Table 2, the net charge-offs of derivatives varied widely from year to year. The dollar amount of charge-offs for derivatives ranged from a high of $445 million in 1998 to a low of less than $1 million in 2000. The losses are small when compared to the net charge-offs for loans and leases that amounted to $11.5 billion in the 3rd Quarter of 2002.

Table 2. Net Charge-Offs of Derivatives in Selected Periods

PERIODS	DERIVATIVES	
	%	$ (MILL.)
1998 3rd Qtr.	0.11	$445
2000 1st Qtr.	0.00	$0.1
2001 4th Qtr	0.06	$296
2002 3rd Qtr.	0.01	$70

Sources: The data for all banks that issue derivatives are from the "OCC Bank Derivatives Report, Third Quarter 2002," December 2002, Graph 5C.

Mackay (1995) argued that the risk from derivatives is not unique. They include credit, settlement, market, liquidity, operation, and legal risks. He also argues that there is no empirical support for the view that they increase systemic risk. However, given the $56.3 trillion size of derivative portfolios—compared to the $5.1 trillion size of loans and leases—the potential for larger losses in derivatives exits.[11] According to Powell (4/1/0/03), the market's use of credit rating downgrades is a potential source of

---

10. Sender (December 5, 2002).
11. Bank data are from *FDIC Quarterly Banking Profile, Fourth Quarter, 2002.*

large disruptions. Many derivative contracts require the counter-party to maintain an investment grade credit rating. A downgrading serves as a "trigger event" that, for a large bank with a substantial derivatives position, could cause "dislocations in both the bank and derivatives market."

Warren Buffett (2003), Chairman and CEO of Berkshire Hathaway Inc., believes that "derivatives are financial weapons of mass destruction, carrying dangers that, while now latent, are potentially lethal." Berkshire acquired General Re Securities, a derivatives dealer, which lost $173 million, pretax, in 2002. Although General Re was the basis for Buffett's comments, the same issues apply to banks.

General Re invested in or insured derivatives, such as collateralized debt obligations (CDOs), to enhance the derivative's credit ratings. CDOs may be divided into three or more tranches representing various degrees of risk. For example, the equity tranche is the lowest, and it has the most risk. The next level is the mezzanine tranch with medium risk, and the senior tranche with least risk.[12] A few defaults in a pool of 100 companies can wipe out the equity tranche. And that is what happened during the economic decline in 2001 and 2002. There were widespread paper losses that had to be marked-to-market in CDO portfolios.

Buffet's concerns appear to stem from the following issues. First, General Re Securities had 14,384 contracts with 672 counterparties; some of the contracts have maturities of 20 years or more. More important, General Re Securities had trading liabilities of $6.5 *billion*. Second, there was no active market for some of the derivatives contracts they held. Third, those who trade derivatives are paid, in part, on "earnings" based on mark-to-market accounting which allows both counterparties using different models and assumptions to show large profits. Buffet calls this "mark-to-myth." The Federal Reserves *Trading and Capital-Markets Activities Manual* (section 2020.1, 1999), states the "Estimating potential exposure can be subjective, and firms approach its measurement in several different ways." Unfortunately for General Re, they did not pick the right way, or their guesses about the future were wrong.

Finally, Buffet points out that total return swaps that facilitate 100% leverage in various markets, including the stock market, make a joke of margin requirements.

---

12. "Toxic Waste," March 15, 2003.

Mark C. Brickell (1996), who was managing director of J.P. Morgan, discussed the lessons that could be learned from the mistakes made in the early 1990s by Gibson Greetings, Procter & Gamble, Orange County, Barings, and Daiwa. With respect to lessons for dealer in derivatives, he cautioned them against concentration risk. Brickell (1996) said that "It is a basic principle of sound banking to avoid the concentration of risk." Isn't the concentration of having one bank holding over half of the derivatives contracts and seven banks holding 96% excessive concentration?

Real Estate

The growth in real estate loans is of greater concern than derivatives because it is widely associated with bank failures. An FDIC study found that booms and busts in the commercial real estate loans were the main cause of losses at failed and surviving banks in the 1980s and early 1990s.[13] An International Monetary Fund study by Lindgren, Garcia, and Saal (1996) examined IMF member countries during the 1980–1996 period. More than 130 of the 181-member countries experienced banking sector problems. Fluctuations in real estate were specifically mentioned in connection with Finland, France, Japan, Malaysia, Norway, Spain, and Sweden. A World Bank study by Sheng (1996) identified real estate loan losses with banking problems in Argentina, Chile, Columbia, Ghana, Yugoslavia, and elsewhere. Finally, Gup (1998), studying international banking crises, identified real estate loans as contributing to more bank failures than any other category of loans.

The data presented in Table 3 shows that in 2002, mortgage debt accounts for 57% of the net bank loans, up sharply from earlier periods. It also shows that the bank's role in total mortgage lending has increased. Today banks surpass the savings institutions as the primary mortgage lenders. Although not shown in Table 2, about 57% of the bank mortgage loans are for 1–4 family properties, 41% is for commercial and multifamily properties, and 1% is for farm mortgage loans.[14]

---

13. *History of the Eighties*, 1997, Vol. 1.
14. *Federal Reserve Bulletin*, August 2002.

Table 3. Real Estate Loans

YEAR	REAL ESTATE LOANS/TOTAL NET LOANS	BANK MORTGAGE DEBT/TOTAL MORTGAGE DEBT	CONTRACT INTEREST RATE, FIXED, NEW HOMES
1980	26.7%	18.0%	14.4% (1982)*
1988	35.8	20.4	10.0
2000	44.4	24.1	8.0
2002	57.3		5.95 (Dec.)

* Contract interest rate data for 1980 was not available.
Sources: *Statistical Abstract of the United States, 1993, 2001; FDIC Quarterly Banking Profile,* Fourth Quarter, 2002, *Federal Reserve Bulletin,* March 2003.

The demand for mortgages increased, in part, because of the decline in market rates of interest. In 2002, mortgage rates were at their lowest levels in 35 years. The contact rate for fixed-rate mortgages on new homes declined from 14.4% in 1982 to 5.95% in December 2002. But what happens when interest rates increase, say 200 basis points?[15]

Before we can examine the impact of the 200 basis point increase in market rates of interest on the borrower, we have to make some assumptions about valuation of the borrower's assets. Suppose that the borrower is investing in commercial real estate. The intrinsic value of the real estate is the present value of expected future cash flows (an annuity), discounted by the market rate of interest. The holding period of the asset is equal to the term of the loan. There are no taxes. Borrowing here is limited to 100%. However, some home equity loans in the U.S. are made for 125% or more of the value of the underlying property.

The present value of an annuity PV_a (1)

$$PV_a = PMT \sum_{t=1}^{n} [\frac{1}{(1+i)^t}]$$

where
PMT = expected annual income
n = number of years
i = interest rate

---

15. Although this example involves mortgage lending, exactly the same point can be made for leveraged financing. Leveraged financing is of concern to bank regulators. See FDIC: Press Release PR-28-2001, April 9, 2001 (Leveraged Financing) for additional information.

Table 4, Panel A, shows the initial intrinsic value of the real estate asset for selected loan-to-value ratios. The loan is for $1 million. If the loan-to-value ratio is 100%, then the value of the asset is $1 million. If the loan-to-value ratio is 90%, the value of the asset is $1,111,111 ($1,000,000/.90), and so on. The difference between the value of the asset and the amount of the loan represents the borrower's equity in the asset. Studies by von Furstenberg (1969, 1970) and Vandell (1978) reveal that loan-to-value ratios and the amount of borrowers' equity accumulation were statistically significant determinants of mortgage loan defaults. The higher the loan-to-value ratios are associated with greater default rates.

Table 4, Panel A, also shows expected annual income (PMT) for each initial asset values based on a 7% interest rate. Table 4, Panel B, demonstrates the effects of the 200 basis point increase in market rates of interest to 9% on the present value of the annuity, which is the intrinsic value of the real estate asset. It also reveals the difference between the loan amount and the intrinsic value of the asset. When the loan-to-value ratio is 100%, the loan exceeds the value by $157,123, and the owner's put option to default on their loans is deep in the money. The put also is in the money when the loan-to-value ratio is 90%. The put is out of the money at lower loan-to-value ratios.

Simons (1994) found that industrial real estate mortgage defaults were strongly associated with negative equity (e.g., the put option being in the money) and bankruptcy. Kau and Kim (1994), analyzing defaults on property, concluded that "If the house price has fallen low enough, one will then default immediately."

Table 4.

Panel A

25 Year, $1,000,000 Commercial Real Estate Loan At 7% Fixed Rate

	LOAN/ VALUE 100%	LOAN/ VALUE 90%	LOAN/ VALUE 80%	LOAN/ VALUE 70%	LOAN/ VALUE 60%
25-YEAR REAL ESTATE LOAN	$1,000,000	$1,000,000	$1,000,000	$1,000,000	$1,000,000
INITIAL ASSET VALUE*	$1,000,000	$1,111,111	$1,250,000	$1,428,571	$1,666,667
EXPECT. ANNUAL INCOME FROM ASSET**	$85,810	$95,345	$107,263	$122,586	$143,017

Table 4. (*cont.*)

Panel B

INTEREST RATES INCREASE 200 BASIS POINTS TO 9%

	LOAN/ VALUE 100%	LOAN/ VALUE 90%	LOAN/ VALUE 80%	LOAN/ VALUE 70%	LOAN/ VALUE 60%
25-YEAR REAL ESTATE LOAN	$1,000,000	$1,000,000	$1,000,000	$1,000,000	$1,000,000
PV$_a$ @ 9%	$842,877	$936,536	$1,053,602	$1,204,113	$1,404,798
ASSET VALUE LESS LOAN	− $157,123 Default likely	− $ 63,464 Default Possible	$ 53,602	$ 204,113	$ 404,798

* At 90% loan/value, $1,000,000/0.90 = $1,111,111.11; $1,000,000/0.80 = $1,250,000, etc.

** PMT is derived from initial asset values being discounted at 7%.

Elmer and Seelig (1998a) developed a choice-theoretic model to examine single-family mortgage defaults in the U.S. They found income and real estate price shocks, along with insolvency, pay a central role in mortgage defaults. Elmer and Seelig (1998b) found that house appreciation rates and loan-to-value ratios explain some of the rising long-term trend in single-family mortgage fore-closure rates.

Finally, some real estate loans are made without recourse. Thus, the borrower is not at risk if he or she defaults on the loan.

All of these reasons provide incentives for borrowers to exercise their put options to default. However, not all borrowers are equally likely to default. A large corporation, such as IBM, is less likely to exercise its put option on one loan than a small firm or an individual investor or speculator.

Subprime Lending

A significant number of banks have turned to subprime and high loan-to-value lending without having adequate prudential standards. Subprime loans include both consumer and real estate loans. Feldman and Schmidt (1999) found that 29% of the banks in the Federal Reserve Bank of Minneapolis' district offered subprime loans. Donna Tanoue (2000), former Chairman of the FDIC, reported that about 140 FDIC-insured institutions had significant exposure to subprime loans in 2000. These institutions accounted for 1% of all institutions and 20% of the problem institutions—those with CAMEL ratings of 4 or 5. Some banks that deal in subprime lending securitize the loans and retain a residual interest in them. This off-balance-sheet commitment adds to their risk.

Some recent bank failures are associated with subprime lending. These banks include, but are not limited to, BestBank (Boulder, CO), First National Bank of Keystone (Keystone, WV), Superior Bank (Hinsdale, IL), Pacific Thrift and Loan Co. (Woodland Hills, CA), and Peoples National Bank of Commerce (Miami, FL), and Genessee Regional Bank (Rochester, NY).

Consider the case of First Consumer National Bank (FCNB) of Beaverton, Oregon. FCNB operated as a limited purpose "credit card bank" under the Bank Holding Company Act and was a wholly owned subsidiary of The Spiegel Group. The 138-year-old Spiegel Group is a specialty retailer that owns Eddie Bauer, the Spiegel Catalog, and Newport News. In an effort to boost sales, Spiegel aggressively expanded its credit card operations through FCNB, and focused on customers with a Fair Isaac Co. (FICO) score under 680—subprime customers. Spiegel also generated income by selling asset-backed securities (ABS) that were linked to the FCNB credit card receivables, and they guaranteed a minimum return on those ABS notes.[16]

Spiegel's sales soared in 1999 and 2000. But the slump in economic activity in 2001 and 2002 resulted in large charge-offs and losses at FCNB and a liquidity crises at Spiegel that had guaranteed a minimum return on the ABS notes. In May 2002, the Office of the Comptroller of the Currency issued a "Cease and Desist Order" for FCNB, and in March 2003, Spiegel filed for Chapter 11 bankruptcy protection.[17]

The Federal Reserve's January 2002 Senior Loan Officer Opinion Survey on Bank Lending Practices revealed that subprime loan portfolios did not perform up to expectations. For example, 40.7% of the subprime residential mortgage loans did not perform as well as predicted. In contrast, only 12.2% of the standard mortgage loans were below expectations.[18] Donald E. Powell, Chairman of the FDIC said these figures suggest that "the current credit risk models may not be suitable for the newer, more flexible products."[19]

---

16. Merrick (3/18/03).
17. Office of the Comptroller of the Currency, Consent order #2002-40, First Consumers National Bank, Beaverton, Oregon.
18. "Senior Loan Officer Opinion Survey on Bank Lending Practices," January 2002.
19. Powell (11/15/02).

Based on the FDIC's experience, Donna Tanoue (2000), former Chairman of the FDIC, recommended increasing the capital requirements for institutions that have the largest concentrations of subprime loans. An FDIC Press Release (January 31, 2001), recommended that institutions that underwrite subprime pools, such as unsecured or high loan-to-value second mortgages, "may need higher capital standards, perhaps as high as 100% of the loans outstanding depending on the level and volatility of the risk."[20]

Equities and Tax Credits

Banks in Germany, Italy, Spain, and other selected countries can count shareholdings as part of their Tier 1 regulatory capital. Their bank capital benefits when stock markets are soaring. However, European stock markets sold off in 2002, and the unrealized capital gains turned into unrealized capital losses and lower bank capital. Pretzlik (2002) reported that as a result of lower stock prices, five European banks have Tier 1 capital ratios below 6%: Banca Nazionale Navaro, Monete del Paschi di Siena, IntesaBCI, Commerzbank, and HBV.

Similarly, banks in Japan include stockholdings as part of their capital. Consequently, Mizuho Holdings, experienced a significant loss of capital when stock prices declined. Mizuho is the largest banking group in the world with assets of $1.3 trillion. In January 2003, the company announced that it intend to sell about one sixth of the remaining stock portfolio to prevent further losses of capital.[21] Finally, deferred tax credit also counted as part of Mizuho's Tier 1 capital. If tax credits were excluded from their capital, it would cut their capital from 10.1% to 4.8%.[22]

3. CONCLUSION

The title of this article is *The New Basel Accord: Is 8% Adequate?* The answer is "no, it is not adequate." The New Basel Capital Accord makes significant changes in the way various risks are addressed in computing the 8% minimum capital requirement. For example, consider the capital required to make a $100 commercial loan.

---

20. For further discussion, see the FDIC Interagency Guidance (March 1, 1999).
21. Dvorak ((1/22/03). Also see "Revision of Earnings Estimate for FY 2002 (January 2003).
22. Bremmer (12/23/2002); Toritani and Jones (1/16/03).

Under the 1988 Basel Accord, $8 capital is required. Under the Basel II standards, using the Advanced Internal Ratings Based (IRB) approach, the amount of capital required can range from $0.37 to $4.45 for a company with a AAA credit rating.[23] If the company has a B credit rating, the capital can range from $3.97 to $41.65.

Another way to look at this issue is that Basel II has some risk weights that exceed 100%. For example, the risk weights on some commercial real estate loans are 150% or higher. This means that banks holding such loans may need more than the required 8% minimum capital to make and hold such loans. One implication of this is that banks with adequate or excess capital will make such loans. Another possibility is that the bank will issue more capital. Finally, banks may avoid holding loans that require high capital charges.

Basel II does not address the fact that the total risk faced by U.S. banks today is much greater than it was at the time of the 1988 Accord. Since then, both on- and off-balance-sheet risks of U.S. banks have increased dramatically.

Not everyone agrees with the "no" answer. The RMA Capital Working Group (2001), representing the largest banks in the U.S. and Canada, argue that the 1988 Basel Accord was arbitrary, and that the new absolute level of capital should be 2–3% lower. Results of a recent survey of 190 banks in 18 countries revealed that 80% of the respondents believed that there would be a significant reduction in their capital.[24]

This article examined the growth in off-balance-sheet derivatives, and on-balance-sheet real estate loans, subprime loans, and equity shareholding. To put this growth in context, consider a speech by Andrew Crockett, General Manager of the BIS and Chairman of the Financial Stability Forum (December 6, 2002). Crockett distinguished between "microprudential" banking supervision and "macroprudential" supervision. Microprudential supervision focuses solely on individual institutions, whereas macroprudential supervision considers the entire financial system. While it may be rational and prudent for each bank to increase its on-and off-balance-sheet risks, the increase in aggregate risk is not prudent from a macro point of view.

---

23. Burhouse, et al. (2003). The calculations reflect the upper and lower bounds for capital to be held on a $100 loan. The lower bound reflects a high recovery rate (Loss Given Default = 10%) on a one-year loan. The lower bound reflects a low recovery rate (LGD = 90%) on a five-year loan. The Advanced IRB was used in includes a charge for operational risk.
24. Garver (2002).

Given the strong likelihood that market rates of interest will rise in the future from their low levels in early 2003, the data presented here suggest a significant increase in loan defaults and possible bank failures. When economic times are hard for the banks, failures are accelerated by high degrees of financial leverage. In 1990, for example, the failure rate of banks (per 10,000) was 137 compared to 74 for business failures in all industries.[25] To some extent, future bank failures could be averted with higher levels of equity capital.

In comments on the New Basel Accord, Citigroup's Chief Operating Officer for Finance and Risk, J. Fishman, (2001) pointed out that there are "significant opportunity costs" for holding more capital than is economically justified. These costs include higher costs to users of funds and lower returns to investors.

On the other hand, comments by The World Bank (2001) recommended that banks in developing and emerging nations that have fragile and unstable macroeconomic conditions be required to hold capital in excess of what is considered the minimum in advanced markets.

Determining what the appropriate level of capital should be is a topic for additional research, and it is beyond the scope of this article. Let the debate begin.

REFERENCES

All-Bank Statistics, United States, 1896–1955, (1959), Washington, D.C., Board of Governors of the Federal Reserve System, Table B1, p. 53.

Brannigan, Martha, and Kathryn Kranhold, (2002), "Bank of America Seeks Energy-Trading Authority," *Wall Street Journal*, September 13, p. A5.

Bremmer, Brian, (2002), "Japan's Cracked Banking Colossus," *BusinessWeek Online*, December 23, (International, Asian Business) *http://www.businessweek.com* (visited 1/15/03).

Brickell, Mark C., (1996), "The Changing Nature of the Derivatives Market and the Lessons We Have Learned So Far," appears in *Derivatives and Public Policy, Proceedings of a Conference,*" Chicago, Ill, Federal Reserve Bank of Chicago, pp. 40–45.

Buffett, Warren E., (2003), "Letter to Shareholders," Berkshire Hathaway Inc., 2002, Annual Report, *http://www. berkshirehathaway.com/*

---

25. *Statistical Abstract of the United States, 2001,* Table 877; *FDIC Annual Report, 2001,* p. 86.

Burhouse, Susan, John Feid, George Finch, and Keith Ligon, (2003), "Basel and the Evolution of Capital Regulation: Moving Forward and Looking Back," *For Your Information,* Federal Deposit Insurance Corporation, January 14, *http://www.fdic. gov/bank/analytical/fyi/2003/011403fyi.html* (visited 1/23/03).

Citigroup: (2001), J. S. Fishman, Chief Operating Officer, Finance and Risk, letter and comments sent to Basel Committee on Banking Supervision, Bank for International Settlements, May 31, *http://www.bis.org/bcbs/cacomments.htm*

"Core Principles for Effective Banking Supervision," (1997), Consultative Paper, Basel, Switzerland, Bank for International Settlements, April.

Crockett, Andrew, (2002), "Institutions for Stability – Current and Past Experience," a speech before the Monetary Stability Foundations, Frankfurt, Germany, December 6, 2002, *http://www. bis.org/speeches/sp021206.htm*

Dvorak, Phred, (2003), "Mizuho Holdings Expects to Post Widest Net Loss Ever in Japan," *Wall Street Journal,* January 22, p. A2.

Elmer, Peter J., and Steven A. Seelig, (1998), (a) "Insolvency, Trigger Events, and Consumer Risk Posture in the Theory of Single-Family Mortgage Default," *Working Paper Series,* FDIC, Division of Research and Statistics, Working Paper pp. 98–3.

Elmer, Peter J., and Steven A. Seelig, (1998), (b) "The Rising Long-Term Trend of Single-Family Mortgage Foreclosure Rates," *Working Paper Series,* FDIC, Division of Research and Statistics, Working Paper pp. 98–2.

Energy Derivatives: Crude Oil and Natural Gas (Product Summary), (1995), Federal Reserve Bank of Chicago, December.

FDIC Annual Report, 2001, (2002), Washington, D.C., FDIC, p. 86.

FDIC: Interagency Guidance, March 1, 1999 (*Subprime Lending*) *http://www.fdic.gov/news/news/financial/1999/FIL9920a.html*

FDIC: Press Release PR-9-2001, January 31, 2001 (Subprime Lending)
http://www.fdic.gov/news/news/press/2001/pr0901a.html

FDIC: Press Release PR-28-2001, April 9, 2001 (Leveraged Financing) *http://www.fdic.gov/news/news/press/2001/pr2801a.html*

Federal Reserve Bulletin, (2002), Board of Governors of the Federal Reserve System, August, Table 1.54.

Federal Reserve Bulletin, (2003), Board of Governors of the Federal Reserve System, March, Table 1.53.

Feldman, Ron and Jason Schmidt, (1999), "Why all Concerns About Subprime Lending Are Not Created Equal," *Fedgazette,* Federal Reserve Bank of Minneapolis, July.

Garver, Rob, (2002), "Most U.S. Banks Preparing for New Basel Accord: Poll," *American Banker,* December 17, p. 4.

Gup, Benton E., (1998), *Bank Failures in the Major Trading Countries of the World: Causes and Remedies*, Wesport. CT, Quorum Books.

History of the Eighties-Lessons for the Future: An Examination of Banking Crises of the 1980s and Early 1990s, (1997), Washington, D.C., Federal Deposit Insurance Corporation, Vol. 1.

Kau, J. B., and T. Kim, (1994), "Waiting to Default: The Value of Delay," *Journal of the American Real Estate and Urban Economics Association*," 22, pp. 539–551.

Lindgren, C., G. Garcia, and M. I. Saal, (1996), *Banking Soundness and Macroeconomic Policy*, Washington, D.C., International Monetary Fund.

Mackay, Robert J., (1995), "Derivatives and Systemic Risk: Issues, Views, and Analysis," appears in *Research in Financial Services, Private and Public Policy*, George G. Kaufman, editor, Greenwich, CN, JAI Press, pp. 111–169.

Merrick, Amy, (2003), "Spiegel Files for Chapter 11," *Wall Street Journal*, March 18, p. B4.

"OCC Bank Derivatives Report, Third Quarter 2002," (2002), Washington, D.C., Office of the Comptroller of the Currency, December.

Office of the Comptroller of the Currency, Consent order #2002-40, First Consumers National Bank, Beaverton, Oregon, Washington, D.C., May 15, 2002.

Powell, Donald E., (2002), "Federal Deposit Insurance Corporation: Housing Trends and the Economy," Washington, D.C., FDIC, Press Release PR-117-2002, November 5.

Powell, Donald E. (2003), "Remarks before the Federal Reserve Bank of Atlanta," Washington, D.C., FDIC, Press Release, PR-32-2003, April 10.

Pretzlik, Charles, (2002), "Banks Wilt Under the Pressure of Downturn," *Financial Times* (Special Report: Banking In Europe), November 18.

Puwalski, Allen C., (2003), "Derivatives Risk in Commercial Banking," FDIC FYI, Washington, D.C., Federal Deposit Insurance Corporation, March 28.

Quantitative Impact Study 3 Technical Guidance, (2002), Basel Committee on Banking Supervision, Bank for International Settlements, Basel, Switzerland, October.

"Revision of Earnings Estimate for FY2002," (2003), Mizuho Financial Group, January, *http://www.mizuho-fg.co.jp/english/pdf/release/2002/20030123_e.pdf* (visited 1/24/03).

RMA Capital Working Group, (2001), Comments on Basel II, Bank for International Settlements, *http://www.bis.org/bcbs/cacomments.htm*

Sender, Henny, (2002), "A Market Backfires, and Investors Pay," *Wall Street Journal,* December 5, p. C1.

"Senior Loan Officer Opinion Survey on Bank Lending Practices," (2002), Washington, D.C., Board of Governors of the Federal Reserve System, January.

Sheng, A., (1996), *Bank Restructuring: Lessons from the 1980s,* Washington, D.C., The World Bank.

Simons, R. A., (1994), "Industrial Real Estate Mortgage Default Experience of the New York State Job Development Authority Second Loan Program: A Preliminary Investigation," *Journal of the American Real Estate and Urban Economics Association,* 22, pp. 632–646.

Statistical Abstract of the United States, 1989, (1990), Washington, D.C., U.S. Census Bureau.

Statistical Abstract of the United States, 1993, (1994), Washington, D.C., U.S. Census Bureau.

Statistical Abstract of the United States, 2001, (2002), Washington, D.C., U.S. Census Bureau.

Tanoue, Donna, (2000), "Testimony of Donna Tanoue, Chairman, FDIC, on the Recent Bank Failures and Regulatory Initiatives," Before The Committee on Banking and Financial Services, U.S. House of Representatives, February 8.

The FDIC Quarterly Banking Profile, First Quarter, 1989, (1989), Washington, D.C., FDIC, First Quarter.

The FDIC Quarterly Banking Profile, Third Quarter, 1993, (1993), Washington, D.C., FDIC, Third Quarter.

The FDIC Quarterly Banking Profile, Fourth Quarter, 1993, (1994), Washington, D.C., FDIC, Fourth Quarter.

The FDIC Quarterly Banking Profile, Third Quarter, 2002, (2002), Washington, D.C., FDIC, Third Quarter.

"The New Basel Capital Accord," (2001) Consulatative Document, Basel, Switzerland, Bank for International Settlements, January.

"The New Basel Capital Accord: an Explanatory Note," (2001), Basel, Switzerland, Bank for International Settlements, January.

The World Bank, (2001), letter and comments sent to the Basel Committee on Banking Supervision, Bank for International Settlements, June 7.

Toritani, Reiko, and Philip Jones, (2002), "Japanese Banks: Stormy New Year—The Major Banks' Results for the Half Year to September 2002," *Fitch Ratings,* January 16, *http://www. fitchrtings.com*

"Toxic Waste," (2003), *The Economist,* March 15, pp. 68–69.

Trading and Capital-Markets Activities Manual, (2001), Section 2000, Board of Governors of the Federal Reserve System, Washington, D.C., *http://www.federalreserve.gov/boarddocs/SupManual/default.htm#cbem*

Vandell, K. D., (1978), "Default Risk Under Alternative Mortgage Instruments," *Journal of Finance,* 33, December, pp. 1279–1296.

von Furstenberg, G. M., (1969), "Default Risk on FHA Insured Home Mortgages as a Function of the Terms of Financing," *Journal of Finance,* 24, June, pp. 459–477.

von Furstenberg, G. M., (1970), "The Investment Quality of Home Mortgages," *Journal or Risk and Insurance,* 37, September, pp. 437–445.

3

Why and How Banks Fail—Would 8% Capital Make a Difference?

Ben Branch

I am sometimes accused of being a banker. My response is that I am a banker in the same sense that a mortician is a doctor. I have worked over the carcass of several large bank holding companies. During that process, I have learned a lot about how and why banks fail.

MY EXPERIENCES WITH TROUBLED BANKS

My experiences with troubled banks began in the mid-1980s. In one of those chance events that changes your life, I let a stockbroker talk me into taking a flyer on a depressed Texas bank. It was the oddity of a NYSE stock trading for about a dollar a share. Texas at that time was experiencing the adverse impact of a very depressed oil market. BancTexas, then the tenth largest bank in the state, was among the most troubled. I reasoned, naively, that since Texas had just begun to allow interstate banking, some large out-of-state bank would be willing to fix BancTexas' balance sheet in order to enter the Lone Star State's market. Little did I know how much better a deal such banks could get just by waiting.

BancTexas did get a temporary bailout. The FDIC pumped $350 million into the situation, and the workout firm, Hallwood Group, used a rights offering to raise additional capital. The bank initially appeared to have been adequately recapitalized. Unfortunately, for everyone but the regulators, the losses embedded in BancTexas' loan portfolio were much larger than Hallwood or anyone else on the investor side had contemplated. BancTexas rather quickly ran through all of the money it had gotten from the

FDIC and the new investors, and still more bad loans kept revealing themselves. The new BancTexas investors (the ones who had subscribed via Hallwood's rights offering) were essentially wiped out. The FDIC seized most of BancTexas' banks. Unlike subsequent Texas bank deals, the recapitalized BancTexas did not have put back rights for bad loans that came out of the woodwork. Most later deals provided such rights. Note that bad loans are a lot like cockroaches. Once you begin to see them, a lot more are almost sure to follow.

Painful as this BancTexas experience was for me financially, it turned out to be a very useful learning experience. Having personally suffered massive losses as a result of a combination of taking on too much leverage, the BancTexas debacle, and the 1987 Stock Market crash, I badly needed to restore my financial fisc. Accordingly, for my 1988 sabbatical leave, I sought out a learning opportunity with some money attached. Since I taught investments, I thought working in a real-world investment shop would be a useful way to spend a year. Moreover, I would be well paid. I approached two former students who ran money for the Springfield, Massachusetts, insurance company, Monarch Capital. I asked them to see if I could join their team for my sabbatical year. Their boss, the vice chairman of Monarch, quickly hired me. As soon as he learned about my BancTexas experience, he put me in charge of its $8-million-bond position in First Republic bank (FRB), then the largest bank in Texas. FRB was the result of a recent merger of two large Texas bank holding companies, Republic and InterFirst. As with the merger of the Pennsylvanian and New York Central Railroads (to form Penn Central), the merger of two large troubled banks produced one very large troubled enterprise. FRB was soon failed by the regulators. Prior to its failing, however, the Federal Deposit Insurance Corporation (FDIC) had extended a (very controversial) one-billion-dollar loan (the note purchase agreement) that each of the FRB banks was required to guarantee. As a result, when the banks failed, the FDIC was able to use the note purchase agreement as its justification for seizing all of FRB's banks (with the exception of FRB's Delaware chartered credit card bank). The credit card bank was later sold for a substantial sum, the disputed proceeds of which were placed into escrow. (Both the FDIC and FRB claimed ownership.)

The FRB estate was itself very complex, with both junior and senior bankholders who derived from both the Republic and InterFirst banks as well as from subsidiaries. Intercorporate guarantees (between Republic and InterFirst) added further complications. Claims also went back and forth between the FRB estate and the FDIC. For example, everyone claimed the credit card bank escrow, and the FRB creditors claimed the value of the solvent banks that the FDIC had seized.

I was made Monarch's representative on the FRB senior unsecured creditors' committee. To make a long story short, I ultimately became committee chair and later, board chairman of the liquidating corporation when FRB emerged from bankruptcy. Eventually we sorted out all of the inter creditor issues and obtained a full recovery of the pre petition claims for FRB's senior bondholders as a result of a settlement with the FDIC, in which each side took a portion of the credit card bank escrow monies.

While working on the FRB case, I met many of the major FRB creditors who were also substantial creditors in other Texas banks/bankruptcies. These investors fell into two major categories: 1) large institutional investors who had purchased their bonds when they were investment grade and 2) large vulture investors who had come into the situation after the bonds had fallen to very depressed levels. Of the ten largest Texas banks in the late 1980s, nine got into sufficient trouble such that they were either seized by the regulators or forced into a distress merger with a large out-of-state bank. As a result of my conversation with these creditors, I became at least somewhat familiar with a number of the other large problem Texas banks, including M Corp, First City, and Texas American Bank Shares. The stories of each had much in common. For an excellent summary of the banking problems of the Southwest, see the *History of the Eighties,* (1997), pp. 291–336.

I MOVED ON TO THE BANK OF NEW ENGLAND CORPORATION

The successful result obtained in the FRB matter (full recovery for seniors and substantial payout for juniors) led a group of bondholders who also owned Bank of New England Corporation (BNEC) bonds to approach me to see if I was willing to become a trustee in the BNEC case. Normally, in a Chapter 7 bankruptcy, an interim trustee is appointed by the U.S. trustee and becomes permanent trustee at the 341st meeting of the Chapter 7 creditors. The creditors do, however, have the right to elect a replacement in what amounts to a proxy fight among creditors. And that is exactly what these bondholders did. They elected me to be the permanent trustee of BNEC. Ultimately, we were once again able to obtain a full recovery for the senior bondholders, in part as a result of a settlement with the FDIC over some noncash assets that had been sent downstream from the holding company to the bankers, after the banks got into trouble. We are still working to obtain a significant recovery for the remaining creditors via a lawsuit against the former auditors, Ernest and Young. Along the way, I also became familiar with a number of other large-bank bankruptcies in the Northeast, including Bank East, Heritage NIS, and Vangard.[1]

FOUR PROPOSITIONS

Having seen a large number of bank failures up close, I have reached several conclusions, which I will now share. While I do not offer any scientific evidence to support them, I believe the following four propositions to be valid. I leave it to the reader to share or reject my viewpoint.

1. Banks fail because they have made too many bad loans.

Banks can have problems for a number of reasons. They can suffer losses because of: a bad bet on the direction of interest rates, employees who embezzled; too high overhead; speculation with derivatives; and/or overpayment for acquisitions. All of the above can cause losses, but rarely do the losses reach the magnitude that leads to failure, particularly for large banks.

On the other hand, loan losses of sufficient magnitude can easily tank a bank. The typical well-capitalized bank may have tangible equity in the order of 8% of total assets. In a good year a bank may generate a gross interest margin of 3%, loan losses of ½% and other operating expenses of 1% for a net profit equal to 1½% of assets. Now suppose the bank gets into trouble such that loans equal to 10% of its assets are newly determined to be at risk (classified) and that a 50% reserve is established for these recently classified problem loans. That addition to the loan reserve would represent 5% of the bank's assets and over half of what had been its 8% equity. Such an event is all too likely to begin a death spiral. Regulatory capital equal to 3% of assets is much too low for comfort (or the regulators), so the bank must downsize. The only assets it can sell without taking write-downs are its best moneymakers (e.g., securities and loans held at a gain, its credit card, and

---

1. *History of the Eighties, Lessons for the Future: An Examination of the Banking Crisis of the 1980's and Early 1990's*, Washington, D.C., Federal Deposits Insruance Corporation, 1997, Vol. 1.

perhaps mortgage operations). A second year of more bad loans (which is almost inevitable) and the bank is underwater and will be seized by the regulators. The bank may have had other problems, such as a poor acquisition strategy, too much overhead, and an adverse move in interest rates, but the core problem that caused the bank to fail is almost always a portfolio full of problem loans. Moreover, no matter how much capital the bank starts with, it can always find enough bad loans to absorb all of its capital and then some.

2. The loans that caused the bank to fail, accumulated on the books over a period of years.

Bad loans don't appear on the books all at once. They accumulate and tend to go unnoticed for a time. While loans that eventually become recognized as troubled may show some red flags early on, they may continue to perform for at least a while, after they are made. Rarely will the borrower default on payment in the first year, or so, after the loan is granted. The loan itself will often provide some breathing room. The borrower will almost always find a way to service the newly acquired debt for a time. New appraisals that will show deterioration in asset value, if made at all, will not come into play for a while. Rarely will the borrower call attention to the problems without first taking some time to try to fix things. Especially when a bank has poor internal controls or loan-monitoring practices, the problems may not surface right away. The delay may be much longer when the bank is poorly run.

Thus, loans that are recognized by the bank as being troubled are only so identified well after they are put on the books. Moreover, the process usually starts slowly with a small increase in loans identified as problems. Initially, the loss reserve may be viewed as adequate to absorb the increase in problem loans, and no more than a normal amount of new reserve may be added. Thus, the ratio of the dollar value of problem loans to loss reserve may be allowed to decline. The bank seeking to avoid taking losses on its loans may try to work with the borrowers to keep problem loans in pay status and thereby put off the need to classify them and eventually foreclose. These efforts may further delay full recognition of the extent of the problem. Creditors have even been known to swap problems with each other to obscure the nature of their problems.

Ultimately, however, the auditors, or more likely the regulators, or both, will force the issue. But here again delays may occur. The bank may for a time be given the benefit of the doubt, if it or its auditor reports that things are under control or being fixed.

Once the problem becomes obvious to all, the bank has an incentive to pump up regulatory capital by a variety of means. These kinds of measures generally involve robbing Peter to pay Paul when Paul is in the future and Peter is now. A bank in trouble will do almost anything it can get away with to pump up its regulatory capital account, even if only temporarily. They are, however, only putting off the inevitable and digging a deeper hole in the process.

Often as a result of a breakdown in internal controls, loans, which are either put on the books with basic structural problems, or which develop such problems after they are made, may not be recognized as problem loans for some time after they are made. By the time the extent of the problem is recognized, it is often too late to save the bank.

3. Banks that fail are almost always found to have had poorly maintained loan files.

Any lender can tell you how easy it is to lend money. The supply of would-be borrowers is never a problem. The hard part of lending is getting paid back. The first step in successful lending is effective due diligence of loan applications. The second and equally important step is monitoring the loans once they are made.

Most loans are made not only with a promise on the part of the borrower to service the debt as provided in the loan contract but also with representations, warranties, and covenants such as to maintain certain prespecified financial ratios. Appraisals and financial statements are supposed to be updated periodically. Additional borrowing is often limited or required to be subordinated. Collateral is to be maintained properly. Withdrawal of capital via dividends or otherwise is limited. These types of requirements are designed to protect the lender's interest in the assets on which the loan is based as well as to provide an early warning system for any problems that are in the process of arising.

The sooner the lender knows of a problem, the sooner actions can be taken to protect the loan's value. Borrowers are generally honest, decent people who have every intention of repaying their loans. Banks try not to lend to the other kind of applicant. If put on notice early, when they too have something of their own left to lose, borrowers will generally work with the bank to maintain and protect the underlining values.

If, however, the problem is allowed to worsen without attention, the borrower may soon get to the point where the face value of the loan exceeds the value of the underlining asset. At that stage, the borrower has little or nothing to lose from taking large risks, which if successful, may salvage his or her investment, and if unsuccessful, will only add to the lender's losses. The lender, of course, has a very different agenda in these situations.

Well-maintained loan files allow lenders to learn quickly if a loan is getting into trouble. Banks that fail do so, in large part, because they were unaware until very late in the process just how deep their problems were becoming. Poorly maintained loan files are a major factor in the banks not knowing the extent of their problems. Well-maintained loan files provide the raw material for a very useful early warning system.

Had the banks had a better handle on their situations as they developed, they could have done many things to mitigate their difficulties. As mentioned above, the losses on individual loans tend to be containable if the problems are recognized early and appropriate action is taken. Moreover, problems with some loans may lead the lender to identify and begin to deal with other similar loans with similar problems before they would otherwise be recognized. Furthermore, once recognized, a pattern of troubled loans may encourage the lender to revise lending practices and thereby correct the problem to avoid future losses. Equally or even more importantly, a lender who knows early that he or she has problems can begin to take corrective strategic actions in an orderly fashion. Such a lender can, for example, reduce new lending and growth-oriented activity in order to better position itself for dealing with its more difficult circumstances. The bank can reduce its risk-taking and begin an orderly effort to downsize. It can reduce overhead to correspond better its projected smaller size. In this way, the bank may be able to deal more effectively with its problems, successfully ride out the storm, and be positioned to resume growth once its situation is stabilized.

4. The bad loans that caused the bank to fail tended to have a common risk element.

When loans start to go bad in significant numbers and dollar amounts, many of the problem loans are found to have some common characteristic. For example, when the real estate market weakens, many real estate properties serving as collateral for loans, and particularly real estate development projects, may lose value. See ibid., pp. 137–167. Similarly, when the price of crude oil declines dramatically, all aspects of the energy market may be hit, including loans serviced directly or indirectly by the sale of energy.[2] Less Developed Country-(LDC) loans are another group that tends to move in a common fashion. Still other loan types are leveraged buyouts- (LBO) based financing and subprime loans. Any lender with a concentration in any one of these categories may find a lot of problem loans on its books if the sector itself encounters difficulties, especially if the loans were poorly underwritten documents or monitored.

Lenders with a concentration of lending activity in any one of the above-mentioned sectors (or others such as defense contractors, agricultural concerns, etc.) tend to be at high risk from such exposure. A diversified portfolio of loans is no guarantee against large loan losses, but it helps. On the other hand, a concentration of lending activity in any one sector can expose the lender to a world of hurt if something happens that adversely impacts that common risk element.

CONCLUSION

A Bank fails largely because it ends up with an asset portfolio containing a substantial percentage of problem loans. These loans accumulated on its books over an extended period of time. The loan files were generally very poorly maintained such that neither the bank, nor its auditors, nor the regulators could have a very accurate idea of the bank's condition. By the time its problem loan portfolio becomes too obvious to ignore, the bank will have passed the point of no return. Finally, a large percentage of the problem loans, which led to the bank's failure, had a common risk

---

2. ibid., pp. 293–313.

element. No amount of beginning capital is so large that a poorly run bank can't find a way to make enough bad loans to run through all its regulatory capital before it realizes how bad things are.

Accordingly, to avoid failing, a bank should:

1. Establish and maintain high-quality standards in its lending practices.
2. Maintain up-to-date and complete loan files on all of its loans; and timely and accurately monitor loans for signs of adverse changes in credit quality.
3. Take quick and appropriate action to defend the value of any loans that become troubled.
4. Avoid excessive exposure to loans having any common risk element.

REFERENCE

History of the Eighties, Lessons for the Future: An Examination of the Banking Crisis of the 1980's and Early 1990's, Washington, D.C., Federal Deposits Insurance Corporation, 1997, Vol. 1.

4

Basel II: The Roar That Moused

George G. Kaufman*

I. INTRODUCTION

In 1999, the Basel Committee on Banking Supervision issued a consultative paper describing proposed modifications to the capital standards for commercial banks, which had first been introduced by the committee in 1988 and implemented in many industrial countries starting in 1991 (Basel Committee, 2003a). The new proposal became known as Basel II to differentiate it from the earlier Basel I. To a large extent, the proposed Basel II was in response to widespread criticism of Basel I, but it also reflected additional thought and analysis of the role of bank capital regulation. In particular, Basel II added two new "pillars"—supervisory review (pillar 2) and market discipline (pillar 3)—to the single pillar of minimum capital requirement of Basel I.

In response to public comments, the committee revised its proposal twice and issued a third consultative paper (CP3) in early 2003. If approved, the proposed standards are scheduled for implementation in most countries at the beginning of 2007. In preparation, in August 2003, U.S. regulators circulated an Advance Notice of Proposed Rulemaking (ANPR) for the application of Basel II to U.S. banks for public comment by November 2003, and the major features have been incorporated by the European Union in a proposed revision of its Capital Adequacy Directive (CAD) for financial institutions, which must, however, be approved by the European Parliament and the member national parliaments before adoption.

* I am indebted to Bill Bergman, Robert Bliss, Douglas Evanoff and Richard Herring for their helpful comments on earlier drafts of this paper. Prepared for presentation at the annual meetings of the Financial Management Association, Denver, October 10, 2003.

This paper focuses on the proposed two new pillars, which have received far less attention than the capital standards pillar. The chapter concludes that both pillars have major design flaws that make achievement of the capital requirements determined by pillar 1, regardless of their desirability, questionable. These flaws help to explain the recent decision of the U.S. bank regulators to limit the mandatory application of Basel II to only the ten, or so, largest internationally active U.S. banks and why these requirements may be ineffective even for these banks. Thus, although Basel II roared loudly when proposed, it is likely to have only a relatively minor lasting effect on the capital of, at least, most U.S. banks.

2. OVERVIEW OF BASEL AND PILLAR I

The Basel Committee on Banking Supervision was established in 1974 by a number of western industrial countries (G-10), primarily in response to the failure of the Herstatt Bank in Germany that had significant adverse implications for both foreign exchange markets and banks in other countries.[1] The Committee focused on facilitating and enhancing information-sharing and cooperation among bank regulators in major countries, and developing principles for the supervision of internationally active large banks (Herring and Litan, 1995). As losses at some large international banks from loans to less-developed countries (LDCs) mounted in the late-1970s, the Committee became increasingly concerned that the potential failures of one or more of these banks could have serious adverse effects, not only for the other banks in their own countries but also for counterparty banks in other countries, i.e., cross-border contagion. The Committee feared that large banks lacked sufficient capital in relation to the risks they were assuming and that the inadequacy, in large part, reflected the reluctance of national governments to require higher capital ratios for fear of putting their own banks at a competitive disadvantage relative to banks in other countries.

In the 1980s, this concern was particularly directed at Japanese banks, which were rapidly expanding globally, based on valuations of capital that included large amounts of unrealized capital gains from rapid increases in the values of Japanese stocks that they

---

1. Current member countries are Belgium, Canada, France, Germany, Italy, Japan, Luxembourg, the Netherlands, Spain, Sweden, Switzerland, the United Kingdom, and the United States.

owned. Such gains were not included in the capital valuations-permitted banks in most other countries, where equity ownership by banks was more restrictive. Partially as a result, the Committee began to focus more on developing international regulation that centered on higher and more uniform bank capital standards across countries. The capital standards developed and introduced in 1988 became known as Basel I.

Perhaps the most revolutionary aspect of the capital requirements developed in Basel I was relating a bank's capital to the perceived credit risk of the bank's portfolio. Before that, most regulators focused on simple leverage ratios that used only total assets as the base. Basel I also incorporated off-balance-sheet assets in the base as well as on-balance-sheet assets and weighted individual assets by a risk factor. However, the formula constructed was a relatively simple one that treated all banks equally—one size fits all. Individual assets were divided into four basic credit risk categories, or buckets, according to the identity of their counterparty and assigned weights ranging from 0 to 100 percent. The weighted values of the individual on- and off- balance-sheet assets were then summed and classified as "risk-weighted assets." Banks were required to maintain capital of not less than 8 percent of their risk-weighted assets. This capital ratio is referred to as risk-based capital (RBC).

But the arbitrary nature of both the risk classes and risk weights led to widespread criticism that the resulting risk-based capital requirements were neither realistic nor useful and to "gaming" by the banks, as they exploited differences in returns computed on different assets on the basis of the regulator-assigned capital requirements—regulatory capital—vis-à-vis that perceived to be required by market forces—economic capital. Such arbitrage likely results in misallocation of resources and reduced economic and social welfare. In addition, total bank credit risk was measured as the sum of the credit risks of the individual asset components, giving no weight to any gains from diversification across less than perfectly correlated assets. Nevertheless, the capital requirements established by Basel I were implemented by an increasing number of countries, including the United States, starting in 1991 and became the effective capital standards for banks worldwide.

Shortly thereafter, in response to the criticisms of its formula and the avoidance activities of banks, the Basel Committee began to work on improving the capital requirements. The structure of the credit risk weights was modified and their values were determined by three alternative methods, depending on the size and financial sophistication of the bank. In addition, explicit weights were assigned to operational risk and the Basel I weights maintained for market and trading risk.

With respect to credit risk exposure, the most important risk component in the Basel structure, potential losses from default are effectively divided into two components—1) the probability of default (PD) and 2) the loss given default (LGD).[2] The values for these measures are to be stipulated by the regulators for the smaller, least sophisticated banks and progressively shifted to the banks as their sophistication increases. The smallest, least sophisticated banks are permitted to apply the "standardized approach" to compute their risk-weighted assets. Weights are assigned by the regulators for individual assets, based to a large extent on credit ratings that the bank's counterparties have received from private credit rating agencies on their outstanding marketable debt that implicitly reflect both PD and LGD.[3] The standardized approach resembles Basel I but is somewhat more complex. Bank assets are divided into five, rather than four, basic groupings and the risk weights for each group are based more on market evidence and stretch over a wider range. But otherwise, the same criticisms that were directed at Basel I may also be directed at this approach in Basel II. On the other hand, the standardized approach has the virtue of simplicity and, as it applies only to small banks, its failings may not be very costly in terms of any lasting damage to the domestic or international financial markets as a whole.

Larger banks are to rely more on internally generated information—the internal ratings approach (IRB)—in which PD and LGD are explicit. Most would compute their own PD for individual loans but use values for LGD provided by the regulators. This is referred to as the "foundation IRB approach." The largest and most sophisticated banks may use the "advanced IRB approach" (A-IRB), which permits them to determine their own values for both PD and LGD. The models used by the banks to obtain their values need to be evaluated and preapproved by the regulators.

---

2. It appears ironic that the credit risk exposure of banks, which are widely assumed to be beneficiaries of private information on their loan customers, is measured by the ratings assigned to their public debt traded on the capital market, which is widely assumed to have little, if any, private information.

3. In addition, assets are assigned values for maturity and exposure at default.

Although the IRB approaches overcome some of the criticism of the Basel I bucket approach, they are not devoid of criticism. In particular, the loss rates determined by the regulators are subject to large errors so that gaming is still likely, and the models used by the banks to generate their internal values are likely to be too complex and opaque for supervisors (and even many bankers themselves) to understand thoroughly, so the resulting capital amounts will be difficult to evaluate for adequacy and compliance with the requirements. The description of the proposed regulations for the application of A-IRB to large U.S. banks in the ANPR takes more than 30 small-type, three-column pages in the *Federal Register* (*Federal Register*, 2003). As has been frequently noted, although the real world is complex, complexity, per se, does not necessarily achieve reality.

The discussion of pillar 1 also bypasses a number of important issues concerning the definition and measurement of capital, in particular, what is capital; is dividing capital into tiers appropriate and, if so, what should be the criteria; role of "subdebt;" what is the relationship between capital and loan loss reserves; and how should loss reserves be determined over the business cycle (Shadow Financial Regulatory Committee, 2000; Laeven and Majnoni, 2003; and Borio, Furfine, and Lowe, 2001). Failure to consider these issues greatly weakens the usefulness of the recommendations.

Many of the above criticisms of pillar 1 and, in particular, of regulator—rather than market—determined RBC have been made by many parties. The remainder of this paper will focus on pillars 2 and 3, which are both intended to effectively enforce and to supplement the capital requirements determined in pillar 1 and have received far less attention.

3. SUPERVISORY REVIEW (PILLAR 2)

Supervisory review "is intended . . . to ensure that banks have adequate capital to support all the risks in their business" (Basel, 2003, p. 138), determined both by pillar 1 and by supervisory evaluation of risks not explicitly captured in pillar 1, e.g., interest rate risk and credit concentration. "Supervisors are expected to evaluate how well banks are assessing their capital needs relative to their risks and to intervene, where appropriate. This interaction is intended to foster an active dialogue between banks and supervisors such that when deficiencies are identified, prompt and decisive action can be taken to reduce risk or restore capital" (Basel, 2003, p. 138). This supervisory responsibility is spelled out further in three of four key principles developed for supervisory review.

Principle 2 of pillar 2 states that "supervisors should take appropriate supervisory action if they are not satisfied with" (Basel, 2003, p. 142) their review and evaluation of the adequacy of the banks' internal models. Moreover, Principle 3 states that "supervisors should expect banks to operate above the minimum regulatory capital ratios and should have the ability to require banks to hold capital in excess of the minimum" (Basel, 2003, p. 144). Principle 4 states that "supervisors should seek to intervene at an early stage to prevent capital from falling below the minimum levels . . . and should require rapid remedial action if capital is not maintained or restored" (Basel, 2003, p. 144). But nowhere in CP3 are supervisors granted the tools and authority to perform these functions. This makes it less likely that countries not currently granting regulators such powers will introduce them when adopting Basel II.

In contrast, in the U.S., the FDIC Improvement Act (FDICIA) enacted at year-end 1991, the same year as Basel I was implemented in the U.S., not only explicitly granted supervisors the authority to impose such sanctions on banks that failed to maintain minimum capital requirements but required the regulators to impose such sanctions when the capital ratios of banks declined below given threshold levels, or the banks displayed other indications of financial troubles. The system of first discretionary and then mandatory regulatory sanctions in FDICIA is referred to as prompt corrective action (PCA). FDICIA specifies that both RBC and simple capital leverage ratios need to be considered, and the bank regulators defined RBC in accord with Basel I. Banks have to satisfy all three capital measures specified. The mandatory sanctions were included to supplement the discretionary sanctions because the U.S. experience with the banking-and-thrift crises of the 1980s suggested that, for a number of reasons, regulators may not always intervene in troubled institutions in a forceful and timely fashion and instead delay or forbear (Benston and Kaufman, 1994 and Kaufman, 1995).

The structure of discretionary and mandatory sanctions included in PCA is summarized in Table 1. Both sets of sanctions are designed to become progressively harsher and the mandatory sanctions progressively more important as the financial condition of a bank deteriorates, and its capital ratios decline, below the thresholds of each of the five capital tranches or tripwires. The mandatory sanctions are to protect against undue delay and forbearance by regulators in imposing discretionary sanctions (Benston and Kaufman, 1994). The sanctions mimic those that the market typically imposes on unregulated firms facing similar financial difficulties. Shortly after a bank becomes "critically undercapitalized," which is currently defined as a 2 percent equity to asset ratio, the regulators are required to place the institution in receivership or conservatorship (legal closure) and to resolve it at least cost to the FDIC.

Table 1. Summary of Prompt Corrective Action Provisions of the Federal Deposit Insurance Corporation Improvement Act of 1991

| | | | Capital Ratios (percent) | | |
| | | | Risk-Based | | Leverage |
Zone	Mandatory Provisions	Discretionary Provisions	Total	Tier 1	Tier 1
1. Well Capitalized			>10	>6	>5
2. Adequately Capitalized	1. No brokered deposits except with FDIC approval		>8	>4	>4
3. Undercapitalized	1. Suspend dividends and management fees 2. Require capital restoration plan 3. Restrict asset growth 4. Approval required for acquisitions, branching, and new activities 5. No brokered deposits	1. Order recapitalization 2. Restrict inter-affiliate transactions 3. Restrict deposit interest rates 4. Restrict certain other activities 5. Any other action that would better carry out prompt corrective action	<8	<4	<4
4. Significantly Undercapitalized	1. Same as for Zone 3 2. Order recapitalization* 3. Restrict inter-affiliate transactions* 4. restrict deposit interest rates* 5. Pay of officers restricted	1. Any zone 3 discretionary actions 2. Conservatorship or receivership if fails to submit or implement plan or recapitalize pursuant to order 3. Any other Zone 5 provision, if such action is necessary to carry out prompt corrective action	<6	<3	<3
5. Critically undercapitalized	1. Same as for Zone 4 2. Receiver/conservator within 90 days 3. Receiver if still in Zone 5 four quarters after becoming critically undercapitalized 4. Suspend payments on subordinated debt 5. Restrict certain other activities				<2**

*Not required if primary supervisor determines action would not serve purpose of prompt corrective action if certain conditions are met.
**Tangible equity.
Source: Board of Governors of the Federal Reserve System.

The purpose of the sanctions is not to punish the bank, per se, but to provide incentives for owners and managers to turn the bank around and return it to greater profitability and a stronger capital position. Without similar PCA-type authority, it is unlikely that bank regulators in other countries can achieve the control over a bank's capital that pillar 2 envisions. Indeed, the early experience with PCA in the U.S. suggests that some regulators may not be using their authority as vigorously as intended in the legislation and that supervisory review needs to be supplemented by other forces, including market discipline, which is pillar 3 in the Basel II proposal (Kaufman, 2003b).

4. MARKET DISCIPLINE (PILLAR 3)

Market discipline may be defined as actions by stakeholders to both monitor and influence the behavior of entities to improve their performance (Bliss and Flannery, 2002). Pillar 3 in Basel II is intended "to complement the minimum capital requirements (Pillar 1) and the supervisory review process (Pillar 2) . . . [and] to encourage market discipline by developing a set of disclosure requirements which will allow market participants to assess . . . the capital adequacy of the institution" (Basel, 2003, p. 154). Unfortunately, the requirements for effective market discipline are not discussed in the section on market discipline in CP3. Rather, the section discusses in great detail what information on a bank's financial and risk positions need be disclosed to the public (Lopez, 2003).

But disclosure and transparency is a necessary, but not sufficient, condition for effective market discipline. What is required is, at least, some at-risk bank stakeholders. Stakeholders not at risk would have little or no incentive to monitor and influence their banks and thus have little, if any, use for the information disclosed about the financial performance of the banks. While market discipline is likely to encourage disclosure, disclosure, per se, is less likely to encourage market discipline in the absence of a significant number of at-risk stakeholders. Because of the fear of substantial economic harm caused by the failure of large banks, governments and bank regulators in almost all countries have tended to avoid failing such institutions and, where they have, protected all depositors and other creditors in a de facto policy termed "too-big-to-fail" (TBTF), (Kaufman, 2003a). Thus, few de facto at-risk stakeholders have existed in even privately owned banks, no less state-owned banks. However, the U.S. has taken steps in recent years to enhance market discipline by reversing the policy of blanket protection of debt stakeholders and converting the largest stakeholders —depositors, creditors, and shareholders—to at-risk status. FDICIA prohibits the FDIC from protecting any uninsured stakeholder at failed banks, in which doing so is not a least-cost resolution to it. But there is an exception.

If there is evidence that not protecting uninsured depositors and/or other creditors at a failed bank "would have serious adverse effects on economic conditions or financial stability; and . . . any action or assistance . . . would avoid or mitigate such adverse effects," the regulators can petition the Secretary of the Treasury to permit such protection. This provision is called the Systemic Risk Exception (SRE) and replaces TBTF. But obtaining permission to do so is not easy. There are a number of significant before-and-after hurdles that need to be cleared. To invoke SRE, a recommendation must be made in writing to the Secretary of the Treasury by two-thirds of both the Board of Directors of the FDIC and the Board of Governors of the Federal Reserve System that protection of at least some uninsured stakeholders is necessary to avoid the serious adverse effects cited in the FDICIA legislation. The Secretary must consult with the President before agreeing with the recommendation, must retain written documentation for review, and must, again in writing, notify the Banking Committees of both the House of Representatives and the Senate (Kaufman, 2003a).

After any protection is provided, a review of the need for the action taken and the consequences must be completed by the General Accounting Office (GAO), and any losses suffered by the FDIC in providing the assistance must be paid "expeditiously" through a special assessment on all insured banks based on their asset size. These barriers appear sufficiently high and difficult to clear to make the SRE exception an exception rather than the rule, as was the case with TBTF before FDICIA, and thereby to increase the number of large and assumably sophisticated, at-risk stakeholders. Since 1992, no SREs have been requested or granted, and uninsured depositors and creditors have experienced losses, in all failures with resolution losses, except in a few small bank resolutions where protecting the uninsured depositors did not increase the loss to the FDIC. In some resolutions, losses to unprotected depositors exceeded 40 percent and other creditors even more (Kaufman, 2003b). On the other hand, since 1992, no large money center bank has encountered insolvency, so the SRE has not really been tested.

Another way to increase the importance of at-risk claimants is to require banks to issue a minimum amount of subordinated debt (subdebt), (Shadow Financial Regulatory Committee, 2000; Evanoff and Wall, 2002, Basel Committee, 2003b, Benston et al., 1986).[4] Such debt would be both de jure as well as credibly de facto unprotected and therefore at risk. Thus, the interest yield spread (at which it is either sold initially in the primary market or traded later in the secondary market) would reflect investors perceptions of the financial strength of the issuing institution (Jagtiani et al., 2002). These market determined yield spreads are likely both to affect investors' attitudes toward the institution and management's actions, and to serve as a signal to regulators of market perceptions. Such signals would supplement the information regulators obtain from their own examinations and other sources and, in some proposals, would automatically feed into PCA and possibly trigger sanctions on the institution when the yield spreads become sufficiently large. Unfortunately, to date, regulators in neither the U.S. nor the other Basel countries have viewed these proposals favorably and implemented them.

5. CONCLUSIONS

The coming of Basel II was announced with great fanfare and has already been incorporated in a notice of proposed rulemaking in the U.S. and a proposed, revised CAD in the EU countries. But, particularly in the U.S., praise by the industry, regulators, and scholars has been much more muted and has become progressively even more muted through time, as the details are examined more closely.[5] Indeed, U.S. bank regulators have recently effectively rejected Basel II as a requirement for all but the largest 10, or so internationally active banks, which would be required to use the advanced IRB approach. All other banks may compute their RBC on the basis of the current Basel I, although they can adopt the advanced IRB approach if they wish and their supervisors concur.

---

4. Since the Depositor Preference Act of 1993 in the U.S., all bank debt is subordinated to deposits at domestic offices and the FDIC. Thus, for this proposal, the term "subdebt" is no longer necessary in the U.S., except at the bank holding company level.

5. Increasing criticism has also been voiced by the European Central Bank and the Institute of International Finance, the major trade association representing large banks in major countries.

The rejection in the U.S. centers primarily on the complexity of computations and doubts about the adequacy of the RBC requirement, the inadequacies of pillars 2 and 3 analyzed in this paper, and the existence of PCA in the U.S. to which all banks are subject. For example, Federal Reserve Vice-Chairman, Roger Ferguson has stated that "for the United States banking authorities, pillar II of Basel II requires nothing new . . . [and] considerable information is publicly disseminated—for example, through our Call Reports—and is available for counterparties" (Ferguson, June 10, 2003, p. 3). Similar views have been expressed by the Comptroller of the Currency (Hawke, 2003a and b). That is, despite its well-recognized shortcomings, the U.S. already has a more effective system in place.

Moreover, to the extent the advanced IRB approach may compute lower capital requirements for the largest banks that will use it, even after addition of operational risk, as it appears likely to do and to be its major appeal, these banks are still subject to the minimum leverage ratio constraint, which is unaffected by Basel II. Indeed, the ANPR specifically states that "the Agencies are not proposing to introduce specific requirements or guidelines to implement Pillar 2. Instead, existing guidance, rules, and regulations would continue to be enforced" (*Federal Register*, 2003, p. 45,905).

This paper supports much of the criticism of proposed Basel II, particularly with respect to pillar 1. However, regardless of the complexity or desirability of RBC computed according to pillar 1, the provisions of pillars 2 and 3 are inadequate to enforce them. Although pillar 2 discusses the need for supervisors to intervene promptly, if either a bank's capital or the model used to compute capital are perceived inadequate, and to impose remedial action, no powers are explicitly recommended for supervisors to effectively enforce this mandate. What appears necessary in countries that do not currently provide for such powers is the introduction of a system of PCA similar to that required in the U.S. since the enactment of FDICIA in 1991. Pillar 3 proposes to enhance market discipline by increasing financial disclosure requirements for banks. But disclosure is most effective if there are substantial bank stakeholders at risk. Presently, few stakeholders, particularly de jure uninsured depositors, view themselves at risk, as regulators have tended to protect them in nearly all large bank failures in almost all countries. What is necessary to enhance market discipline further is to increase the number and importance of stakeholders who perceive themselves at risk de facto as well as de jure. This requires scaling back TBTF, as has been attempted in the U.S. with the introduction of SRE. Adoption of a subdebt requirement would expedite this process.

Thus, on the other hand, until the Committee proposes more substantial pillars for enhancing supervisory review and market disciple, Basel II will encounter difficulties in fulfilling many of the grand promises made at its introduction, particularly outside the United States. On the other hand, however, regardless of its short-comings, Basel II has both increased our knowledge of the nature and measurement of risk in banking and the sensitivity of bankers, regulators, analysts, and the public to risk management. This is no small feat in itself and may represent Basel II's major lasting contribution. Indeed, the Basel proposals may make their greatest lasting contribution by continuing to be an ongoing process that is never implemented.

REFERENCES

Basel Committee on Banking Supervision, *The New Basel Capital Accord* (Consultative Document), (2003a), Basel, Switzerland: Bank for International Settlements, April.

Basel Committee on Banking Supervision, *Markets for Bank Subordinated Debt and Equity in Basel Committee Member Countries* (Working Paper No. 12), (2003b), Basel, Switzerland: Bank for International Settlements, August.

Benston, George J., Robert A. Eisenbeis, Paul M. Horvitz, Edward J. Kane, and George G. Kaufman, (1986), *Perspectives on Safe and Sound Banking*, Cambridge, MA: MIT Press.

Benston, George J. and George G. Kaufman, (1994), "The Intellectual History of the Federal Deposit Insurance Corporation Improvement Act of 1991," in George Kaufman, ed., *Reforming Financial Institutions and Markets in the United States*, Boston: Kluwer Academic, pp. 1–18.

Bliss, Robert R. and Mark J. Flannery, (2002), "Market Discipline in the Governance of U.S. Bank Holding Companies: Monitoring vs. Influence," *European Finance Review*, Vol. 6, No. 3, pp. 361–395.

Borio, Claudio, Craig Furfine, and Philip Lowe, (2001), "Procyclicality of the Financial System and Financial Stability: Issues and Policy Options," in *Marrying the Macro- and Microprudential Dimensions of Financial Stability* (BIS Papers No. 1), Basel: Bank for International Settlements, March.

Evanoff, Douglas D. and Larry D. Wall, (2002), "Subordinated Debt and Prompt Corrective Regulatory Action" in George Kaufman, ed., *Prompt Corrective Action in Banking: 10 Years Later*, Amsterdam: Elsevier Science, pp. 3–29.

Federal Register, (2003), "Risk-Based Capital Guidelines: Proposed Rule and Notice" Washington, D.C., August 4, pp. 45,900–45,988.

Ferguson, Roger W., (2003), "Basel II: Scope of Application in the United Sates," Washington, D.C.: Board of Governors of the Federal Reserve System, June 10.

Ferguson, Roger W., (2003), "Testimony Before the Subcommittee on Financial Institutions and Consumer Credit Committee on Financial Services, U.S. House of Representatives," Washington, D.C.: Board of Governors of the Federal Reserve System, June 19.

Hawke, John D., (2003a), "Testimony Before the Committee on Financial Services, U.S. House of Representatives," Washington, D.C., Comptroller of the Currency, February 27.

Hawke, John D., (2003b), "Remarks Before the Committee on Banking, Housing, and Urban Affairs, U.S. Senate" (NR2003-50), Washington D.C.: Comptroller of the Currency, June 18.

Herring, Richard J. and Robert E. Litan, (1995), *Financial Regulation in the Global Economy*, Washington, D.C.: Brookings Institution.

Jagtiani, Julapa, George Kaufman, and Catharine Lemieux, (2002), "The Effect of Credit Risk on Bank and Bank Holding Company Bond Yields," *Journal of Financial Research*, Winter, pp. 559–575.

Kaufman, George G., (1995), "The U.S. Banking Debacle of the 1980s," *The Financer*, May, pp. 9–26.

Kaufman, George G., (2003a), "Too-Big-To-Fail: Quo Vadis?" in Benton Gup, ed., *Too-Big-To-Fail: Policies and Practices*, Westport, CT, Praeger.

Kaufman, George G., (2003b) "FDIC Losses in Bank Failures: Has FDICIA Made a Difference?" *Working Paper*, Chicago: Loyola University Chicago, August.

Laeven, Luc and Giovanni, Majnoni, (2003), "Loan Loss Provisioning and Economic Slowdowns: Too Much, Too Late?" *Journal of Financial Intermediation*, April, pp. 178–197.

Lopez, Jose A., (2003), "Disclosure as a Supervisory Tool: Pillar 3 of Basel II," *FRBSF Economic Letter*, August 1.

Shadow Financial Regulatory Committee, (2000), *Reforming Bank Capital Regulation*, Washington, D.C.: American Enterprise Institute.

5

Basel II Creates an Uneven Playing Field

Benton E. Gup[1]

The 1988 Basel Capital Accord provides a minimum capital requirement of 8% of risk-weighted assets for internationally active banks in order to 1) ensure an adequate level of capital and 2) competitive equality. It is the second point, *competitive equality*, that is addressed here. Competitive equality referred to the fact that at that time, banks in the major trading countries had significantly different capital ratios. Those with lower capital ratios had lower costs of funds and a competitive advantage in the loan markets of the world. Thus, one of the purposes of the 1988 accord was to even the playing field in terms of capital requirements, thus attempting to create competitive equality. It was successful. By the turn of the century, the 8% capital standard had been adopted in more than 100 countries with internationally active banks.[2]

The 8% capital standard is a "one-size-fits-all" measure. It focuses on credit risk, which is a good starting point; but banks face a wider variety of risks. Accordingly, in 1996, an amendment was introduced that allowed banks to deal with trading/market risks. And in 1999, the Basel Committee on Banking Supervision proposed a "New Capital Adequacy Framework" to replace the 1988 accord. The end product will be the new Basel Capital Accord (Basel II), which is expected to be adopted in 2006. The good news is that Basel II will provide greater flexibility and risk sensitivity

---

1. Testimony before the U.S. House of Representatives, Committee on Financial Services, Subcommittee on Financial Institutions and Consumer Credit, June 19, 2003.
2. "The New Basel Capital Accord," Press Release, January 16, 2001.

than the 1988 accord. The bad news is that it will create competitive inequality, which was one of major reasons behind the framing of the 1988 accord.

Basel II provides three options for calculating risk-weighted assets for credit risk.[3]

1. The *standard approach*, which is similar to the 1988 accord. However, some adjustments to the risk weights are made for sovereign exposures, nongovernmental public-sector entities, and multilateral development banks. A 100% risk weight means a full capital charge equal to 8% of that value. A 50% risk weight means a capital charge of 4% ($0.5 \times 8\%$) of that value. For corporate lending, Basel II provides risk weights of 20%, 50%, 100%, and 150%.

2. The *foundation internal ratings-based (IRB) approach*, under which bank supervisors provide the estimates of the values used in establishing losses—for example, loss given default (LGD), exposure at default (EAD), and maturity (M)—that are used in the models.

3. The *advanced internal ratings-based (A-IRB) approach.* The A-IRB approach is similar to the foundation IRB approach, but the bank provides the probability of default (PD), LGD, EAD, and M. The range of risk weights under the foundation and advanced IRB approaches is greater than under the standard approach. Credit risk mitigation and securitization are considered under both approaches.

BANK CAPITAL

Table 1 shows the total risk-based capital ratios for all FDIC-insured commercial banks in 2002. The ratios range from 17% for the smallest banks to 12% for the largest ones. There are 80 large banks with assets greater than $10 billion, and 7,807 smaller banks. The small banks have excess capital. The capital for the large banks exceeds the 8% minimum, and provides a cushion for growth. During the 1997–2002 (4th Qtr.) period, large bank assets increased 66%. During that same period, the assets of smaller banks remained virtually unchanged.

---

3. "Overview of the New Basel Capital Accord," April 2003.

Table 1. Total Risk-Based Capital Ratio at FDIC-Insured Commercial Banks

Full Year 2002

	LESS THAN $100 MILLION IN ASSETS	$100 MILLION TO $1 BILLION IN ASSETS	$1 BILLION TO $10 BILLION IN ASSETS	GREATER THAN $10 BILLION IN ASSETS
12.78% Average capital ratio for all banks	17.10%	14.20%	14.53%	12.12%
7,887 banks	4,168	3,314	325	80

Source: *FDIC Quarterly Banking Profile*, Fourth Quarter, 2002, Table III-A, *http://www2.fdic.gov/qbp/2002dec/cb3.html.*

Federal banking regulators are expected to require about twenty of the largest commercial banks to use the Advanced IRB approach. The other banks will be given a choice of using the Advanced IRB approach or continuing to use the 1988 Basel Capital Accord standard. Because the smaller banks have excess capital and less need to enter the national and international capital markets than the larger banks, the 1988 Basel Capital Accord will work for them. That leaves about 60 large banks in a quandary. Which approach should they use?

One factor affecting their decision is the cost of implementing Basel II that ranges from $10 million for small banks to $150 million, or more, for large banks.[4] For example, Credit Suisse First Boston estimated that the initial costs of complying with Basel II would range from $52 million to $75 million, plus substantial costs for maintaining the systems.[5]

Stock market and debt market values are important, too. Some bankers whose stocks are actively traded believe that they must choose the Advanced IRB approach if they want to be considered major league players by equity analysts and shareholders. Otherwise, they will be considered minor league players, and it could adversely affect the price of their stocks. The issue of whether a bank is a major league player appears to be of greater concern to equity analysts than to credit rating agencies.

---

4. Petrou (2003).
5. Ervin (2003).

DIFFERENT METHODS OF CALCULATING CREDIT RISK GIVE DIFFERENT CAPITAL REQUIREMENTS

Large banks will probably select the Advanced IRB method for calculating risk-weighted assets because it gives them the greatest potential for reducing the amount capital that they must allocate for credit risk. Thus, a bank using the Advanced IRB method for calculating risk may have lower capital requirements for a loan than a bank using the 1988 Basel Accord standards. By way of illustration, consider a $100 commercial loan with a 1-year maturity. An FDIC study by French, Stark, Cave, and Feid (2003) revealed that under the Standard Approach—which is similar to the 1988 Basel Accord standards, the loan has a 100% risk weight, and the capital charge is $8. Under the Advanced IRB approach, if the loan has an initial S&P rating of "A+," a 10% loss given default (LGD), and a 0.3 probability of default (PD), it would have a 1.72 risk weight that equates to a capital charge of $0.14 ($8 × 0.0172 = $0.1376).

The LGD, PD, and EAD used in the Advanced IRB method to evaluate a particular loan may vary from bank to bank depending on the underlying assumptions, judgments, quality, and quantity of the data, and the models they use. It is possible that some banks using the Advanced IRB method may understate the risks to minimize the initial risk capital required in order to price a loan below their competitors. Even if such banks don't "game" the system, the Advanced IRB typically produces lower capital requirements. To the extent that capital is taken into account in pricing loans, this creates an uneven playing field for the 7,800+ banks using the 1988 Basel Accord standard.

REAL ESTATE

Real estate loans are singled out because they constitute a larger percentage of the loan portfolios of the larger regional banks than of the largest banks in our system. The risk weights assigned by Basel II to real estate loans appear to be excessive in light of the changes that have occurred in that industry. The past and the present are discussed below.

An FDIC study, *History of the Eighties* (1997, Vol. 1), found that real estate loans were the main cause of losses at failed and surviving banks in the U.S. in the 1980s and early 1990s. An International Monetary Fund study by Lindgren, Garcia, and Saal (1996) found that real estate loans contributed to banking sector problems in Finland, France, Japan, Malaysia, Norway, Spain, and Sweden. A World Bank study by Sheng (1996) identified real estate losses with banking problems in Argentina, Chile, Columbia, Ghana, Yugoslavia, and elsewhere. Finally, Gup (1998), studying international banking crises, identified real estate loans as contributing to more bank failures than any other category of loans. The bottom line is that real estate lending can be risky. Why?

THE 1985–1991 PERIOD

In order to answer that question for real estate loans in the U.S., we examine one of the worst periods in banking history and then contrast it to 2002. As shown in Table 2, 1,260 FDIC-insured commercial banks failed during the 1985–1992 period. During this period, real estate loans expressed as a percentage of net loans and leases increased from 27% to 44%.

In order to examine the failed banks in greater detail, we focus on 1991.[6] Table 3 shows that most of the banks that failed were small: 69% had assets of less than $100 million and 23% had assets of $100 million to $1 billion. Stated otherwise, 92% of the banks that failed were small community banks. Table 3 also reveals that most of the failed banks were located in the Northeast and Southwest.

Bad real estate loans were a major factor in many of the failures. Figure 1 shows a map of troubled real estate loans by state in 1991. The darkest color on the map depicts states with 8% or more troubled real estate assets. They are located primarily in the Southwest and Northeast. Banks located in Texas, Connecticut, and Massachusetts accounted for the greatest concentration of failures. Other parts of the country fared better.

The map in Figure 1 and the data in Table 3 provide unique insights. The real estate problems were highly concentrated in selected states. Because small banks serve their local communities, they were impacted the most by downturns in their real estate markets in the sense that they could not diversify their real estate loan risk. The same was true for the larger banks that failed. However, the composition of loans and charge-offs rates of loans differed substantially between small and large banks (see Table 5).

---

6. 1991 was selected because the data were complete and consistent in the sources cited in Tables 2-5. Data for 1992 was not consistent.

In the early 1990s, bank operations were restricted geographically. It was not until 1994 that the Riegle-Neal Interstate Branching Efficiency Act was passed that allowed interstate bank acquisitions.

In 1991, commercial and industrial loans accounted for 27% of total loans and leases, and real estate loans accounted for about 43%. However, as shown in Table 4—FDIC Assets in Liquidation—C&I loans exceeded real estate loans. This suggests that commercial loans also contributed significantly to bank failures and that bad real estate loans were not the sole cause.

Table 2. FDIC-Insured Bank Failures, Deposits, and Real Estate Loans

YEAR	BANK FAILURES (1,260)	BANK DEPOSITS AT FAILED BANKS $ BILL. ($180)	TOTAL REAL ESTATE LOANS AT ALL BANKS $ BILL.	NET LOANS AND LEASES $ BILL	REAL ESTATE LOANS/NET LOANS AND LEASES %
1992	120	$41	$868	$1,977	43.9%
1991	124	54	851	1,998	42.6
1990	168	15	830	2,055	40.4
1989	206	24	762	2,004	38.0
1988	200	25	675	1,886	35.8
1987	184	6	600	1,779	33.7
1986	138	7	515	1,728	29.8
1985	120	8	439	1,608	27.3

Annual Report 2002, FDIC, p. 111; FDIC, "Real Estate Loans," Table CB12, *http://www2fdic. gov/hsob/hsobRpt.asp.*

Table 3. 1991 Failed Banks by Asset Size and Location

BANK ASSET SIZE	1991 FAILED BANKS
Greater than $10 billion	2 (1%)
$1 billion–$10 billion	9 (7%)
$100 million–$1 billion	28 (23%)
Less than $100 million	85 (69%)
Total	124 100%
Northeast	45 (36%)
Southwest	38 (31%)

"Banks Failures and Assistance," 1991, FDIC, *http://www.fdic.gov/bank/historical/bank/ 1991/index.html.*

Table 4. 1991 FDIC End-of-Year Assets in Liquidation

ASSET TYPE	BOOK VALUE ($ BILLIONS)
Commercial Loans	$15.3
Mortgage Loans	12.8
Other Loans	1.4
Real Estate Owned	6.0
Judgments	1.9
Securities	0.3
Other Assets	5.6
Total	$43.3

Managing the Crisis: The FDIC and RTC Experience, 1998. Table 15-4.

Table 5. Percent of Real Estate Loans Charged-Off (Net), Year-end 1991

	ALL BANKS	ASSETS LESS THAN $100 MILLION	ASSETS $100 MIL-LION–$1 BILLION	ASSETS $1–10 BILLION	ASSETS GREATER THAN $10 BILLION
All Real Estate Loans	0.98%	0.26	0.45	1.02	1.54
Construction & development	3.02	0.45	1.43	3.12	4.38
Commercial	1.24	0.40	0.62	1.18	2.21
Multifamily residential	2.01	0.51	0.56	1.58	3.75
1–4 Family	0.20	0.18	0.18	0.28	0.14
Home equity lines of credit	0.14	0.27	0.11	0.15	0.10

Source: *The FDIC Quarterly Banking Profile*, Fourth Quarter, 1991, page 4.

REAL ESTATE LENDING 2002

The dynamics of real estate lending have changed dramatically as a result of deregulation and changes in technology.

Figure 1.[7]

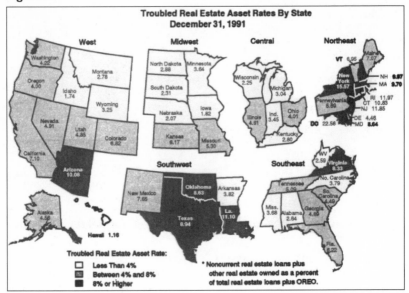

Geographic Diversification

As a result of the previously mentioned Riegle-Neal Act, and other laws deregulating banking activities, such as Gramm-Leach-Bliley, large banks today enjoy geographic and product diversification that allows them to limit their loan risk in specific markets. No longer is a bank limited to one city or one state. It can expand throughout the United States to obtain an optimal allocation of its loan portfolio.

Securitization

Securitization of loans benefits both the sellers and the buyers. The sellers can reduce their balance-sheet risks and increase their fee income. Fannie Mae, for example, buys home mortgages and mortgage-related products from banks and other financial institutions. Fannie Mae also guarantees some mortgage products. The buyers can diversify their loan portfolios by buying loans from different geographic areas, and with different degrees of risk.

---

7. *The FDIC Quarterly Banking Profile,* Fourth Quarter, 1991, Chart F.

Derivatives

Derivatives are widely used by about 400 banks to hedge interest rate and credit risks.[8] The *Fannie Mae 2002 Annual Report*[9] does an outstanding job explaining how this Government Sponsored Enterprise (GSE) uses derivatives to hedge interest rate and credit risk. Table 6, from Fannie Mae's 2002 Annual Report, illustrates the type of instruments used, what they are hedging, and the purposes of the hedged transactions. The annual report of Fannie Mae should be read by all real estate lenders to gain insights about how to mitigate the risks associated with such loans.[10]

Table 6. Fannie Mae's Use of Derivatives

TABLE 24: PRIMARY TYPES OF DERIVATIVES USED		
Derivative Hedging Instrument	Hedged Item	Purpose of the Hedge Transaction
Pay-fixed, receive-variable interest-rate swap	Variable-rate debt Anticipated issuance of debt	To protect against an increase in interest rates by converting the debt's variable rate to a fixed rate.
Receive-fixed, pay-variable interest-rate swap	Noncallable fixed-rate debt	To protect against a decline in interest rates. Converts the debt's fixed rate to a variable rate.
Basis swap or spread-lock	Variable-rate assets and liabilities	To "lock-in" or preserve the spread between variable-rate, interest-earning assets and variable-rate, interest-bearing liabilities.
Pay-fixed swaption	Variable-rate debt	To protect against an increase in interest rates by having an option to convert floating-rate debt to a fixed rate.
Caps	Variable-rate debt	To protect against an increase in interest rates by providing a limit on the interest cost on our debt in a rising rate environment.
Receive-fixed swaption	Noncallable fixed-rate debt	To protect against a decline in interest rates by having an option to convert fixed-rate debt to floating-rate debt.
Foreign currency swaps	Foreign currency–denominated debt	To protect against fluctuations in exchange rates on non-U.S. dollar-denominated debt by converting the interest expense and principal payment on foreign-denominated debt to U.S. dollar-denominated debt.

Source: *Fannie Mae 2002 Annual Report, page 63.*

Loan-to-Value (LTV) Ratios

The *Fannie Mae 2002 Annual Report* (page 71) states that "LTV ratio is a strong predictor of credit performance. The likelihood of default and the gross severity of a loss in the event of a default are lower as the LTV ratio decreases, all other factors held equal." This is true for both residential and commercial real estate.

---

8. "OCC Bank Derivatives Report, Third Quarter 2002," December 2002.

9. See pages 61–63 in the *Fannie Mae 2002 Annual Report.*

10. Also see Poole (2003) for a discussion of the GSEs role in the housing markets and financial stability.

The average loan to price ratio on new single family homes in the U.S. in 2002 was 77.8%, not much different from the 75.0% in 1991.[11] Data are not available for commercial and other real estate LTVs. Nevertheless, the same principle applies—high LTVs are associated with high risk.

Credit Scores

In recent years, credit scores developed by Fair Isaac & Co. (FICO scores) have become widely used as an indicator of credit quality for retail borrowers.[12] The FICO scores range from 150 to 950. Scores below 620 are considered subprime. The higher the score the better and less likely the chance of default.

BANK FAILURES AND LOANS CHARGED-OFF IN 2002

Ten FDIC insured banks failed in 2002, the largest number of bank failures since 1994. The failures reflected slow economic growth and problems with subprime lending.

The data presented in Table 7 shows the loans that were charged-off in 2002. Notice that all real estate loans had a charge-off rate of 0.15%, while C&I loans and loans to individuals had charge-off rates of 1.76% and 3.34%, respectively. This may suggest that the real estate market has suffered less than the other markets. It also may suggest that the real estate lenders have taken advantage of the risk mitigation techniques described above. In either case, it appears that real estate today is not as risky as it was during the 1985–1992 period. Accordingly, the Basel II risk weights for real estate need to be adjusted to level the playing field.

Finally, it is interesting to note that Fannie Mae and Freddie Mac, whose portfolios consist primarily of single-family and multi-family mortgage products, are required to hold far less regulatory capital (about 3%) than commercial banks (about 8%). However, the risk weight for home mortgages in the Basel II Standard approach could be as low as 40%. That risk weight translates into a regulatory capital charge of 3.2% ($40\% \times 8\% = 3.2\%$). The capital

---

11. *Federal Reserve Bulletin*, May 2003, A 32; U.S. Department of Commerce, *Statistical Abstract of the United States, 1993*, Table 811.

12. For additional information, see *http://www.myfico.com*.

charge under the IRB Approach could range from 7.2% to 21.5% depending on the assumptions made about the probability of default (PD) and the loss given default (LGD).[13]

Both Fannie and Freddie make the point that the U.S. government does not guarantee their debts. Nevertheless, the capital markets seem willing to accept their low capital ratios. This suggests that the capital markets consider their real estate lending to be relatively low risk because of their portfolio management techniques they use.

CONCLUSIONS

The main point made here is that Basel II creates an uneven playing field for the large, but not the largest, banks in the U.S. Bank regulators will require our largest banks to use the costly and complex Advanced IRB approach to comply with Basel II. Some of the other large banks believe that if they don't use that approach, it will have adverse consequences in the capital markets. If they want to be considered in the same league as the largest banks, they will have to comply with the same standards. And in this post-Enron, WorldCom, HealthSouth period of accounting skullduggery, stock analysts and investors will want to know which Basel II approach banks are using. The Securities and Exchange Commission Reg FD (Fair Disclosure) requires companies that disclose material nonpublic information to disseminate it broadly. Therefore, there is little doubt that all banks that are active in the capital markets should state in their annual reports which IRB method they use.

Another major point is that our largest banks are not as heavily invested in real estate loans as the large banks. For example, commercial real estate accounts for less than 2% of the loans at Citibank and J.P. Morgan Chase, while it accounts for more than 20% of the loans at Colonial and Regions banks. The fact that the Basel II risk weights on commercial real estate loans is 150%, or higher, means that banks holding such loans may need more than the required 8% minimum capital to make and hold such loans. One implication of this is that banks with adequate or excess capital will make such loans. Another possibility is that the bank will issue more capital. A third implication is that banks may get out of that business because of the high capital charges.

---

13. *"Basel Briefing 5"* (May 2003), p. 22.

As a corollary, we should ask if the high capital charges on real estate are necessary. The answer is yes, and no. There is no doubt that highly concentrated loan portfolios consisting of high LTV real estate loans are very risky. That was the case in the late 1980s and early 1990s in the U.S., and it still may be the case in some foreign countries. However, in the U.S. today, real estate loan portfolios can be diversified geographically and by products, hedged with derivatives, and have less risk by having lower LTVs and higher FICO scores. These techniques will make future real estate bubbles less of a threat to financial stability than they were in the past. Fannie Mae and Freddie Mac provide examples of how such techniques can be used. In such cases, the Basel II capital risk weights are excessive.

One final thought concerning the statistical methodology of the Advanced IRB approach that permits each bank to have different capital charges for the same type of loan. As previously noted, the capital charge for home mortgages can range from 7.2% to 21.5% or more depending on the assumptions made about the probability of default (PD) and the loss given default (LGD).[14] Simply stated, the IRB methodology depends too much on past data to predict future losses. Looking at the real estate problems of the 1980s in Texas and in Massachusetts, to predict future real estate bubbles in the 21st century is analogous to driving down a steep, winding mountain road by only looking out the back window. A crash is inevitable.

Because the risk management techniques used today are dynamic, the data and the new and existing variables in the IRB models need to be updated constantly. This is a costly and time-consuming process. A bank that can afford to develop models that are advantageous to them will probably have the lowest capital charges and a competitive advantage. Stated otherwise, once again there will be *competitive inequality* in bank capital. Recall that ensuring *competitive equality* was one of the two reasons given for enacting the 1988 Basel Capital Accord.

---

14. *"Basel Briefing 5"* (May 2003), p. 22.

Table 7. Total Loans and Percentage Charged-Off, 2002

	$ BILLIONS	PERCENTAGE OF TOTAL LOANS AND LEASES	PERCENTAGE OF LOANS CHARGED-OFF
Total Loans and leases	$4,163.4	100%	1.11%
All real estate loans	2,068.0	49.7	**0.15**
Construction and development	207.4	5.0	0.17
Commercial real estate	555.8	13.3	0.15
Multifamily residential	71.9	1.7	0.07
Home equity loans	214.6	5.2	0.19
1–4 Family	945.9	22.7	0.14
Commercial and Industrial	912.0	21.9	**1.76**
Loans to Individuals	703.6	16.9	**3.34**
Credit card loans	275.8	6.6	6.38
Other loans to Individuals	427.8	10.3	1.46
Other loans and leases	479.8	11.5	0.58

Source: *Quarterly Banking Profile*, Fourth Quarter, 2002, Washington, D.C., Federal Deposit Insurance Corporation, 2003, Table V-A.

REFERENCES

Annual Report 2002, (2003), Washington, D.C., Federal Deposit Insurance Corporation.

"Banks Failures and Assistance," 1991, 1992, FDIC.

"Basel Briefing 5," KPMG, (2003), May.

Ervin, D. Wilson, (2003), Testimony on behalf of Credit Suisse First Boston and The Financial Services Roundtable, Hearings on the New Basel Accord before the Subcommittee on Domestic and International Monetary Policy, U.S. House Committee on Financial Services, February 27.

Fannie Mae 2002 Annual Report, (2003), Washington, D.C., Fannie Mae.

Federal Reserve Bulletin, (2003), May.

French, George, William A. Stark, Jason C. Cave, and John Feid, (2003), "Risk-Based Capital Requirements for Commercial Lending: The Impact of Basel II, *FYI,* FDIC, April 21, http://www.fdic.gov/bank/analytical/fyi/2003/042103fyi.html.

Gup, Benton E., (1998), *Bank Failures in the Major Trading Countries of the World: Causes and Remedies,* Wesport, CT, Quorum Books.

History of the Eighties-Lessons for the Future: An Examination of Banking Crises of the 1980s and Early 1990s, (1997), Washington, D.C., Federal Deposit Insurance Corporation, Vol. 1.

Lindgren, C., G. Garcia, and M.I. Saal, (1996), *Banking Soundness and Macroeconomic Policy,* Washington, D.C., International Monetary Fund.

Managing the Crisis: The FDIC and RTC Experience, (1998), Washington, D.C., Federal Deposit Insurance Corporation, Table 4.

"OCC Bank Derivatives Report, Third Quarter 2002," (2002), Washington, D.C., Office of the Comptroller of the Currency, December.

"Overview of the New Basel Capital Accord," (2003), Consultative Document, Basel Committee On Banking Supervision, Bank For International Settlements, Basel, Switzerland, April.

Petrou, Karen Shaw, (2003), "Policy Issues in Complex Proposals Warrant Congressional Scrutiny, "Testimony before the Domestic and International Monetary Policy, Trade and Technology Subcommittee on Financial Services, U.S. House of Representatives, February 27.

Poole, William, (2003), "Housing in the Macroeconomy," *Review,* Federal Reserve Bank of St. Louis, May/June, pp. 1–8.

Quarterly Banking Profile, Fourth Quarter, 2002, (2003), Washington, D.C., FDIC.

"Real Estate Loans," (2003), FDIC, Table CB12, *http://www2fdic. gov/hsob/hsobRpt.asp.*

Sheng, A., (1996), *Bank Restructuring: Lessons from the 1980s,* Washington, D.C., The World Bank.

The FDIC Quarterly Banking Profile, Fourth Quarter, 1991, (1992), Washington, D.C., FDIC.

The FDIC Quarterly Banking Profile, Third Quarter, 2002, (2002), Washington, D.C., FDIC,

The FDIC Quarterly Banking Profile, Fourth Quarter, 2002, (2003), Table III-A.

"The New Basel Capital Accord," (2001), Press Release, Basel Committee on Banking Supervision, Bank for International Settlements, Basel, Switzerland, January 16.

U.S. Department of Commerce, (1994), *Statistical Abstract of the United States, 1993,* Washington, D.C.

6

Market Discipline: Is It Fact or Fiction?

Benton E. Gup[1]

The Bank for International Settlements (BIS) is an international organization that fosters cooperation among central banks and other agencies with an eye toward monetary and financial stability. The Basel Committee on Banking Supervision is part of the BIS. In January 2001, the Basel Committee on Banking Supervision issued a proposal for a new Basel Capital Accord that is based on three complementary "pillars": 1) minimum capital requirements, 2) supervisory review, and 3) market discipline.[2]

The new accord is to be implemented by participating banks in 2006. The Basel Committee's consultative document on market discipline states that "an appropriate level of timely disclosures will have benefits for well-run institutions, investors and depositors, for financial stability more generally, and will help support the effective and efficient operation of the capital markets."[3] The disclosures refer to capital, credit risk, market risk, operations risk, and other factors. But the Basel Committee never provides a clear definition of "market discipline."

The remainder of this chapter is divided into six parts. Part 1 defines market discipline. Part 2 explains that market discipline is based on information. Part 3 deals with insiders and outsiders who

---

1. This paper was presented at the International meeting of the Financial Management Association in Dublin, Ireland, June 6, 2003. George G. Kaufman was the discussant, and his comments follow this article in the appendix. An earlier version of this paper appeared on the Social Science Research Network (SSRN). It was in the "Top Ten Download" list for Banking & Financial Institutions (11/7/03), and International Finance (10/22/03).

2. Basel Committee on Banking Supervision, Press Release, "The New Basel Capital Accord," January 16, 2001. For additional details, see: Basel Committee on Banking Supervision, Consultive Document, *The New Basel Capital Accord, Bank for International Settlements, Basel, Switzerland, January 2001.*

3. Basel Committee on Banking Supervision, Consultive Document, *Pillar 3 (Market Discipline)*, Bank for International Settlements, Basel, Switzerland, January 2001, 3.

can exert market discipline. Part 4 examines whether market discipline works for banks. Part 5 looks at the implications of market discipline when the true condition of a firm is not known and when there are different interpretations of the information. Part 6 is the conclusion.

I. WHAT IS MARKET DISCIPLINE?

Survival of the Fittest

What is market discipline? It is not a new concept in banking, but its meaning has changed over time. The concept has been traced back to the free-banking era in Scotland (1695–1845), and it began in the United States in 1838. During this time it was assumed that rational depositors with sufficient information would invest in safe banks, and banks that were not safe would fail. Leathers and Raines (2000), writing about the history of market discipline, say that in the extreme form, "market discipline means total reliance upon competitive market forces imposing losses and ultimately failure on suppliers that do not operate efficiently."[4] However, market discipline may not be a panacea. They go on to say "Even in nonbanking sectors, where it is widely accepted that the social interest can be served by the regulating force of market competition, no theory of competitive markets promises market stability."

Debt and Equity Market Reactions

While it is clear that market discipline in the Darwinian sense of the survival of the fittest does work, that is not the way it is defined by bank regulators. A 1999 Staff Study by the Federal Reserve defines direct and indirect market discipline.[5] Direct market discipline is the cost of borrowed funds, which reflects the bank's risk profile. The study claims that cost provides an *ex ante* incentive for the bank to refrain from taking on more risk. Private parties, or government regulators, who monitor the secondary market prices of interest-rate-sensitive instruments in order to assess bank risk, exert indirect market discipline.

---

4. Leathers and Raines (2000), 164.
5. "Using Subordinated Debt as an Instrument of Market Discipline," 1999.

Silvano Tittonel (2002), Member of Secretariat, Bank for International Settlements, Basel Committee on Banking Supervision, said, "Market discipline is the third pillar of the new framework for capital adequacy, and complements capital requirements (Pillar 1) and the supervisory review process (Pillar 2) to promote the safety and soundness in banks and the financial system. The Basel Committee aims to encourage market discipline by developing a set of disclosure recommendations (and requirements) which will allow market participants to assess key pieces of information on the scope of application, capital risk exposures, risk assessment and management processes, and therefore the capital adequacy of the bank."

Andrew Crockett (2001), General Manager of the Bank of International Settlements and Chairman of the Stability Forum, said that market discipline is playing a greater role in ensuring financial stability because of the increased reliance on institutions' own assessment of risks, on the qualitative aspects of risk control processes, and on disclosure. Crocket uses the term "market discipline" to denote internal and external governance mechanisms in a free-market economy in the absence of direct government intervention. He goes on to say that for market discipline to be effective, participants require information, the ability to process it, incentives, and a mechanism to invoke the discipline.[6]

Academics also have various definitions of market discipline. Benink and Wihlborg (2002) say that banks are given incentives by debt and equity market participants. Scott (1991) and Rose (1999) go further, and claim that market discipline occurs when market participants "punish" banks for making bad decisions. The punishment may come in the form of having to pay higher rates on CDs and other borrowed funds, and lower stock prices. They focus primarily on the financial markets to provide discipline.

The strongest definition presented here is from Bliss and Flannery (2000) who state that the concept of market discipline requires investors to *evaluate* the true condition of a firm and that the managers *respond* to the investor feedback impounded in the security prices. Similarly, Ward (2002) states that market participants must change their behavior in response to new information. That requires the acquisition, processing, and acting on the information, and that may be costly to do.

---

6. For additional comments on the requirements for market discipline and the results of prior studies, see Gup (2000).

Market signals, per se, are not market discipline. The key to market discipline is that management must do something in response to the market signals. Otherwise, market discipline is like closing the barn door after the horse is out. Consider the case of Farmer Mac (the Federal Agricultural Mortgage Corporation), the largest issuer of unrated debt in the U.S. In June 2002, the bids on default swaps for Farmer Mac increased from 60 basis points to 200 basis points signaling credit markets concern over rising delinquencies.[7] The rising delinquencies in agricultural and rural mortgages were caused by a faltering economy, and there is little that Farmer Mac can do to change the state of the economy. Increasing its credit standard, when the economy has bottomed out, does not seem like a good strategy.

Also, consider the following CD announced by Schwab Bond-Source (January 29, 2003). LaSalle Bank, N.A., a subsidiary of ABN AMRO Bank N.V., offered a step-up coupon, FDIC-insured CD, in early 2003, with a fifteen-year maturity in 2/12/18. The bank's credit rating by Moody's is Aa3, and S&P is A+. The CD is callable 2/12/04 at par and at any interest date, thereafter. If not called, the coupon resets annually to the following: 4.125, 4.25, 4.50, 4.75, 5.00, 5.50, 6.00, 6.50, 7.00, 8.00, 9.00, 10.00, 11.00, and 12.00. The yield to maturity ranges from 4.00% to 6.23%, depending on if and when the CD is called. By way of comparison, the U.S. 10-year Treasury constant maturity rate in January 2003 was 4.05%, and the AAA corporate bond rate was 6.17%.[8] What if any information does this bondlike CD convey about the bank? The point is that even FDIC-insured CDs can be complex, and the rates paid may not offer any insights about the true condition of the bank.

Litigation

Litigation is another means of administering discipline by investors and others. Litigation usually takes place after disclosure (or failure to disclose), and the legal process may take years. For example, during the 1982–2002 period, more than 1,000 corporations have been named as defendants in asbestos-related law suits,

---

7. Wiggins (June 4, 2002). For information about Farmer Mac, see *http://www.farmermac. com.*

8. *Economic Indicators* (February 2003, p. 31).

and more than have sought bankruptcy protection. One article called this "The $200 Billion Miscarriage of Justice."[9] Some of the firms never produced asbestos, and some of the plaintiffs are not sick from asbestos.

The Private Securities Litigation Reform Act of 1995 tended to have a chilling effect on investor's lawsuits concerning disclosure.[10] In March 2002, the Bush administration announced that it favors legislation that will make class-action lawsuits more business-friendly—which would make it hard for people to sue companies, and provide less market discipline.[11]

2. MARKET DISCIPLINE IS BASED ON INFORMATION

Providing Information

Market discipline requires timely, accurate, and relevant information. However, there are serious issues to be resolved concerning the frequency of reporting, the materiality of the information, how to deal with proprietary information, and how, and to whom, information is distributed. Some of these issues fall under the purview of the Securities and Exchange Commission Regulation (SEC) Fair Disclosure (Reg FD) and the Sarbannes-Oxley Act. Reg FD was enacted in 2000 to curb the selective disclosure of material nonpublic information, such as "earnings information," by issuers to analysts and institutional investors. Reg FD requires that the disclosure of material information be done publicly.

Unfortunately, SEC regulations do not solve all the problems. For example, are private plant and factory tours, which may convey a competitive advantage but not material information, permissible under Reg FD?[12] While the intent of Reg FD is good, some analysts believe that it has chilled corporate communications and contributed to "boilerplate" disclosures, as companies err on the side of caution.[13] A study by Agrawal and Chada (2002) found that sell-side analyst's forecasts of earnings were less accurate after Reg FD

---

9. Parloff (2002).
10. D'Avolio, Gildor, and Shleifer (2001).
11. Office of Management and Budget, Statement of Administration Policy, "H.R. 2341—Class Action Fairness Act of 2002," March 12, 2002; For a discussion of the bill, see VandeHei (2000).
12. Unger (December, 2001).
13. ibid.

was enacted. The forecasts were worse for small firms than for large ones. Corporate information is commonly disseminated in SEC Form 8-K filings, through web casts, and in press releases.

The Sarbanes-Oxley Act of 2002 was signed into law in July 2002. It makes the most significant changes in corporate governance since the Securities Act of 1933 and the Securities Exchange Act of 1934. The purpose of the new law is to protect investors by improving the accuracy and reliability of corporate disclosures. The law created an independent Public Company Accounting Oversight Board to oversee the audit of public companies to protect the interest of investors and to further the public interest in providing informative and accurate information. Another part of the law requires executive certification or the accuracy and completeness for annual and quarterly reports submitted to the SEC. The Sarbanes-Oxley Act also deals with corporate and criminal fraud and provides criminal penalties for defrauding shareholders of publicly traded companies. In March 2003, the U. A. Attorney for the Northern District of Alabama charged the Vice President of Finance of HealthSouth with conspiracy to commit wire and securities fraud in a $1.4 billion scandal, and four former CFOs pled guilty to fraud charges.[14] Part of the charge was under the "executive certification" clause of the Sarbanes-Oxley Act. This should send a strong signal to those who certify financial statements.

Interpreting Information

The other side of the coin is how the information is used. The New York Clearing House Association (2001) said: "In order for the disclosure mechanism to function effectively, the user must be able to understand and act on the information provided. Given the dramatic increase, both in scope and complexity, of available information in the public domain and the dynamic changes in bank portfolios, disclosures become outdated almost instantaneously, which renders it nearly impossible for a user to have up-to-date information with regard to a bank's risk profile."

---

14. "HealthSouth Officer Charged. . . .," (March 31, 2003). Emery Harris was the V. P. for Finance who was charged with conspiracy to commit wire and securities fraud. William T. Owen, Weston L. Smith, Michael D. Martin, and Malcolm McVay, all former Chief Financial Officers of HealthSouth, pled guilty to fraud charges.

With respect to banks, the Australian Prudential Regulation Authority (2001) said that "while the purpose of disclosure is to improve market understanding, increases in the volume and detail of disclosed information carry some risk of confusing and hindering an assessment of the risk profile and capital adequacy of a disclosing bank, especially amongst less financially aware market participants."[15] As will be explained later, even sophisticated investors may not be able to "see the forest through the trees." There are ambiguities in the data that can be materially misleading.

Pro forma earnings are one example of information that companies disclose, but they can be materially misleading. Pro forma earnings are regular earnings before taking into account extraordinary items. There is no generally accepted accounting principles (GAAP) definition of pro form earnings—it is whatever a company wants it to be. Pro forma earnings can be used to turn accounting losses into profits, and they can be misleading. The SEC found that Trump Hotels & Casino Resorts' press release of quarterly earnings on October 25, 1999, "was fraudulent because it created the false and misleading impression that the Company had exceeded earnings expectations primarily through operational improvements, when in fact it had not."[16] The net income figure excluded an $81.4 million one-time charge resulting in higher than expected earnings.

3. INSIDERS AND OUTSIDERS

Market discipline involves insiders and outsiders. *Insiders* are examiners and auditors who are responsible for bank examinations and audits. Insiders also include directors and managers who have a duty to act on behalf of the shareholders. Finally, there are employees of the firm that also may be stockholders. By definition, insiders have access to information that is not readily available to outside debt and equity investors. *Outsiders* include credit-rating agencies, security analysts, debt and equity investors, and customers.

---

15. Australian Prudential Regulation Authority, "Submission to the Basel Committee on Banking Supervision, The New Basel Capital Accord," May 2001, 43.
16. United States Securities & Exchange Commission, Press Release, January 16, 2002.

Insiders

BANK REGULATORS/EXAMINERS: Bank regulators and examiners are concerned with the safety and soundness of the banks they supervise. Part of the examination process is the early detection of problem banks and banks that are going to fail. However, an FDIC study stated that "the record shows that 260 failed banks were not identified as requiring increased supervisory attention within 24 months of failure. Of these, 141 were not detected as troubled banks within 18 months of failure; 57 were not detected within 12 months of failure; and 9 were not detected within 6 months of failure."[17] This is not a good track record.

In September 1999, the First National Bank of Keystone, West Virginia, was closed amid allegations of fraud. A total of $515 million in loans were sold, yet remained on the books. The bank had grown from $85 million in 1990 to $1.1 billion in 1999 by making high-risk subprime loans. The bank had only $15 million of uninsured deposits in about 500 accounts.[18] Market discipline did not work here. Neither did the bank regulators who spotted internal control problems and audit deficiencies as many as eight years before the failure but didn't act on them, until it was too late. Representative James A. Leach (2000), Chairman of the House Banking and Financial Services Committee said that the Keystone case brought to light problems of coordination between bank regulators (OCC and the FDIC) regarding examinations.

The effectiveness of regulatory and auditor oversight was called into question again in 2002 in connection with the $691 million in foreign exchange trading losses at Allied Irish Banks PLC. The fraud went on for several years, but there were no *red flags* raised in the internal audit reports and risk assessments.[19]

When a bank is significantly undercapitalized, federal bank regulators must take Prompt Corrective Action (PCA) requiring the affected bank to correct the situation.[20] The banks are required to remedy their capital shortfall and take other actions to restore them to a sounder financial condition. Table 6-1 lists the PCA Enforcement Actions by the OCC during the 1998–2001 period.[21] All of the banks listed had less than $1 billion in assets.

---

17. "Bank Examination and Enforcement," (1997).
18. FDIC Press Release, PR-52-99 (9-03-99).
19. Beckett and Mollenkamp (March 18, 2002).
20. See 12 U.S.C. § 1831o and 12 C.F.R. Part 6, for details on the laws.
21. The OCC web site states that this list may not be complete.

NextBank, for example, had $700 million in assets and $554 million in deposits, of which $29.4 million was uninsured in about 2,000 accounts.[22] The noninsured depositors did not enforce market discipline on these banks.

Table 1. PCA Enforcement Actions by the Office of the Comptroller of the Currency

YEAR	BANK	LOCATION
2001	NextBank N.A.	Phoenix, AZ
	Sinclair National Bank	Gravette, AR
2000	Metropolitan Bank	New York, NY
	Prairie National Bank	Belle Plaine, MN
1999	None	
1998	Monument National Bank	Ridgecrest, CA
	The Malta National Bank	Malta, OH
	Western American National Bank	Bedford, TX

Source: Office of the Comptroller of the Currency, *www.occ.treas.gov* (visited 3/18/02).

AUDITORS: Paul Volcker (1997), former Chairman of the Board of Governors of the Federal Reserve System, said, "Market discipline can be very important. We like to use it. But I remind those who want to rely on it wholly of some simple facts. I can't remember any banks that failed who didn't have a clean auditing statement, sometimes as little as two weeks before they failed. Markets are prone to excessive exuberance in all dimensions—not just the banking world."

Consider the case of Superior Bank, FSB. The summary of a GAO report stated that the key events leading to Superior's failure were associated with its strategy of large-scale lending and securitization of subprime loans.[23] The "paper profits" resulted in overstating its capital levels. The profits were largely attributable to the value assigned the residual interests that resulted from their securitization activities. The report goes on to explain that Superior's external auditor, Ernst & Young, failed to detect the improper valuation, until the OTS and FDIC insisted that the issue be resolved at Ernst & Young's national headquarters. The OTS was ineffective because of the apparent high earnings and the expec-

---

22. FDIC Press Release, PR-16-2002 (2-7-02).
23. United States General Accounting Office, *Bank Regulation* (2002).

tation that the owners of the bank would provide additional capital, if needed. This, combined with communication and coordination problems between the OTS and FDIC, contributed to their delayed response. Their response was a Prompt Correct Action (PCA) in February 2001. Superior Bank was closed on July 27, 2001. Where were the Superior Bank's directors? Why did they let this happen?

The GAO report concludes that the failure of Superior Bank illustrates what happens when banking supervisors do not recognize that a bank has a particularly complex and risky portfolio. The same problem existed with the recent failures of BestBank and Pacific Thrift and Loan (FDIC), and Keystone Bank (OCC).

MANAGEMENT/ENRON: Enron Corporation's failure in 2001 provides another example of the breakdown in safeguards and accounting problems. Enron provided products and services related to natural gas, electricity, and communications to wholesale and retail customers. Its revenues in 2000 were $101 billion, making it the 7th largest firm in the *Fortune* 500 listing, and was a major trader of energy derivatives. Enron made extensive use of off-balance-sheet Special Purpose Entities (SPE) to shield debts. Arthur Anderson gave the opinion that Enron's accounting system was adequate and fairly represented the financial condition of the firm. Arthur Anderson was wrong, and they failed in their oversight. Maybe it was the large consulting fees Arthur Anderson received from Enron that contributed to their lack of professional responsibility.

On November 19, 2001, Enron filed the Form 10-Q and refined the restated earnings and reduced its shareholder equity by $1.2 billion. On November 12, 2001, Standard & Poor's downgraded Enron's senior unsecured debt rating to BBB-, which was a "Trigger Event" that resulted in $690 million in debt becoming payable if Enron did not post additional collateral by November 27, 2001. Its stock price plunged on the news. The low stock price was another "Trigger Event" that required Enron to repay, refinance, or cash collateralize additional credit facilities amount to $3.9 billion in connection with certain partnership agreements.[24]

Enron's credit ratings were downgraded to junk status by the other credit-rating agencies on November 28, 2001.

---

24. According to Enron's Form 10-Q (filed 11/19/01), the "Trigger Event's" included the stock price falling below $59.78 in the case of the Osprey partnership, and $34.13 in the case of the Marlin partnership. As of November 16, 2001, Enron's stock price was $16 per share.

Enron was unable to meet the financial requirements triggered by the low stock prices and downgrading, and declared Chapter 11 bankruptcy on December 2, 2001.

Banks and other types of businesses use SPEs. Some banks use SPEs to hold securitized assets. PNC Financial Services used an SPE to remove problem loans from its balance sheet in order to improve their financial statements.[25]

Boston Chicken, the fast-food chain, filed for bankruptcy in 1992. It, too, used SPE to hide risks from the stockholders.[26]

MANAGEMENT/XEROX: Xerox Corporation is another example of a major firm that used various "accounting actions" and "accounting opportunities" to distort their operating revenue by more than $3 billion and their pretax earnings by half that amount over the 1997–2000 period.[27] The Securities and Exchange Commission charged the company with fraud. The SEC settled with Xerox a $10 million fine and required it to restate its earnings.

MANAGEMENT/JAPANESE BANKS: Some large Japanese banks have found a way to turn bad debts into equity by using debt-for-equity swaps.[28] The debt-for-equity swaps are used to exchange some of their loans to heavily indebted companies for shares of their common or preferred stock. This action appears to reduce the banks' bad loans and raise their core capital ratios. Officially, the big Japanese banks have about 10% capital-adequacy ratios. However, analysts claim that if they subtract the public funds invested in the banks, deferred taxes, and property revaluations, the capital-adequacy ratios are about 2%, far below the 8% required by the Basel Accord. This is another example of substituting form for substance.

One can argue that the directors and management failed to act in the best interest of the outside stockholders they represent in the cases cited above.

---

25. Beckett, et al. (January 30, 2002).

26. Richards and Thurm (March 13, 2002).

27. United States Securities & Exchange Commission Press Release, "Xerox Settles SEC Enforcement Action Charging Company with Fraud," (2002-52), April 11, 2002.

28. "Surreal," (April 20, 2002).

EMPLOYEES: Finally, employees who are stockholders of firms that are about to be bankrupt firms may not have insights about its true condition. Bank managers of the Bank of New England were buying stock in the bank as late as a year before it failed.[29]

Outsiders

CREDIT-RATING AGENCIES: The credit-rating agencies are the first "outsiders" to be examined. There are three SEC "Nationally Recognized Statistical Rating Organizations," or credit-rating agencies—Moody's Investor Service, Standard & Poor's, and Fitch —that provide credit ratings on corporate security issues. Critics argue that the SEC recognition gives them a monopoly and shields them from their bad calls. They are not strictly independent of the organizations that they rate because they are paid by them to do the ratings. Part of their power stems from the fact that the SEC uses their credit ratings to assess the value of securities held as capital by securities firms. Similarly, banks are commonly limited to holding investment grade securities, and under the new Basel accord, their ratings will be used to assess bank portfolios. The problem is exacerbated by the increased use of collateralized debt obligations (CDOs) that present unique problems for credit-rating agencies. Because CDOs are actively managed, their rating depends as much on the quality of the manager as it does on the underlying assets.[30]

The biggest problem is that the credit-rating agencies' record of finding corporate problems before other investors is marred. They failed to sound the alarm in the case of the New York debt crises and the bankruptcy of Orange County California.[31] In the case of Enron, all three major credit-rating agencies downgraded Enron's debt after the company filed the Form 10-Q, not before. Enron's debt did not fall below investment grade until a few days before it went bankrupt. One reason for the delay was the proposed merger with Dynergy, which was subsequently called off. Another is that the agencies' claim that they were duped by incomplete and misleading information. Critics argue that they should have asked more questions and downgraded the debt earlier.[32]

---

29. Litan (1997, 289).
30. "Badly Overrated," (May 10, 2002).
31. Wayne (April 23, 2002).
32. Borrus, McNamee, and Timmons (April 8, 2002).

Credit-rating agencies have no greater access to information than most investors. Equally important, the information that they have received may not be transparent. The problem of misleading accounting terms, such as pro forma earnings, and misleading accounting statements is not limited to the U.S. A recent article from the *Wall Street Journal* found that a careful examination of five European firms' balance sheets left "investors confused."[33]

Finally, Gropp and Richards (2001) found that changes in credit ratings had a greater impact on stock prices than on bond prices. Thus, the rating changes provided information to the markets. However, we do not know if the rating changes or the changes in market prices affected the firm's behavior.

STOCK ANALYSTS: Stock market analysts are the second group of outsiders examined here. Ten of the 15 analysts who followed Enron recommended it as a "buy," even as it was being investigated by the Securities and Exchange Commission in October and November 2001, shortly before it went into bankruptcy on December 2, 2001.[34] Similarly, some analysts recommended WorldCom, even as its stock plummeted in 2002.[35]

Thomas Bowman (2002), President and CEO of the Association for Investment Management and Research (AIMR), said that "maintaining a "buy" recommendation in the face of falling stock prices is NOT *prima facie* evidence of a lack of independence, objectivity, or a reasonable basis for a recommendation." He goes on to point out that companies such as Texaco that have gone bankrupt, turned out to be good investments. However, he does not say that they were good investments at their peak prices before their stock prices fell. Enron's stock price was about $38 per share in early November, and it fell to a low of $0.11 per share on January 29, 2002.

Some stock analysts said that they did not have complete and accurate information about Enron.[36] Others argue they may be influenced by the amount of investment banking fees their firms earned from Enron.[37] In addition, analysts may not want to be branded as "controversial" by questioning the value of a popular stock.

---

33. "Scrutinizing European Firms' Balance Sheets" (2002).
34. Gordon (February 28, 2002).
35. Sidel (June 27, 2002).
36. White (February 28, 2001).
37. Smith and Lucchetti (February 26, 2002).

Enron was only one stock out of the thousands of stocks that analysts follow. A study by Barger, Lehavy, McNichols, and Trueman (2001) of over 360,000 stock recommendations over the 1986–1996 period found that a portfolio of stocks with the most (least) favorable consensus analysts' recommendations provided an average annual return abnormal gross return of 4.13 (-4.19) percent after controlling for market risk, size, book-to-market, and price momentum effects. They conclude that the market is semi strong inefficient (before transaction costs). Simply stated, the consensus stock analysts' recommendations are generally correct.

The analyst's recommendations may have been generally correct because the market went up over that period, and the analysts were overly optimistic. The three-to-five-years earnings forecasts for each of the S&P 500 corporations compiled by analysts averaged almost 12 percent during the 1985–2001 period.[38] Actual earnings increased 7 percent over the same period.

DEBT AND EQUITY INVESTORS: Citigroup and J. P. Morgan Chase & Co. made large loans to Enron, and they knew what Enron was doing was wrong. Neal Batson, the court-appointed bankruptcy examiner for Enron said that "Citi and J. P. Morgan had actual knowledge of the wrongful conduct in these transactions."[39] However, Manhattan District Attorney Robert Morgenthau said in a news conference in July 2003, that they did not have enough evidence to show that Citi and J. P. Morgan committed fraud. Instead of exercising market discipline, two of our largest banks *contributed* funds to the wrongdoing. The word "contributed" is underscored because they agreed to a $236-million Enron settlement with the SEC, and $53 million paid to the Manhattan District Attorney, New York City, and New York State. In addition, they may lose their rights as Enron creditors of $4.2 *billion.*

Alliance Capital Management Holding LP, the nation's largest publicly held asset-management firm, invested in Enron for the Florida State pension fund and lost $282 million.[40] Alliance bought the Enron at high prices and sold it at low prices. In

---

38. Greenspan (March 26, 2002).
39. Thornton and France (August 11, 2003); United States Securities & Exchange Commission, Press Release "SEC Settles Enforcement Proceedings Against J.P. Morgan Chase and Citigroup," (2003-87), July 28, 2003. The SEC settlement with Citigroup had an additional $19 million in connection with fraud at Dynergy Inc; JPMorgan Chase, Press Release, July 28, 2003; Citigroup, Press Release, July 28, 2003.
40. Krahnhold (April 23, 2002).

September 2001, Alliance was Enron's largest shareholder, holding about 43 million shares. Frank Savage, a senior executive and director of Alliance, sat on Enron's board of directors.[41] Florida sued Alliance.

In a later development, Alliance had acquired 10.9% of World-Com, which subsequently was accused of misrepresenting $3.8 billion in expenses.[42]

The California Public Employees' Retirement System is known for pursuing corporate governance in companies in which it invests. According to their web site, "The California Public Employees' Retirement System (known as "CalPERS") has long been a leader in the corporate governance movement. As the largest public retirement system in the U.S., CalPERS' Board of Administration has concluded that "good" corporate governance leads to improved long-term performance. CalPERS' also strongly believes that "good" governance requires the attention and dedication not only of a company's officers and directors, but also its owners. CalPERS is not simply a passive holder of stock. We are a "shareowner," and take seriously the responsibility that comes with company ownership."[43]

CalPERS was a substantial investor in Enron as well as a partner in some of its SPEs (e.g., JEDI, Joint Energy Development Investments LP). A *New York Times* article reporting on CalPERS' relationships with Enron was titled "Even a Watchdog is Not Always Fully Awake."[44] If we can't depend on CalPERS or on large investors like Alliance Capital to look out for the public interest and enforce market discipline, or on large and respected creditors like Citigroup and J. P. Morgan Chase & Co—whom can we count on? It is not reasonable to assume that individual investors would have greater insights or access to inside information.

Next consider the role of individual investors. A few individual investors take a strong role in corporate governance. Warren Buffett, Carl Ican, and Martin Ebner are three such individuals.[45] Unfortunately, three out of over 80 million investors is not a very big number, so their influence is limited to a few companies.

---

41. Abelson and Gilpin (December 7, 2002).
42. O'Brian (June 27, 2002).
43. *www.calpers-governance.org/forumhome.asp* (visited 3/14/02). CalPERS "Corporate Governance Core Principles & Guidelines are available from its web site.
44. Henriques (February 5, 2002).
45. Fairlamb (March 18, 2002).

Most investors who buy debt and equity securities are not actively involved in corporate governance, and they may not find it difficult to determine if the interest rates paid on debt securities or the stock prices are signaling good or bad information about the issuer. By way of illustration, consider the Freddie Mac variable rate medium-term notes due February 28, 2012.[46] The note has a nominal interest rate of 10.125%, which is about 400 basis points above what Freddie Mac normally pays on a 10-year note. That rate is paid only when the London Interbank Offered Rate (LIBOR) is below 7%. If LIBOR goes above 7%, Freddie Mac pays no interest. The note is callable at par, plus accrued interest. These notes may not be very liquid. It is not clear what this subordinated debt signals about Freddie Mac, except that it has very sophisticated financing.

CUSTOMERS: Arthur Anderson LLP was the auditor for Enron. As a consequence of its role in Enron's failure, and with accounting problems at other firms, such as Waste Management, Sunbeam, and Cendant, many of its major customers dropped it as an auditor. The list of customers dropping Anderson includes, but is not limited to, the U.S. Government, Freddie Mac, Ford, Delta Airlines, Banco Santiago, and SAP. In that context, the original definition of market discipline worked, and Anderson may not survive. But does market discipline work in other cases?

4. DOES MARKET DISCIPLINE WORK FOR BANKS?

The evidence on what market discipline means, and its effectiveness is mixed. Brickell (1996) claims that because the Bank of England let Barings Bank close in 1995, after large losses from derivatives trading, it put other banks on notice that "firms cannot expect to be routinely relieved of responsibility for their errors. The financial systems is strong enough to withstand such failures."[47]

Some studies focus on effects of subordinated debt. Silverberg (1985) argued that investors in subordinated debt were in a better position to assess risk and exercise market discipline than depositors. Most deposits are insured, but the debt holders have their money on the line. Hence, capital discipline is likely to be superior to depositor discipline. It should be noted that before

---

46. Cohen (April 29, 2002); Freddie Mac, Variable Rate Medium-Term Notes Due February 28, 2012, issued January 28, 2002, (CUSIP Number 3129242Z5).
47. See Gup (1998) for a discussion of Barings, pages 50–51.

Continental Illinois bank failed, the uninsured depositors had a "silent run" on that bank. However, advocates of using subordinated debt to provide market discipline ignore the fact that both bank regulators and rating agencies treat the subordinated debt as though it were equity for purposes of capital regulation. They can call it whatever they want to, but debt by any other name is still debt, and it increases a firm's financial leverage ratio and its risk.

Gilbert (1985) reviewed the results from prior studies, and found the following: First, the potential for market discipline is greatest for large banks that rely more on the debt and equity markets than small banks.[48] Second, depositors are not as efficient in evaluating risks as are debt and equity investors. Third, the disclosure of adverse information, such as problem-bank classifications, does not generally cause disruptions in the market. Finally, and most important, he found virtually no evidence of market signals on changes in portfolio behavior or risk.

A 1999 Federal Reserve Staff Study, "Using Subordinated Debt as an Instrument of Market Discipline," reviewed the literature as of that date and found risk measures (CAMELS ratings and accounting measures) to be positively and significantly associated with rates, and the cost issuing CDs reflected a risk premium.[49] With respect to subordinated debt, they found that some debt holders may have been relying on presumed implicit government guarantees.

Bliss and Flannery (2000) agree that the market can monitor the risk of U.S. bank holding companies. However, they did not find any strong evidence that either debt or equity investors regularly influence the management behavior. They state that the concept of market discipline requires that investors *evaluate* the true condition of a firm, and that the managers *respond* to the investor feedback impounded in the security prices. They do admit that some beneficial influences, such as refraining from taking action, are not measurable. Flannery (1998) finds that market discipline may help for *large, traded* U.S. financial firms. Unfortunately for the advocates of market discipline, most banks in the U.S. are small. About 7,400 of our 7,900 banks have less than $1 billion in assets, and 4,200 have less than $100 million in assets. Market discipline will not help them.

---

48. Also see Eisenbeis and Gilbert (1985).
49. "Using Subordinated Debt as an Instrument of Market Discipline," 1999.

Birchler and Hancock (2003) found evidence that yield spreads on banks' subordinated debt was not a good measure of bank risk. But Krainer and Lopez (2003) find that debt and equity market data are useful to banks' supervisors.

Greenspan (2000) claims that private market discipline works well for derivatives dealers. They must maintain strong credit ratings to participate in the credit markets. He said this before the Enron debacle. As previously noted, Enron was a very large energy trading company specializing in energy derivatives.

Federal Reserve Governor Susan Schmidt Bies (2002) said the following in connection with regulating large, complex firms. ". . . it has become clear in recent months that some companies have not been completely transparent in the application of accounting and disclosure standards to specific transactions. In these situations . . . . . As a result, the market was not able to appropriately discipline the risk-taking activities of these firms on a timely basis because it lacked the information from either financial statements or other disclosures to do so."

5. IMPLICATIONS

True Condition Is Unknown

History has shown that insiders—auditors, directors, examiners, and some inside shareholders—may not know the true condition of their troubled firms or banks. Likewise, outsiders—credit-rating agencies, and debt and equity investors—are similarly uninformed. There are several possible explanations for why they were uninformed. First, top-level managers may try to conceal and confuse other insiders and outsiders, as was the case with Enron. Second, there may be some degree of complicity between the insiders. Again, Enron provides an example. Arthur Anderson allowed Enron to twist accounting rules to its advantage because of the large fees paid. Even if it did comply with GAAP, the information provided was not transparent. The widespread use of SPEs was designed to hide debt and other relationships that outside investors might not like.

Some Enron investors had more information than others. CalPERS, CSFB, Citigroup, JPM Chase, and Merrill Lynch all invested in Enron's LJM partnerships that were SPEs used to hide debts. They had detailed information that was not available or disclosed to the shareholders. If these sophisticated investors invested in an Enron SPE, and three of them even underwrote Enron securities, and they didn't foresee Enron's problems, how is the "average investor" supposed to invoke market discipline?

Different Interpretations of Information

In general terms, the current definition of market discipline means that good or bad information about a firm is reflected in the prices or interest rates of its securities. What happens when inside and outside investors have adequate information to make decisions, and they disagree about whether the news is good or bad?

Consider the Hewlett-Packard and Compaq merger. In September 2001, Hewlett-Packard's CEO, Carleton (Carly) Fiorina offered to buy Compaq Computer Corporation for about $21 billion—the largest high-tech merger to date. Both firms were earning less than their cost of capital. [50] Nevertheless, it was hoped that the merger would result in increased efficiencies. Was that good news or bad news? The answer is that it was good news for some and bad news for others. Several of Carly's own board members, including Walter B. Hewlett and David W. Packard, were against it, as were CalPERS, UBS Warburg, Wells Fargo & Co., and other institutional investors who considered it bad news. On the other hand, other institutional investors (e.g., Barclays Global Investors, Putnam Investment Management, and Alliance Capital management) supported the merger. In addition Institutional Shareholder Services (ISS, a proxy advisory firm) recommended that investors vote for the merger on March 19, 2002.[51] On March 6, 2002, the Federal Trade Commission approved the merger.

Hewlett-Packard Company won the proxy fight to buy Compaq Computer Corp by a small margin of 2.8 percent of the voting shareholders. Walter Hewlett claims that Carly improperly swayed Deutsche Bank AG's Deutsche Asset Management to switch its vote on 17 million shares from a no vote to being in favor of the deal. The 17 million shares was not large enough to change the outcome

---

50. Colvin (January, 2002).

51. For additional information about the merger battle, see Park and Kerstetter (December 24, 2001); Burrows and Park (March 18, 2002); Park and Burrows (March 25, 2002). Advertisements *against the merger* appeared in the *Wall Street Journal*, March 12, 2002 (C12, and C13); March 15, 2002 (C7, and C9); and advertisements *for the merger* March 12, 2002, C22. This listing is for purposes of illustration and is not intended to be complete.

of the vote.[52] This outcome can be interpreted to support market discipline, or to say that it is not effective because both insiders and outsiders disagreed on whether the merger is good or bad.

Faster Is Not Better

Another concern is that the speed of failure may be increasing. Consider the case of Barings Brothers and Co., Ltd. In a twenty-eight day period, a rouge trader speculating on Japanese stocks on the Singapore futures exchange brought down the bank in 1995. It had losses of $1.4 billion versus capital of $500 million.[53]

Consider Enron. It grew from a small gas pipeline company in 1985 to a gigantic, highly regarded derivatives trader in 2001. On October 16, 2001, Enron announced its third-quarter results in a press release, stating that it would have nonrecurring charges of $1.01 billion after taxes. In November, it further restated earnings, and it declared Chapter 11 bankruptcy on December 2, 2001. Enron's stock price declined from a high of $90 per share in September 2000, to about $38 per share at the time of the October 2001 announcement, to $0.01 per share on May 20, 2002. Is that market discipline or investors bailing out?

The unknown true conditions of a firm's different interpretations of data and the increased speed of failure do not lend much support to relying on market discipline as a tool for corporate governance.

6. CONCLUSION

Market discipline is a good idea, but its time is yet to come. The Enron, Global Crossing, WorldCom, and Tyco debacles had some impact on market discipline and corporate governance. Responding to investor fears about shoddy accounting practices at Enron, Krispy Kreme Dougnuts Inc. was one of the first companies that took steps to boost investor confidence. Krispy Kreme announced that it was changing its method of reporting the construction of its $35 million Illinois doughnut mixing plant from "an off-balance-sheet synthetic lease" to a mortgage that will appear on the balance sheet. This was done to avoid the appearance of doing something improper.[54] It is also adding two outside directors to its board of

---

52. Tam (April 18, 2002).
53. Gup (1998).
54. Morse (2002); Lubove and MacDonald (2002).

directors, and has revealed various transactions by insiders.[55] And General Electric Corporation provided greater disclosure of its $56 billion invested SPEs. However, the increased disclosure did not satisfy all. GE was criticized because it acts as a financial institution and a manufacturing firm, so it should disclose its loan loss reserves and default rates.[56]

A greater emphasis is going to be placed on the disclosure requirements of public companies in three areas: liquidity and capital resources, including off-balance-sheet arrangements; trading activities, including non-exchange traded contracts; and relationships and transactions on terms that would not be available from clearly independent third parties.[57]

In addition, corporate stock options are coming under closer scrutiny.[58] Stock options boost earnings because they are not considered an expense, but at the same time, they provide benefits to the issuer. Employee stock options and share repurchases have exceeded dividend payments in recent years.[59] They are an increasingly common way of using cash that is not needed for investments and distributing wealth to employees. Warren E. Buffet criticized stock options because executives, unlike shareholders, profit from the options, even if the stock price declines.[60] Options can be repriced, or canceled and reissued at a later date and lower price. Some argue that this is an incentive for management to drive down the price of the stock during this period. All of this suggests that investors want greater disclosure.

Although the public wants accounting reform, it may not happen. Paul Volcker (2002), former Fed Chairman, and Chairman of the International Accounting Standards Committee, said "The issue we face is how far the newfound zeal for reforms will go, and whether it will persist for as long as Enron, Global Crossing, Xerox, WorldCom and other accounting scandals fade from the front pages. The historical record affords no comfort on that score. In the face of earlier difficulties, the accounting firms and their trade associations firmly resisted meaningful reform. They

---

55. Lloyd (March 8, 2002).
56. Morgenson (March 17, 2002).
57. United States Securities and Exchange Commission, Press Release 2002-13 (January 22, 2002). The Press Release contains links to a petition for interpretive guidance from the five major accounting firms and the American Institute of Certified Public Accountants, and an Appendix that provides details about the proposed disclosures.
58. Henry, et al. (March 4, 2002); Gleckman, et al. (March 4, 2002).
59. Liang and Sharpe (1999).
60. Norris (March 11, 2002).

have satisfied themselves with weak oversight bodies, usually dominated by the profession itself. That pattern is clearly reasserting itself in current lobbying efforts in the halls of Congress."

Nevertheless, Congress did enact the Sarbanes-Oxley Act of 2002.[61] This law created the Public Company Accounting Oversight Board to oversee the audit of public companies. It also provided for greater corporate disclosure and other features enhancing corporate governance, including a code of ethics for senior financial offices of publicly traded companies and penalties for violations of the Act.

Finally, Federal Reserve Chairman Alan Greenspan (2001), said that "market discipline in one form or another was a major governor of bank risk-taking in the early years of the Republic . . . But if market discipline was such an attractive governor for managing risk, why were the nineteenth and early twentieth centuries punctuated by those periodic banking collapses known to historians as *panics?*" Why did informed investors, security analysts, and regulators fail to spot Enron before it failed? Did it work in the case of Hewlett-Packard-Compaq? Why should we expect market discipline to work now?

REFERENCES

Abelson, Reed, and Kenneth N. Gilpin, (2001), "2 Enron Roles Raise Questions of Allegiance," *The New York Times On the Web*, December 7, *http://www.nytimes.com* (visited 12/7/02).

Agrawal, Anup, and Sahiba Chadha, (2002), "Who is Afraid of Reg FD? The Behavior and Performance of Sell-Side Analysts Following the SEC's Fair Disclosure Rules," University of Alabama, Working Paper, February.

Australian Prudential Regulation Authority, (2001), "Submission to the Basel Committee on Banking Supervision, The New Basel Capital Accord," May, *http://www.bis.org.* (visited 3/13/02).

"Badly Overrated," (2002), *Economist*," May 10, pp. 69–70.

"Bank Examination and Enforcement," (1997), *History of the Eighties: Lessons for the Future*, Vol. I, Washington, D.C., Federal Deposit Insurance Corporation, Retrospect, p. 433.

---

61. Public Law No: 107-204.

Barber, Brad, Reuven Lehavy, Maureen McNichols, and Brett Trueman, (2001), "Can Investors Prophet from Prophets? Security Analyst Recommendations and Stock Returns," *Journal of Finance*, Vol. 56, No. 2, April, pp. 531–653.

Basel Committee on Banking Supervision, (2001), Consultative Document, *The New Basel Capital Accord*, Bank for International Settlements, Basel, Switzerland, January.

Basel Committee on Banking Supervision, (2001), Consultative Document, *Pillar 3 (Market Discipline)*, Bank for International Settlements, Basel, Switzerland, January.

Basel Committee on Banking Supervision, (2001), Press Release, "The New Basel Capital Accord," Bank for International Settlements, Basel, Switzerland, January 16.

Beckett, Paul, and Carrick Mollenkamp, (2002), "Regulators, Auditors Were Silent As Allied Irish Banks' Losses Rose," *Wall Street Journal*, March 18, p. C15.

Beckett, Paul, Susan Pulliam, and Carrick Mollenkamp, (2002), "PNC Shakes Up Banking Sector: Investors Exit," *Wall Street Journal*, January 30, pp. C1, C2.

Benink, Harald, and Clas Wihlborg, (2002), "The New Basel Capital Accord: Making it Effective with Stronger Market Discipline," *European Financial Management*, Vol. 8, No. 1, pp. 103–115.

Bies, Susan Schmidt, (2002), Remarks by Governor Susan Schmidt Bies, "Strengthening the Financial System of the 21st Century Through Sound Accounting and Disclosure," at the Symposium on Building the Financial System in the 21st Century, Rüschlikon, Switzerland, (Board of Governors of the Federal Reserve System, Washington, D.C.), February 28.

Birchler, Urs. W., and Diana Hancock, (2003), "What Does the Yield on Subordinated Bank Debt Measure?" presented at the BIS, Banking and Financial Stability: A workshop on Applied Banking Research, Rome, Italy, March 20–21, *http://www.bis. org/bcbs/events/wkshop0303/index.htm* (visited 4/18/03).

Bliss, Robert R., and Mark J. Flannery, (2000), "Market Discipline in Governance of U. S. Bank Holding Companies: Monitoring vs. Influencing," Federal Reserve Bank of Chicago, Working Paper WP 200-03.

Borrus, Amy, Mike McNamee, and Heather Timmons, (2002), "The Credit-Raters: How They Work and How They Might Work Better," *BusinessWeek*, April 8, pp. 38–40.

Bowman, Thomas A., (2002), President and Chief Executive Officer of The Association for Investment Management and Research before the United States Senate Committee on Governmental Affairs, Enhancing Analysts Independence and Improving Disclosure to Investors, February 27.

Brickell, Mark C., (1996), "The Changing Nature of the Derivatives Market and the Lessons We Have Learned So Far," appears in *Derivatives and Public Policy, Proceedings of a Conference,*" Chicago, Ill, Federal Reserve Bank of Chicago, pp. 40–45.

Burrows, Peter, and Andrew Park, (2002), "Compaq and HP: What's an Investor To Do?" *BusinessWeek,* March 18, pp. 62–64.

Citigroup, Press Release, (2003), "Citigroup Statement on Enron Settlements with the SEC, Federal Reserve, OCC, and Manhattan DA," July 28, *http://www.citigroup.com* (visited 8/28/03).

Cohen, Marilyn, (2002), "Interest Rate Chicken," *Forbes,* April 29, p. 130.

Colvin, Geoffrey, (2002), "One Number That Won't Lie," *Fortune,* January 21, p. 42.

Crockett, Andrew, (2001), "Market Discipline and Financial Stability," Speech before the Bank for International Settlements at the Banks and Systemic Risk Conference, Bank of England, London, May 23–25.

D'Avolio, Gene D., Efi Gildor, and Andrei Shleifer, (2001), "Technology, Information Production, and Market Efficiency," appears in *Economic Policy for the Information Economy,* Federal Reserve Bank of Kansas City, pp. 125–160.

Economic Indicators, (2003), Washington, D.C., Government Printing Office, February.

Eisenbeis, Robert A., and Gary G. Gilbert, (1985), "Market Discipline and the Prevention of Bank Problems and Failures," *Issues in Bank Regulation,* 8, Winter, pp. 16–23.

Fairlamb, David, "Rebel in a Bow Tie," (2002), *BusinessWeek,* March 18, pp. 52–53.

FDIC Press Release, (1999), "FDIC Approves Assumption of Insured Local Deposits of First National Bank of Keystone, Keystone, West Virginia," PR-52-99, September 3.

FDIC Press Release, (2002), "FDIC Approves the Payout of Insured Deposits of NextBank National Association, Phoenix, Arizona, PR-16-2002, February 7.

Flannery, Mark J., (1998), "Using Market Information in Prudential Bank Supervision: A Review of the U.S. Empirical Evidence," *Journal of Money, Credit, and Banking,* August pp. 273–305.

Freddie Mac, Variable Rate Medium-Term Notes Due February 28, 2012, issued January 28, 2002, (CUSIP Number 3129242Z5), *http://www.frediemac.com/debt/*.

Gilbert, Gary G., (1985), "An Analytical Framework for Improved Disclosure in Banking," appears in Federal Reserve Bank of Chicago *Proceedings, Conference on Bank Structure and Competition,* May 1–3, pp. 552–562.

Gleckman, Howard, Dean Foust, Michael Arndt, Kathleen Kerwin, (2002), "Tax Dodging: Enron Isn't Alone," *BusinessWeek,* March 4, pp. 40–41.

Gordon, Marcy, (2002), "Analysts Didn't See Enron Warning," *http://www.washingtonpost.com,* February 28 (visited 2/28/02).

Greenspan, Alan, (2000), "Banking Evolution," appears in Federal Reserve Bank of Chicago, *The Changing Financial Industry Structure and Regulation: Bridging States, Countries, and Industries,* May, pp. 1–20.

Greenspan, Alan, (2001), "The Financial Safety Net," appears in Federal Reserve Bank of Chicago Proceedings, *The Financial Safety Net: Costs, Benefits, and Implications for Regulation,* pp. 1–8.

Greenspan, Alan, (2002), "Corporate Governance," remarks by Chairman Alan Greenspan at the Stern School of Business, New York, NY, Federal Reserve Board, March 26.

Gropp, Reint, and Anthony J. Richards, (2001), "Rating Agency Actions and the Pricing of Debt and Equity of European Banks: What Can We Infer About Private Sector Monitoring of Bank Soundness," *European Central Bank Working Paper Series,* Working Paper No. 7, Frankfurt, Germany, August.

Gup, Benton E., (1998), *Bank Failures in the Major Trading Countries of the World: Causes and Remedies,* Westport, CT: Quorum Books, pp. 50–51.

Gup, Benton E., (2000), "Market Discipline and the Corporate Governance of Bank: Theory vs. Evidence," appears in *The New Financial Architecture: Banking Regulation in the 21st Century,* B. E. Gup, ed., Westport, CT Quorum Books, pp. 187–206,

"HealthSouth Officer Charged with Conspiracy to Commit Wire & Securities Fraud," United States Attorney, Northern District of Alabama, Press Release, March 31, 2003. *http://www.usdoj.gov/usao/aln.*

Henriques, Diana, B., (2002), "Even a Watchdog is Not Always Fully Awake," *New York Times,* February 5, *http://www.nytimes.com* (visited 2/5/02).

Henry, David, Michelle Conlin, Nanette Byrnes, Michael Mandel, Stanley Holmes, and Stanley Reed, (2002), "Too Much of a Good Incentive," *BusinessWeek,* March 4, pp. 38–39.

JPMorgan Chase, Press Release, "JPMorgan Chase Resolves Enron-related Regulatory Matters," July 28, 2003, www.*http://jpmorganchase.com* (visited 8/27/03).

Krainer, John, and Jose A. Lopez, (2003), "Forecasting Bank Supervisory Ratings using Securities Market Information," presented at the BIS, Banking and Financial Stability: A workshop on Applied Banking Research, Rome, Italy, March 20–21, *http://www.bis.org/bcbs/events/wkshop0303/index.htm* (visited 4/18/03).

Kranhold, Kathryn, (2002), "Florida Panel May Sue Alliance Over Pension's Enron Losses," *Wall Street Journal*, April 23, p. B2.

Leach, James A., (2000), "Opening Statement of Rep. James A. Leach, Chairman, House Banking and Financial Services Committee, Hearing on Recent Failures," February 8.

Leathers, Charles G., and J. Patrick Raines, (2000), "Market Discipline for Banks: A Historical Review," appears in *The New Financial Architecture: Banking Regulation in the 21st Century*, B. E. Gup, ed., Westport, CT., Quorum Books, pp. 163–185.

Liang, Nellie, J., and Steven B. Sharpe, (1999), "Share Repurchases and Employee Stock Options and their Implications for S&P 500 Share Retirements and Expected Returns," Board of Governors of the Federal Reserve System, Finance and Economic Discussion Series, No. 1999-59, November.

Litan, R. E., (1997), "Institutions and Policies for Maintaining Financial Stability," appears in *Maintaining Financial Stability in a Global Economy*, Kansas City, MO, Federal Reserve Bank of Kansas City.

Lloyd, Mary Ellen, (2002), "Krispy Kreme Takes Steps to Increase Investor Confidence," *Wall Street Journal*, March 8, p. A4.

Lubove, Seth, and Elizabeth MacDonald, (2002), "Debt, Who Me?" *Forbes*, February 18, pp. 65–57.

Morgenson, Gretchen, (2002), "Annual Reports: More Pages, But Better?" *New York Times on the Web*, *http://www.nytimes.com*, March 17, (visited March 17, 2002).

Morse, Dan, (2002), "Krispy Kreme Goes Extra Mile to Explain New Mortgage Plan," *Wall Street Journal*, February 13, p. B7.

New York Clearing House Association, (2001), Comments Re: "The Proposed New Basel Accord," May 31, *http://www.bis.org*, (visited 5/8/02).

Norris, Floyd, (2002), "Stock Options are Faulted by Buffett," *New York Times on the Web*, *http://www.nytimes.com*, March 11, (visited 2/11/2002).

O'Brian, Bridget, (2002), "WorldCom Buffets Alliance Capital," *Wall Street Journal*, June 27, p. C19.

Office of Management and Budget, Statement of Administration Policy, (2002), "H.R. 2341—Class Action Fairness Act of 2002," March 12.

Park, Andrew, and Peter Burrows, (2002), "The HP Fight is Still Too Close to Call," *BusinessWeek*, March 25, p. 35.

Park, Andrew, and Jim Kerstetter, (2001), "Carly's Last Stand," *BusinessWeek*, December 24, pp. 63–70.

Parloff, Roger, (2002), "The $200 Billion Miscarriage of Justice," *Fortune*, February 17, *http://www.fortune.com* (visited 1/16/03).

Richards, Bill, and Scott Thurm, (2002), "Boston Chicken Case Mirrors Enron Failure," *Wall Street Journal*, March 13, pp. C1, C13.

Rose, Peter S., (1999), *Commercial Bank Management*, 4th ed., Boston, MA.; Irwin/McGraw-Hill.

Sarbannes-Oxley Act of 2002, Public Law 107-204.

Schwab BondSource, New Issue Alert (Charles Schwab & Co.), LaSalle National Bank N.A., Step-up Coupon FDIC Insured CD, January 29, 2003.

Scott, William L., (1991), *Contemporary Financial Markets and Services*, St. Paul, MN: West Publishing Co.

"Scrutinizing European Firms' Balance Sheets," (2002), *Wall Street Journal*, February 25, pp. A11, A14.

Sidel, Robin, (2003), "Some Untimely Analyst Advice On World-Com Raises Eyebrows," *Wall Street Journal*, June 27, p. A12.

Silverberg, Stanley C., (1985), "Deposit Insurance and the Soundness of Banks," appears in Federal Reserve Bank of Chicago Proceedings, *Conference on Bank Structure and Competition*, May 1–3, pp. 447–451.

Smith, Randall, and Aaron Lucchetti, (2002), "Analysts' Picks of Enron Stock Face."

"Scrutiny," *Wall Street Journal*, February 26, pp. C1, C15.

"Surreal," (2002), *Economist*, April 20, p. 74.

Tam, Pui-Wing, (2002), "H-P Claims Vote Approved Deal With Compaq," *Wall Street Journal*, April 18, p. A3.

Thornton, Emily, and Mike France, (2003), "For Enron's Bankers, A 'Get out of Jail Free' Card," *BusinessWeek*, August 11, p. 29.

Tittonel, Silvano, (2002). Member of the Secretariat, Basel Committee on Banking Supervision, e-mail message to Benton E. Gup concerning market discipline, March 18.

United States General Accounting Office, (2002), *Bank Regulation: Analysis of the Failure of Superior Bank, FSB, Hinsdale, Illinois*, Statement of Thomas J. McCool, before the Committee on Banking, Housing, and Urban Affairs, U.S. Senate, GAO-02-419T, February 7.

Unger, Laura S., (2001), "Special Study: Regulation Fair Disclosure Revisited," United States Securities & Exchange Commission, Washington, D.C., December.

United States Securities & Exchange Commission, (2002), Press Release, "SEC Brings First Pro Forma Financial Reporting Case—Trump Hotels Charged With Issuing Misleading Earnings," (2002-6), January 16.

United States Securities & Exchange Commission, (2002), Press Release, "SEC Issues Statement on Disclosure Requirements for Public Companies," (2002-13), January 22.

United States Securities & Exchange Commission, (2002), Press Release, "Xerox Settles SEC Enforcement Action Charging Company with Fraud," (2002-52), April 11.

United States Securities & Exchange Commission, (2003), Press Release "SEC Settles Enforcement Proceedings Against J.P. Morgan Chase and Citigroup," (2003-87), July 28.

"Using Subordinated Debt as an Instrument of Market Discipline," (1999), Staff Study 172, Board of Governors of the Federal Reserve System, December.

VandeHei, Jim, (2002), "Bush's Cherished Tort-Reform Plans Survive Enron—Barely,' *Wall Street Journal,* March 14, pp. A20.

Volcker, Paul A., (1997), "The 1980s in Retrospect," appears in *History of the Eighties: Lessons for the Future,* Vol. II, Washington, D.C., Federal Deposit Insurance Corporation, pp. 89–91.

Volcker, Paul A., 2002. "A Litmus Test for Accounting Reform," *Wall Street Journal,* May 21, pp. A18.

Ward, Jonathan, (2002), "The New Basel Capital Accord and Developing Countries: Problems and Alternatives," Working Paper No. 04, Version, 2.0, Cambridge University, UK.

Wayne, Leslie, (2002), "Credit Raters Get Scrutiny and Possibly a Competitor," *The New York Times on the Web,* April 23, *http://www.nytimes.com* (visited 4/23/02).

White, Ben, (2002), "Analysts Say Enron Lied to Them," *http://www.washingtonpost.com,* February 28, pp. E01. (visited February 28, 2002).

www.calpers.org (California Public Employees' Retirement System is known as "CalPERS").

APPENDIX
COMMENTS ON GUP'S PAPER,
"MARKET DISCIPLINE: IS IT FACT OR FICTION?"
GEORGE G. KAUFMAN

In this paper, Gup casts doubt about the effectiveness of market discipline, not only in banking but in almost all industries. He demonstrates convincingly that both banks and other firms have failed. From this, Gup concludes that market discipline is not a "panacea" that produces "market stability" and that "market discipline is a good idea, but its time is yet to come."

I am not convinced by Gup's arguments. Let me stand back and examine what we mean by market discipline and what we expect market discipline to do for firms. All firms are disciplined by something or someone with respect to what and how to produce, and what prices to charge. In the absence of any discipline whatsoever, firms would be able to continuously do whatever the owner wants without limit. But in actuality, they can do so only as long as the owner's funds (be they private or government) are not completely dissipated.

Most firms are disciplined by the private market place. And the market is a tough regulator! If for whatever reason firms misjudge and generate losses that dissipate their capital, the market forces them out of business and encourages new entry by owners willing to risk their capital. But, at times, the outcome of market discipline is inconsistent with the political, social, or economic goals of society as a whole, e.g., it produces an "unfair" distribution of income or not fully priced externalities such as the production of pollutants, physical harm, or broad averse effects of firm failure. Then, society often switches to government discipline with respect to what and how to produce, and what to charge.

In the United States, we have both market and government discipline (although only a few but highly visible industries operate primarily under government discipline). This is a good situation. It provides for a healthy tension between the two and keeps either from going off the deepend. If market discipline is perceived not to work effectively in an industry, society will switch more to government discipline. Likewise, if government discipline is perceived not to work effectively, society will switch more to market discipline. U.S. history is replete with examples of such switches back and forth, although not generally to the extreme of either.

If not market discipline for an industry, then what? Opponents of market discipline are obligated to raise and to answer this question. That is, if Gup believes that the time has not yet come for market discipline, for what type of discipline has it come? To answer this question, it is useful to examine what one can reasonably expect from market discipline. This would include:

- Encourage efficiency
- Encourage responsiveness to changes in market forces
- Encourage orderly exit of inefficient or unlucky firms when their capital is exhausted
- Encourage entry of new hopeful firms whose owners have, and are willing to risk, capital
- Focus on firm profitability as a measure of performance

My reading is that government discipline does more poorly on most, if not all, of these criteria for the large majority of industries. If not, why do we have so much market and so little government discipline? Unless one argues that it is a result of a massive conspiracy, it reflects revealed preference. Thus, my bottom line paraphrases Winston Churchill in that market discipline is the worst of all systems of discipline except for any other system tried to date.

I have a few more specific comments on the paper:

- Market discipline is not an "invention" that suddenly occurred in Scotland in 1695 and in the U.S. in 1838. It is an ongoing and developing process that has existed in one form or another since earliest times.
- Market discipline does not mean no firm failures, nor is it immune to fraud or bad behavior by owners/managers. In time, market discipline will catch up with all firms. This may take time, but probably no longer than government discipline takes, on average.
- The failed Superior Bank was a privately held bank owned by only two parties. Thus, the usual rules of corporate governance and disclosure do not necessarily hold.
- Credit-rating agencies do have better access to firm information than private investors, but they may not analyze it very well.
- Mandating subdebt at banks need not increase leverage. Subdebt holders will demand a minimum of equity to protect them. Subdebt will primarily substitute for other debt or deposits. After all, most firms in the U.S. are not regulated by the government but operate with far more equity and less debt than government-regulated banks.

7

The New Basel Capital Accord and Questions for Research

Marc Saidenberg and Til Schuermann[1]

I. INTRODUCTION

There are two sets of reasons often given for capital regulation in financial institutions broadly and banks in particular. One is the protection of consumers from exploitation by opaque and better-informed financial institutions; for banking, the objective would be depositor protection. The second is systemic risk.[2] Banks are often thought to be a source of systemic risk because of their central role in the payments system and in the allocation of financial resources,[3] combined with the fragility of their financial structure.[4] Banks are highly leveraged with relatively short-term liabilities, typically in the form of deposits, and relatively illiquid assets, usually loans to firms or households. In that sense, banks are said to be "special" and hence subject to special regulatory oversight.

There is a tight linkage between deposit insurance and capital regulation. Deposit insurance is designed to overcome the asymmetry of information in the banking system (Diamond and Dybvig

---

1. We would like to thank Larry Wall for his encouragement and patience and Darryll Hendricks and Beverly Hirtle for their helpful and insightful comments. An earlier version of this paper appeared on *FMA Online*. All remaining errors are ours.
2. Not all observers agree that systemic risk should be an important objective of bank capital regulation. See, for example, Benston and Kaufman (1995).
3. In many countries, banks control 70% or more of the assets in the financial system. In the U.S., however, the bank share of total assets has fallen to little more than 20% (Basel Committee on Banking Supervision 1996, p. 126).
4. For an interesting cross-sectoral comparison, see Joint Forum (2001).

(1983), Dewatripont and Tirole (1994)). The bank knows more about the riskiness of its activities than do its depositors. A depositor, therefore, is unable to tell a good bank from a bad one. Because banks are highly leveraged institutions, depositors have a strong incentive to show up at the bank first to withdraw their funds in case they doubt the financial health of a particular bank. Those at the end of the line may get nothing. In short, deposit insurance is designed to prevent depositors from overreacting to bad news about banks.[5]

The creation of such a safety net comes at a cost, namely moral hazard. Depositors no longer have an incentive to monitor (or pay to monitor) banks since their deposits are guaranteed up to the coverage limit (currently $100,000 per individual per institution in the U.S.). Banks have an attendant incentive to increase risk. Hence the name of the game in designing a safety net has been to balance the need to prevent bank panics (and other social costs to bank failure such as credit crunches) with the moral hazard brought on by the very presence of the safety net. The regulation of bank capital is often justified to achieve this balance.[6]

The literature on the general rationale for capital regulation in financial institutions is extensive and has been the subject of several recent surveys (Santos (2001), Ball and Stoll (1998), Berger, Herring and Szegö (1995)). Bank regulators have long regarded the prevention of systemic risk as the fundamental rationale for imposing capital requirements on banks. The assumption is that shareholders will not take into account the social costs of systemic risk in their capital decisions and so will tend to hold less capital than if these spillover costs were considered.

Capital requirements are intended to mitigate the risks of adverse selection by ensuring that the financial firm has at least some minimal level of resources to honor its commitments to its customers. Capital requirements are intended to mitigate moral hazard by ensuring that the owners of a financial institution have a

---

5. Bank runs and panics were quite real and prevalent in the U.S. in the 19th and early 20th centuries. In the years preceding the creation of the FDIC (i.e., 1930–33), the number of bank failures averaged 2,000 per year (Mishkin 1997).

6. Santos (2001), in a survey of the bank capital regulation, points out the necessity of jointly considering the problems of deposit insurance pricing, lender of last resort, and bank capital standards and regulation. "In general, the optimal regulation encompasses a menu of regulatory instruments, designed to extract information from banks and minimize the cost of 'bribing' the lower quality banks to mimic the higher quality ones." (Santos, 2001, p. 59.) In short, while the information asymmetry inherent in banking is a real issue, deposit insurance may not be the only solution, and if deposit insurance is chosen, its design matters in determining banking stability and efficiency.

stake in ensuring that the firm does not engage in fraud and conforms to the conduct of business rules, if only to avoid fines or loss of equity value. To be effective in this role, capital requirements must be sensitive to the risks to which an institution is exposed.

Formal and systematic bank capital regulation is relatively new. The 1988 Basel Capital Accord, or Basel I (Basel Committee on Banking Supervision (BCBS) (1988)), which set minimum capital standards for internationally active banks, was really the first international accord of its kind. It succeeded at raising capital levels at a time when they were quite low. Aside from defining what types of capital were eligible, Basel I set a capital ratio at 8% of risk-adjusted assets. It was the risk adjustment of the assets which became the focus of concern and current regulatory reform resulting in the new Basel Capital Accord, or Basel II (BCBS (2001)).

The new Basel Capital Accord for bank capital regulation is designed to better align regulatory capital to the underlying risks by encouraging more and better systematic risk management practices, especially in the area of credit risk. Compliance with an even more risk-sensitive capital ratio is only one of three pillars under the accord. Revisions to the new accord also introduce banks' internal assessments (subject to supervisory review—Pillar 2) of capital adequacy and market discipline (through enhanced transparency—Pillar 3) as key components of prudential regulation. It may therefore come as no surprise that underlying the accord is some formal economic modeling. Both the models and their implication for implementation of the accord open the door to many research questions. We see these questions falling into three groups: the impact of the proposal on the global banking system through possible changes in bank behavior; a set of issues around risk analytics; issues brought about by Pillar 2 (supervisory review) and Pillar 3 (public disclosure).

The rest of the paper will proceed as follows. In Section 2 we expand on some of the problems that Basel I brought with it; Section 3 will provide an overview of the main objectives of Basel II, details of which are provided in Section 4. In Section 5 we will cover the questions the new accord raises for the research community. Section 6 provides some final comments.

2. PROBLEMS WITH BASEL I

To understand and appreciate the basic goals of Basel II and the strategy for achieving these goals, it is important to understand the shortcomings of the current Basel Capital Accord (Basel I). Under the current Accord, capital requirements are only moderately related to a bank's risk taking. The requirement on a credit exposure is the same whether the borrower's credit rating is triple-A or triple-C. Moreover, the requirement often hinges on the exposure's specific legal form. For example, an on-balance sheet loan generally faces a higher capital requirement that an off-balance sheet exposure to the same borrower, even though financial engineering can make such distinctions irrelevant from a risk perspective.

This lack of risk sensitivity under the current Accord distorts economic decision making. Banks are encouraged to structure transactions to minimize regulatory requirements or, in some cases, to undertake transactions whose main purpose is to reduce capital requirements with no commensurate reduction in actual risk taking. As an example, no capital charge is assigned to loans or loan commitments with a maturity of less than one year. Perhaps not surprisingly, 364-day facilities have risen in popularity. The corollary to this problem is that the current system fails to recognize many techniques for actually mitigating banking risks. A closely related concern is that the current Accord is static and not easily adaptable to new banking activities and risk management techniques. Lastly, some banks may have been reluctant to invest in better risk management systems because they are costly and would not provide tangible regulatory capital benefits.

The lack of risk sensitivity also impedes effective supervision. Although both banks and supervisors have been working to improve their assessments of capital adequacy, these assessments tend to center on comparisons of actual capital levels against the regulatory minimums. Bank examiners continue to focus on these ratios in part because they are part of the legal basis for taking supervisory actions. Reflecting supervisors' emphasis on regulatory capital ratios, financial markets and rating agencies tend focus on them as well. Consequently, in some cases supervisors and even the banks themselves may have limited information about a bank's overall risk and capital adequacy. In this setting, it is difficult to ensure that banks and supervisors will respond to emerging problems in a timely manner.

3. OBJECTIVES OF THE NEW BASEL ACCORD

Broadly speaking, the objectives of Basel II are to encourage better and more systematic risk management practices, especially in the area of credit risk, and to provide improved measures of capital adequacy for the benefit of supervisors and the marketplace more generally. At the outset of the process of developing the new Accord, the Basel Committee developed the so-called three pillars approach to capital adequacy involving (1) minimum capital requirements, (2) supervisory review of internal bank assessments of capital relative to risk, and (3) increased public disclosure of risk and capital information sufficient to provide meaningful market discipline. Although the Committee's proposals have evolved considerably over the past several years, these fundamental objectives and the three-pillar approach have held constant.

It is hardly necessary to emphasize the importance of banks and banking systems to financial and economic stability.[7] The ability of a sound and well-capitalized banking system to help cushion an economy from unforeseen shocks is well known, as are the negative consequences of a banking system that itself becomes a source of weakness and instability. A critical potential weakness of financial markets is that risks are in many cases under-estimated and not fully recognized until too late, with a concomitant potential for excessive consequences once they have been fully realized. This is why the Basel Committee's efforts to promote greater recognition of risks and more systematic attention to them are vitally important.

The essence of Basel II is a focus on risk differentiation and the need for enhanced approaches to assessing credit risk. Some critics have argued that it is preferable to downplay differences in risk, and indeed forbearance can sometimes appear the most expedient strategy. But experience has also shown that this will not work as an overall approach because ignoring risks inevitably leads to larger problems down the road. Thus, one of the key messages of Basel II is that bankers, supervisors, and other market participants must become better attuned to risk and better able to act on those risk assessments at the appropriate time. Bank supervisors must get better at addressing issues pre-emptively rather than in crisis mode. Significant attention to risk management is one of the primary mechanisms available to help banks and supervisors do that.

---

7. For a broad cross-country study analyzing the real economic impact of banking crises, see Caprio and Klingebiel (1996).

Basel II seeks to provide incentives for greater awareness of differences in risk through more risk-sensitive minimum capital requirements. The Pillar 1 capital requirements will, by necessity, be imperfect measures of risk as any rules-based framework will be. The objective of the proposals is to increase the emphasis on assessments of credit and operational risk throughout financial institutions and across markets.

Perhaps even more important in the long run is the second pillar of the new Accord. Pillar 2 requires banks to systematically assess risk relative to capital within their organization. The review of these internal assessments by supervisors should provide discipline on bank management to take the process seriously and will help supervisors to continually enhance their understanding of risk at the institutions. The third pillar of Basel II provides another set of necessary checks and balances by seeking to promote market discipline through enhanced transparency. Greater disclosure of key elements of risk and capital will provide important information to counterparties and investors who need such information to have an informed view of a bank's profile.

4. KEY ELEMENTS OF THE PACKAGE

While the way minimum regulatory capital requirements are computed has changed substantially, what actually counts towards capital has not; the numerator in the capital-asset ratio remains unchanged.[8] The New Accord outlines two new approaches to assessing credit risk and for the first time specifies a capital charge for operational risk. In this section we will briefly provide details on both, including a description of the calibration effort that the Basel Committee has undertaken with participants in industry.[9]

4.1. Pillar 1: Credit Risk

In order to allow for evolution of credit risk management methods and practices the New Accord introduces a range of approaches for assessing credit risk: a standardized and an internal ratings-based (IRB) approach, the latter having two versions. The standardized approach incorporates modest changes in risk sensitivi-

---

8. See Board of Governors of the Federal Reserve System (2002) for review of eligible capital.
9. See Basel Committee on Banking Supervision (2002) for detailed descriptions of each element of the minimum capital requirements.

ties to improve risk sensitivities through readily observable risk measures such as external credit ratings. This simple rules-based approach is designed to address some of the most blatant short-comings of the current Accord.

Compared to the current Accord, the IRB approach is fundamentally different in concept, design, and implementation. Consistent with the Basel Committee's objectives, it is intended to produce a capital requirement more closely linked to each bank's actual credit risks—a lower-quality portfolio will face a higher capital charge, a higher-quality portfolio a lower capital charge. Such an approach is essential to creating the correct incentives for both banks and supervisors.

The IRB approach is based on four key parameters used to estimate credit risks:[10]

1. *PD*   The probability of default of a borrower over a one-year horizon
2. *LGD*   The loss given default (or 1 minus recovery) as a percentage of exposure at default
3. *EAD*   Exposure at default (an amount, not a percentage)
4. *M*   Maturity

There are two variants of IRB available to banks, the foundation approach and the advanced approach.[11] They differ principally in how the four parameters can be measured and determined internally, but an essential feature of both approaches is their use of the bank's own internal information on an asset's credit risk. For the foundation approach only *PD* may be assigned internally, subject to supervisory review (Pillar 2). *LGD* is fixed and based on supervisory values. *EAD* is also based on supervisory values in cases where the measurement is not clear. Finally, a single average maturity of three years is assumed for the portfolio. In the advanced approach all four parameters are determined by the bank and are subject to supervisory review.

The IRB at heart provides a continuous mapping from the basic set of four input parameters (*PD, LGD, EAD* and *M*), plus some other observables such as borrower type, to a minimum capital requirement. This mapping is based on the same analytical framework as most credit portfolio models.[12] Gordy

---

10. Section III.B, § 23 – 30, of Basel Committee on Banking Supervision (2001a)
11. For qualification conditions, please see Basel Committee on Banking Supervision (2001a).
12. See also Section 5.2.4 below.

(2003) demonstrates that such a risk-bucketing approach, i.e. capital requirements which only depend on the characteristics of an individual exposure, is consistent with an asymptotic single risk factor credit portfolio model, itself based on the Merton (1974) options-based model of firm default.

Risk-weighted assets (RWA) is computed as a function of the basic set of four input parameters: $RWA = K(PD, LGD, M) \times 12.5 \times EAD$, where 12.5 is just the reciprocal of 8% (the overall level of minimum capital as a percentage of RWA).[13] The risk weight function $K(\cdot)$ steepens quickly for low (annual) probabilities of default and then becomes relatively flatter for low quality credits.

A critical issue with respect to the IRB approach is the reliability of the credit risk parameters supplied by banks, upon which the capital charges are based—specifically the estimated PDs, LGDs, and EADs described above. If these estimates prove unreliable, the IRB approach would provide little, if any, improvement in risk sensitivity over the current Accord. Thus, it is essential that prior to IRB implementation supervisors ensure that a bank's internal processes for determining internal risk ratings, PDs, LGDs, and EADs are credible and robust. To support this objective, Basel II will require that banks comply with a set of minimum operational requirements in each of these areas. Although these standards are a critical element, they may have little consequence unless supervisors have the ability to validate and enforce them.

4.2. Pillars 2 and 3: Supervisory Review and Public Disclosure

Pillar 2 promotes the supervisory review process and is regarded as an essential element of the new Accord. Pillar 2 encourages banks to develop internal economic capital assessments appropriate to their own risk profiles for identifying, measuring, and controlling risks. The emphasis on internal assessments of capital adequacy recognizes that any rules-based approach will inevitably lag behind changing risk profiles of complex banking organizations. The banks' internal assessments should give explicit recognition to the quality of the risk management and control process and to risks not fully addressed in Pillar 1.

Much of the focus has been on the principle that banks should hold capital above the regulatory minimums, with the recognition that the capital buffer should reflect risks that either are not fully

---

13. Basel Committee on Banking Supervision (2003) and Saunders and Allen (2002).

captured (e.g. concentration risk) or not taken into account (e.g. interest rate risk, business risk) in Pillar 1. Additionally, the capital buffer should also reflect factors external to the bank (e.g. business cycle effects).

Pillar 3 represents the Basel Committee's efforts to promote market discipline through enhanced transparency and is integral to the success of the New Basel Accord. In particular, Pillar 3 will provide enhanced public disclosures of capital adequacy and risk information. The Pillar 3 framework has undergone a number of substantive changes since first proposed. The Committee has maintained throughout the Accord revision process that the dis-closures should be mandatory for all banks given the increased reliance on internal assessments of risks. The Committee has tried to strike a balance and ensure that the disclosures are meaningful and sufficiently detailed to allow for comparisons across institutions and over time while not becoming burdensome or prescriptive.

4.3. Calibration Effort

Implicitly or explicitly, the calibration of risk weights involves (1) estimating the volatility or uncertainty in portfolio credit losses over a time horizon taken to be one year, and (2) given this estimated volatility, determining the level of capital needed to achieve possible target solvency probabilities.

The Basel Committee balanced two broad empirical approaches—one direct and another survey-based—for calibrating IRB risk weights. The Committee looked to survey data from banks and trade groups. This approach uses the economic capital requirements from banks' internal economic capital systems, thus building upon research already conducted within the private sector. The Committee collected information on banks' internal economic capital allocations. For each institution these data were used to estimate the implied risk weights attributed by each bank to loans having particular *PD*, *LGD* and maturity.

The Committee also looked to direct or model-based calibration of risk weights to support the survey evidence. This method involved using formal credit risk models to estimate the required capital associated with an individual loan within a large, well-diversified portfolio. Key assumptions, such as correlation parameters, reflected a range of values based on industry practice and independent research conducted with borrower default data from multiple countries. These credit risk modeling exercises produced results comparable to those obtained from the survey evidence.

The development of appropriate risk weight functions and their specific parameters, to a minimum capital requirement, is indeed a challenge. In part, these difficulties reflect the limited historical data with which to estimate key credit risk parameters. In addition to these empirical issues, the Committee has also faced a number of fundamental policy tradeoffs. The Basel Committee has a stated objective of ensuring that the capital within the banking system does not either fall or rise significantly with the introduction of the new Accord. The Committee also sought to address the concern that the introduction of a risk-sensitive capital requirement would be excessively volatile or pro-cyclical. Exercises such as a series of Quantitative Impact Studies were conducted to address these issues.

4.4. Operational Risk: 3 Flavors

Throughout the Accord revision process, the Basel Committee maintained that there must be an explicit capital charge for operational risk, and that this charge should be risk sensitive. Operational risk is defined as "the risk of direct of indirect loss resulting from inadequate or failed internal processes, people and systems or from external events" (Basel Committee on Banking Supervision (2001), §547). Both the unbundling of the minimum capital requirement into risk sensitive measures of credit and market risk, and the importance of operational risk warranted an explicit capital charge for operational risk. Developing a capital charge for operational risk is challenging both because of a lack of agreed methodology, and because of limited historical loss data.

In response to these challenges, the Basel Committee developed three approaches for measuring operational risk capital requirements. The Basic Indicator and Standardized approaches provide simple ways to determine a capital requirement, based on a percentage of gross income. Through the Advanced Measurement approach (AMA) the Committee sought to provide flexibility for banks to use their own internal measurement approaches subject to meeting rigorous qualitative and quantitative standards. One of the key objectives of the AMA is to provide incentives for banks to develop improved measures of operational risk and to encourage operational loss data collection efforts to use as a basis for calibrating the regulatory capital requirements. This is spelled out in BCBS (2002).

5. QUESTIONS FOR RESEARCH ON THREE FRONTS

In designing the specifics of the New Basel Accord, regulators made use of advances in the academic literature, particularly in the area of risk management. In turn, the regulatory proposals have become fertile ground for more research. We see these research questions falling into three groups: (1) what is the impact of the proposal on the global banking system through possible changes in bank behavior; (2) a set of issues around risk analytics; (3) issues brought about by Pillar 2 (supervisory review) and Pillar 3 (public disclosure).

5.1 Impact of Proposal on Banking System and Bank Behavior

A stated goal of the New Basel Accord is to keep the overall level of capital in the global banking system from changing significantly, assuming the same degree of risk. Obviously that does not mean that the capital levels of each bank will remain unchanged. The calibration effort discussed in Section 4.3 described how the Basel Committee has gone about ascertaining the impact of the New Accord on the banking system. These calibrations are conducted under ceteris paribus assumptions; it is unclear how bank behavior might change once the new Accord is in place. This raises several questions.

One is: how will Basel II impact banks domiciled and/or operating in the emerging markets? Much like the 1996 Market Risk Amendment to Basel I (BCBS (1996)), Basel II was designed with large, internationally active banks in mind. For market risk this has created some perverse incentives, namely that the standardized approach often yields much lower regulatory capital levels than the internal models approach, precisely the opposite of what was intended. For example, the charge for interest rate risk reflects, for instruments of 1-2Y maturity, a yield change of only 90 basis points. While this may indeed be a large movement in the G-7 fixed income markets, it occurs with much greater regularity in many emerging markets. If the risk-sensitive parameter values of the standardized approach for credit risk in the New Basel Accord are similarly "too low," the Accord will lack the desired incentive to have banks migrate toward the IRB approach. It remains an open question just how different the impact between the standardized and IRB approaches are in the emerging market context, and whether that difference provides the right incentives.

A second example is the Accord's impact, if any, on the business cycle, the so-called pro-cyclicality debate. The basic concern is that tying banks' capital to dynamically changing credit ratings will result in pro-cyclical behavior on the part of the banks. When the business environment softens, firms (borrowers) become riskier as predicted by the credit risk (internal ratings) models, which often have obligor profitability as a driver. As a result, banks need to hold more capital against loans to those firms. Yet firms may need additional funds precisely during those challenging times to ensure that they are in a viable position when demand resumes.

Of course, bank lending is already pro-cyclical (Lown, Morgan and Rohatgi (2000)), and it is not clear that the new Accord will necessarily exacerbate this pro-cyclicality. Business cycle fluctuations can have a major impact on credit portfolio loss distributions. Carey (2002), using re-sampling techniques, shows that mean losses during a recession such as 1990/91 in the U.S. are about the same as losses in the 0.5% tail during an expansion. Bangia et al. (2002), using a regime switching approach, find that capital held by banks over a one-year horizon needs to be 25–30% higher in a recession than in an expansion.

To be sure, it is not clear how to detect pro-cyclicality, even if it were to exist. Are losses higher in a recession because of a bad draw from the loss distribution or because cyclical factors affecting the loss distribution have shifted? Allen and Saunders (2002) make the important distinction between ex post loss realization (the loss distribution is fixed) vs. ex ante changes in credit exposure (the entire loss distribution shifts in response to macroeconomic factors). Allen and Saunders (2002) and Borio, Furfine and Lowe (2001) claim that the New Basel Accord would exacerbate pro-cyclicality, while Carpenter, Whitesell and Zakrajsek (2001) argue otherwise. All of these studies are conducted under a similar ceteris paribus assumption as the calibration effort under the Quantitative Impact Studies.[14] Yet, analogous to a Lucas-style critique, the very introduction of the New Basel Accord will likely influence bank behavior. For all banks, the increased transparency achieved by disclosing many of those risk metrics to the market

---

14. Basel Committee for Banking Supervision (2002).

through Pillar 3 may affect their behavior. For some banks, the output of the risk calculations under the New Basel Accord may serve as useful inputs to many decision points for bank management, including capital allocation between different lending activities, risk-based pricing and performance measurement.

More recently, the creation of a bifurcated capital framework for the U.S. (advanced IRB for the large, internationally active banks, no change from the current standard for the remaining institutions) has opened the door to a set of questions related to competitiveness, as highlighted in the "U.S. Advanced Notice of Proposed Rule Making" (see Federal Reserve Board (2003)). For example, would such a bifurcated approach lead to an increase in industry consolidation as larger banks, seeking to lever capital efficiencies, acquire smaller banks? Importantly, what are the competitive implications of continuing to operate under a regulatory framework that is not risk sensitive? The potential and channels for changing bank behavior is an important issue that merits more research.

5.2. Risk Analytics

This may be the largest grouping of attendant research questions. We will distinguish between validation of models, the four IRB parameters of *PD*, *LGD*, *EAD* and *M*, correlations and portfolio aggregation, operational risk metrics and finally, coherent risk measures. We will briefly give some highlights in each area.

5.2.1. RISK ANALYTICS: VALIDATION
In Section 4.1 we laid out some of the key elements of the credit risk portion of the New Basel Accord, in particular the IRB (internal ratings based) approach to estimating credit risk. Of the four parameters or variables, the probability of default (*PD*), loss given default (*LGD*), exposure at default (*EAD*) and maturity (*M*), *PD* arguably serves as the cornerstone. At a practical level, banks implement *PD* estimates through a rating tool, where each obligor is assigned a credit rating, effectively a summary measure of the obligor's creditworthiness. The key question here may simply be: how do we recognize a good or bad rating system? Backtesting à la VaR models for market risk is going to be very hard for the simple reason that defaults, the event forecast by rating tools, happen rarely. Lopez and Saidenberg (2000) point out that judging the performance of a model from a single year's results is difficult because of the

limited number of defaults and because common macroeconomic conditions affect all borrowers. Thus making inference about long-run default behavior based on data from a single year is misguided. Moreover, this dependence on common factors makes it difficult to assume *across* year independence. This dependence will affect test statistics, which typically make *iid* assumptions.[15]

More broadly, there are two key related, yet distinct, elements in the evaluation (or validation) of banks' internal ratings systems by banks or supervisors. The first is the accuracy of the ratings systems or models, which refers to whether the ratings reflect the actual credit quality of the bank's borrowers on an ex ante basis. However, since the credit quality of borrowers is never truly known, absolute evaluations of accuracy may not be possible. Evaluations of accuracy relative to other ratings system, such as by independent ratings agencies, other firms' internal ratings, or model-generated ratings, are possible and should be evaluated.

The second element of internal rating systems or models evaluations is their consistency. The intuition here is that if a ratings system is well defined, then ratings across time and across borrowers should be predictable. That is, based on new information at a different point in time or for a new borrower, the system should generate a rating that is reasonable related to those already assigned.

5.2.2. Risk Analytics: *PD*

The *PD* is a real number defined on the unit interval; however, credit ratings, such as those assigned by rating agencies, are discrete.[16] What is the appropriate mapping from one to the other? How many buckets or ratings should a rating system have? How does one know if there are too few or too many? Even if the bank can answer these questions for themselves, how should supervisors examine and monitor these rating systems?

Another relevant aspect of *PD* and rating is the process of ratings migration. Credit migration or transition matrices characterize the past changes in credit quality of obligors (typically firms) and are a convenient summary of credit behavior in a portfolio; the default probability is simply the last column of this matrix. There are different methods for estimating this matrix from ratings histories from either public bonds or internal customers, some less

---

15. However, it may be reasonable to make conditional independence assumptions, where the conditioning could be the state of the economy.

16. For a review of the use of rating systems at U.S. banks, at least through the late 1990s, see Treacy and Carey (2000).

efficient than others. Schuermann and Jafry (2003) explore whether and by how much it matters which of these methods are used (it can matter a lot) for annual migration matrices. In addition, these matrices are known to exhibit non-Markov behavior (Lando and Skodeberg (2002)) and sensitivity to the business cycle (Nickell, Perraudin and Varotto (2000) and Bangia et al. (2002)).

5.2.3. Risk Analytics: *LGD*, *EAD* and *M*   There are several ways of measuring *LGD*:

1. Market *LGD*: observed from market prices of defaulted bonds or marketable loans soon after the actual default event.
2. Workout *LGD*: the set of estimated cash flows resulting from the workout and/or collections process, properly discounted, and the estimated exposure.
3. Implied Market *LGD*: *LGD*s derived from risky (but *not* defaulted) bond prices using a theoretical asset-pricing model.

Banks typically have the second type at their disposal, though it is helpful to compare such estimates, whenever possible, against the other two types. A critical assumption with all three methods is the appropriate discount rate. It is by no means obvious which discount rate to apply. In principle the correct rate would be for an asset of similar risk. Importantly, once the obligor has defaulted, the bank is an investor in a defaulted asset and should value it accordingly. Inappropriate candidates include the coupon rate (set ex ante of default, so too low) and the bank's hurdle rate (unless the bank only invests in very risky assets like defaulted debt instruments, probably too low). Estimating reliable risk-adjusted return measures on recoveries remains an important task.

We do know a little about what drives the variability in *LGD*. It matters where the debt instrument is in the capital structure of the defaulted firm and whether the debt is secured (Altman and Kishore (1996), Gupton, Gates and Carty (2000)). *LGD*s exhibit strong business cycle sensitivities (Frye (2000), Altman, Brady, Resti and Sironi (2002), Hu and Perraudin (2002)), and there is some systematic variation by industry (Altman and Kishore (1996)), although the recent default experience in the telecommunications and broadcasting sectors may have changed some of those results in non-trivial ways. Little is known about recovery variability in the emerging markets.

There are fewer empirical studies on *EAD*. For a term loan, *EAD* is rarely ambiguous. This is not the case for facilities such as lines of credit where a borrower is theoretically able to draw down at will up to the committed line of the facility. Moreover, as financial distress worsens, a borrower will typically draw down as much as possible on existing unutilized facilities in order to avoid default. In the foundation sub-approach of IRB, *EAD* is also based on supervisory values in cases where the measurement is not clear. For instance, *EAD* is 75% for irrevocable undrawn commitments. However, under the advanced sub-approach, *EAD* may be determined by the bank via a model.

For facilities where exposure and hence *LGD* are uncertain, the loan equivalency factor (*LEQ*) represents a quantitative estimate of how much of the commitment will be drawn down by a defaulting borrower. *LEQ*s should be differentiated across both credit quality and facility type. Empirical work on this topic is sparse. As part a broader study of loan performance, Asarnow and Marker (1995) analyze the performance of large corporate commitments at Citibank from 1988–1993 and show the importance of credit (debt) rating, particularly at the speculative end. More recently, Araten and Jacobs (2001) evaluate the behavior of over 400 facilities from defaulted borrowers over a six-year period and find a highly significant increase in *LEQ*s relative to time-to-default across all rating grades and a somewhat weaker relationship between *LEQ*s and ratings grades. They note that similar to *LGD*s, observed or realized *LEQ*s are widely dispersed.

5.2.4. RISK ANALYTICS: CORRELATIONS AND PORTFOLIO AGGREGATION

The model building component around the IRB approach is largely focused on exposure-level risk modeling: what is the *PD* and *LGD* of a particular obligor or facility? To compute risk (and capital) at portfolio level, one needs to make some assumption about the joint default (loss) process or distribution. Broadly there are two approaches to computing joint losses: direct estimation with data or indirectly through a structural model of firm valuation and default. The binding constraint typically is data availability: defaults are rare, joint defaults even more so.

The direct approach would take a large data set with a long history and proceed to computing default and loss correlations directly within a time window large enough, say monthly or quarterly, to capture sufficient simultaneous default events. To do this properly, one really needs large amounts of data, typically restricting the application of this approach to consumer banking portfolios such as credit card.

The indirect approach uses a structural model of default, e.g. the Merton model. Since default data is very sparse, the idea is to focus modeling effort instead on the default process in a space where the data is denser. The Merton model, for example, looks at evolution of a firm's balance sheet to arrive at a distance-to-default measure. This broad modeling approach is elegant in the sense that any structural approach is, but also tricky to implement. There may be a large class of observationally equivalent structural models which explain the default process; how does one choose between them? The Merton model is indeed widely used, and there is some evidence that it does well.[17] Moreover, the final capital value determined by the New Basel Accord implicitly assumes a single-factor Merton-type model, where the asset correlation is a weighted average of 12% and 24%.[18]

Recently there has been exciting progress in the area of modeling joint default and loss. One method in particular holds great promise: the computation of the joint distribution using copulas. A copula is a function that links the marginals to the joint distribution. Beyond allowing for the aggregation of diverse marginal distributions which capture some of the essential features found in risk management, like fat tails, copulas also allow for richer dependence structure than allowed for by simple models like the multivariate normal. For a review of the theory, see Nelsen (1998). Embrechts, McNeil and Straumann (1999, 2002) were among the first to introduce this toolkit to the finance literature. Li (2000) provides an application to credit risk and credit derivatives.[19] These methods are now being put to the test, and we eagerly anticipate their reported performance.

5.2.5. RISK ANALYTICS: OP RISK METRICS Arguably, the timing and degree to which an internal models approach to computing capital has become part of the regulatory process is inversely

---

17. For a discussion of the power of Merton default prediction models see Falkenstein and Boral (2001) and Gemmill (2002) who find that the Merton model generally does well in predicting default (Falkenstein and Boral) and credit spreads (Gemmill).
18. See also Gordy (2002)
19. Wang (1999, 2002) proposes an application to insurance with particular emphasis to enterprise-wide risk management (Wang, 2002).

related to the level of difficulty in modeling the risk types and how much data is available. An internal models approach for market risk became embedded in the regulations with the 1996 amendment to the first Basel Accord (BCBS (1996)). In the New Basel Accord, the IRB approach allows for some, though not complete, internal modeling of credit risk capital. Operational risk capital is new territory for capital regulation, and this is driven to some extent by the difficulty in modeling this risk type.[20]

Large, institution-threatening operational risk events are by definition rare. Smaller ones may or may not be relevant for learning about the operational risk event data generating mechanism. And therein lies one of the fundamental issues in modeling operational risk: the events are both rare and hard to identify. Moreover, one can think of many examples where it is not obvious whether an event should be classified as an operational risk event or part of market or credit risk. For instance, if in the process of marking-to-market the options book the institution used a "wrong" or "mis-specified" model, is that market or op risk? Another example would be the classification of credit card losses due to fraud as either credit or operational risk.

Given that data on operational risk events is so sparse, banks will likely want to supplement their own internal data with external sources. In a recent paper, de Fontnouvelle, DeJesus-Rueff, Jordan and Rosengren (2003) use two publicly available databases to show how economic capital estimates could be computed. They explicitly control for the reporting bias likely to exist in the databases. For instance, while some losses may indeed be too large to hide, moderate (but still substantial) losses may be under-reported. Once the bias is corrected they find that, for large internationally active banks, risk capital attributable to operational risk is typically larger than it might be for market risk.

When it comes to formal modeling, several (Embrechts, Klüppelberg and Mikosch (1997), papers collected in Embrechts (2000)) have argued that the toolkit of insurance risk may be a useful place to look. One example is extreme value theory (EVT) which seeks to model extreme events outside the range of historical experience. In its basic formulation, the probabilistic theory assumes that the underlying event process is *iid*, and by focusing on the tail of the observed distribution we can make inference about the very far, not-yet-seen tail.

---

20. See also Netter and Poulsen (2003) for an overview.

However, there is a sharp developmental contrast between the probabilistic and statistical aspects of EVT. The probability theory is elegant and voluminous, whereas the statistical theory remains largely skeletal. This is particularly unfortunate because empirical applications must rely on statistical inference.[21] For instance, if this insurance approach is indeed promising, then those risks could be insured much like other events are insured by property and casualty insurers. A proper understanding of the event generating process is needed to appropriately price those contracts.

5.2.6. Risk Analytics: Relevant Risk Summaries If the broad regulatory goal is to make capital regulation more sensitive to the underlying risk, what measure of risk is the right one to target? Many of the risk measurement tools are variants of VaR (value-at-risk). VaR is defined as the loss to the portfolio due to an adverse market move that is only exceeded $\alpha\%$ of the time (e.g. $\alpha = 2.5\%$, 1%). It is thus a scalar measure (a summary) of a very high dimensional problem.

Christoffersen and Diebold (2000) and Berkowitz (2001) argue that rather than focusing on just one number such as VaR, risk managers and, implicitly, regulators should focus on the whole density function of returns, perhaps using techniques such as those laid out in Diebold, Gunther and Tay (1998) and Berkowitz (2001). Nonetheless, interest in a simpler summary measure continues. What standards should such a summary measure meet and how do the regulatory approaches currently in use measure up to these standards?

Artzner, Delbaen, Eber, and Heath (1997, 1999) lay out a set of criteria necessary for what they call a "coherent" measure of risk. They include homogeneity (larger positions bring greater risk), monotonicity (greater returns come with greater risk), sub-additivity (the risk of the sum cannot be greater than the sum of the risks) and the risk-free condition (as the proportion of the portfolio invested in the risk-free asset increases, portfolio risk should decline). Importantly, VaR does not satisfy the sub-additivity condition, implying that a firm could concentrate all of its tail risks in one exposure in such a way that the risk borne by that exposure appears just beyond the overall portfolio VaR threshold.

---

21.   See also Diebold, Schuermann and Stroughair (1998) for a more extensive assessment of the use of EVT in risk management.

One potential solution to this shortcoming is to include the expected shortfall or exceedence. It answers the simple question: how bad is bad? Borrowing from the insurance literature, authors such as Embrechts, Klüppelberg and Mikosch (1997), Artzner, Delbaen, Eber, and Heath (1997, 1999), Neftci (2000) and Basak and Shapiro (2001), among others, suggest ways for looking at the beyond-VaR region.

The expected shortfall measure describes the expected loss given that $VaR(\alpha)$ has been exceeded. Taking the mean is a very simple summary statistic of the beyond-VaR tail. However, the risk manager (and regulator) might care differently about the probability mass being piled up near the VaR threshold or further away (i.e. deeper into the tail), prompting one to consider estimating higher moments of the tail region (standard deviation, skewness, and so on). It becomes clear again that the information loss from attempting to summarize the portfolio risk in a single number from the whole density could be substantial.

5.3. Pillars 2 and 3: Supervisory Review, Disclosure and Market Discipline

Estrella (2000) provides a thoughtful discussion of the difficulties and trade-offs encountered in design of regulation for financial institutions. They include the different goals and objective functions of the different constituencies; the desire for both simplicity (emphasis on rules) and flexibility (emphasis on supervision); at the same time we want to allow for market forces to provide a powerful monitoring and correction mechanism.[22] The framework of the New Basel Accord is partly motivated by wanting to strike a balance among these apparently competing forces.

The second pillar can be thought of as the main load-bearing column of the regulatory framework. In the words of Estrella (1998, p. 192), this pillar would allow regulators to reap "the benefits of informed supervision. Mechanical formulas may play a role in regulation, but they are in general incapable of providing a solution to the question of how much capital a bank should have." Especially for a large, complex financial institution, the supervisory review is likely to be far more important than the rules-based approach. It would enable the supervisor to evaluate the adequacy

---

22. Estrella (2000) and Santos (2001) stress that risk and capital are hard to determine in the presence of safety net such as deposit insurance, and that the two design problems (capital adequacy, deposit insurance) should be addressed simultaneously (Santos (2001)).

of an institution's internal risk management and capital decision processes along a number of dimensions. Importantly, this pillar should be a flexible approach that allows for differences across institutions. Such differentiation is necessary to accommodate variations in business mix, risk profile, legal structure, and level of sophistication.

The third pillar would leverage market judgements on capital adequacy. In the end, the market's judgement of capital for the holding company (and potentially individual subsidiaries) will be decisive, through its influence on pricing and access to funding. While it is attractive from a theoretical standpoint to place great weight on the market's consensus, in practical terms there are too many limitations in current accounting conventions and disclosure standards for this pillar to be sufficient on its own.

The basic idea behind Pillar 3 is for the banks to tell market participants the relevant and important risk measures. Financial institutions are particularly opaque, however, making assessments by rating agencies and equity analysts more difficult. Morgan (2002) measures this opacity by showing that bond raters disagree more about banks and insurance companies than about any other kind of firm. Moreover, in Section 5.2.6, we showed how hard it is to agree on the relevant summary statistic for a bank's risk profile.

To some degree, the disclosure experiment has already been running for market risk. Several papers have examined the accuracy and information content of VaR model estimates with subsequent bank performance. Berkowitz and O'Brien (2002) compare daily VaR forecasts with next day trading results using a sample of large U.S. banks containing confidential supervisory data, i.e. data which is *not* available to market participants. While the VaR models provide a conservative estimate of the 99% tail on average, there is substantial variation across institutions. Moreover, they demonstrate that a simple GARCH model based on daily trading P&L outperforms the VaR models. Jorion (2002) and Hirtle (2003) examine the information content of VaR reporting. Both studies suggest that such disclosures are indeed informative. Jorion (2002) reports that VaR disclosures predict variability in trading revenues. Similarly Hirtle (2003) finds that reported market risk capital is useful for predicting changes in market risk exposure over time for individual banks; however, such disclosures provide little information about differences in market risk exposure across banks. Estrella, Park and Peristiani (2000) examine the problem of predicting bank failure and find that the basic leverage ratio is no worse than the Basel I risk-based capital measure. The more risk sensitive measures in Basel II should prove to be more informative.

It may be fair to say that a consensus is emerging that information reaching the public through disclosure is actually informative, whether it is through rating agencies (credit ratings), the debt markets (credit spreads on bonds), or equity markets (stock volatility). There is a rich literature on how credit spreads on subordinated bank debt could shed light on a bank's riskiness. For example, De Young, Flannery, Lang and Sorescu (2001) find that subordinated debt yields indeed incorporate information about the bank (see also Evanoff and Wall (2000)). However, Hancock and Kwast (2001) point to some pitfalls (low liquidity) of using this financial instrument to evaluate the conditions of banks. Krainer and Lopez (2003) is an example of the latter; they examine whether equity market variables such as default probabilities implied by return volatility are useful to supervisors who have access to privileged information in assessing the condition of banks holding companies. The short answer is yes.

Of course disclosure and building the necessary infrastructure to measure and report the information is not costless. Just what the direct and indirect benefits are to such measurement and reporting (to internal as well as external constituencies) is an area of inquiry where a lot of work remains to be done. Just recently Baumann and Nier (2003) have found some encouraging results, namely that it pays to disclose: disclosure decreases stock return volatility, increases market value, and increases the usefulness of company accounts in predicting valuations.

6. FINAL COMMENTS

Given its objectives and strong analytical foundations the New Basel Accord opens the door to many research questions. This paper has broken down some of these questions into to three groups: the impact of the proposal on the global banking system through possible changes in bank behavior; a set of issues around risk analytics such as model validation, correlations and portfolio aggregation, operational risk metrics and relevant summary statistics of a bank's risk profile; issues brought about by Pillar 2 (supervisory review) and Pillar 3 (public disclosure). The output of the risk calculations under the New Basel Accord may also change bank behavior as some of the internal risk metrics are disclosed to the public. With this in mind, our view for a research agenda going forward is one focused less on regulatory design. Instead the agenda might be better oriented towards understanding the Accord's likely impact on the banking system, possible changes in bank behavior through different uses of the risk measurement framework, and important analytical issues around model development and validation in both credit and operational risk narrowly and the development of relevant risk summary statistics more broadly. Without a doubt, given its scope and complexity, the Accord continues to provide many opportunities for researchers to contribute to the policy debate and implementation of these proposals.

REFERENCES

Allen, L. and A. Saunders (2002), "A Survey of Cyclical Effects in Credit Risk Measurement Models," mimeo, Stern School of Business, NYU; available at *http://pages.stern.nyu.edu/~asaunder/procyclicality_allensaunders.pdf.*

Altman, E.I. and V.M Kishore, 1996, "Almost Everything You Wanted to Know about Recoveries on Defaulted Bonds," *Financial Analysts Journal*, November/December, pp. 57–64.

Altman, E., B. Brady, A. Resti and A. Sironi, 2002, "The Link between Default and Recovery Rates: Implications for Credit Risk Models and Procyclicality," forthcoming, *Journal of Business*.

Araten, Michel and Michael Jacobs Jr., 2001, "Loan Equivalents for Revolving Credits and Advised Lines." *RMA Journal*, May, pp. 34–39.

Artzner, P., Delbaen, F., Eber, J.M., Heath, D., 1999, "Coherent Measures of Risk," *Mathematical Finance* 9, pp. 203–228.

Artzner, P., Delbaen, F., Eber, J.M., Heath, D., 1997, "Thinking coherently," *Risk* 10 (11), pp. 68–71.

Asarnow, Elliot and James Marker (1995), "Historical Performance of the U.S. Corporate Loan Market: 1988–1993," *Commercial Lending Review*, Spring, pp. 13–32.

Ball, Clifford A. and Hans R. Stoll, 1998, "Regulatory Capital of Financial Institutions: A Comparative Analysis," *Financial Markets, Institutions & Instruments* 7 (3), pp. 1–57.

Bangia, A., F.X. Diebold, A. Kronimus and C. Schagen and T. Schuermann, 2002, "Ratings Migration and the Business Cycle, With Applications to Credit Portfolio Stress Testing," *Journal of Banking & Finance*, 2002, (26: 2/3), pp. 445–474.

Basel Committee on Banking Supervision, 1988, "Internal Convergence of Capital Measurement and Capital Standards," *http://www.bis.org/publ/bcbs04A.pdf*, July.

Basel Committee on Banking Supervision, 1996, "Amendment to the Capital Accord to Incorporate Market Risks (No. 24)," January.

Basel Committee on Banking Supervision, 2001a, *The New Basel Capital Accord*, *http://www.bis.org/publ/bcbsca.htm*, January.

Basel Committee on Banking Supervision, 2001b, *The Internal Ratings Based Approach*, *http://www.bis.org/publ/bcbsca.htm*, May.

Basel Committee on Banking Supervision, 2002, *Quantitative Impact Study 3 Technical Guidance*, *http://www.bis.org/publ/bcbsca.htm*, January.

Basel Committee on Banking Supervision, 2003, *Third Consultative Paper*, *http://www.bis.org/bcbs/bcbscp3.htm*, April.

Basak, S. and A. Shapiro, 2001, "Value-at-Risk Based Risk Management: Optimal Policies and Asset Prices," 2001, *Review of Financial Studies*, 14(2), pp. 371–405.

Baumann, U. and E. Nier, 2003, "Disclosure in Banking: What Matters Most?" presented at the Federal Reserve Bank of New York Conference "Beyond Pillar Three in International Banking Regulation: Disclosure and Market Discipline of Financial Firms," October 2003.

Benston, George J. and George Kaufman, 1995, "Is the banking and payment system fragile?" *Journal of Financial Services Research*, 9.

Berger, A.N., R.J. Herring and G.P. Szegö, 1995, "The Role of Capital in Financial Institutions," *Journal of Banking & Finance*, 19, pp. 393–430.

Berkowitz, Jeremy, 2001, "Testing the Accuracy of Density Forecasts, applications to Risk Management," *Journal of Business and Economic Statistics*, 19, pp. 465–474.

Berkowitz, Jeremy and Paul O'Brien, 2002, "How accurate are Value-at-Risk Models at Commercial Banks?," *Journal of Finance* 57 (3).

Board of Governors of the Federal Reserve System, 2002, *Capital Adequacy Guidelines*, 12 CFR 225, appendix A.

Borio, C, C Furfine and P Lowe, 2001, "Procyclicality of the Financial System and Financial Stability: Issues and Policy Options," *BIS Working Papers*, no 1.

Calem, P. and R. Rob, 1999, "The Impact of Capital-Based Regulation on Bank Risk-Taking," *Journal of Financial Intermediation* 8, pp. 317–352.

Caprio, G. and D. Klingebiel, 1996, "Bank Insolvencies: Cross-Country Experience," World Bank, Policy Research Paper #1620, July.

Carey, M. (2002), "A Guide to Choosing Absolute Bank Capital Requirements," *Journal of Banking & Finance* 26 (5), pp. 929–951.

Carpenter, S.B., W. Whitesell and E. Zakrajšek (2001), "Capital Requirements, Business Loans and Business Cycles: An Empirical Analysis of the Standardized Approach in the New Basel Accord," Federal Reserve Board, Finance and Economics Discussion Series # 2001-48.

Christoffersen, P. and F.X. Diebold, 2000, "How Relevant is Volatility Forecasting for Financial Risk Management?," *Review of Economics and Statistics* 82, pp. 12–22.

Crouhy, M., D. Galai and R. Mark, 2001, *Risk Management*, New York: McGraw Hill.

DeYoung, R., M. Flannery, W. Lang and S. Sorescu, 2001, "The Informational Content of Bank Exam Ratings and Subordinated Debt Prices," *Journal of Money, Credit and Banking* 33(4), pp. 900–925.

Dewatripont, M. and J. Tirole, 1994, *The Prudential Regulation of Banks*, Cambridge, MA: MIT Press.

Diamond, D.W. and P.H. Dybvig, 1983, "Bank Runs, Deposit Insurance and Liquidity," *Journal of Political Economy* 91, pp. 401–419.

Diebold, F.X., T.A. Gunther and A.S. Tay, 1998, "Evaluating Density Forecasts," *International Economic Review* 39, pp. 863–883.

Diebold, F.X., T. Schuermann and J. Stroughair, 1998, "Pitfalls and Opportunities in the Use of Extreme Value Theory in Risk Management," Ch. 1 in A.-P. N. Refenes, A.N. Burgess and J.D. Moody (eds.), *Advances in Computational Finance*. Amsterdam: Kluwer Academic Publishers.

Embrechts, P., C. Klüppelberg and T. Mikosch, 1997, *Modelling Extremal Events for Insurance and Finance*, New York: Springer Verlag.

Embrechts, P., A. McNeil and D. Straumann, 1999, "Correlation and Dependence in Risk Management: Properties and Pitfalls," Working Paper, ETH Zürich. Forthcoming in M. Dempster (Ed.), 2001, *Risk Management: Value at Risk and Beyond*, Cambridge, UK: Cambridge University Press.

Embrechts, P. (editor), 2000, *Extremes and Integrated Risk Management*, London, UK: Risk Publications.

Estrella, A., 1998, "Formulas or Supervision? Remarks on the Future of Regulatory Capital," *Federal Reserve Bank of New York Economic Policy Review*, October, pp. 191–200.

Estrella, A., 2000, "Regulatory Capital and the Supervision of Financial Institutions: Some Basic Distinctions and Policy Choices," in A. Santomero, S. Viotti and A. Vredin (eds.) *Challenges for Modern Central Banking*, Stockholm: Swedish Riksbank (forthcoming).

Estrella, A., S. Park and S. Peristiani, 2000, "Capital Ratios as Predictors of Bank Failures," *Federal Reserve Bank of New York Economic Policy Review* 6 (2), pp. 33–52.

Evanoff, D. and L. Wall, 2000, "Sub-debt Yield Spreads as Bank Risk Measures," Federal Reserve Bank of Atlanta Working Paper #2000-24.

Falkenstein, E. and A. Boral (2001), "Some empirical results on the Merton Model," *Risk Professional*, April 2001.

Federal Reserve, Board of Governors, 2003, "U.S. Advanced Notice of Proposed Rule Making," available at *http://www.federalreserve.gov/boarddocs/press/bcreg/2003/20030804/default.htm*.

de Fontnouvelle, P., V. DeJesus-Rueff, J. Jordan and E. Rosengren, 2003, "Using Loss Data to Quantify Operational Risk," Federal Reserve Bank of Boston Working Paper 03-5.

Frye, J., 2000, "Depressing Recoveries," Federal Reserve Bank of Chicago working paper, an abridged version appeared in *Risk*, November.

Gemmill, G. (2002), "Testing Merton's Model for Credit Spreads on Zero-Coupon Bonds," Faculty of Finance, City University Business School; available at *http://www.staff.city.ac.uk/g.gemmill/working_papers/credit_spread.pdf*.

Gordy, M.B., 2003, "A Risk Factor Model Foundation for Ratings-Based Capital Rules," *Journal of Financial Intermediation*, 12, pp. 199–232.

Gupton, G., D. Gates, and L. Carty, 2000, "Bank Loan Loss Given Default." *Moody's Special Comment*, November.

Hancock, D. and M.L. Kwast, 2001, "Using Subordinated Debt to Monitor Bank Holding Companies: Is it Feasible?," *Journal of Financial Services Research* 20(2/3), pp. 147–197.

Hirtle, B., 2003, "What Market Risk Capital Reporting Tells Us About Bank Risk," *Federal Reserve Bank of New York Economic Policy Review*, 9(3), pp. 37–54.

Hu, Y-T and W. Perraudin, 2002, "The Dependence of Recovery Rates and Defaults," CEPR working paper.

Joint Forum, 2001, *Risk Management Practices and Regulatory Capital, Cross-Sectoral Comparison*, November; available at *http://www.bis.org/publ/joint03.pdf*.

Jorion, P., 2002, "How Informative are Value-at-Risk Disclosures?," *Accounting Review* 77 (October), pp. 911–931.

Lando, D. and T. Skødeberg, (2002), "Analyzing Ratings Transitions and Rating Drift with Continuous Observations," *Journal of Banking & Finance* 26 (2-3), pp. 423–444.

Li, David X., 2000, "Default Correlation: A Copula Approach," *Journal of Fixed Income*, March, pp. 43–54.

Lopez, J.A. and J. Krainer, 2003, "Incorporating Equity Market Information into Supervisory Monitoring Models," forthcoming in *Journal of Money, Credit and Banking*.

Lopez, J.A. and M. Saidenberg, 2000, "Evaluating Credit Risk Models," *Journal of Banking & Finance* 24 (1/2), pp. 151–167.

Lown, C.S., D.P. Morgan, and S. Rohatgi, 2000, "Listening to Loan Officers: Commercial Credit Standards, Lending and Output," *Federal Reserve Bank of New York Economic Policy Review* 6 (2), pp. 1–16.

Merton, R., 1974, "On the pricing of corporate debt: the risk structure of interest rates," *Journal of Finance* 29, pp. 449–470.

Mishkin, F.S., 1997, "Evaluating FDICIA," *Research in Financial Services: Private and Public Policy* 9, pp. 17–33.

Morgan, D.P., 2002, "Rating Banks: Risk and Uncertainty in an Opaque Industry," *American Economic Review* 92 (4), pp. 874–888.

Neftci, S.N., 2000, "Value at Risk Calculations, Extreme Events and Tail Estimation," *Journal of Derivatives* 8, pp. 23–37.

Nelsen, Roger B., 1998, *An Introduction to Copulas*, Lecture Notes in Statistics, 139, New York: Springer Verlag.

Netter, Jeffry M. and Annette B. Poulson, 2003, "Operational Risk in Financial Service Providers and the Proposed Basel Capital Accord: An Overview," Terry College of Business, University of Georgia, Department of Banking and Finance Working Paper. available at *http://papers.ssrn.com/paper.taf?abstract_id=369581*.

Nickell, P, W. Perraudin and S. Varotto, 2000, "Stability of Rating Transitions," *Journal of Banking & Finance*, 24, pp. 203–227.

Santos, J.A.C., 2001, "Bank Capital Regulation in Contemporary Banking Theory: A Review of the Literature," *Financial Markets, Institutions & Instruments* 10 (2), pp. 41–84.

Saunders, Anthony and Linda Allen, 2002, *Credit Risk Measurement-New Approaches to Value at Risk and Other Paradigms*, 2nd Ed., New York: John Wiley & Sons.

Schuermann, T. and Y. Jafry (2002), "Estimating Credit Migration Matrices: Measurement Matters," mimeo, Federal Reserve Bank of New York.

Treacy, W.F. and M. Carey, 2000, "Credit Risk Rating Systems at Large U.S. Banks," *Journal of Banking & Finance*, 24, pp. 167–201.

Wang, Shaun S., 1999, "Aggregation of Correlated Risk Portfolios:

Models & Algorithms," Casual Actuarial Society Theory of Risk Working Paper; available at *http://casact.org/cofor/Wang.pdf.*

Wang, Shaun S., 2002, "A Set of New Methods and Tools for Enterprise Risk Capital Management and Portfolio Optimization," CAS Forum Summer 2002; available at *http://www.casact. org/pubs/forum/02sforum/02sf043.pdf.*

8

The New Basel Accord and Advanced IRB Approaches: Is There a Case for Capital Incentives?

Christine Brown and Kevin Davis

INTRODUCTION

One defining feature of the New Basel Accord is the proposal to apply different approaches for determining regulatory capital requirements for different types of banks. Those banks that have suitably sophisticated, internal ratings-based (IRB) approaches for measuring and managing credit risk will be regulated under the advanced or Foundation IRB approach, while other banks will be regulated under a Standardized approach. For both approaches, the capital charge is 8 percent of risk-weighted assets (RWA), but the method of calculating RWA varies between the two approaches. In the former case, a bank's own internal model will be used (in conjunction with regulatory parameters) to determine RWA, while in the latter case, a formula-based approach (much like the current approach) prescribed by the Basel committee is applied.

Significantly, the RWA (and corresponding capital charge) calculated for a given loan portfolio will differ between the two approaches, with the advanced approach leading to lower capital charges. This is a stated objective of the architects of the New Accord, but one that has been advanced without detailed justification. Since there are potentially significant effects on competitive neutrality, this objective warrants further investigation.

In this paper, we assess the main argument that has been advanced for such capital incentives (i.e., concessions) and find it wanting. We provide a possible alternative justification based on an analysis of bank incentives to undertake the significant expenditures required to implement advanced IRB risk management systems. To the extent that deposit insurance agencies (or taxpayers) capture some part of the benefits from improved bank risk management techniques, regulatory capital concessions may be justified. However, an alternative response to this effect would be to adjust the price of deposit insurance for banks meeting the standards of the advanced approach, raising the question (which we address) of why capital concessions are the preferred regulatory response.

In the following section, we outline and assess the case made for capital concessions in the New Basel Capital Accord and compare the initially anticipated magnitude of such concessions with the estimated effects found in the Basel Committee's third Quantitative Impact Study (QIS3). We then (in Section 2) examine the costs and potential benefits involved in introducing advanced risk management systems and address the question of whether banks would make socially optimal investment decisions in such technology without regulatory capital concessions. Section 3 presents an analysis of why the existence of (explicit or implicit) deposit insurance might lead to socially suboptimal investment by banks, and Section 4 attempts to quantify the extent of capital concessions that might be justified. An alternative policy response of adjustments to the price of deposit insurance is considered in Section 5, and issues relevant to the preference for capital incentives are discussed in Section 6. Section 7 contains concluding remarks.

I. CAPITAL CONCESSIONS IN THE NEW ACCORD

An important feature of the distinction between the IRB and Standardised approaches is the desire to better align regulatory capital charges for specific activities with credible economic capital estimates made by banks using advanced risk management systems (ARMS). Banks with systems meeting specified regulatory standards will be regulated under the IRB approach with regulatory capital charges based (partially) on the output of the bank's internal models. There could be potentially large differences between the capital charges for specific loan categories arising from the IRB approach relative to the Standardised approach. For example, the capital charge for residential mortgages in the new standardised approach results from proposed regulatory assignment of a risk weight of 35%. Some banks have "reported IRB housing risk weights averaging around 15% of the housing risk weight proposed in the standardised approach." (Australian Prudential Regulatory Authority [APRA], 2002)

Kupiec (2001) studies some of the implications of different risk weights (and capital charges) for particular assets between the two regulatory approaches. These may include the development of clienteles, as particular types of borrowers migrate to banks regulated under the approach that involves a comparative advantage in risk weight assigned to that borrower. Such effects are important and have significant implications for the impact of the new accord on competition in financial markets. They result from variations across asset categories in the risk weight differential between the IRB and the Standardised approach. Our approach focuses upon an additional potential competitive effect that is independent of such portfolio composition effects and would result if the risk-weight differential in the two approaches were constant across all asset categories.

To illustrate, consider the case of two banks undertaking identical activities. The architects of Basel 2 have proposed a system that would result in a different amount of capital required for those banks if one is regulated under the IRB approach and the other regulated under the Standardised approach. The former would face a lower capital requirement. This differential treatment has been proposed on the grounds of providing an incentive for banks to introduce advanced risk management systems (ARMS) that qualify them for regulation under the IRB approach.

The Basel Committee motivated the introduction of the dual (IRB and Standardised) approach using an argument based around bank incentives: "The new framework is intended to align capital adequacy assessment more closely with the key elements of banking risks and to provide incentives for banks to enhance their risk measurement and management capabilities." (Basel, 2001, para 2)

A clear statement of their general objectives for capital concessions can be found in the following statement: "In respect of the IRB approaches, the Committee's ultimate goals are to ensure that the overall level of regulatory capital generated is sufficient to address the underlying credit risks and is such that it provides capital incentives relative to the standardised approach (e.g., for the foundation IRB approach in the aggregate, a reduction in risk-weighted assets of 2% to 3%)." (Basel Committee, 2001, para 48)

Justification of the need for, and appropriate size of, capital concessions beyond such general comments is difficult to find in Basel Committee publications. Implicit appears to be some perception that business decisions of banks regarding introduction of ARMS will not be socially optimal, thus warranting some form of regulatory incentive. While this may be so, no evidence nor analysis appears to be forthcoming in support, and the testimony before the U.S. Senate of Kevin Blakely of KeyCorp, regarding compliance costs of the new accord, are instructive. "Before one accepts the large figures attributed to Basel II compliance, one must subtract the costs of building the risk management systems that a good financial institution would invest in, regardless. We do not believe the gap between the two is significant." (Blakely, 2003, p. 8)

Adapting ARMS to comply with IRB requirements may involve banks in additional costs, but that does not explain why banks would not introduce such systems for their own management purposes if they were indeed value-adding. Only if the extant (standardised) capital adequacy requirements, or some other market or regulatory imperfections, adversely distorted bank decision making (regarding adoption of new systems) would some regulatory incentive seem warranted. There is no evidence, nor theory, of which we are aware to suggest that capital adequacy requirements have such an effect. As we explain later, deposit insurance pricing that does not adjust appropriately to changes in bank risk may create such distortions and justify capital concessions.

While the Basel Committee envisaged capital incentives in the order of 2–3%, calibrating the risk weights to achieve such an outcome has proved somewhat difficult, particularly given the diversity of bank portfolio composition and internal modeling techniques. Consequently, more recent versions of the accord proposals have involved an interim floor on the capital requirement resulting from use of the IRB approach: "the Committee has proposed that banks using these approaches also be subject to a declining floor on their new capital requirement for the first two years following formal implementation. This floor is calculated using the rules of the existing Accord and would equal 90% of the calculation in the first year and 80% in the second year." (Basel Committee, 2002, para 52)

The results of the QIS3 study indicate the rationale for imposing such a transitional floor and suggest that the capital concessions may be significantly greater than originally suggested. Table 1 illustrates the estimated change in capital requirements under the Basel Committee proposals (as calibrated in late 2002) for two different groups of banks, where each bank calculated the capital charge on its existing portfolio under both approaches. The figures demonstrate clearly that the capital requirement for credit risk for the Foundation IRB approach would be significantly lower than for the Standardised approach. Potentially significant effects on competitive neutrality could be anticipated and would be aggravated by induced changes in portfolio composition reflecting risk-weight differentials between the approaches for various asset categories.

Table 1. Changes in capital requirements: Standardised and IRB Foundation approaches

	GROUP 1*		GROUP 2*	
	Standardised	Foundation IRB	Standardised	Foundation IRB
Overall credit risk	0%	-7%	-6%	-27%
Operational risk	10%	10%	7%	7%
Overall change	10%	3%	1%	-19%

* Group 1 banks are large, diversified, and internationally active with Tier 1 capital in excess of 3bn Euros, and Group 2 banks are generally smaller and, in many cases, more specialised.
Source: Basel Committee (2003b, p. 5).

2. BANK INVESTMENT IN RISK MANAGEMENT SYSTEMS

Recent years have seen significant developments in the measurement and management of credit risk. Banks and third party vendors have developed complex advanced risk management systems (ARMS) drawing on advances in finance theory, technology and past experience.[1] Such systems hold promise of better assessment and pricing of credit risk and improved management of credit portfolios, providing (temporary) competitive advantages to those banks that expend resources on development and implementa-

---

1. See Crouhy, Galai and Mark 92000) for a comparative analysis of models used in the measurement and management of credit risk. They also detail the third party vendor applications of these models.

tion of such systems. Competition in banking can be expected to induce adoption of such systems by banks seeking competitive advantage or in order to prevent loss of market share to other users of such systems.

ARMS for credit risk are typically of the internal ratings-based approach in which counterparties are assigned risk classifications based on estimates of probability of default (PD). Also important for the management of credit risk are estimates of loss given default (LGD) based on characteristics of the facility, collateral, etc. Such information can be utilized, in conjunction with historical data, to estimate the economic capital required to support particular loans and for the credit portfolio in aggregate.

Although all banks have some form of credit risk management system in place, they range from rudimentary, judgment-based, approaches to highly advanced, technical approaches. Development and implementation of such advanced systems, as used by a small number of large banks and requisite for regulation under the IRB approach, is a costly exercise. Data requirements are extensive as are information systems requirements. It is therefore not surprising that only a small number of banks are expected to be able to satisfy requirements for the IRB approach. Some commentators have suggested that around forty banks worldwide could quickly achieve that status—a figure compatible with the statement of Federal Reserve Vice Chairman Roger Ferguson that, for the USA, "we expect about twenty banks to adopt the advanced version of Basel II before or shortly after the initial implementation date." (Ferguson, 2003, p. 9) In terms of size, this latter statement is indicative of banks with assets in 2003 in excess of U.S. $60–70 billion. Worldwide, some 100–120 banks are of that size, suggesting that (based on size alone) initial estimates of likely candidates for IRB status may have been too low.

Reliable estimates of the cost of implementing ARMS, which meet IRB requirements, are, not surprisingly, difficult to come by and subject to wide variance. Informal discussions with bankers have produced ballpark estimates ranging between U.S.$10 and U.S.$100 million. and the incremental costs will vary between banks, depending upon the current state of their systems. Specific estimates are available in testimony before the U.S. Senate Committee on Banking, Housing, and Urban Affairs. "The monetary cost of complying with the Basel II rules will be significant. For

Credit Suisse Group, our holding company, we estimate that our initial costs will be $70mm to $100mm just to implement the system, plus substantial ongoing costs." (Ervin, 2003, p. 8)

"A recent survey of the cost of Basel implementation for the larger banks expected to use the advanced models indicates that it will reach $200 million per bank." (Petrou, 2003, p. 14)

These are sizable amounts which suggest that only larger banks will be able to afford introduction of such systems. Affordability itself, however, is not the key issue. Like any investment project, it can be expected that banks will evaluate introduction of such systems using capital budgeting techniques—comparing costs with the present value of expected future benefits. If introduction of such systems has a positive Net Present Value, it can be expected that banks will make the requisite investment.

What benefits flow from such an investment? Clearly the ability to make better risk assessment and correctly price loans is the key attraction. A bank with a competitive advantage in this area may be able to make loans on terms, which generate above normal economic profits and which thus more than compensate for the initial outlay on the systems. Better identification of high- and low-quality borrowers can lead to better loan selection, lower expected losses, and lower dispersion of loan portfolio losses. Improved risk-based pricing will see the spread between rates charged to higher-versus lower-quality borrowers widen.

Alternatively, in a highly competitive environment, banks will be forced to make such outlays to avoid a decline in the quality of their loan book as other adopters of the new technology are better able to identify borrower quality, price loans, and select borrowers accordingly. In such an environment, competition will prevent lenders from making above normal economic profits, and the costs of introducing such systems will be reflected in the pricing of loans. Lower expected losses on the aggregate loan portfolio can be expected to offset the costs of introducing such a system, and better risk identification will lead to high-quality borrowers no longer incurring the externality of higher interest rates imposed by being indistinguishable from low-quality borrowers.

This outcome can be demonstrated in the context of a simple illustration of loan pricing. Consider an initial situation in which no bank in a competitive market is able to distinguish between two groups of good and bad borrowers. The former group never defaults, while the latter group always defaults, and repays nothing. The common interest rate (r) charged to all borrowers will be given by:

$$r = p + c + r_k$$

where p is the expected loss per dollar lent, c is operating costs per dollar lent, and r_k is the weighted average cost of capital. This competitive loan rate ensures that each bank has an expected return on loans equal to its cost of capital. Suppose that a new borrower assessment technology becomes available and (assuming for simplicity that it is leased) involves additional operating costs of x per dollar lent. The new technology enables the bank to identify the good borrowers who have a probability of default of zero. The competitive rate charged to this group now becomes

$$r_g = 0 + c + x + r_k.$$

Substituting for $c + r_k$ from the previous equation gives

$$r_g = r + x - p.$$

In this simple example, good borrowers benefit from a lower cost of borrowing (i.e., $r_g < r$), as long as x < p. Bad borrowers lose because they are appropriately excluded (in this example where they have a 100% default rate) from the market. The resource costs of the new technology are met through the interest rate charged to good borrowers, but this is lower than before the technology was introduced because of the lower expected loss on the portfolio. Any bank, which did not adopt the new technology, would find itself unattractive to good borrowers (since its loan rate of r exceeds that of r_g charged to such borrowers by other banks), and would attract only bad borrowers and hence make losses.

As this example illustrates, it might a priori be expected that profit maximising banks will optimally introduce new risk management systems for which the expected benefits exceed the costs. Why then are capital concessions proposed in the New Basel Accord to give incentives for banks to adopt such systems?

We suggest two possible explanations which could justify the use of capital concessions. The first stems from noting that introduction of systems that will qualify a bank for advanced status is an investment project, which involves largely sunk costs. As explained by the real options literature, it may be optimal to defer undertaking such a project, even though it has a positive NPV, if the passage of time involves resolution of some elements of uncertainty associated with such a project. In this case, the pace of technological progress in the development of risk management systems, the potential for lower cost systems, and the uncertainty about the effectiveness of extant systems, may create some "real option" characteristics. If so, adoption of advanced risk management systems, while optimal from the private perspective of bank owners, may be slower than is viewed as optimal from a social perspective.

Our preferred explanation, however (which may justify capital incentives), is based upon noting that some part of the benefits from introduction of ARMS may accrue to regulators/deposit insurers, rather than to the bank, thereby creating a wedge between private and social cost benefit calculations. We consider this explanation and its implications for the appropriate size of capital concessions in the next section.

3. DEPOSIT INSURANCE AND CAPITAL CONCESSIONS

We adopt an option-pricing framework common in the literature on deposit insurance. Where an insurance or guarantee scheme operates, the insurer or government has, in effect, written a put option giving the bank owners the right (exercised when the bank is insolvent) to put the bank's assets to the insurer at a strike price equal to the deposit obligations (including interest due).

For ease of exposition, consider a bank engaged in lending to only one homogeneous group of borrowers over a one year horizon. It has no operating costs and no need to hold liquid assets. It raises \$D of deposits (offering to repay $\$De^r$ in one year) and \$E of owner's equity (capital) and can make $A = D + E$ of loans. In book value terms:

$$A_{BV} = D_{BV} + E_{BV}.$$

If loans are priced such that they have a zero NPV, then book value equals market value:

$$A_{BV} = A_{MV}.$$

Consider now the introduction of advanced risk management systems. There are two potential effects arising from this. First, the bank can better select borrowers and may be able to make loans, which have a positive NPV. Then, $A_{MV} > A_{BV}$ and $E_{MV} > E_{BV}$. Since the market value of the bank's assets is greater, there would need to be larger unexpected losses before insolvency occurs. The deposit insurer benefits since the value of the put option (insurance) written has declined. Bank owners benefit from the introduction of the new risk management techniques, but some part of the total benefit accrues to the insurer, unless the deposit insurance premium is reduced appropriately.

A similar effect occurs if the introduction of ARMS reduces the volatility of total repayments by borrowers. There may be better loan monitoring and management practices, better loan portfolio composition, or ability to use credit derivatives. The variance of losses may be reduced and reflected in a lower volatility of the market value of the bank's assets. This also reduces the value of the put option, which has been written by the deposit insurer. Unless the lower value of the put option is reflected in the insurance premium charged, or offset by a reduction in the bank's capital ratio, some part of the benefit is captured by the deposit insurer/government when insurance/guarantees exist.

The result of these effects is that expenditure by banks on ARMS, which will (ceteris paribus) reduce the probability of bank failure, will reduce claims on the deposit insurer. If deposit insurance is initially fairly priced such that the deposit insurer breaks even, the effect of ARMS introduction will result in the deposit insurer making excess profits. One response is to reduce insurance premiums such that "fair" pricing is reestablished at the now lower probability of bank failure. Another response is to allow banks to increase leverage to reestablish fair pricing but to restore the original probability of bank failure.

Figure 1 illustrates these arguments. Initially, the bank has deposit repayment obligations at the end of the period of De^r. Funds raised from contributed equity of E and deposits of D have been invested in assets (loans) with a zero NPV such that the market value of assets $(A_{MV}{}^0)$ equals the book value $(A_{MV}{}^0 = A_{BV} = D + E)$. Given the volatility of end-of-period asset value, σ_0, (which reflects the potential losses experienced on the loan portfolio) the value of the put option written by the deposit insurer is P_0, which is derived from an option-pricing model using strike price of De^r, volatility σ_0, and where the underlying variable is the current market value of the bank's assets. P_0 is the put option value at the asset value of $A_{MV}{}^0 = (D + E)$.

Figure 1. The value of the put option for varying volatility and asset levels.

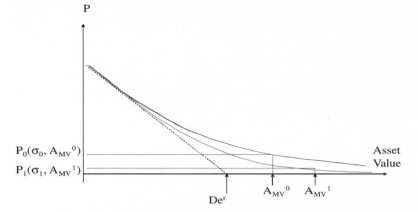

Introduction of ARMS has two effects as outlined above. First, the option-pricing curve is shifted down because of the lower volatility of end-of-period asset value, here denoted by σ_1. Second, the asset value at which the option is now valued is shifted to the right to A_{MV}^1, where $A_{MV}^1 > A_{MV}^0$, reflecting the fact that the bank is now undertaking positive NPV loans. P_1 is the put option value after the change. If the price of deposit insurance is adjusted to reflect the lower risk, bank equity increases in value by $A_{MV}^1 - A_{MV}^0 + (P_0 - P_1)$ and the insurer does not benefit. However, if the deposit insurance premium is unchanged, then bank equity increases by $(A_{MV}^1 A_{MV}^0)$ and the insurer benefits by $(P_0 - P_1)$.

Since some part of the benefit arising from the introduction of the advanced risk management system accrues to the put option writer, there would appear to be an argument for some recognition of this effect. Note that this could occur in two ways. One is by reducing the option premium (insurance fee) charged to the bank to reflect the lower put option value. The other is by allowing the bank to increase its leverage (reduce its capital ratio) such that the value of the put option remains unchanged.

4. CALCULATING CAPITAL CONCESSIONS

In what follows, we assume that deposit insurance premiums are not adjusted and consider what size capital concession might be warranted to offset the reduction in the fair value of the put option provided by the deposit insurer. Subsequently, we return to the question of why capital concessions, rather than changes in insurance premiums, are proposed. We also focus on the case where introduction of ARMS reduces bank asset volatility rather than on the case of gains from selection of positive NPV loans. As noted earlier, these latter gains may arise but may be quickly lost in a competitive banking market where many banks adopt the new technology. In the current context, an approximate way to allow for such gains, if thought important, would be to consider larger reductions in asset volatility arising from ARMs.

Merton (1977) demonstrates that if the cost of the guarantee per dollar of insured deposits is written as $g = p(T)/D$, where $p(T)$ is the value of the put option with strike price equal to the value of deposits plus interest, De^{rT}, then

$$g(d,T) = N(h_2) - \frac{1}{d} N(h_1),$$ (1)

where

$$h_1 = \frac{\ln d - \frac{1}{2}\sigma^2 T}{\sigma \sqrt{T}}, \quad and\, h_2 = h_1 + \sigma \sqrt{T},$$ (2)

($d = D/A$ is the current deposit-to-asset ratio; T is the maturity date of the put option; r is the risk-free rate; A is current market value of the bank; σ^2 is the instantaneous variance of the return on the bank's assets; and $N(.)$ is the univariate cumulative normal distribution function.) The deposit-to-asset ratio (d) and the volatility of the underlying assets (σ) are the two key determinants of the appropriate cost of deposit insurance per dollar of deposits given by equation (1).

There are a number of alternative option-based models for pricing deposit insurance in the literature, which differ in terms of how the characteristics of the deposit insurance contract is modeled. Since our focus in this paper is on the *change* in fair deposit insurance premiums that is warranted for a given change in asset volatility, we adopt the Merton (1977) model, which captures the essential sensitivity of the deposit insurance premium to changes in asset volatility.

In order to gain some estimate of appropriate capital concessions, the model is calibrated as follows. First, we assume an asset volatility of 4.0% p.a., which is similar to the value chosen by Merton (1977) based on the volatility of money market instruments, although higher than the average of around 2.5% estimated by Pennacchi (1987) for a sample of 23 large U.S. banks in 1981–82. A deposit/assets ratio of 0.945 is chosen based on an assumption of an average risk-weighted assets to total assets ratio of 0.69 (in line with figures observed for major banks) and a risk-weighted capital ratio of 8%. These figures give a 14.6 basis point cost of deposit insurance using the Merton (1977) model. While this is below the minimum premium in the U.S. (of 23 basis points) for banks, which pay premiums, most banks are currently exempt from paying premiums. In addition, using these figures, if we assume a market risk premium of 5% p.a., this calibration gives rise to a risk-neutral probability of default equal to 8.2% p.a. corresponding to an actual probability of default of 0.41% p.a. (using the approach of Crouhy, Galai, and Mark (2000)), which is within the range estimated by Jackson, Perraudin, and Saporta (2002).

Using knowledge of the option-pricing model and its properties, we conclude that the value of the deposit insurance as given by equation (1) will be positively related to asset volatility and positively related to the deposit-to-asset ratio. This can be seen by differentiating equation (1) with respect σ to and d respectively with explicit expressions given in equations (3) and (4).

$$\frac{\partial g}{\partial \sigma} = \frac{n(h_1)\sqrt{T}}{d}, \; where\, n(h_1) = \frac{1}{\sqrt{2\pi}} e^{\frac{1}{2}h_1^2} \tag{3}$$

$$\frac{\partial g}{\partial d} = \frac{N(h_1)}{d^2} \tag{4}$$

Figure 2 shows the value of the deposit insurance premium against the deposit-to-asset ratio for two levels of asset volatility: high (σ_H) and low (σ_L), and illustrates the relationships given in equations (3) and (4).

If we assume a fixed deposit insurance premium, then in order to keep the value of the put option constant, the appropriate regulatory response to a reduction in the asset volatility from introduction of ARMS is to allow the deposit-to-asset ratio d to increase—the "capital concession." This is shown in Figure 2 as the value of the deposit guarantee remaining constant for a decrease in volatility from σ_H to σ_L and an increase in the deposit-to-assets ratio from d_0 to d_1. For the calibration of the model as given above, with an initial asset volatility of 4% and a value of d equal to 0.945, the cost of deposit insurance is 14.6 basis points.

We consider a reduction in σ from 0.04 to 0.035 as a result of introducing ARMS. Although this choice of a decline in of 0.5% p.a. is somewhat arbitrary, a change of this magnitude is not

Figure 2. Fair insurance premium per dollar of insured deposits plotted against the deposit-to-asset ratio for low volatility of assets (σ_L) and high volatility of assets (σ_H).

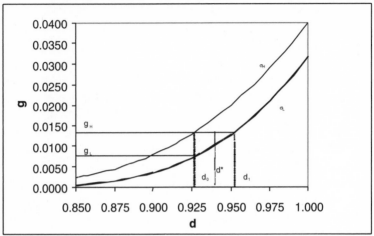

inconsistent with prior cross-section estimates of differences in bank asset volatility. Pennacchi (1987), for example, estimates bank asset volatilities ranging from 1.63% p.a. to 3.40% p.a. (a difference of 1.73% p.a.) for a sample of 23 large U.S. banks in 1981–82. An increase in d from 0.945 to 0.954 is required in order to hold the insurance premium fixed at 14.6 basis points. This is equivalent to a reduction in capital of 16.4% (from $5.50 per $100 of assets to $4.60 per $100 of assets). In the context of the Basel Accord risk-weighted asset framework, it would be equivalent to a decline in the average risk weight in this example from 0.69 to 0.58.[2] Table 2 gives a range of (σ, d) pairs for which the fair deposit insurance premium from equation (1) remains constant at 14.6 basis points. Included in that table is the value of $N(h_2)$, which represents the risk-neutral probability of default given by the Merton (1977) model. As the volatility decreases, the value of d increases in order to keep the insurance premium constant. However, as d increases, the risk-neutral probability of default also increases, as Table 2 illustrates. The value of the insurance premium is constant because the discounted expected payoff on the put option remains constant: the probability of default

---

2. A capital/assets ratio of 5.5% corresponds to an average risk weight of 0.69 if the bank has capital/risk weighted assets equal to 8%.

increases, but the cash flow in the event of default is lower because of the lower volatility of assets. Therefore, the contingent liability of the deposit insurer is constant and regulatory risk has not increased.

Table 2. The relationship between volatility, leverage, and the risk-neutral probability of default holding insurance value constant (g = $0.00146).

d	0.927	0.936	0.945	0.954	0.962	0.971
sigma	0.050	0.045	0.040	0.035	0.030	0.025
$N(h_2)$	0.068	0.074	0.082	0.091	0.103	0.120

The preceding calculation illustrates the maximum decline in the capital requirement (to reflect the assumed decline in bank asset volatility), which is possible without increasing regulatory risk. If such a change occurs, the put option provided by the deposit insurer remains fairly priced at the preexisting premium. (Alternatively, where deposit insurance was previously provided at a subsidized price, banks do not experience any change in the deposit insurance subsidy.) If the decline in the capital charge is less than this value, banks will now be paying a premium in excess of the fair value of the deposit insurance—given the initial assumption of fair pricing.

These arguments are illustrated in Figure 2, If the deposit-to-asset ratio is allowed to increase from d_0 to d_1 (a decrease in the capital ratio) for a reduction in volatility of the assets from σ_H to σ_L, the value of the deposit guarantee remains fairly priced at a value of g_H. If the increase in d is less, the deposit guarantee becomes overpriced.

Assuming that the deposit guarantee remains fairly priced, benefits to banks from the introduction of ARMS must arise from direct benefits, such as the new ability to make positive NPV loans, or from benefits arising from the increased leverage allowed. There is one main benefit arising from the allowed increase in leverage. Increased leverage gives rise to a tax shield from the tax deductibility of debt (deposits), if minimum capital requirements constrain capital structure choice. We assume for our calculations that the tax rate is t = 30 percent and that the tax shield is equal to tD.

Thus, there is an incentive for the bank to outlay the fixed costs, $C, of introducing ARMS, when the benefits arising from the increased debt tax shield for a given change in capital ratio and improved ability to make positive NPV loans outweigh these fixed costs. As we have noted earlier, competition may prevent banks from making positive (rather than zero) NPV loans, and some part of the costs of new credit risk management technology may be passed on to borrowers. (Better discrimination of borrowers means that poorer-quality borrowers face increased loan interest rates, and good borrowers face lower rates, with the additional costs of ARMS captured in the average margin of loan rates over the cost of capital to the bank. On average, loan interest rates charged may fall, if the decline in expected loan losses or effect of lower economic capital requirements outweigh the costs of ARMS introduction.)

We consider a worst case scenario where banks are unable to recoup any of the costs of ARMS from charges to customers. The question posed is then the following one. Since introduction of ARMS has desirable effects on bank failure probability, and benefits flow to the deposit insurer, what level or type of incentives can be provided by regulators to induce introduction of ARMS by transfer of deposit insurer benefits to the banks. Where banks can capture loan pricing benefits or pass ARMS introduction costs on to loan customers, the required incentives will be less than those estimated here.

There is an overall gain to the bank if the tax shield gain (TS) plus loan pricing gains (NPV_{loans}) exceed the fixed costs of ARMS introduction (C) as shown in equation (5).

$$C + TS + NPV_{loans} > 0. \tag{5}$$

As noted previously, we assume that the gain from positive NPV loans is zero. Since the tax shield is tD, the change in the value of the tax shield can be written as $t(d_1 - d_0)A$. Equation (5) then reduces to[3]

$$-C + t(d_1 - d_0)A > 0 \qquad (6)$$

In order to gain some idea of the maximum costs that an institution might profitably incur to introduce ARMS, note that equation (6) implies a break-even ratio of ARMS implementation costs to assets (C/A) of:

$$\frac{C}{A} = t(d_1 - d_0) \qquad (7)$$

Setting $t = 0.3$ and $(d_1 - d_0) = 0.09$, gives $C/A = 0.027$ or an implementation cost/asset ratio of around 2.7%, for the parameter values we have chosen. Thus, for example, if implementation costs are \$100 million, an institution with an asset size of around \$37 billion would find it just as worthwhile to undertake the expenditure.

Note, however, that this calculation assumes that the capital ratio is decreased (d increased) by around 16% in order to keep the price of deposit insurance fairly priced. Suppose instead that the increase in d was only from 0.945 to 0.95, an increase of 0.05 rather than 0.09. In addition to a reduction in leverage-related benefits, the bank owners would now incur a cost of overpriced deposit insurance. Referring to Figure 2, if, for example, the allowed increase in d was from d_0 to d^*, the cost to the bank (each year) is given by $g(\sigma_H, d_0)d_0 A - g(\sigma_L, d^*)d^* A$. Assuming that this cost is perpetual and discounting at the cost of equity (r), the project acceptance condition now becomes:

$$-C + t(d^* - d_0)A - \frac{g(\sigma_H, d_0)d_0 A - g(\sigma_L, d^*)d^* A}{r} > 0 \qquad (8)$$

and the breakeven implementation cost/asset ratio becomes:

$$\frac{C}{A} = t(d^* - d_0) - \frac{g(\sigma_H, d_0)d_0 - g(\sigma_L, d^*)d^*}{r} \qquad (9)$$

---

3. In a classical tax system, the gain from leverage can be approximated as the product of the tax rate and the dollar value of the debt (assuming that the interest on the debt and the discount rate for the tax savings are equal). In an integrated tax system or a dividend imputation system, the tax advantages to increased leverage are lower, and consequently, the capital concessions required to satisfy equation (9) may have to be larger.

For $d0 = 0.945$, $d* = 0.95$, $\sigma_H = 0.04$, $\sigma_L = 0.035$, $g(\sigma_H, d_0) = 14.62$ basis points and $g(\sigma_L, d*) = 11.38$ basis points. Assuming that r = 0.15, for these parameters there is no positive breakeven implementation cost/asset ratio. The (reduced) leverage gains are more than outweighed by the cost of now overpriced deposit insurance.

These indicative calculations illustrate the importance of appropriate adjustment of the minimum capital ratio to compensate banks for the benefits which would otherwise accrue to the deposit insurer. Without such adjustments, bank investment in ARMS may be inhibited. For example, to take an extreme case, if the bank's outlays on ARMS only reduced volatility and there was no change in either the minimum capital ratio nor the cost of deposit insurance, there would be no incentive whatsoever for the bank to undertake such outlays. Of course, the numerical results derived above depend crucially on the assumption that the only effect of introducing ARMS is to reduce the volatility of bank asset value. If the introduction of the risk management system results in the bank making positive NPV loans, or if introduction costs can be passed onto customers, then the introduction of advanced systems results in a gain to the bank from this source.

Petrou (2003) estimates that the cost of implementation of ARMS to qualify for advanced IRB status will reach \$200 million per bank. Given the uncertainty surrounding such estimates, Table 3 gives the relationship between various levels of fixed costs, \$C, and the minimum size of the institution for which introduction of ARMS will be a positive NPV investment. The calculations assume that asset volatility is reduced as a result of the introduction of ARMS, and the regulator response is to allow an increase in the deposit-to-asset ratio such that the fair value of the insurance premium remains constant. We set the initial asset-to-deposit ratio to 0.945 and the tax rate to 0.3. For example, for an initial asset volatility of 4%, an initial asset-to-deposit ratio of 0.945, and a reduction in asset volatility from 4% to 3.5%, for fixed costs of \$100 million, a bank of asset size slightly larger than \$37 billion would benefit from the introduction of ARMS. If fixed costs are \$200 million, the minimum viable size is \$74 billion. From the bank's perspective, the capital incentive is sufficient to incur the cost of introduction of the advanced risk management systems, even assuming that the gain from positive NPV loans is zero.

Table 3. Minimum size required ($b) for the benefits from capital concessions to be greater than the cost of implementing ARMS, for a range of assumed costs ($m) and initial asset volatilities. These results are derived under the assumption that the allowed capital concession keeps the fair insurance premium constant, and d is initially set at 0.945 before the reduction in volatility for each case. We have also assumed that there is no benefit to the bank from positive NPV loans.

Panel A: Initial asset volatility = 0.05				
Change in volatility	Costs ($b)	50	100	200
	0.005	20.83	41.67	83.33
	0.010	11.11	22.22	44.44
	0.015	7.25	14.49	28.99
	0.020	5.56	11.11	22.22
Panel B: Initial asset volatility = 0.04				
Change in volatility	Costs ($b)	50	100	200
	0.005	18.52	37.04	74.07
	0.010	9.80	19.61	39.22
	0.015	6.41	12.82	25.64
	0.020	4.90	9.80	19.61
Panel C: Initial asset volatility = 0.03				
Change in volatility	Costs ($b)	50	100	200
	0.005	15.15	30.30	60.61
	0.010	7.94	15.87	31.75
	0.015	5.38	10.75	21.51
	0.020	4.07	8.13	16.26

These estimates are suggestive of the size of institutions which might qualify for IRB status, although they are potentially an overestimate of minimum feasible size and hedged with considerable uncertainty about appropriate parameter values. As noted earlier, there are approximately 120 banks worldwide with assets in excess of $60–70 billion.

5. ADJUSTING THE PRICE OF DEPOSIT INSURANCE

An alternative regulatory response to the reduction of asset volatility (or better quality loan book) that results from ARMS might be to adjust the deposit insurance premium charged to banks. In this case, the value of the put option granted by the insurer or the government decreases, and the premium paid by the bank is reduced. (In addition, the probability of default decreases.) There is an overall benefit to the bank if the reduction in value (and thus cost) of the put option is greater than the cost, $C, of introducing the risk management system. Assume that the only regulatory response is to lower the insurance premium; that is, there are no capital concessions. Referring to Figure 2, if the insurance premium is reduced to its fair value for a drop in volatility from σ_H to σ_L and an initial deposit-to-asset ratio of d_0, then the premium drops from $g(d_0, \sigma_H)$ to $g(d_0, \sigma_L)$. We assume that the bank can claim deposit insurance costs as a taxable expense such that the change in after-tax cash flows is $(1-t)[g(d_0, \sigma_H) g(d_0, \sigma_L)]D$. Then provided $(1-t)[g(d_0, \sigma_H) ~ g(d_0, \sigma_L)]D > C$, the bank is better off incurring the cost, $C, to introduce ARMS.

The change in the value of the put option (Δp), where p = g.D, for a given change in volatility of assets is given by

$$\Delta p = D\sqrt{T}n(h_1)\Delta\sigma \tag{10}$$

(D is the size of the institution (insured deposits), and p is the value of the put option.) We can calculate the present value of the change in the value of the put option payments, after tax at the rate, t, as a perpetuity, assuming the change in volatility is permanent as

$$PV(\Delta p) = \frac{1}{r}D\sqrt{T}n(h_1)\Delta\sigma(1-t) \tag{11}$$

where r is the appropriate discount rate.

Therefore, the reduction in the put value for a given decrease in the volatility of assets is greater than the costs involved in implementing the risk management system if

$$D > \frac{rC}{n(h_1)\sqrt{T}\Delta\sigma(1-t)} \text{ or } A > \frac{rC}{n(h_1)\sqrt{T}\Delta\sigma(1-t)} \tag{12}$$

Equation (12) can be used to estimate the minimum size of the institution for which the benefits of a reduction in the value of the put option (and insurance premiums charged) outweigh the costs of introduction of the risk management system. (As before, this will be an overestimate of the size if banks can recoup part of the introduction costs from loan customers.) The minimum size depends on the discount rate, the initial volatility of assets (refer to equation (2), where it can be seen that h_1 is a function of volatility), the leverage ratio, the size of the change in volatility ($\Delta\sigma$), and the tax rate (t). Table 4 gives the minimum size for a discount rate of

15% (assumed to be the cost of equity capital), a deposit-to-asset ratio of 0.945, assumed initial asset volatilities of 5% (panel A), 4% (panel B), 3% (panel C), and a tax rate of 30%.

Table 4. Minimum asset size required ($b) for the reduction in the value of the deposit guarantee to be greater than the costs of implementing risk management system, for a range of assumed costs ($m) with d = 0.945. These results are derived assumed that the price of deposit insurance is adjusted (and remains fairly priced) to reflect the lower volatility of assets.

Panel A: Initial asset volatility = 0.05				
Change in volatility	Costs ($b)	50	100	200
	0.005	11.09	22.19	44.37
	0.010	5.55	11.09	22.19
	0.015	3.70	7.40	14.79
	0.020	2.78	5.55	11.09
Panel B: Initial asset volatility = 0.04				
Change in volatility	Costs ($b)	50	100	200
	0.005	15.90	31.80	63.59
	0.010	7.95	15.90	31.80
	0.015	5.30	10.60	21.20
	0.020	3.97	7.95	15.90
Panel C: Initial asset volatility = 0.03				
Change in volatility	Costs ($b)	50	100	200
	0.005	34.60	69.21	138.41
	0.010	17.30	34.60	69.21
	0.015	11.53	23.07	46.14
	0.020	8.65	17.30	34.60

The relationships depicted in Table 4 are as expected. The higher the volatility of the institution (implying a more valuable deposit guarantee), the smaller the size at which the reduction in the put option value will exceed the costs of implementing the risk management system. Or, for a given cost and initial asset volatility, the greater the reduction in volatility, the smaller the minimum size of the institution for which the expenditure becomes worthwhile.

Note that for an initial asset volatility of 4% and fixed costs of $100m and a volatility reduction to 3.50%, an institution of approximately $32 billion in assets would find it worthwhile to implement advanced systems if the deposit premium were adjusted fairly. This figure is not too dissimilar to the estimate of $37 billion minimum size calculated for similar parameters in the case where capital concessions were allowed.

6. REGULATORY INCENTIVES AND RISK MANAGEMENT

The preceding calculations highlight some of the issues involved in providing capital incentives for banks, which adopt ARMS. First, it is clear that accession to IRB status will be limited to relatively large banks—because of the significant costs involved in introducing ARMS (and making them compliant with the requirements of the new accord). Second, it is possible that capital concessions may provide competitive advantages to recipient banks over and above those obtained directly from introduction of such systems. This would occur if capital concessions (increased leverage) were not just an offset to lower inherent risk but allowed an increase in the riskiness of the banks involved, which was not offset by either a price response by uninsured depositors or by higher deposit insurance premiums.

Third, properly calibrated capital concessions can be interpreted as providing recipient banks with compensation for the decline in risk faced by the deposit insurer in lieu of a reduction in deposit insurance premiums. These would align the private cost benefit calculation undertaken by banks considering investment in ARMS with a social cost benefit calculation. There may, however, be tax benefits associated with such a response which warrant further attention.

Fourth, an alternative to capital concessions exists in the form of reductions in deposit insurance premiums for banks adopting ARMS. That this alternative has not been recommended may reflect a number of complications associated with the operation of deposit insurance schemes. One is that some countries do not have an explicit scheme of deposit insurance, and hence, adjustments to insurance premiums are impossible. If there is implicit deposit insurance, ultimately paid for by the taxpayers, introduction of ARMS reduces the taxpayer subsidy. A second complication is that few deposit insurance schemes have accurate risk-based pricing. Hence, appropriate adjustments may be difficult to determine and implement. A third complication arises because even where an explicit deposit insurance scheme exists, not all deposit claims are insured. For example, in the U.S., foreign deposits and that portion of deposits above the insurance ceiling remain uninsured. In such circumstances, adjustments to an aggregate capital requirement may have quite different effects across banks with different proportions of insured versus uninsured deposits. To the extent that large banks likely to consider adopting ARMS have a smaller proportion of insured to total deposits than other banks, the effect of capital concessions may be relatively more valuable.

In addition to these factors, institutional factors are also relevant. Prudential supervision and deposit insurance are not always colocated in the one institution. Verification of the quality of a bank's risk management systems is likely to be the province of prudential regulators, and independent deposit insurers may be reluctant to base insurance premium decisions on such an assessment.

A further explanation for the advocacy of capital concessions may lie in the fact that regulators perceive the current level of bank risk to be approximately correct from a public policy perspective. Reducing insurance premiums for banks, which adopt ARMS, would compensate those banks for expenditures undertaken, but would also mean that the probability of failure of such banks was reduced below the current level. Alternatively, capital concessions also provide compensation but (if calibrated correctly) restore regulatory risk back toward its original level. Depending on the size of the capital concession (even that which keeps the insurance premium at its fair value), the probability of bank failures could increase, although the severity of failure and the size of the insurer payout would be lower because of the lower asset volatility.

7. CONCLUSION

We have argued that capital incentives for banks introducing advanced risk management systems can be justified on the basis of compensating banks for expenditures, which would otherwise confer benefits on deposit insurers. Better risk management systems, which imply a lower risk of bank failure, *ceteris paribus*, reduce the fair value of deposit insurance. Banks will not take this social benefit into account in decisions regarding introduction of ARMS. Consequently, adoption of such systems may be slower than is socially optimal unless banks are compensated in some way for the social benefits.

In principle, regulators could respond in (at least) two ways. Deposit insurance premiums could be reduced for those banks introducing such systems. Alternatively, capital incentives could be provided. Either approach, if calibrated appropriately, will maintain deposit insurance premiums at their fair value (or keep the extant deposit insurance subsidy constant). The latter approach (of capital incentives), however, works to offset the reduction in bank failure probability, otherwise resulting from the introduction of ARMS. In contrast, reducing deposit insurance premiums would not offset that decline in bank failure probability.

Either approach involves significant issues of competitive neutrality of regulation. Banks will introduce ARMS if they perceive doing so to be value-adding (either from first mover advantages or mimicking the actions of others to prevent deterioration of their competitive position). Even where competition amongst adopters of ARMS prevents banks deriving above normal economic profits, such systems will be introduced if benefits exceed costs—with costs being recouped through more accurate loan pricing and margins. In such circumstances, non-adopters may face a competitive disadvantage in some loan markets due to their inability to accurately grade and price loans.

Providing further competitive advantage through capital concessions is thus a potentially contentious issue, although, as we have argued, one which may be justified on the grounds of spill-over social benefits from the introduction of ARMS. Calculating the appropriate size of such concessions is a difficult task but one which is necessary and for which this paper has provided some preliminary estimates.

In conclusion, however, the case for capital concessions is reduced by the tendency for (explicit or implicit) deposit insurance to be provided in many countries at a subsidised rate, and perhaps disproportionately so for large banks where "too big to fail" issues may be significant. In such situations, the case for providing capital concessions to large banks, which introduce ARMS, rather than using the opportunity to reduce the size of extant subsidy would seem to be not yet proven.

REFERENCES

Australian Prudential Regulatory Authority (2002), "APRA's Views On Basel II: Managing The Transition," *APRA Insight*, 2nd Quarter, pp. 3–6, *http://www.apra.gov.au/Insight/Insight-2nd-Quarter-2002.cfm*

Basel Committee on Banking Supervision (2001), Consultative Document Overview of The New Basel Capital Accord, January, *http://www.bis.org/publ/bcbsca02.pdf*

Basel Committee on Banking Supervision (2002), Overview Paper for the Impact Study, October, *http://www.bis.org/qisover.pdf*

Basel Committee on Banking Supervision (2003b), Supplementary Information on QIS 3, May, *http://www.bis.org/bcbs/qis/qis3sup.pdf*

Blakely, Kevin (2003), "Statement of Kevin Blakely," *U.S. Senate Committee on Banking, Housing, and Urban Affairs, "A Review of the New Basel Capital Accord,"* June, 18, *http://www.senate.gov/~banking/_files/blakely.pdf*

Crouhy, M., D. Galai and R. Mark (2000), "A Comparative Analysis of Current Credit Risk Models," *Journal of Banking and Finance*, 24, pp. 59-117.

Ervin, D. Wilson (2003), "Statement of D. Wilson Ervin," *U.S. Senate Committee on Banking, Housing, and Urban Affairs, "A Review of the New Basel Capital Accord,"* June, 18, *http://www.senate.gov/~banking/_files/ervin.pdf*

Ferguson, Roger (2003), "Statement of Roger Ferguson," *U.S. Senate Committee on Banking, Housing, and Urban Affairs, "A Review of the New Basel Capital Accord,"* June, 18, *http://www.senate.gov/~banking/_files/ferguson.pdf*

Jackson, P., W. Perraudin and V. Saporta (2002), "Regulatory and 'Economic' Solvency Standards for Internationally Active Banks," *Journal of Banking and Finance*, 26, pp. 953–976.

Kupiec, P (2001), "Is the New Basel Accord Incentive Compatible?" *Presented at workshop, Basel 2: An Economic Assessment*, Basel 17–18, May 2002, *http://www.bis.org/bcbs/events/b2eakup.pdf*

Merton, R. C. (1977), "An Analytic Derivation of the Cost of Deposit Insurance and Loan Guarantees," "An Application of Modern Option Pricing Theory," *Journal of Banking and Finance*, 1, pp. 3–11.

Pennacchi, George G. (1987), "A Reexamination of the Over- (or Under-) Pricing of Deposit Insurance," *Journal of Money, Credit and Banking*, August, 19, 3, pp. 340–360.

Petrou, Karen Shaw (2003), "Statement of Karen Shaw Petrou," *U.S. Senate Committee on Banking, Housing, and Urban Affairs, "A Review of the New Basel Capital Accord,"* June, 18, *http://www.senate.gov/~banking/_files/petrou.pdf*

9

Pro-cyclicality, Banks' Reporting Discretion, and "Safety in Similarity"

Pipat Luengnaruemitchai
Department of Economics
University of California, Berkeley
lpipat@econ.berkeley.edu

James A. Wilcox
Haas School of Business
University of California, Berkeley
jwilcox@haas.berkeley.edu

The authors thank Michael Dooley, Luis Dopico, Mark Flannery, George Kaufman, Joe Peek, and participants at seminars at Berkeley and at the 2003 FMA annual meeting for helpful comments. Steve Egli and Ryan Stever provided excellent research assistance. Any remaining errors are ours. The authors express their appreciation for financial support from the Anandamahidol Foundation and the Kruttschnitt Family Chair, respectively.

Pipat Luengnaruemitchai
Department of Economics
University of California, Berkeley
lpipat@econ.berkeley.edu

James A. Wilcox
Haas School of Business
University of California, Berkeley
jwilcox@haas.berkeley.edu

Abstract

During recessions, either declines in actual capital or increases in required capital may intensify pressures on banks. One way for banks to boost their capital ratios is by reducing their lending. However, one effect of systematic reductions in the supply of bank loans during recessions would likely be to accentuate the magnitudes of macroeconomic fluctuations. To reduce this source of "pro-cyclicality," it has been proposed that Basel II include "escape clauses." Such clauses might, for example, operate so as to raise required bank capital during macroeconomic expansions and reduce it during downturns.

Apart from formal escape clauses, pro-cyclicality might be reduced or even reversed in practice if banks exercise sufficient discretion in reporting their charge-offs and loan loss provisions. We propose two hypotheses about the past cyclicality of such discretion. We hypothesize that individual banks tended to report fewer charge-offs and provisions when the banking system was troubled than when it was generally healthier. That suggested our second hypothesis: Banks tended to cluster more when the banking industry was troubled. Banks would maximize the value of their reporting discretion by clustering more then; being similar to other banks raised the likelihood that a bank would be able to exert reporting discretion when it encountered difficulties, because other, similar banks, and thus the banking system as a whole, would likely be troubled at the same time.

We found some support for our hypotheses at large U.S. banks. During the late 1980s, when banking was troubled and bank capital ratios were low, individual banks reported fewer charge-offs, ceteris paribus, when the capital ratios of their peers were lower. During the late 1990s, in contrast, when capital ratios were higher, charge-offs at individual banks were not systematically related to the capital ratios of peer banks. We also found that the equity and the asset betas of individual banks tended to cluster more when banking was more troubled than they did when banking was less troubled.

"We must all hang together, or assuredly we shall all hang separately."

Benjamin Franklin, July 4, 1776

I. INTRODUCTION

Banks may come under capital pressure either because of declines in their capital or because of increases in required capital. Pressures on bank capital may reduce lending and output. Basel reformers have become concerned that the constant application in practice of a fixed set of capital regulations over the business cycle could accentuate the magnitudes of macroeconomic fluctuations. That is, bank capital rules might then contribute to economies' "pro-cyclicality." If bank capital requirements are revised promptly on the basis of expected losses on bank assets, then increases in expected losses in and around recessions could raise banks' capital requirements and thereby make bank lending more pro-cyclical than otherwise. In order to ameliorate the pro-cyclicality of bank capital rules, "escape clauses" of some sort might be included in the reform of the Basel Capital Accord. These clauses might, for example, require banks to hold more capital during economic expansions so that they would have it available to be drawn down during economic downturns.

Determining whether bank supervision and regulation as a whole has been, or will be, pro-cyclical or countercyclical is problematic. Some elements of bank regulation, such as prompt revision of required capital in light of changed estimates of expected losses, may have pro-cyclical effects. Other elements may have countercyclical effects. For instance, "discretion" in the amounts of charge-offs and loan loss provisions reported by banks during troubled times might reduce, or even reverse, pro-cyclicality attributable to increases in amounts of required capital and associated decreases in the supply of bank loans. Banking supervision and regulations, either explicitly or implicitly, might allow banks to report fewer charge-offs and provisions for actual and expected loan losses when an entire banking system is under considerable stress than would otherwise be the case. Such discretion would prop up earnings, retained earnings, and reported capital ratios. Such discretion might have countercyclical effects, as opposed to the pro-cyclical effects that might emanate from rigid application of banking supervision and regulation.

Bank supervisors might be skeptical of being asked to help manage, and be seen as helping to manage, macroeconomic outcomes. Discretion in banks' reporting of loan loss provisions and charge-offs might exacerbate losses to banks and deposit insurers and confound appropriate application of countercyclical monetary policy. Allowing banks discretion in their reporting might (1) reduce the discipline of banks' credit monitoring, (2) lead ultimately to larger amounts of problem loans, and (3) divert credit from its most efficient uses. In addition, monetary authorities may recognize that bank supervisors might respond to contractionary monetary policy by allowing banks to exercise more discretion, for example, by permitting banks to avoid charging off or "evergreening" loans. To the extent that the amounts and effects of such reporting discretion are hard to quantify, monetary policy would be that much harder to conduct.

Monetary authorities might compensate for the anticipated effects of increased reporting discretion by imposing stricter monetary policies than they would otherwise. The effects of the even-tighter monetary policy would be felt most keenly by borrowers whose loans would not benefit from the reporting discretion, such as variable-rate business borrowers with good credit ratings and borrowers at banks that do not engage in reporting discretion.

We seek empirical estimates of the extent to which the reported amounts of loan loss provisions and charge-offs at U.S. banks have varied, relative to the amounts that would have been expected in light of the conditions of their loan portfolios. More specifically, we seek estimates of the effects of the condition of banking generally on the amounts of charge-offs and provisions reported by individual banks. We use data for loan delinquencies, capital, earnings, and other bank variables for the 30 largest U.S. banks in each year from 1976 through 2001. We also examined the 1999 data for nine large Japanese banks.

We examine two hypotheses. The first hypothesis relates to discretion in banks' reported amounts of loan charge-offs and loss provisions; the second relates to banks' "safety in similarity." Bank supervisors monitor and promote the safety and soundness of individual banks and thereby the banking industry. They may, however, apply different standards when problems are isolated in a few banks than when the banking industry generally is more troubled. When the banking industry generally is in good condition, bank supervisors might be more insistent that a troubled bank adhere to standard reporting requirements for loan charge-offs and provisions (and for other inputs to a bank's financial statements). If an individual bank had sufficiently poor management, low earnings (perhaps due to large expected future loan losses), or heavy loan losses (and as a result had low capital ratios), supervisory action might follow the established norms for severity and speed. If the condition of the bank were sufficiently dire, to preclude larger losses later, bank supervisors might close the bank.[1]

In contrast, when the banking industry was generally quite troubled, bank supervisors might be attuned to the (1) macroeconomic repercussions of widespread reductions in bank lending, (2) stability of the financial system, and (3) repercussions of widespread bank failures on bank supervisors and their organizations. In light of these considerations, we hypothesized that bank supervisors might grant banks more discretion in reporting charge-offs and provisions when the banking system is generally troubled than when problems are confined to a few banks. We refer to this as our "reporting discretion hypothesis."

We also hypothesize that supervisors are more likely to close atypical banks than to close average banks. Individual banks may employ business strategies that profit from differentiation from the strategies and markets of their competitors. During relatively good times, the value to an individual bank of reporting discretion is reduced because of relatively large earnings and relatively small amounts of charge-offs and provisions. In contrast, when the banking industry is generally troubled, banks benefit from "safety in similarity." By being similar to each other, individual banks increase the odds that they are troubled at the same time as the industry, generally. Since the likelihood of reporting discretion rises as the banking industry becomes more troubled, a similar bank would be able to exercise reporting discretion when that discretion is most valuable to the bank, which is when the bank itself is troubled. This is our "safety in similarity hypothesis."

---

1. If an individual bank is large enough ("too big to fail," TBTF), regulators may relax standards in order to increase the chances of the bank's survival, to minimize disruptions to the bank's continuing deposit and credit operations, and to avoid closing a large bank during the regulators' tenure. TBTF may have applied during the 1980s in the U.S. to about a dozen banks. It is not clear how many (if any) banks TBTF applied to since then. TBTF may mean too big to cease operations or be liquidated. It need not preclude formal insolvency or a shotgun marriage to another institution. The 10th largest U.S. bank in 2001 was Sun Trust Bank (Atlanta, GA), which had about $100 billion in assets and 1.6% of all U.S. commercial bank assets.

To confront our hypotheses with data, we estimated bank charge-off and provision equations and computed measures of bank similarity. We also examined how each varied over time. Our econometric estimates are consistent with banks exercising greater reporting discretion during troubled times. During the late 1980s, capital ratios at large U.S. banks were generally low and potentially overstated due to reporting discretion. At that time, the lower the capital ratios at peer banks, the smaller the reported charge-offs at individual banks. During the late 1990s, average bank capital ratios were higher. At that time, the capital ratios of peer banks had no detectable effects on the charge-offs reported by individual banks. Consistent with our hypothesis that banks seek safety in similarity, we found that banks chose market betas and asset betas that clustered together more when banking was troubled.

Section II presents a brief literature and historical review of related issues. Section III details the data and methodology that we use. Section IV presents statistical results that address (1) the cyclicality of bank capital regulation and (2) the discretion (or management) in bank accounting based on data from the era of U.S. bank and thrift crises in the 1980s and early 1990s and from the Japanese banking crisis since the 1980s. Section V summarizes the chapter and discusses some of its implications.

II. LITERATURE AND HISTORICAL REVIEW

In this section, we provide (1) a brief review of literature that is closely related to our reporting discretion hypothesis and (2) some preliminary evidence that banks tend to cluster more when the banking industry is troubled.

The literature on the cyclicality and cyclical effects of bank capital requirements has sprung up and expanded considerably in recent years. Ranging from Bernanke and Lown (1991) through Van der Heuvel (2002), numerous studies have documented the effects in the U.S. on banks and on the economy of pressures on bank capital. Bliss et al. (2002) succinctly argue that the simple model of how expansionary monetary policy increases bank assets may be incomplete, because banks are subject both to reserve and to capital requirements. When capital requirements are binding, injection of reserves may not increase bank lending and may even reduce it.

Some accounting studies conclude that individual banks use loan loss provisions, charge-offs, and allowances to manage their reported amounts of regulatory and generally accepted earnings and capital. For instance, Ahmed et al. (1999) use the 1990 change in capital adequacy regulation to construct tests of capital and earnings management on loan loss provisions. The authors find evidence that loan loss provisions are used for capital management, but they do not find evidence that banks use loan loss provisions to manage reported earnings or to signal future earnings to outsiders.

There is also literature on the laxity of bank supervisors in the U.S. and in Japan. For instance, Kane (1987, 1989) trumpets the dangers of capital forbearance at savings and loans. Hayakawa (2001) details the reticence of Japanese supervisors to close any banking institutions. Pilling (2002) notes that the reported amounts of nonperforming loans at Japanese banks are widely regarded as hugely underestimating the true amounts. Ioannidou (2002) finds that the Federal Reserve's simultaneous roles of being banking supervisor and central bank compromise the latter, in that indicators of monetary policy affect the Fed's actions as banking supervisor. Those same monetary policy indicators do not, however, affect the actions of the U.S. bank supervisors that are not responsible for monetary policy (the OCC and the FDIC).

Next, we present some evidence about reporting discretion at Japanese banks and about clustering by U.S. banks. To do so, we use two different measures: capital ratios for Japanese banks and the standard deviations of equity betas for U.S. banks. Figure 1 shows the ratio of total capital to risk-weighted assets for 9 large Japanese banks in 1999. The narrow range (between 10 and 13 percent) across these banks fits the hypothesis of reporting discretion. It may be that the conditions of these Japanese banks and the Japanese banking system are sufficiently dire that they cannot attract private capital. As a result, it may be that individual banks are implicitly permitted to cap the amount of problem loans that they report so that they report having enough capital to satisfy Basel capital minimums.

Figure 1. Total Risk-Weighted Capital Ratios at 9 Large Japanese Banks, 1999

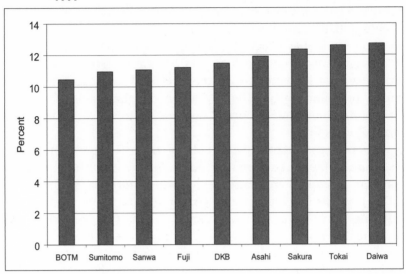

Source: Morgan Stanley Dean Witter (1999).

Figure 2. Total Risk-Weighted Capital Ratios at 5 Large Japanese Banks, 2002

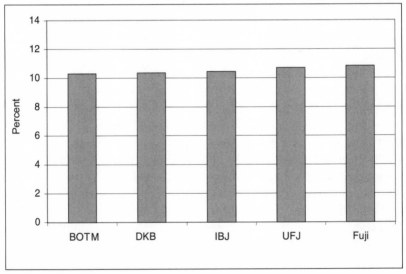

Source: Merrill Lynch (2002).

Figure 2 shows the ratio of total capital to risk-weighted assets for 5 large Japanese banks in 2002. Several developments have taken place between 1999 and 2002. The number of large banks fell as some of the weak large banks merged. These mergers can be described either as the takeover of weak institutions by slightly stronger ones or as mergers among roughly similar weak institutions. Ibison (2002) concludes that Japanese banking is now dominated by even larger institutions, each with unclear corporate histories and ethos and each with high levels of inherited nonperforming loans. The range across capital ratios for the 5 large Japanese banks is even narrower (between 10 and 11 percent) in 2002 than in 1999, which may suggest that even more reporting discretion has been exercised more recently. Not only does our hypothesis suggest that reported charge-offs and capital ratios may not be trustworthy, but it also suggests that until the backlog of unreported bad loans is cleared, lower reported charge-offs might indicate worsened, and not improving, banking conditions.

Figures 3 through 7 are based on data for the 30 largest U.S. banks in each year. Figure 3 presents average rates of return on assets (ROA) and average capital ratios for those banks for each year from 1976 through 2001. These data highlight that banking conditions were noticeably worse before the middle of the 1990s and have been markedly better since. Until the middle of the 1990s, banks' ROAs and capital ratios were lower than since. (Moreover, the evidence presented in Section IV below suggests that the reported capital ratios in the late 1980s may have been overstated.) After the early 1990s, both ROAs and capital ratios rose markedly.

Figures 4 through 7 provide preliminary evidence that a generally weaker U.S. banking industry was associated with banks clustering more. Our data source did not have sufficient data to permit us to calculate capital ratios for individual banks before 1986. For each year from 1976 through 1985, we calculated capital ratios for the 30 largest U.S. banks as follows: We subtracted the difference between the national aggregate bank capital ratio for 1986 and the weighted average for the 30 largest U.S. banks for 1986 from the national aggregate bank capital ratio for each year from 1976 through 1985. We used the resulting data series as our measure of the weighted average capital ratio for the 30 largest U.S. banks.

Figure 4 compares (weighted by assets) average capital ratios with (weighted by assets) average equity betas. Lower average equity betas are associated with (1) lower volatility relative to the stock market and, typically, (2) less total risk taking. Figure 4 shows that when average capital ratios were relatively low (ranging from 4.7 to 6.0 percent between 1976 and 1991), average equity

Figure 3. Average Equity Capital Ratio and Average ROA for Large U.S. Banks

Annual, 1976–2001

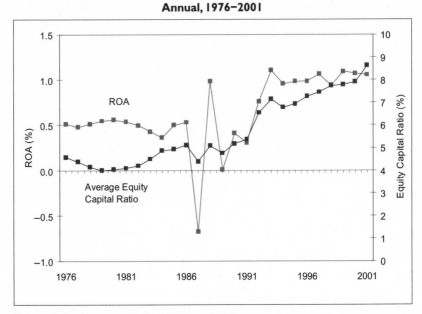

Source: Federal Reserve Bank of Chicago (2003).

betas were also low (ranging from 0.70 to 1.32). In contrast, when average capital ratios were higher (ranging from 7.0 to 7.8 percent between 1992 and 2001), average equity betas were also higher (ranging from 1.01 to 1.55). Although estimates of the average equity betas are somewhat volatile, Figure 4 generally does support the hypothesis that banks reduce their (systematic) risks during troubled times.

Banks' equity betas may reflect not only their assets but also their leverage. Figure 5 compares average capital ratios and average asset betas, which measure the underlying volatility of the market values of banks' assets. Banks' leverage fell considerably over this period as their capital ratios rose. When average capital ratios were low, average asset betas were also low (ranging from 0.038 to 0.073 between 1976 and 1991). In contrast, when average capital ratios were higher, average asset betas were also higher (ranging from 0.079 to 0.116 between 1992 and 2001). Thus, Figure 5 also supports the hypothesis that banks held less risky assets during troubled times.

Figures 6 and 7 compare average bank capital ratios with the standard deviations (across banks) of their equity betas and their asset betas, respectively. We calculated betas from banks' own

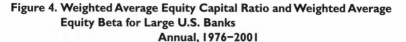

Figure 4. Weighted Average Equity Capital Ratio and Weighted Average Equity Beta for Large U.S. Banks
Annual, 1976–2001

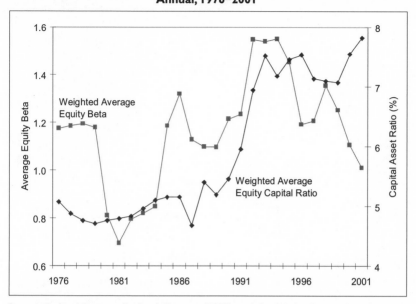

Source: Federal Reserve Bank of Chicago (2003) and Center for Research in Security Prices (2003).

total equity returns, total returns on a broad market index, and the banks' leverage ratios. Lower standard deviations of equity and asset betas imply that banks are more clustered. When average capital ratios were low, standard deviations of equity betas (ranging from 0.18 to 0.25 between 1976 and 1991) and standard deviations of asset betas (ranging from 0.011 to 0.019 between 1976 and 1991) were also low. When average capital ratios were higher, standard deviations of equity betas (ranging from 0.24 to 0.42 between 1992 and 2001) and standard deviations of asset betas (ranging from 0.020 to 0.038 between 1992 and 2001) were also higher. Thus, Figures 6 and 7 support the hypothesis that banks more tightly mimicked each other when banking generally was more troubled.

III. DATA AND METHODOLOGY

We use ordinary least squares (OLS) regressions to estimate equations that indicate reporting discretion at Japanese and U.S. banks. We use data on capital ratios, operating income, provisions for loan losses, and loan charge-offs for the 9 largest Japanese banks in

Figure 5. Weighted Average Equity Capital Ratio and Weighted Average Asset Beta for Large U.S. Banks
Annual, 1976–2001

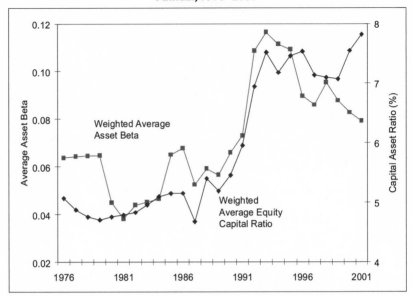

Source: Federal Reserve Bank of Chicago (2003) and Center for Research in Security Prices (2003).

1999 from Morgan Stanley Dean Witter (1999). We also use panel data for the financial statements for the 30 largest U.S. banks for each year from 1976 through 2001, the period for which Reports of Condition and Income Reports (Call Reports) are publicly available from the Federal Reserve Bank of Chicago database.

Thus far, we have not analyzed the hypothesis of "safety in similarity" econometrically. The figures discussed in Section II use accounting data for the largest 30 U.S. banks for each year from 1976 through 2001 and data for the stock prices and returns for the 40 largest U.S. bank holding companies (BHCs) for the same period. We obtained stock price data from the Center for Research in Security Prices (CRSP). Our datasets for accounting data and stock prices do not overlap exactly. Using the S&P 500, we computed equity betas for each BHC over the time period and the mean and standard deviation across the 40 largest BHCs. We used the average capital ratios from our accounting data to impute the average asset beta for the 40 largest BHCs.

We hypothesize that banks have more reporting discretion when the banking industry is troubled. That implies that the amounts of charge-offs and provisions would be a function of the

Figure 6. Weighted Average Equity Capital Ratio and Weighted Standard Deviation of Equity Betas for Large U.S. Banks
Annual, 1976–2001

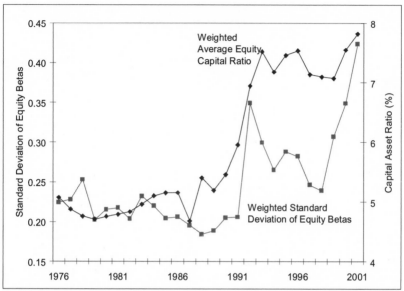

Source: Federal Reserve Bank of Chicago (2003) and Center for Research in Security Prices (2003).

bank's own conditions regardless of industry conditions. It also implies that the impact of industry conditions would rise as the condition of the banking industry deteriorated.

We tested our hypotheses with variations of equation (1) for Japanese and U.S. banks, for different time periods, and for sample periods of varying length:

$$y_t^i = \sum_{j=1}^{2} \alpha_j \cdot y_{t-j}^i + \sum_{k} \sum_{j=0}^{2} \beta_{jk} \cdot x_{t-j}^k + \sum_{j=0}^{2} \gamma_j \cdot OK_{t-j} \qquad (1)$$

We use two measures of y_t^i: loan loss provisions and charge-offs. We scale provisions by risk-weighted assets for Japanese banks and by gross loans for U.S. banks. We scale charge-offs by risk-weighted assets for Japanese banks and by gross loans for U.S. banks.

To allow for lags, we included y_t^i lagged by one year and lagged by two years as independent variables. The x_{t-j}^k variables control for various conditions at each bank. For each, we included two annual lagged terms, as well as the contemporaneous term.[2] As control variables we include operating income, nonaccrual loans, allow-

---

2. For allowances for loan losses and total equity capital, we included only the two lagged variables and not the unlagged variable.

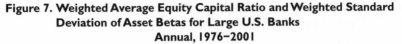

Figure 7. Weighted Average Equity Capital Ratio and Weighted Standard Deviation of Asset Betas for Large U.S. Banks
Annual, 1976–2001

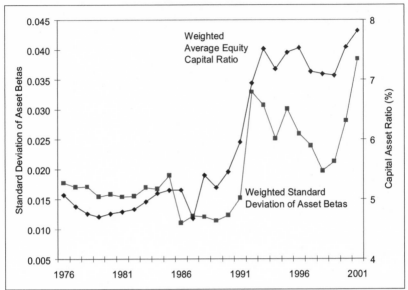

Source: Federal Reserve Bank of Chicago (2003) and Center for Research in Security Prices (2003).

ance for loan losses, and bank capital. For Japanese banks, we scale operating income by risk-weighted assets. For U.S. banks, we define operating income as earnings before income tax and provisions, and scale by total assets. We scale nonaccrual loans by gross loans. We scale the allowance for loan losses by gross loans. For Japanese banks, we use (Basel) total capital and scale it by risk-weighted assets. Total capital includes subordinated debt and the allowance for loan losses. For U.S. banks, we use total equity capital and scale by total (unweighted) assets.

We also included the variable "Other banks—Capital to Assets Ratio" (OK_{t-j}) and its two annual lags. For each bank in each year, we calculate the values for this variable as the average of the capital to assets ratio across all other banks in the sample for that year (29 in the case of the U.S. data). Within any given year, the variation in this variable is minimal across banks. However, this variable captures the evolution of reported capital ratios for the banking industry across time.

Absent reporting discretion, once we control for a bank's own condition (capital, etc.), reported charge-offs and provisions would not rise with the average capital ratio at other banks. Absent reporting discretion, charge-offs and provisions might be negatively related to other banks' capital ratios: Troubles in other banks that are reflected in reduced capital ratios might be correlated with factors that would raise charge-offs and provisions for a bank. Obtaining positive coefficients on the variable that measures reported capital at other banks then can be taken as support for the hypothesis that banks exercise more reporting discretion when other banks are in more trouble.

IV. RESULTS

Tables 1 through 6 provide results for regressions of bank charge-offs and provisions for loan losses in Japan and in the U.S. Tables 1 and 2 provide the results for truncated versions of equation (1) for 9 large Japanese banks in 1999. Tables 3 and 4 provide the results for similar regressions for the 30 largest U.S. banks in each year for various sample periods from 1977 through 2001. Tables 5 and 6 provide the results of regressions that include larger numbers of control variables for the 30 largest U.S. banks in each year for sample periods from 1985 through 2001.

The regressions reported in Tables 1 and 2 use as explanatory variables only a (Japanese) bank's operating income (divided by risk-weighted assets) and a bank's own total capital ratio. We do not find either charge-offs or provisions to be significantly affected by operating income. However, we do find that bank capital ratios significantly and positively affect reported charge-offs and provisions. This is consistent with banks' acknowledging more bad loans, not just when loans "sour" but when their own reported capital ratios are high enough to withstand sour loans.

Table 1. Relation of Charge-Offs to Operating Income and Capital
Dependent Variable: Charge-offs/Risk-Weighted Assets
Large Japanese Banks, 1999

		(1)
1.	Constant	−0.05*
		(2.29)
2.	Operating income/risk-weighted assets	0.13
		(0.19)
3.	Total capital ratio	0.60**
		(3.19)
	Number of observations	9
	R-squared	0.63
	F-statistic	5.10

Absolute value of t-statistics in parentheses.
** denotes significance at the 1 percent level.
* denotes significance at the 5 percent level.

Table 2. Relation of Loan Loss Provisions to Operating Income and Capital
Dependent Variable: Loan Loss Provisions/
Risk-Weighted Assets
Large Japanese Banks, 1999

		(1)
1.	Constant	−0.01
		(0.85)
2.	Operating income/risk-weighted assets	−0.21
		(0.63)
3.	Total capital ratio	0.23*
		(2.47)
	Number of observations	9
	R-squared	0.54
	F-statistic	3.48

Absolute value of t-statistics in parentheses.
** denotes significance at the 1 percent level.
* denotes significance at the 5 percent level.

Using specifications similar to those in Tables 1 and 2, Tables 3 and 4 provide results based on data for 30 large U.S. banks in each year during 1977–2001 and for three smaller subsamples (1978–1983, 1986–1991, and 1994–1999). Each of these three subsamples is associated with distinct conditions for the U.S. banking system, generally. The 1978–1983 period includes high inflation, high unemployment, a double-dip recession, but relatively few bank loan charge-offs. The 1986–1991 subsample also includes a recession but is distinguished by its severe banking crisis and historically high charge-offs. The 1994–1999 subsample includes a long and vigorous economic expansion, low inflation, and low charge-offs.

The dependent variables in Tables 3 and 4 are charge-offs and provisions. Each is scaled by gross loans (as opposed to risk-weighted assets). We scale the independent variables by total assets. Also, we include the capital to assets ratio for the other 29 banks, lagged one year, instead of the capital ratio for each bank, which we use in Tables 1 and 2. Looking across the columns of Tables 3 and 4, we see that the relations of reported charge-offs and provisions to earnings and capital vary across the subsamples. In particular, the larger coefficients in the earlier, more troubled period for banking supports the hypothesis that reporting discretion varies inversely with the overall condition of banking.[3] A larger positive relation between reported charge-offs and provisions and earnings is consistent with lower earnings "allowing" banks to acknowledge fewer of its bad loans by reporting fewer charge-offs and provisions. Concomitantly, when their earnings are higher, banks may reduce any accumulated backlog of under-reported charge-offs or provisions.

---

3. The results for charge-offs and provisions for loan losses are broadly similar across Tables 3 and 4. Thus, we do not discuss them separately and refer to both as "reported bad loans."

Table 3. Relation of Charge-Offs to Earnings and Other Banks' Capital
Dependent Variable: Charge-offs/Gross Loans
30 Largest U.S. Banks Each Year, Annual, 1977–2001

		1978–1983	1986–1991	1994–1999	1977–2001
		(1)	(2)	(3)	(4)
1.	Constant	−0.02	−0.02	0.00	0.01**
		(1.31)	(1.34)	(0.80)	(2.82)
2.	Earnings before income tax and provision /assets	1.29**	0.41	0.27**	0.67**
		(5.60)	(1.73)	(3.49)	(10.43)
3.	Other 29 banks' average equity capital/ assets, lagged 1 year	0.29	0.55*	−0.00	−0.07*
		(0.91)	(2.09)	(0.02)	(2.52)
	Number of observations	180	180	180	750
	Number of banks	35	56	69	106
	R-squared	0.18	0.07	0.10	0.15
	F-statistic	16.04**	4.27*	6.16**	54.50**

Absolute value of t-statistics in parentheses.
** denotes significance at the 1 percent level.
* denotes significance at the 5 percent level.

Table 4. Relation of Loan Loss Provisions to Earnings and Other Banks' Capital
Dependent Variable: Loan Loss Provisions/Gross Loans
30 Largest U.S. Banks Each Year, Annual, 1977–2001

		1978–1983	1986–1991	1994–1999	1977–2001
		(1)	(2)	(3)	(4)
1.	Constant	−0.03	−0.09**	−0.00	0.01*
		(1.33)	(4.53)	(0.45)	(2.31)
2.	Earnings before income tax and provision /assets	1.71**	0.75*	0.52**	0.93**
		(5.37)	(2.13)	(5.97)	(10.49)
3.	Other 29 banks' average equity capital/ assets, lagged 1 year	0.39	1.91**	−0.00	−0.15**
		(0.87)	(4.86)	(0.01)	(4.06)
	Number of observations	180	180	180	750
	Number of banks	35	56	69	106
	R-squared	0.17	0.21	0.25	0.15
	F-statistic	14.77**	15.79**	18.04**	56.91**

Absolute value of t-statistics in parentheses.
** denotes significance at the 1 percent level.
* denotes significance at the 5 percent level.

The signs and significance of the coefficients on capital at other banks are not as stable across subsample periods as those for earnings. The estimated effects of other banks' capital were insignificant when industry-wide charge-offs were low (1978–1983 and 1994–1999). In contrast, during the 1986–1991 period, charge-offs and provisions were lower when other banks had lower capital ratios, which is consistent with our reporting discretion hypothesis.

Tables 5 and 6 provide the results of regressing the same dependent variables on more control variables for the 30 largest U.S. banks in each year during 1985–2001 and for two smaller subsamples (1986–1991 and 1994–1999). The regressions in Tables 5 and 6 cover a shorter time period (1985–2001) than the regressions in Tables 3 and 4 (1977–2001) because of data limitations. We allowed for, but do not report in Tables 5 and 6, individual bank-fixed effects.

Table 5. Relation of Charge-Offs to Banks' Own Conditions and Other Banks' Capital
  Dependent Variable: Charge-offs/Gross Loans
  30 Largest U.S. Banks Each Year, Annual, 1985–2001

		1986–1991	1994–1999	1985–2001
		(1)	(2)	(3)
1.	Constant	−0.06*	0.00	0.00
		(2.00)	(0.35)	(1.58)
2.	Charge-offs/gross loans, lagged 1 year	0.05	0.00	0.21**
		(0.52)	(0.02)	(4.58)
3.	Charge-offs/gross loans, lagged 2 years	−0.27**	0.00	−0.18**
		(2.85)	(0.00)	(4.08)
4.	Earnings before income tax and provision/ assets	0.00	0.42**	0.32**
		(0.00)	(6.24)	(5.19)
5.	Earnings before income tax and provision/ assets, lagged 1 year	−0.16	−0.14	−0.06
		(0.71)	(1.51)	(0.82)
6.	Earnings before income tax and provision/ assets, lagged 2 years	0.18	−0.20**	−0.09
		(1.02)	(3.06)	(1.69)
7.	Nonaccrual loans/gross loans	0.13**	0.43**	0.13**
		(2.68)	(5.83)	(5.44)
8.	Nonaccrual loans/gross loans, lagged 1 year	0.12	0.00	0.07
		(1.67)	(0.02)	(1.95)
9.	Nonaccrual loans/gross loans, lagged 2 years	0.07	0.05	−0.03
		(1.05)	(0.86)	(1.11)

Table 5. Relation of Charge-Offs to Banks' Own Conditions and Other Banks' Capital (*cont.*)
Dependent Variable: Charge-offs/Gross Loans
30 Largest U.S. Banks Each Year, Annual, 1985–2001

	1986–1991	1994–1999	1985–2001
	(1)	(2)	(3)
10. Allowance for loan and lease losses/gross loans, lagged 1 year	0.19*	0.21**	0.15**
	(2.54)	(2.76)	(4.12)
11. Allowance for loan and lease losses/gross loans, lagged 2 years	0.00	−0.22**	0.09*
	(0.05)	(3.35)	(2.38)
12. Equity capital/assets, lagged 1 year	−0.05	−0.02	−0.05
	(0.42)	(0.63)	(1.74)
13. Equity capital/assets, lagged 2 years	−0.23	0.01	0.01
	(1.78)	(0.31)	(0.42)
14. Other 29 banks' average equity capital/assets	0.55*	0.06	0.03
	(2.62)	(0.91)	(0.57)
15. Other 29 banks' average equity capital/assets, lagged 1 year	0.83**	−0.01	0.05
	(2.81)	(0.19)	(0.91)
16. Other 29 banks' average equity capital/assets, lagged 2 years	0.12	−0.03	−0.11
	(0.36)	(0.24)	(1.88)
Number of observations	178	179	504
Number of banks	55	69	101
R-squared	0.63	0.53	0.59
F-statistic	12.13**	7.12**	37.98**

Absolute value of t-statistics in parentheses.
** denotes significance at the 1 percent level.
* denotes significance at the 5 percent level.

Table 6. Relation of Loan Loss Provisions to Banks' Own Conditions and Other Banks' Capital
Dependent Variable: Loan Loss Provisions/Gross Loans
30 Largest U.S. Banks Each Year, Annual, 1985–2001

	1986–1991	1994–1999	1985–2001
	(1)	(2)	(3)
1. Constant	0.08	0.02*	0.01
	(1.66)	(2.06)	(1.29)
2. Loan loss provisions/gross loans, lagged 1 year	−0.10	0.59**	−0.12
	(0.47)	(4.71)	(1.62)

Table 6. Relation of Loan Loss Provisions to Banks' Own Conditions and Other Banks' Capital (*cont.*)
Dependent Variable: Loan Loss Provisions/Gross Loans
30 Largest U.S. Banks Each Year, Annual, 1985–2001

		1986–1991	1994–1999	1985–2001
		(1)	(2)	(3)
3.	Loan loss provisions/gross loans, lagged 2 years	−0.12	0.01	0.09
		(0.83)	(0.12)	(1.71)
4.	Earnings before income tax and provision/assets	0.53	0.42**	0.56**
		(1.79)	(5.72)	(5.67)
5.	Earnings before income tax and provision/assets, lagged 1 year	0.36	−0.29**	0.17
		(0.97)	(2.77)	(1.47)
6.	Earnings before income tax and provision/assets, lagged 2 years	−0.02	0.11	0.09
		(0.07)	(1.37)	(1.01)
7.	Nonaccrual loans/gross loans	0.53**	0.20*	0.51**
		(6.62)	(2.53)	(12.63)
8.	Nonaccrual loans/gross loans, lagged 1 year	0.24	−0.13	−0.110
		(1.95)	(1.36)	(1.86)
9.	Nonaccrual loans/gross loans, lagged 2 years	0.06	0.07	0.00
		(0.50)	(1.22)	(0.09)
10.	Allowance for loan and lease losses/gross loans, lagged 1 year	−0.45*	−0.18*	−0.18*
		(2.27)	(2.14)	(2.13)
11.	Allowance for loan and lease losses/gross loans, lagged 2 years	0.15	−0.18*	−0.05
		(0.81)	(2.33)	(0.65)
12.	Equity capital/assets, lagged 1 year	0.23	−0.01	−0.04
		(1.08)	(0.21)	(0.81)
13.	Equity capital/assets, lagged 2 years	0.23	0.02	0.02
		(1.10)	(0.57)	(0.43)
14.	Other 29 banks' average equity capital/assets	−1.29**	0.01	−0.30**
		(3.86)	(0.21)	(3.29)
15.	Other 29 banks' average equity capital/assets, lagged 1 year	−0.06	−0.16*	0.28**
		(0.14)	(2.23)	(3.01)
16.	Other 29 banks' average equity capital/assets, lagged 2 years	−0.88	−0.14	−0.11
		(1.58)	(1.15)	(1.10)
	Number of observations	178	179	504
	Number of banks	55	69	101
	R-squared	0.62	0.62	0.53
	F-statistic	11.66**	10.49**	28.92**

Absolute value of t-statistics in parentheses.
** denotes significance at the 1 percent level.
* denotes significance at the 5 percent level.

Tables 5 and 6 validate the earlier results. The (sums across rows within columns of the) estimated coefficients on the earnings variable are generally positive in each column of Tables 5 and 6. Similar to the results in Tables 3 and 4, the earnings coefficients are least significant during 1986–1991 and are less significant in the regression for charge-offs and more significant in the regression for provisions. The estimated coefficients on other banks' capital also generally follow the results for charge-offs in Tables 3 and 4. They do, however, less clearly validate the results for provisions. Mirroring the results in Tables 3 and 4, the estimated effects of other banks' capital (and its one-year lag) on charge-offs are both positive and significant during 1986–1991, but are insignificant during 1994–1999.

In contrast, the estimated effects of other banks' capital (summed over all lags) on provisions conflicted with the results shown in Tables 3 and 4. The signs and significance of coefficients on other banks' capital do not fit the pattern across time periods that is consistent with either reporting discretion or its absence. Visual examination of average charge-offs and provisions during 1986–1991 reveals that provisions are far more volatile during that period (and charge-offs far smoother) than during other periods. One possibility is that, during this period, bank supervisors exogenously imposed a more stringent set of standards for reporting charge-offs and provisions.

The remaining results in Tables 5 and 6 are mixed. Some do not have ready interpretations; some follow the predictions of economic theory; and some are just plain insignificant. For example, the estimated coefficients on nonaccruals and allowances comport with theory. The coefficients for nonaccruals are consistently positive and significant in both Tables 5 and 6. More nonaccruals later lead to more provisions and more charge-offs. The estimated coefficients on loan loss allowances (lagged one-year) in the charge-off equations are consistently positive and significant, indicating that larger stocks of loss reserves imply that banks later will take larger charge-offs but can make smaller provisions.

The lagged own-capital coefficients are generally not statistically significant. On the other hand, Table 5 shows that banks tended to record higher charge-offs, ceteris paribus, when other banks had more capital. During the troubled 1986–1991 period, then, individual banks tended to report fewer charge-offs as the capital ratio of their peer banks fell. During the less troubled period that followed, 1994–1999, individual banks showed no such tendency to reduce reported charge-offs as a function of the condition of peer banks.

V. SUMMARY AND IMPLICATIONS

Banks typically come under capital pressure either because large loan losses reduce their capital or because changes in rules and regulations raise the amounts of capital that they are required to hold. In turn, capital pressures can lead to reductions in banks' supply of loans. The Basel Accord may be revised in such a way that required capital promptly rises as expected loan losses rise, for example, during recessions. In that case, bank lending might become more pro-cyclical than when required capital responds less to current conditions. To reduce the pro-cyclicality of a revised Basel Accord, some argue for including "escape clauses." Such clauses might, for example, require bank capital to rise during expansions but perhaps allow it to fall during downturns.

In a similar way, discretion in banks' reporting of charge-offs and provisions may reduce the pro-cyclicality that some have warned about and might have countercyclical effects on the macroeconomy. Banks may be permitted to exercise more discretion in their reporting of charge-offs and provisions when the banking system is generally troubled than when problems are isolated in a few banks. Such discretion may encourage clustering by banks because of "safety in similarity."

Reforms in the U.S. such as the prompt corrective action (PCA) clauses of FDICIA seek to minimize future banking and deposit insurer crises and losses. PCA generally insists that restrictions on troubled banks become increasingly severe as the bank's capital declines below various trigger ratios. In part, PCA is designed to reduce both the need and opportunities for regulatory forbearance. However, PCA and similar triggered policies might be undermined by reporting discretion that allows banks to avoid PCA being triggered. The hypothesis of reporting discretion posits that underreporting of problems will occur when banks and their supervisors find it preferable to keep reported capital ratios above some target.

To test our hypotheses, we analyzed measures of bank similarity and loan provisions and charge-offs both for Japanese and U.S. banks. We found evidence of reporting discretion both for the U.S.

in the late 1980s and for Japan in 1999. Thus, the evidence suggests reporting discretion did take place during troubled, pre-FDICIA years. We also find that, during troubled times, banks tend to cluster more.

We found little evidence of reporting discretion in U.S. banks by the late 1990s. That does not mean that reporting discretion will not emerge during future banking crises. Since FDICIA was enacted, banking has been quite profitable and capital ratios rose to their highest levels in more than a generation.

Because of the macroeconomic repercussions of banking difficulties, it may, after all, be socially optimal that reporting discretion of the sort discussed here does emerge. If so, it may also be preferable that it be practiced consciously and consistently so that the policies of both private-sector banks and public-sector policy makers can better coordinate general policies and specific responses. Acknowledging and measuring the magnitudes of reporting discretion in the past is a first step toward more coherent policies in both sectors.

REFERENCES

Ahmed, Anwer S., Carolyn Takeda and Shawn Thomas. "Bank Loan Loss Provisions: a Reexamination of Capital Management, Earnings Management and Signaling Effects." *Journal of Accounting and Economics 28* (1999) pp. 1–25.

Bernanke, Ben and Cara S. Lown. "The Credit Crunch." *Brookings Papers on Economic Activity* (1991, No. 2) pp. 205–239.

Bliss, Robert, George Kaufman and John Smith. "Explaining Bank Credit Crunches and Procyclicality." The Federal Reserve Bank of Chicago. *Chicago Fed Letter* 179 (July, 2002).

Hayakawa, Yoshihisa. "Crisis and Regulation: the Japanese Case." In *Financial Regulation: A Guide to Structural Reform.* Edited by Douglas Arner and Jan-juy Lin. Sweet & Maxwell Asia, Hong Kong (2003) pp. 241–256.

Ibison, David. "Merging Two Bad Banks Doesn't Create a Good One." *Financial Times.* London (September 30, 2002) P. V.

Ioannidou, Vasso P. "Does Monetary Policy Affect the Central Bank's Role in Bank Supervision?" Tilburg University, Center for Economic Research. *Discussion Paper Series number 54* (2002).

Kane, Edward J. "Dangers of Capital Forbearance: the Case of the FSLIC and Zombie S&Ls." *Contemporary Policy Issues 5* (1987) pp. 77–83.

Kane, Edward J. *The S&L Insurance Mess: How Did it Happen?* Urban Institute Press, Washington, D.C. (1989).

Merrill Lynch. "Japanese Banks: FY3/02 Results for Major Banks." Merrill Lynch Global Securities Research and Economics Group (June 5, 2002).

Morgan Stanley Dean Witter. "Japanese Banks, to Reorganize or Nationalize? A Question of Survival." *Japan Investment Research* (July, 1999).

Pilling, David. "Japan Bank's Bad Loans Warnings Fall on Deaf Ears." *Financial Times* (September 25, 2002) p. 4.

Van de Heuvel, Skander J. "Does Bank Capital Matter for Monetary Policy?" *Federal Reserve Bank of New York, Economic Policy Review* (May, 2002) pp. 259–265.

10

The Inadequacy of Capital Adequacy Policies for Financial Institution Regulation

Benton E. Gup

WHAT IS CAPITAL?

Disagreement over what constitutes capital leads to confusion over capital adequacy. The accountant views capital as book valued assets minus liabilities with some adjustments for off-balance-sheet transactions. The stock holder views capital as current stock prices multiplied by shares outstanding, the latest valuation of the firm by those trading. The regulatory analyst, concerned with insolvency and resolution costs, views capital as "market adjusted" assets minus liabilities. The lawyer sees capital adequacy as a lower limit, which merits discretionary or mandatory regulator actions if violated. The legislator sees capital as a way to achieve safety and soundness in the financial sector. The economist views capital as a present value of a discounted earnings stream. These different views will seldom, if ever, produce identical measures of capital. Although some overlap may sporadically occur, each view results in a very different "measure" of capital. Different measures of capital, however, produce different measures of capital adequacy. So although no accountant, stockholder, regulatory analyst, lawyer, legislator, or economist would oppose a regulated institution having "adequate capital," the words mean different things to different people.

With trillions of dollars at stake in regulated financial institutions worldwide, debates continue as to what should be counted or not counted as capital, whether assets should be "marked to market," evaluated on a "fair value basis," or simply kept in book value form. The measurement of capital remains a heated and controversial issue.

With such disagreements about the nature of capital, it is somewhat surprising that capital adequacy has become such an important part of financial regulatory policy. Regulators appear to embrace capital as THE prominent regulatory tool, attracted by what it is intended to represent, a measure of solvency, its conceptual simplicity, and practical implementation. If last quarter's "measured capital" exceeds a predetermined regulatory limit, then the regulator pronounces the firm "adequately capitalized."

All things held equal, competitive financial firms seek to maximize their net worth over time, factoring risks and various constraints into consideration. This maximization results in a messy stochastic optimal control problem, because the future is unknown, and networth is not so much measured but estimated. Firms adjust portfolios to choose expected returns and variances that reflect their risk management capabilities and risk appetites. Financial institutions have become well acquainted with this problem. Unfortunately legislators and regulators have been slow to accept the fact that economic capital or networth is not directly observed in quarterly income and balance-sheet statements, and further refinement of accounting concepts will not address this problem.

The financial literature tells us that when economic net worth is positive, an institution is solvent. But is this really so? When economic net worth is negative, an institution is supposedly insolvent, but finance also tells us that solvency depends on the future, an unknown future, a future with many possible states. Regulators understandably want to know whether a regulated institution is solvent or insolvent today based on normal business conditions, but they also want to know whether the institution can survive a period of economic stress. Can a firm be solvent today if the future is characterized as business-as-usual conditions and "insolvent" today if the future holds a period of economic stress? Suppose both future states are equally likely?

Although regulators are not happy to admit it, they still cannot distinguish precisely between liquidity and insolvency. They cannot determine precisely when many of the failed U.S. banks and thrifts actually became insolvent even years after their resolutions!

While regulators, legislators, accountants, creditors, stockholders and others legitimately desire the comfort of balance sheets, accounting conventions, and an ability to directly measure capital, capital remains a fuzzy target and capital adequacy an elusive measure.

Capital by its nature is a conditional random variable.[1] The net worth of an institution today remains only an estimate dependent upon the future. To say an institution today is worth $30 billion without including some estimate of the possible dispersion about the $30 billion is to provide a less than complete answer. Perhaps it is worth $30 billion plus or minus a standard error of $5 billion. Assuming a normal probability distribution the probability that the firm is worth between $25 billion and $35 billion is 69 percent, and the probability that it is insolvent is greater than zero!

Regulators would naturally like to state with reasonable certainty that an institution is adequately or inadequately capitalized. Firms and industry analysts would like to do the same. However, it is impossible to do this unless we consider the extent of our uncertainty. Clearly the probability that capital may be adequate depends upon whether the standard error of capital is $5 billion, $10 billion, or more. Obtaining unbiased, efficient, and consistent estimators of existing and future capital, and its conditional standard errors, is challenging and unfortunately, largely ignored.

The current regulatory focus takes us far afield from what capital is supposed to be. Regulators have approached capital principally from an accounting and legal perspective. Using a

---

1. A random variable is an economic or statistical variable that takes on multiple (or a continuum of) values, each with some probability that is specified by a probability distribution. A probability distribution is a specification of the probabilities for each possible value of a variable. In this paper, it is assumed that capital (net worth) has a probability distribution conditional upon each future state of the world. It follows that any assessment of solvency must be stochastic. For example, given business-as-usual conditions, a firm has a 1 percent chance of being insolvent. Under more deleterious conditions, a firm might have a 25 percent chance of being insolvent. If the probability distribution is normal, only two parameters (mean and standard error of networth) may be necessary to estimate the probability of insolvency, the probability that capital may slip below a regulatory standard, or the Enterprise Wide Risk. Economic theory suggests that a firm will choose a portfolio of investments that affects both the mean and standard error of its current and future net worth.

bottom-up approach that mimics firm, level decisions, regulators continue to produce cumbersome regulatory models that frequently ignore the uncertainties associated with estimating conditional net worth and its conditional probability distributions. One exception to this is the structured internal models approach, but this has yet to be fully implemented. Capital adequacy, conceptually a function of potential future losses, has become but a crude extension of last quarter's spreadsheet measures. As a result, capital becomes an easily gamed and ineffective buffer.

Fortunately, the existing inadequacies of capital adequacy models have generated much discussion and some promising alternatives. These alternatives have a common element; they treat capital as a conditional random variable, and they look to the future. Before these new approaches become accepted, however, they must be validated. They must complement current examination processes and on-site supervision. Examiners, in turn, must become more conversant with statistical inference and risk management. Alternatives must be accessible and easy to use. They must be sufficiently flexible to be adjusted when necessary. They must use available information efficiently. Most importantly, the new alternatives will require change, a change in the regulatory culture and the infusion of statistics, finance, and economics into the existing accounting and legal capital standards.

Future capital standards will go beyond off-site regulatory models to incorporate the regulated entity's own projections and confidence intervals, the firm's own precommitments, and capital market information. Future regulators will synthesize such estimates before setting "capital standards." Ultimately, this process will incorporate underwriting, off-balance-sheet valuations, risk pricing, and regulatory perceptions of risk management.

What forces will bring such changes?

Insightful comments and discussions regarding capital standards from academics, private banks, and central banks may evoke changes. Frustrations that existing capitalization standards distort risk taking may induce legislative and regulatory changes, but these phenomena will more likely lag a large institution failure. After pronouncing that certain financial institutions are adequately capitalized, regulators will be forced to admit that existing standards simply didn't work when the institutions fails.

Is this an unnecessarily pessimistic view? I think not. Large financial institution failures have become more frequent, and there is little reason to suspect that similar events will no longer occur. But won't capital standards protect against such failures? Recall that small- and medium-sized banks and thrifts had to be resolved only months after sporting capital/asset ratios that exceeded 15 percent during the 1980s. By all appearances such institutions appeared "adequately capitalized." Future regulators will undoubtedly hesitate to resolve larger institutions as they have done in the past but not before existing capital adequacy measures of such institutions prove inadequate.

The term "capital adequacy" became so pervasive in both legislative and regulatory parlance, over the last three decades, that the casual industry observer might assume that capital as a concept and a measure is well understood. This is not the case. "Capital" and "Capital adequacy" have been moving targets that elude easy definition and measurement. From a regulatory perspective, setting of minimal capital standards and enforcement of capital rules have become second nature and therein lay the danger. Amid such widespread acceptance, it is easy to forget that such regulatory tools have had a comparatively short-lived and relatively unsuccessful history.

Elected officials empower regulators to determine whether the capital held by a regulated entity is adequate. They ask, "Does today's capital provide a sufficient buffer for unanticipated future losses?" They hope to hear, "Yes, the institution is adequately capitalized." They desire a simple and to the point answer. The regulator checks the box and is done with it.

Unfortunately, the question is much more complicated than it appears, and the answer depends to a very great extent upon whether capital today and capital in the future is correctly defined and measured.[2]

In 2001, the Basel Committee on Banking Supervision, (Bank of International Settlements [BIS]) issued its Consultative Document, The New Basel Accord, or Basel II, in which it declared "minimum capital standards" to be its "First Pillar" of regulation (Pillars 2 and

---

2. Calem, P. S. and Rob, R. (1996), Calem and Rob (1996) design a dynamic (discrete time) model of portfolio choice and analyze the impact of capital-based premia under the perfect audit hypothesis. They show that regulation may be counterproductive; a tightening in capital requirement may lead to an increase in the risk of the portfolios chosen by banks, and similarly, capital-based premia may sometimes induce excessive risk taking by banks.

3 deal with bank supervision and market discipline, respectively).[3] The BIS use of the word "pillar" suggests a sound foundation upon which a fair regulatory structure may evolve. As a principle, but not necessarily a practice, capital is the net worth of an institution and, as such, appears to provide a good basis for assessing its financial health.

Unfortunately, financial regulation uses the concept of net worth to justify its preoccupation with capital but fails to address the fact that the true net worth of any regulated firms is unobservable. Using proxies like book value historical capital, "mark to market" capital, and risk-weighted assets minus liabilities, presents a lingering estimation problem that distorts all comfort that capital adequacy measures should afford. This paper explores several alternatives to the standard definitions for capital adequacy and its estimation. It suggests that continued reliance upon current standards and rules may be perilous.[4]

Four sections follow. The first provides a broad historical perspective that blends a literature review and synthesis of historical regulatory experiences in different financial industries. The second introduces the concept of capital as a conditional random variable. The third discusses alternative procedures recently suggested as alternatives to current capital adequacy approaches. The fourth section concludes.

I. HISTORICAL PERSPECTIVE: CAPITAL ADEQUACY

The Beginnings

The Federal Reserve Act of 1913 was the first U.S. law to establish minimal capital requirements for financial institutions, but technically, Congress did not require nor direct the Federal Reserve to

---

3. Basel Committee (1999 and 2001).
4. See J. C. Santos (2000) for an extensive literature review on capital adequacy. For additional literature review see C. Karacadag and M. Taylor (2000); L. Allen and A. Saunders (2002); A. Saunders (2000). For alternative approaches to capital adequacy see P. Kupiec and J. O'Brien (1997); C. Taylor (2002). For discussions of capital adequacy and estimation see P. Swamy, T. Lutton, and P. Bartholomew (2001). They provide a rigorous way to estimate capital as a conditional random variable that complements the precommitment approach. For other alternatives to traditional estimates of capital adequacy see J. Stein, S. Usher, D. La Gattuata, and J. Yourn (2001). This procedure is now being implemented by the National Economic Research Associates (2002) and by major financial institutions using proprietary models.

enforce strict capital levels at existing institutions. The "adequacy of capital structure" appears as a phrase in the Banking Act of 1933 and subsequent revisions in 1935 and 1936. This law required regulators to consider capital adequacy as an essential part of regulation but refrained from defining capital adequacy, preferring to leave it in the hands of the regulators. The first risk-based capital standards emerged during the 1950s and 1960s in the Federal Reserve System. Called the "Form for Analyzing Bank Capital," the Federal Reserve introduced the concept of the ABC form, a way to factor probability of loss into the assessment of bank assets and liabilities.[5] Never formally implemented in bank holding companies, the concept remained alive and resurfaced in the late 1980s as risk-based capital.

Securities and Exchange Commission: Early Attempts at "Marking to Market"

In 1975, the Securities and Exchange Commission issued rule 15C 3-1 that required broker-dealers to calculate the market value for their net worth on a day-to-day basis. Perhaps the first such explicit capital adequacy rule, net worth/assets had to exceed 2 percent. In other words, if a broker-dealer had to liquidate all assets, "a capital cushion" of 2 percent should be sufficient to protect brokerage accounts and creditors. Starting with book value, capital broker dealers proceed to make a series of adjustments intended to "mark to market" all assets and liabilities.

The Bank of International Settlements

In the aftermath of serious disturbances in the financial markets during the early 1970s (notably the failure of Bankhaus Herstatt in West Germany), central bankers banded together at the Bank of International Settlements and undertook what was to become a three-decade study of capital adequacy. With the full and active support of the U.S. Federal Reserve, the BIS concluded that the best way to ensure financial stability was to promulgate international capital standards as a basis for measuring capital adequacy on a microprudential, bank-by-bank basis, reminiscent of the ABC

---

5. See George Morgan (1992).

form. Oddly, BIS placed little emphasis on macroprudential regulation, given their articulated concerns at the time for safeguarding the financial sector as a whole.[6] Many studies followed before capital adequacy was ready for implementation. Technically, the BIS did not act until 1988, when the Group of Ten Countries (G 10) Governors set forth Basel I, the first in an evolving set of capital adequacy rules that would require banks to maintain "risk-based" capital adequacy ratios of 8 percent.[7]

Between 1993 and 1999, the BIS heard numerous complaints and criticisms of its "one size fits all" capital adequacy measures from bankers, academics, and regulators. In June 1999, the Basel Committee initiated additional study of capital adequacy to address these problems. In January 2001, it published a more extensive Consultative Document, "The New Basel Capital Accord." "Capital Adequacy" retained the same conceptual basis as Basel I—capital standards had to be developed and enforced on a bank-by-bank basis, but Basel II expanded on the "one size fits all" methods required in Basel I.

Basel II urged regulators to consider capital models employed by regulated entities and not rely exclusively on off-site regulatory models. Basel II seemed to admit that such advanced internal ratings-based (IRB) approaches might better characterize, monitor, and measure capital than traditional off-site regulatory models or book value financial ratios for large complex models.[8] Basel II allows the large internationally-active banks to employ their own internal ratings models based on their own experience and assessment of the probability of default, loss given default, the correlation factor, and time to maturity. Notwithstanding, each bank is still expected to provide inputs of these in-house assessments to a prescribed model that the Basel Committee has constructed for its use.[9]

---

6. Borio (2003).

7. Basel I separated capital into two tiers.

Total Capital = Tier I Capital + Tier II Capital.

Tier I capital consisted of equity + disclosed reserves. Tier II = undisclosed reserves + revaluation reserves + general loan loss reserves + capital debt instruments + subordinated debt.

Basel I set the minimum value of the ratio of Total capital to risk-weighted assets to be 8% of which Tier I Capital had to be at least 4%. Basel I would ultimately be adopted by 100+ countries but not implemented until 1993.

8. The minimum capital standards under Basel II have become mired in the complexity of trying to integrate financial instruments, risks, and "fair value" accounting at the most basic business level. This complexity has begun to interfere with computational tractability and appears to be leading regulators in the wrong direction.

9. J. DeCamps, J. Rochet, B. Roger (2002).

U.S. Banks and Thrifts: 1981–1990

Prior to 1981, U.S. banking regulators did not enforce capital adequacy in any systematic fashion. Regulators did required minimum amounts of capital for obtaining bank charters but did not enforce fixed capital guidelines after the firm received its charter.[10] Technically, U.S. regulators only began enforcing explicit capital requirements, and even then, they only did so in a limited fashion after 1982.[11] Those capital levels imposed consisted of legislatively sanctioned accounting constructs that included "good will" and other intangibles. For the most part, these were simply book value leverage ratios, devoid of any risk or market value adjustments. In some sense, the ABC form reemerged in risk- based requirements regulators proposed during the Savings and Loan Crisis in 1986 and the Banking Crisis that had begun to emerge. Ultimately, regulators only began to enforce "risk-based" requirements in the form of "asset haircuts" in 1990, after much of the damage from the Savings and Loan Crisis and the Banking Crises had already occurred. U.S. bank and thrift regulators had to resolve roughly 2000 failed U.S. depository institutions during the period 1987–1992. By the late 1980s, U.S. regulators appeared overwhelmed and insurance funds were insufficient to deal with the numbers of problem institutions. Congress stepped into the fray in 1989 and again in 1991 to help regulators and replenish deposit insurance funds.[12] The prominent solution at the time seemed to be that thrifts and banks had to hold more capital.

---

10. H. Baer and J. McElravey (1992).

11. G. Gorton and A, Winton (1995).

12. Financial Institutions Reform, Recovery, and Enforcement Act of 1989 (FIRREA) and the Federal Deposit Insurance Corporation Improvement Act of 1991 (FDICIA). FIRREA recognized that the losses associated with the Savings and Loan failures were so severe that taxpayers would be required to make whole all insured deposits at failed thrifts. FDICIA required that banks and thrifts regulators impose similar capital requirements. Commercial banks faced two different capital requirements: a capital-asset (leverage ratio) and a risk-based capital ratio. FDICIA provided a 15 element matrix of capital criteria that included 5 categories of capitalization and 3 types of capital ratios. Regulators would declare a bank could be declared: well capitalized, adequately capitalized, undercapitalized, significantly undercapitalized, and critically undercapitalized based upon its last quarter's total capital to risk-based asset ratio, Tier I capital to risk-based asset ratio and Tier 1 Leverage ratios. See Saunders (2000) and Federal Reserve Board of Governors (2003).

Congress, Depository Institutions and Capital Adequacy: Post-1991

The U.S. Congress passed capital adequacy legislation in 1991 to provide regulatory capital standards that looked surprisingly like the Basel I standards. For example an "adequately capitalized bank" had to have total capital/risk-based assets above 8% and Tier I risk-based assets above 4% (similar to Basel I), but in addition had to have a Tier I to total assets ratio above 4%. The Federal Deposit Insurance Corporation Improvement Act of 1991 (FDICIA) imposed not just capital standards but mandated specific regulatory actions for violations. These directed regulators to restrict brokered deposits, suspend dividends and management fees, require a capital restoration plan, restrict asset growth, require approval for acquisitions and new activities, order recapitalization, suspend payment on subordinated debt, raise insurance premiums, and ultimately place an offending institution into receivership depending upon the severity of the capital violations.

By 1991, Congress legitimately began to fear that insolvencies may not be limited to thrifts and banks. It turned its attention to other financial institutions including government-sponsored enterprises (GSEs) and insurance companies.

Congress, GSEs and Capital Adequacy

In 1992, Congress passed legislation to set capital adequacy standards for Fannie Mae and Freddie Mac, nondepository GSEs. Compared to post-FDICIA banks and thrifts, these two GSEs held exceptionally low book value capital asset (leverage) ratios. By FDICIA standards, these two GSEs were undercapitalized, but Congress also recognized that the same capital standards might not be applicable to non-depository financial intermediaries.

Congress created a regulatory agency, The Office of Federal Housing Oversight (OFHEO), in 1992, to ensure that these enterprises were adequately capitalized using two standards: a minimum capital standard, roughly 2.5% of assets, and a risk-based capital standard, to be developed by OFHEO. OFHEO would finally develop a risk-based capital (RBC), stress-based capital adequacy standard by year-end 2002, while monitoring minimal capital ratios dictated by the 1992 Act. In early 2003, the Director of OFHEO declared Fannie Mae and Freddie Mac "adequately capitalized" because both institutions held sufficient book value capital to exceed minimum capital and risk-based capital standards.

Insurance and Capital Adequacy: 1990–Present

Similar developments concerning capital adequacy were taking place in the insurance industries. In 1993, the National Association of Insurance Commissioners proposed the NAIC life insurance model intended to reflect asset risk, insurance risk, interest rate risk, and business risk. The model produces Total Capital/Risk Based Capital ratios. If the insurance manager produces a ratio that exceeds one, the insurance firm is considered adequately capitalized. Again, a tangible measure of capital was to be compared to a standard to monitor capital adequacy.

A similar model was produced in 1994 for property and casualty insurers. It used slightly different risk weights that included two types of underwriting risks but, like the NAIC model, produced a simple ratio to determine capital adequacy—Total Capital/Risk-Based capital—and like the NAIC model, provided a simple indicator for capital adequacy monitoring.

Why Were Regulators Preoccupied with Capital Adequacy?

Throughout the period from the 1970s to 2002, capital adequacy remained the focus regulators concerned with safety and soundness. Why?

Saunders (2000) suggests why regulators did so. He lists four reasons why financial regulators developed, enforced, and emphasized capital standards and capital adequacy for regulated institutions.[13]

1. Capital absorbs unanticipated future losses.[14]
2. Capital "protects" uninsured creditors and liability holders in the event of insolvency and possible liquidation.
3. Capital protects federal and state insurance funds and taxpayers.
4. Capital allows a financial institution to acquire plant and other additional real investments necessary to provide a flow of services.

Regulators continue to view capital as the primary protection against insolvency, a shield against unanticipated future economic and financial stress.[15]

---

13. A. Saunders (2000).
14. K. Froot and J. Stein (1998). Froot and Stein discuss how capital may become a buffer but only if it is net worth.
15. A. Berger, R. Herring, and G. Szego (1995) discuss this phenomenon and the roles capital plays in financial institutions.

Regulators demand that each financial institution holds sufficient amounts of capital (today), risk-weighted or other, to decrease its likelihood of insolvency (future), and thereby maintain the safety and soundness of the financial sector and minimize systemic risk. The appeal of capital, so defined and measured, to both regulators and elected officials is consequently understandable. Unfortunately capital so defined and measured offers little hope of monitoring of capital adequacy and net worth in the context of an uncertain future.

Capital and Book Value Accounting

Every firm, even regulated financial institutions, that produces an income and balance sheet provides a measure of book value capital: For reasons that will become apparent later let us subscript capital with a time index, t. The book value capital at any period t may be expressed in its simplest form as:

$$C_t = A_t - Lt + OBS_t$$

where t is a time index (t=1,2,3, . . . T), C is the book value of capital, A is the book value of assets on balance sheet, L is the book value of liabilities and OBS is the net value of off-balance-sheet activities. The subscript "t" becomes very important and must be included.

The book value capital, Ct, consists of four well-understood components: the par value of shares,[16] the surplus value of shares,[17] retained earnings,[18] and loan loss reserves.[19]

The book value of capital is time dimensional and represents only a very crude form of the net worth of an institution. The book values of long term securities, mortgages, and loans reflect only the historic of these assets as independent entities—values when the loans were made and securities purchased. Book value capital includes nonperforming assets not written off as losses. Book value capital and its components change over time, but Ct, as it is

---

16. (face value of common stock shares multiplied by the shares outstanding)

17. (the difference between the price the public paid for common stock when initially offered and their par values times the number of shares outstanding)

18. (the accumulated value of past profits not paid out in dividends to shareholders)

19. (a special cash reserve set aside out of retained earnings to meet expected and actual losses on the portfolio)

observed, clearly refers only to historical values. It has no probability distribution. It is as it is reported, assuming no accounting improprieties and known with certainty.

Of course, book values may deviate substantially from true economic value or net worth of a firm, particularly during periods of interest rate and credit volatility, lax examinations and enforcement, and economic cycles. Deviations may also become notable to the extent that the future returns from such assets are jointly determined. Technically, book values have little bearing on risk, since risk has to do with the future and book values essentially have to do with history. Furlong and Keeley (1990), Kim and Santomero (1988), Koehn and Santomero (1980), Rochet (1992), Thakor (1996) have noted the distortion of banks' assets allocation that could be generated by the wedge between market assessment of asset risks and book valuation similar to Basel I.[20]

The Inadequacy of Book Capital to Provide a Buffer Against Future Losses

Taking a forward-looking perspective, it is easy to see why book value capital from last quarter has lacks the ability to buffer or cushion against future losses the farther into the future the regulator looks. If the market values of assets decrease relative to liabilities during a long stressful period, then book values from last quarter may substantially overstate market values today and give the impression that the institution holds more capital than it actually does. The savings and loan and banking crisis provide ample illustrations of how the book values of capital and market values may diverge in any period of time. Many of the failed institutions held book value leverage ratios that exceeded 15 percent only a year or two prior to resolution. By the time of resolution, such "book-valued assets" had so eroded in terms of market values that the market value of liabilities swamped the market value of assets resulting in enormous resolution costs.

Stock Prices and Capital

Because the stock of large financial institutions like major banks and government-sponsored enterprises are traded with some frequency, analysts have recognized that some "market valuation of

---

20. F. Furlong and N. Keeley (1990); D. Kim. and A. Santomero (1988); M. Koehn and A. Santomero (1980); J. Rochet (1992); J. Santos (2000); A.V. Thakor (1996).

traded assets and liabilities can be used to "adjust" potential distortions associated with book value capital, some analysts suggest a "marked to market" approach as a regulatory alternative—simply multiply the market value of shares outstanding by the number of shares. Theory suggests that the price of a stock in period t is a function of the expected dividend income stream it will produce.

$$P_t = (D_{t+1})/(1+k)+(D_{t+2})/(1+k)^2+(D_{t+3})/(1+k)^3+.....(D_{t+n})/(1+k)^n.$$

Where n=> infinity, D is expected dividends, and k is the discount rate or requires return on the stock. The "market value of the firm," MV, becomes a simple aggregation:

$MV_t = P_t*SO_t$, which may be greater, equal, or less than its capital C_t.

Financial analysts have long noted that the MV_t does not necessarily equal C_t.

A dramatic example of this discrepancy appears in market to book value ratios. Saunders and Wilson (1995) show that from 1913 to 1993 the MV/BV ratio for banks varies from .6 to 2.5, with the highest peak just prior to the Panic of 1929![21] Although seemingly heretical, the Market Value of a firm in period "t" may not have much to do with economic net worth!

Marked to Market vs. Book Value Capital

Unfortunately, not all assets held by a financial firm are traded frequently. Investors and traders do not necessarily view the future from the same perspective as a regulator. The regulator is more likely to consider the long term and more stressful environment than do traders and investors. The "market value" of assets less liabilities today, MV_t, should not necessarily be confused with true economic net worth.

The market prices on any given day only reflect what investors and traders who engage in transacting stocks might believe. Consequently "marked to market" measure introduces variability into the calculation of earnings and net worth that affects unrealized capital gains and losses of stockholders, but not enterprise earnings.

---

21. A. Saunders and B. Wilson (1995).

Critics of the "mark to market" approach warn that rates of return to the enterprises do not necessarily reflect the changes in stock prices, or rates of return to the stockholders and traders. Temporary interest rate spikes and headlines cause noticeable and dramatic volatility in traded stock prices that can overstate variability in enterprise earnings. The volatility of stock prices during 2001–2003 gives regulators serious concerns, particularly when actual earnings of the enterprises bear little relationship to stock price volatility. In addition, because market valuations tend to vary pro-cyclically, the net worth of institutions based on such measures would correspondingly rise and fall with the market and/or the economy as a whole. If regulators were to enforce such capital cycles, they could exacerbate the underlying economic cycles, asking firms to increase capital during recessions and reduce capital during expansions. As a result, regulators have been reluctant to rely solely on MV capital measures.[22]

2. ECONOMIC NET WORTH: CAPITAL AS A CONDITIONAL RANDOM VARIABLE

Let's start with the economic and finance definition of capital that would serve as a measure of capital adequacy if it were observable. Define capital in period t as economic net worth or net-worth capital (NWC_t.)

Distinguish NWC_t from C_t or MV_t

NWC_t is the difference between the market value of a firm's assets and liabilities adjusted for off-balance-sheet activities and the on-going value of the firm. It is a valuation of the worth of the entity as a whole if it were to be put on the market in period t. It is unobservable. Assume it possesses a probability distribution.

Regulators actually require two measures of NWC. They need estimates of NWC_{t0}, which is the net worth of capital today, and NWC_{t0+n}, the net worth of capital in the future. Such measures do not appear in the firm's balance sheet. However, conditional estimates may be constructed. Ideally, the estimators used to construct such estimates would have desirable statistical and forecasting properties. For example, the estimators would be unbiased, consistent, efficient, admissible, and coherent estimators of NWC.

---

22. Saunders (2000) includes a list of arguments that discuss why regulators historically have been opposed to against Market Value accounting, pp. 400–401.

Conditional Best Guesses at Net Worth

Call the conditional estimates of NWC at the two time periods in question: $E\ (NWC_{t0}|\theta)$ and $E\ (NWC_{t0\ +n}|\varphi)$.

$E\ (NWC_{t0}|\theta)$ is the best guess of the economic net worth of a firm today, period t0, based upon a firm's existing portfolio, current economic conditions, and assumptions θ.

$E\ (NWC_{t0+n}|\varphi)$ is the best guess of the economic net worth of a firm today, period t0, based upon how the firm may evolve its portfolio, future economic conditions, and assumptions θ. Note that φ might reflect different assumptions than θ. For example, φ might reflect an economic stress environment, optimistic or pessimistic scenarios, economic expansions or contractions, where as θ typically connotes "business as usual" or baseline assumptions.

Both estimates provide numerical values of the conditional expectations—best guesses of the true value of the firm. Best guesses, by definition, reflect the means of probability distributions, each of which has a 50% likelihood of occurring given assumptions.

Capital Adequacy and the Conditional Present

Assume that the manager of a firm believes NWC_{t0} is normally distributed. For the illustration, suppose the best guess of a firms net worth is $E\ (NWC_{t0}|\ \theta) = \$35$ billion, that is the manager is 50 percent sure that the true value is $35 billion. If the manager knows the variance of this distribution is $9 billion squared and the standard error is $3 billion, then we say:

$NWC_{t0} \sim N\ (\$35\ billion, \$9\ billion\ squared|\ \theta)$.

This becomes statistical shorthand that says that the manager is 68 percent sure that the true value of the firm lies between $32 billion and $38 billion, 16 percent sure that the value exceeds $32 billion, and believes that this firm has only a .5% chance of being insolvent. From where do such probability estimates come? They come from the probability distribution of net worth and embody the existing portfolio, risk appetite, market values of assets and liabilities, and the uncertainty that surrounds the best guess of net worth. From this distribution emerges a basic concern of the regulator. Is the institution insolvent?

The chance of insolvency may be expressed as:

$$\Pr\left((NWC_{t0}|\theta) < 0\right) = .005\%.$$

If the regulator imposes an upper limit on the probability of insolvency, say λ_{t0}, the manager could evaluate the capital adequacy of the firm in question: Let $\lambda_{t0} = .1\%$. By definition the manager of the firm in question would conclude that the firm is adequately capitalized today because

$$\Pr\left((NWC_{t0}|\theta) < 0\right) = .005\ \% < (.1\% = \lambda_{t0}).$$

If the manager and regulator agreed with this assessment of NWC, then both would concur that they are 99.9% certain that the firm today is solvent. This is basic to any assessment of capital adequacy. Is the firm solvent? In this case, the answer is most assuredly so. The regulator examines this probability using all the information in θ both on-site examination and supervision, and off-site assessments that monitor book, marked to market, and third party assessments of financial health. In principle, if not always in practice, these may be used to construct estimates of both $E\ (\sigma)$ and σ to assess the probability of insolvency. Even if the E (NWC) were to increase between t0-1 and t0, the $\Pr\left((NWC_{t0}|\theta) < 0\right.$ could increase relative to $\Pr\left((NWC_{t0-1}|\theta) < 0\right)$, in which case the regulator could surmise that an increase in risk of insolvency had occurred. Further investigation might reveal the cause.

Capital and the Conditional Future

The probability of insolvency today, however, is not sufficient to determine capital adequacy. The regulator requires some assurance that the firm may be able to handle unanticipated events or stresses during some specified future period. This requires the regulator to have some understanding of the probability distribution of future net worth, NWC_{t0+n}. By analogy to the conditional present, suppose that the regulator and firm agree that future capital, NWC, is normally distributed, specifically,

$$NWC_{t0+n.} \sim N\ (\$27\ \text{billion},\ \$100\ \text{billion squared}).$$

In this case, the firm, the regulator, the capital market analyst, the competitor, could potentially all make a best guess of the net worth of the firm in period t0+n.

$E\ (\text{NWC}_{\text{to+n}}|\varphi) = \$27$ billion

But the variance is greater, σ^2, is $100 billion squared and the standard error becomes

$\sigma = \$10$ billion.

The chance of insolvency may be expressed as:

$\Pr\ ((\text{NWC}_{\text{to+n}}|\varphi) < 0) = .3\%$.

It would not be reasonable to suppose that the conditional probability of insolvency today was less than the conditional probability of insolvency assigned under a stress test for some future period, say 10 years.

If the regulator imposes an upper limit on the probability of insolvency, say $\lambda_{\text{tt0+n}}$, $= 1\%$, the manager and regulator could evaluate the future capital adequacy of the firm in question.

$\Pr\ ((\text{NWC}_{\text{t0+n}}|\varphi) < 0) = .3\% < (1\% = \lambda_{\text{t0+n}})$.

In this case, both would concur that the firm today is adequately capitalized to handle stress with a fair degree of certainty conditional on φ. Of course, each period between t0 and t0+n reflects different distributions and assumptions. Moreover, these distributions will not be independent if the firm seeks to optimize an inter-temporal objective function that maximizes E $(\text{NWC}_{\text{t0+n}}|\varphi)$ subject to regulatory and σ constraints. The true income (losses) to the firm between period t0 and t0+1 for example will become

True Income (losses) $= \text{NWCt}_{\text{o+1}} - \text{NWC}_{\text{t0}}$.

Illustration of Capital Adequacy and Probability

With knowledge of the probability distributions associated with the economic net worth of a firm in period t0 and t0+n, capital adequacy becomes estimable and related to how probability varies with NWC. Let us view capital adequacy from the perspective of the future value net worth as shown in Chart 1.

Using a cumulative distribution function in Chart 1, a regulator or a financial institution manager could assess the base probability that NWC, either today or in the future, is less than

Chart 1. Illustration of Probability and Future Capital
$NWC_{t_0+n} \sim N$ ($27 billion, $100 billion squared)

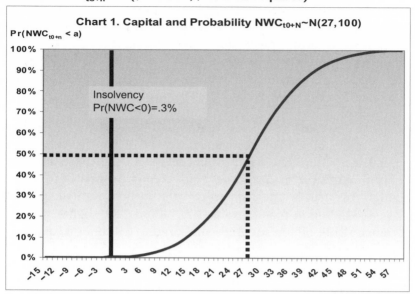

Chart 1. Capital and Probability $NWC_{t_0+n} \sim N(27, 100)$

$Pr(NWC_{t_0+n} < a)$

Insolvency
$Pr(NWC<0)=.3\%$

required capital. Consider two constraints. One capital requirement is that capital exceeds a legislated minimum. Assume that
this minimum is $25 billion. A second capital requirement is that
capital exceeds a risk-based capital requirement that comes from a
stress test. Using the information in Chart 1, the probability that
capital is less than 0 (the firm is insolvent) is .3 percent. The
probability that the firm has less than the RBC constraint of $19
billion is 21.2 percent, and the probability that NWC < minimum
capital ($25 billion) is 42.1 percent.

Note how the probabilities may be read directly off the vertical
axis in Chart 1. The estimated probability that Pr (NWC_{t_0+n}) = $27
billion, for example, is 50%. This makes sense because $27 billion
is the best guess or mean at the future value of NWC. Technically,
either comparative simple or complex models may be used to
estimate the expected value and its variance.[23]

---

23. The degree of complexity, ironically, does not negate the importance of considering
future net worth a conditional random variable with a probability distribution. A growing
number of capital adequacy models delve into extraordinary detail to "mark to market"
every asset within a portfolio to provide a "net worth" measure. Such valuations may be
useful but not to the exclusion of considering the variance and covariance of such assets and
liabilities in future periods. The accounting and "trading" focus of such models often
ignores the fact that decisions made by the regulated entities change with economic
conditions. The taking of more or less risk becomes part of that probability distribution and
variance of future NWC. To ignore variance is in some sense to ignore risks.

$E \ (NWC_{t0+n}|\varphi$ and $\sigma^2 = E(NWC_{t0+n} - E \ (NWC_{t0+n}|\varphi))^2$.

Suppose the regulator took an even more pessimistic view of NWC and employed a more stressful set of conditions. Chart 2 compares the initial probability assessments in terms of capital adequacy with the more stressful test.

NWC_{t0+n}. ~N ($15 billion, $144 squared).

Note how the curve-linear segmented line in Chart 2 reflects higher probabilities of insolvency, capital below the minimum capital levels, and the RBC capital levels. In the more stressful environment, the probabilities can change appreciably. Even though this firm is still likely to be solvent, because its expected NWC is $15 billion (compared to $27 billion), the slightly greater variance ($144 billion squared compared to $10 billion squared) increases the probability from .3 percent to 10.6%.

Table 1. Comparison of Estimated Probabilities of Insolvency

	BASE	STRESS	DIFFERENCE	Δ PROBABILITY
Pr (NWC < 0)	0.3%	10.6%	(0.102)	Increase
Pr (NWC < 19)	21.2%	63.1%	(0.419)	Increase
Pr (NWC < 25)	42.1%	79.8%	(0.377)	Increase

Charts 1 and 2 provide a relatively simple way to evaluate capital adequacy using probability.

Capital Adequacy: Will More Capital Always Reduce the Likelihood of Insolvency?

Table 2 provides estimates of the probabilities of insolvency, i.e., Pr $(NWC_{t0+n}<0)$ for different normal distributions of NWC. It provides estimates for expected values of NWC from $18 billion through $30 billion and for standard errors that range from $1 billion to $15 billion. Table 2 illustrates why more capital does not necessarily reduce the risk of insolvency, if that capital is also associated with a higher standard deviation.

For example, consider two cases:

Case 1. $E \ (NWCto_{+n})$ = 24 and σ = 9........Pr $(NWC_{t0+n}<0)$ =.4%.

Case 2. $E \ (NWCto_{+n})$ = 27 and σ = 2........Pr $(NWC_{t0+n}<0)$ =1.2%.

**Chart 2. Illustration of Probability and Future Capital
Comparison of Two Portfolios
NWC_{to+n}. ~N ($27 billion, $100 billion squared).
NWC_{to+n}. ~N ($15 billion, $144 squared).**

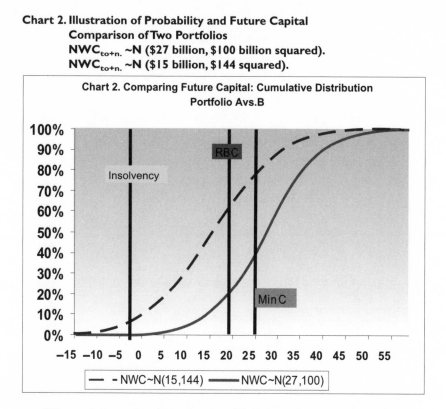

What might make Case 2 occur? A financial institution seeking to maximize expected net worth might find a speculative strategy perfectly acceptable. If it assigned a low cost to an increase in the probability of insolvency from .4% to 1.2%, it might be perfectly willing to embark upon a growth strategy closer to Case 2 than Case 1. Moreover, if the regulator had chosen a 5 percent probability of insolvency upper limit, the firm could be compliant with the regulatory rule, as well, even though it chose a strategy with a higher likelihood of insolvency.

Table 2. The Importance of Standard Deviations and NWC

σ \ E(NWC)	18	19	20	21	22	23	24	25	26	27	28	29	30
1	0.0%	0.0%	0.0%	0.0%	0.0%	0.0%	0.0%	0.0%	0.0%	0.0%	0.0%	0.0%	0.0%
2	0.0%	0.0%	0.0%	0.0%	0.0%	0.0%	0.0%	0.0%	0.0%	0.0%	0.0%	0.0%	0.0%
3	0.0%	0.0%	0.0%	0.0%	0.0%	0.0%	0.0%	0.0%	0.0%	0.0%	0.0%	0.0%	0.0%
4	0.0%	0.0%	0.0%	0.0%	0.0%	0.0%	0.0%	0.0%	0.0%	0.0%	0.0%	0.0%	0.0%
5	0.0%	0.0%	0.0%	0.0%	0.0%	0.0%	0.0%	0.0%	0.0%	0.0%	0.0%	0.0%	0.0%
6	0.1%	0.1%	0.0%	0.0%	0.0%	0.0%	0.0%	0.0%	0.0%	0.0%	0.0%	0.0%	0.0%
7	0.5%	0.3%	0.2%	0.1%	0.1%	0.1%	0.0%	0.0%	0.0%	0.0%	0.0%	0.0%	0.0%
8	1.2%	0.9%	0.6%	0.4%	0.3%	0.2%	0.1%	0.1%	0.1%	0.0%	0.0%	0.0%	0.0%
9	2.3%	1.7%	1.3%	1.0%	0.7%	0.5%	0.4%	0.3%	0.2%	0.1%	0.1%	0.1%	0.0%
10	3.6%	2.9%	2.3%	1.8%	1.4%	1.1%	0.8%	0.6%	0.5%	0.3%	0.3%	0.2%	0.1%
11	5.1%	4.2%	3.5%	2.8%	2.3%	1.8%	1.5%	1.2%	0.9%	0.7%	0.5%	0.4%	0.3%
12	6.7%	5.7%	4.8%	4.0%	3.3%	2.8%	2.3%	1.9%	1.5%	1.2%	1.0%	0.8%	0.6%
13	8.3%	7.2%	6.2%	5.3%	4.5%	3.8%	3.2%	2.7%	2.3%	1.9%	1.6%	1.3%	1.1%
14	9.9%	8.7%	7.7%	6.7%	5.8%	5.0%	4.3%	3.7%	3.2%	2.7%	2.3%	1.9%	1.6%
15	11.5%	10.3%	9.1%	8.1%	7.1%	6.3%	5.5%	4.8%	4.2%	3.6%	3.1%	2.7%	2.3%

Fixed Capital Standards and Perverse Incentives

Any firm faced with decision making under risk must consider how it will adjust its decisions when faced with changes in the economic environments in light of capital standards. As a simple illustration of this concept a consider a firm with an existing book of business, portfolio, and an ability to assess its net worth. Let us say that its existing portfolio is such that Portfolio A results in the following net worth

Portfolio A $NWC_{to+n.}$ ~N ($27 billion, $100 billion squared).

Given all its assets, expected returns, covariance among returns, Portfolio A yields an expected net worth of $27 billion with a standard deviation of $10 billion. Assume that the regulator imposes minimum capital requirements of $25 billion and RBC capital of $19 billion. We note that the firm estimates the probabilities of insolvency, failing to meet RBC levels, and failing to meet minimum capital levels as .3%, 21.2%, and 46%, respectively.

Your research group suggests that a slightly different portfolio could provide the following:

Portfolio B $NWC_{to+n.}$ ~N ($24 billion, $64 billion squared).

Given all its assets, expected returns, covariances among returns, Portfolio B yields an expected net worth of $24 billion with a smaller standard deviation of $8 billion. As a decision maker, you note that the firm will be worth $3 billion less, but there is less uncertainty associated with Portfolio B. See Table 3.

Table 3. Comparison of Mean and Standard Deviation of A and B

	E (NWC)	σ
Portfolio A	27	10
Portfolio B	24	8

Portfolio B represents a hedge that lowers the likelihood of insolvency from .3% to .1%, and assuming all else equal, Portfolio B presents a lower risk of insolvency. However, before Portfolio B would be chosen by a purely risk averse decision maker, consider the implications of the capital constraints. See Table 4.

Table 4. Probabilities of Violating Capital Rules

	PR(NWC<0)	PR(NWC<19)	PR(NWC<25)
Portfolio A	0.3%	21.2%	46.0%
Portfolio B	0.1%	26.6%	59.9%

So, as a decision maker, you must choose between Portfolio A and B. Portfolio B has a lower likelihood of insolvency, but it also has a lower projected capital. Portfolio A has a higher projected capital, higher likelihood of insolvency, but lower likelihood of violating the RBC or Minimum Capital constraints. So, which do you choose? Chart 3 provides an illustration of the complex relationships involving probability assessments and capital rules.

Note how Portfolio B (the top line) makes it more likely that the firm will violate both the RBC rule and the Minimum Capital rule. A trade-off results when the regulatory constraints enter the objective function. Should the decision maker choose Portfolio A with a smaller likelihood of violating capital constraints or Portfolio B with a smaller likelihood of insolvency but a larger likelihood of violating capital rules.

The cumulative density function for Portfolio B shifts, pivots, and changes shape. Portfolio B produces smaller probabilities that NWC will fall below $14 billion, but higher probabilities that NWC

Chart 3. Illustration of Why Capital Standards May Increase
Risk of Insolvency
Comparison of Two Portfolios
Portfolio A NWC$_{to+n.}$ ~N ($27 billion, $100 billion squared)
Portfolio B NWC$_{to+n.}$ ~N ($24 billion, $64 billion squared)

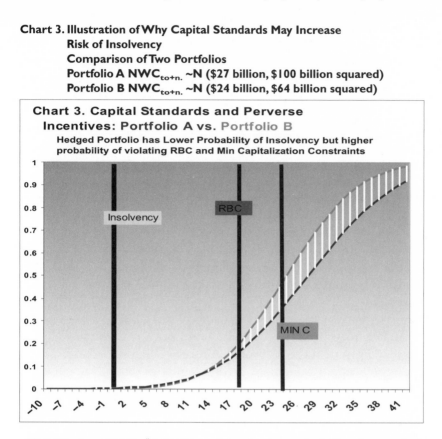

Chart 3. Capital Standards and Perverse Incentives: Portfolio A vs. Portfolio B

Hedged Portfolio has Lower Probability of Insolvency but higher probability of violating RBC and Min Capitalization Constraints

will fall below NWC>$14 billion. Clearly the probability that capital will fall below regulatory capital rules increases with portfolio B. This might cause the decision maker to choose A to avoid the violating capital constraints.

Worse yet, regulators technically would only observe the selection of Portfolio A with little understanding that B could have lowered the likelihood of insolvency. Chart 3 illustrates a second phenomenon. The more binding the capital constraints become (the more minimum capital exceeds $25 billion and RBC exceeds $19 billion), the greater the likelihood that Portfolio A will be chosen over Portfolio B (the hedging strategy). Although this chart provides only a simple numerical illustration, it does raise a fundamental question, "Can safety and soundness regulation be improved by raising regulatory capital constraints?" Chart 3 suggests the answer may be "no."

The same types of arguments and illustrations may be formulated to show that increasing regulatory constraints may only encourage speculation, with higher mean values of NWC at t0+n, but with greater conditional variances and higher likelihoods of insolvency.

The Present and Future Valuation Combined

It is, of course, possible that a firm may be adequately capitalized today, assuming business as usual conditions, but inadequately capitalized to handle the future stress scenario. Regulators ideally should have the flexibility and discretion to distinguish between the two and develop a strategy with the firm for achieving compliance with both. Remember compliance here is defined in terms of acceptable conditional probability levels. The prominent strategy would be guided by the least costly methods of achieving compliance.

Taken together, these two estimates of capital adequacy (conditional Present and conditional Future) could be used to produce desirable capital adequacy. If the regulator and the regulated entity could agree upon the θ or σ, then the firm and the regulator could choose jointly upon acceptable probability levels and lower limits for capital that would conform to business conditions, and safety and soundness.

Regulatory Risk Assessment and Safety and Soundness

Consider regulatory risk management compared to firm level risk management. Loss estimates to society that result from insolvency may differ considerably from losses to stockholders and creditors. The regulator must consider each in the establishment of capital standards. Regulators could establish upper bounds on the probability of losses and estimate risk levels of each with information from distributions of NWC, and potential economic impact multipliers. To illustrate this, suppose a firm had a $NWC_{to}=\$500$ million. If it were to become insolvent, stockholders might loose $500 million with limited liability. Creditors would likely lose far less, depending upon government guarantees. Assume the regulator had determined from a macroeconomic analysis that prior to its resolution, a large financial institution could inflict $1 billion threat (loss) to a regional/national economy in the process of becoming insolvent.

Suppose further that the likelihood of the institution of being insolvent today is only .5 percent. The risk "premium" imposed by society becomes:

$1 billion × .005 = $5 million.

This premium could be administered as a capital charge—the costs of taking systemic risks. If the institution subsequently adjusted its portfolio to lower the likelihood of its insolvency, to say .001 from .005, then its risk premiums would fall to $1 million.

The $4 million margin might provide sufficient incentive to do so. If the probability of its insolvency over a longer period, say 10 years, is 1% then its risk premiums could be adjusted accordingly, or the firm could alter its portfolio to lower the likelihood of insolvency over this future period. Note in all cases, however, the risks managed by the regulators requires a knowledge of the probability distribution of capital where the mean might be $500 million, but the losses that concern the regulator are not limited to stockholder and creditor losses. These losses are the losses that the economy might sustain.

In either case, regulators and regulated firms view capital adequacy two perspectives: the probability distributions of NWC_{to} and NWC_{to+n}. Both appear essential to estimating capital adequacy. Both simultaneously satisfy "fair value" accounting concepts and disclosure. Regulators could rely on such measures to monitor the financial health of an institution.[24]

Potential Benefits of Capital Adequacy Using Probability Distributions

Such information increases the knowledge of NWC and would eliminate proxy variables and arbitrary "risk weights" employed by current capital adequacy models. If everyone agreed that the expected net worth was actually declining and variances increas-

---

24. Note, however, that focusing of book value capital does not help. For example, the Office of Federal Housing Enterprise Oversight provides a model of capital adequacy that "freezes" the current portfolio of Fannie Mae and Freddie Mac and explores a stress test that permits both changes in prepayment and default associated with interest rate and housing prices changes. The period t0+n is 120 months in the future. OFHEO provides and estimate of $E(C_{t0+n}|\theta)$, i.e., the "book value of capital" under the stress test. If $E(C_{t0+n}|\theta)$, remains positive, the Enterprise in question is considered solvent. OFHEO makes no estimates of market values. It could, however, require both Fannie Mae and Freddie Mac to provide their estimates. It could also modify its model and estimate NWC using capital markets information and independent assessments for valuing the Enterprise portfolios.

ing, regulators, creditors, stockholders, and justice officials would take note of the increase in risks. Forbearance would be less defensible and be replaced by more timely prompt corrective regulatory triggers. Regulatory actions would not be based on last quarter's financial ratios or MVt estimates, but upon current and future distributions of NWC. Regulators would propitiously resolve institutions as

$$\Pr((\text{NWC}_{\text{to}}|\theta) <0) => 100\%$$

and

$$\Pr((\text{NWC}_{\text{to}}|\varphi) <0)) => 100\%.$$

In such a system, "too big to fail" becomes less onerous. Who would keep insolvent institutions operating to prevent economic losses that may well have already occurred? Financial signals would become less murky and dissonant. Implicit and explicit government guarantees would become unnecessary and redundant.

Is this possible? Do we have the capability of actually estimating the distributions of current and future capital? Section 3 addresses these questions.

3. ALTERNATIVES TO TRADITIONAL CAPITAL ADEQUACY

Capital Adequacy and Modeling Net Worth

To make capital adequacy computationally tractable, assuming capital is regarded as net worth with a probability distribution, let us start with the financial institution itself and its decisions under uncertainty.

Financial institutions, like banks, managed risk before modern risk management tools were developed. This translated to an ability to assess net worth, project cash flows with certain confidence, and provide a best guess as to what net worth would be in the future. Advances in statistics, economic, finance, computers, financial engineering, and risk management techniques have only enhanced these abilities. Financial institutions now routinely develop their own risk management tools and software, but also purchase it from vendors. Risk management continues to reconcile practical market experience with scientific disciplines at the asset, portfolio, and firm level.[25]

As a result financial institutions are better able now to quantify potential losses than ever before, and the key to risk measurement is the ability to estimate or otherwise assign reasonable probability distributions for returns (losses) on financial assets. From the perspective of the individual financial institution, the potential losses or risk are borne by the stockholders and its creditors.

It is therefore reasonable to expect that each financial institution, with capable internal risk management systems, provides the regulator with conditional best guesses for NWCt0+n and an associated standard error. In the previous section, we discussed how just these two parameters provide the basis for constructing conditional density functions for current and future net worth. Note that contained with these parameters lays all interest rate risk, credit risk, operations risk, and other risks expressed implicitly in the conditional density functions. Indeed, the change in expected NWC and its standard error, with respect to interest rates, credit quality, operation practices, and other variables, becomes the basis for evaluating such risks.[26]

Do others, outside the individual firms, have access to data that would allow the estimation of NWC and its standard deviation? Although there is, of course, no particular reason to assume that regulators, brokers, or independent third party analysts are any better at estimating such parameters, each has a reasonable set of tools to do so. Lutton (2000) provided such an evaluation system for peer groups of banks in the OCC.[27]

Of course, more complex relationships may be developed and generalized that feature econometric approaches to risk measurement with nonproprietary data. See Swamy et al. (2001) for a more theoretically justified approach to net-worth estimation.

---

25.   An example of such a firm is BlackRock, Inc. Two of its principals B. Golub and L. Tilman (2000) recount the development and logic of such risk management practices and theories. Another example of a textbook that features detailed applied risk management procedures and software is S. Benninga (2000).

26.   An excellent nontechnical discussion of this is found in Golub and Tilman (2000). A more technical discussion relevant to interest rate risk is found in Swamy et al., 2001.

27.   Virtually any linear in parameter multivariate econometric equation that features net earnings to equity or asset ratios produces conditional means and variances capable of estimating future losses. T. Lutton (1999).

These and other studies should be considered preliminary inquiries in a rapidly expanding field that employs less cumbersome models that may be quickly reestimated and simulated to synthesize information.

Combining Results of Multiple Models

Indeed, regulatory analysts, academics, and consultants routinely construct and build models to provide slightly different information than that contained in regulated firm models. It is now becoming more an issue of whether and how to distill the results of multiple models than finding such models. Regulators may soon be in the position to explore prominent solutions that may arise if they can access individual institution models.

Assume that we have three forward-looking models. Model 1, the regulator's model, produces and estimates distributions of NWC based upon a set of assumptions denoted $\theta 1$ and $\varphi 1$. Model 2 is the regulated firm's model(s) and produces a distribution for NWC with a slightly different set of assumptions than the regulator. These are denoted $\theta 2$ and $\varphi 2$. Model 3 is a model of NWC available from an external source such as a specialized consulting firm with assumptions $\theta 3$ and $\varphi 3$.

Step 1 Try to reconcile the assumptions concerning the nature of the distributions and the information implicit in each model $\theta 1 = \theta 2 = \theta 3$. Focus on estimated net worth of a firm today that would provide a basis for synthesizing information and standardizing assumptions. Presumably, such models would include book value capital or marked to market capital and consider an expected discounted cash flow stream under baseline assumptions as part of the evaluation of the distribution of NWC_{t0}:

Step 2 Compare the three estimates of net worth from each model, the variance of each distribution, and if possible, the covariance across models. Assuming normal distributions, the expected net worth of multiple models becomes a simple, weighted average:

$E(NWC_{t0}| \theta 1, \theta 2, \theta 3)$ $E(NWC_{ito}| \theta_i)*w_i$ where i=1,2,3 and $0<w_i<1$ and $\sigma w_i=1$.

Step 3 Construct the variance of NWC_{t0}:

$$\sigma^2 = \Sigma_j \Sigma_i \sigma_{ij} * w_i * w_j \text{ where i=1, 2, 3.}$$

By design, the different models will produce different estimates of the means and variances and covariance associated with networth. Technically, regulators that now rely only on their model and use this procedure by assuming that $w_2=w_3=0$. Firms assess their net worth to the exclusion of other models assuming $w_1=w_3=0$. Assuming each group held equally valuable information $w_1=w_2=w_3$. Alternatively, if one model produced better results on average than others, different weights might be constructed from an optimizing algorithm that solved for the optimal weights based upon forecasting errors associated with cash flows or net income projections.

By analogy, the same procedures could be used to construct estimates of the probability distribution for NWC_{t0+n}.

Ultimately, the application of this procedure could be achieved with as few as 4 parameters for each model: the means and standard errors for NWC_{t0} and NWC_{t0+n}.

The Precommitment Approach: The Capital Adequacy Ratio

Kupiec and O'Brien (1997) proposed a "precommitment" approach to capital adequacy in which a bank would propose a self-imposed lower limit for capital (risk-weighted or other). This precommitted limit would serve as a regulatory capital standard for that bank, subject to discussion and agreement with regulators. If the bank were to suffer losses that eroded capital to a point below that limit, banks would pay a penalty payment to the regulators providing an incentive to allocate reasonable amounts of capital.[28] Kupiec and O'Brien consider capital a conditional random variable that reflects net worth but fail to address precisely how the firm would measure such net worth. Nevertheless, they postulated that precommitted amounts of capital would emerge from an equilibrium solution in which the firm would choose "optimal" precommitment of capital by considering the probability-weighted penalties that would be associated with violating its precommitments.

Taylor (2002) discusses two limitations of the method.[29] A penalty payment was likely to occur precisely when the bank could least afford it, thereby making the financial condition of the bank even worse. If capital eroded in the system as a whole during a

---

28.   P. Kupiec and J. O'Brien (1997).
29.   C. Taylor (2002).

recession, for example, the imposition of penalties might exacerbate the recession by introducing a credit crunch. Second, Taylor asks, as a practical matter, how the supervisor would be able to determine whether the "precommitted" capital limit was adequate?

In the Kupiec and O'Brien (1997) world, banks could easily game the system, because they enjoyed the distinct benefits of asymmetric information. As a result, the management of the bank would effectively propose its own level of regulatory capital given its anticipated risks, even if that appetite was excessive and compromised by moral hazard. Regulators would lack the same ability to evaluate such risks because they were not privy to the same information. They would no longer be in a position to control capital in individual banks or in the system as a whole. In any case, regardless of the merits of their original proposal, Basel II was sufficiently well underway that the "precommitment" approach sounded too much like starting from scratch and admitting that the regulators were ill-positioned to impose capital adequacy constraints in the first place! Whether too radical, too simple, or too poorly sold, regulators failed to embrace the precommitment approach.

Taylor (2002) provides a regulatory "hook" that Kupiec and O'Brien (1997) did not. He introduces the concept of a Capital Adequacy Ratio (CAR) that provides the regulator with some control of precommitments.

Taylor's CAR consists of two precommitments by the regulated firm. The numerator in this ratio is a precommitted capital limit—a measurable net worth concept that establishes a time-specific, lower limit for capital. The bank assures the regulator that it would not let its net worth fall below this threshold. The second measure is a threshold measure of "loss" that could be tolerated in any given time period, such as a quarter. The CAR consists of a precommitted stock variable (capital) to precommitted flow variable (loss). Technically, since capital is "true net worth," the "true losses" would be the inter-quarter differences in net worth.

Such precommitments may be found within the original Kupiec and O'Brien proposal, but unlike that proposal, Taylor introduces a regulatory capital adequacy parameter (CAR) designed such that the precommitted thresholds of capital in the numerator and loss in the denominator must EQUAL this preset value. CAR values may be varied across banks and over time. Banks that subsequently suffer either larger losses than precommitted or reductions in capital beyond precommitted capital levels would be subject to customarily unpleasant and costly regulatory and supervisory actions.

Taylor treats capital and losses as conditional random variables, each possessing its own distribution. These distributions are known to the bank who will use them, in turn, to obtain reasonable precommitment levels. For simplicity, Taylor illustrates the problem assuming stationary normal distributions where probability is treated as a relative frequency. He postulates, for example, that a bank expects to earn "true income" of $30 million with a standard error of $40 million. The bank expects to be profitable and earn $30 million a quarter, $120 million over the course of a year. He notes that if we assume a normal distribution of net income, a loss of $10 million would be expected only 15.9% of the time. A greater loss, $20 million, would occur more infrequently, only 10.9% of the time, and a $90 million loss, only .1%. See the last row of Table 5. Using this information, the firm could obtain an "optimal" precommitment ratio that satisfied the regulatory imposed CAR. See Table 5 for an illustration of how regulators might set CAR.

Regulators determine the capital adequacy ratios (CAR) that appear in the left-hand column of Table 5. They range from .01 to .2. Taylor's Capital Adequacy Ratio is simple, yet easily generalized. Table 5 provides a simple version and matches precommitment ratios with regulatory standards. Note that capital thresholds vary inversely with precommitted threshold losses.

CAR = Precommitted Threshold Level of Capital/Precommitted Threshold Level of Losses.

This means the precommitted capital thresholds appear in each cell in the table below for any given CAR and loss threshold.

For example, if regulators had set a CAR at .10, then the capital levels associated with a precommitted loss of $50 million would be $500 million. The firm would precommit to sustain no losses greater than $50 million and, consequently, would also agree to post a capital threshold of $500 million, below which it would not slip at any given time, say, a quarter. Similarly, if the firm precommitted to no greater than $10 million and CAR remained at .10, the pre-committed capital could be reduced to $100 million. Alternatively, if the firm precommitted to losses as high as $100 million, then the firm would have to precommit to $1 billion of capital.

Table 5. Capital Thresholds Consistent with Capital Adequacy Ratio and Threshold Losses Acceptable Capital Losses 100 =>10

REGULATORY CAR	100	90	80	70	60	50	40	30	20	10
0.01	$10,000	$9,000	$8,000	$7,000	$6,000	$5,000	$4,000	$3,000	$2,000	$1,000
0.02	$5,000	$4,500	$4,000	$3,500	$3,000	$2,500	$2,000	$1,500	$1,000	$500
0.03	$3,333	$3,000	$2,667	$2,333	$2,000	$1,667	$1,333	$1,000	$667	$333
0.04	$2,500	$2,250	$2,000	$1,750	$1,500	$1,250	$1,000	$750	$500	$250
0.05	$2,000	$1,800	$1,600	$1,400	$1,200	$1,000	$800	$600	$400	$200
0.06	$1,667	$1,500	$1,333	$1,167	$1,000	$833	$667	$500	$333	$167
0.07	$1,429	$1,286	$1,143	$1,000	$857	$714	$571	$429	$286	$143
0.08	$1,250	$1,125	$1,000	$875	$750	$625	$500	$375	$250	$125
0.09	$1,111	$1,000	$889	$778	$667	$556	$444	$333	$222	$111
0.10	$1,000	$900	$800	$700	$600	**$500**	$400	$300	$200	$100
0.11	$909	$818	$727	$636	$545	$455	$364	$273	$182	$91
0.12	$833	$750	$667	$583	$500	$417	$333	$250	$167	$83
0.13	$769	$692	$615	$538	$462	$385	$308	$231	$154	$77
0.14	$714	$643	$571	$500	$429	$357	$286	$214	$143	$71
0.15	$667	$600	$533	$467	$400	$333	$267	$200	$133	$67
0.16	$625	$563	$500	$438	$375	$313	$250	$188	$125	$63
0.17	$588	$529	$471	$412	$353	$294	$235	$176	$118	$59
0.18	$556	$500	$444	$389	$333	$278	$222	$167	$111	$56
0.19	$526	$474	$421	$368	$316	$263	$211	$158	$105	$53
0.2	$500	$450	$400	$350	$300	$250	$200	$150	$100	$50
Pr(Loss>a)	0.1%	0.1%	0.3%	0.6%	1.2%	2.3%	4.0%	6.7%	10.6%	15.9%

If the regulator decides to lower the CAR, to say .08, capital precommitments must rise for any given loss threshold. Note that end-of-period capital and losses are jointly determined. For $100 million, $50 million, and $10 million loss thresholds, capital rises to $1.25 billion, $625 million, and $125 million in Table 5. If the regulator decides to raise CAR, to say .12, capital precommitments fall. For the same loss thresholds, capital falls to $833 million, $417 million, and $83 million.

How should the firm optimally decide on its precommitment levels?

The firm's assessment of precommitments derives directly from its conditional probability distributions of net worth and profitability. Probabilities of losses and net worth levels obtain directly from the firm's view of the conditional probability density functions of capital, the time horizon of its objective function, and the expected costs and benefits from over and under precommitment levels. Any financial institution with reasonable risk-monitoring and management practices should be able to determine such levels. Taylor suggests a simple univariate approach to doing so, but more sophisticated methods are readily available.

For example, Swamy et al. (2001) provides an econometric approach to estimating market values from a model of whole bank returns. Using a stochastic coefficient estimation procedure, they provide both a literature review and a detailed explanation of how a firm might employ mixed information, market valuations, and accounting in such a fashion as to estimate and monitor capital adequacy, and safety and soundness in banking. They distinguish between book valuation, "marked to market" valuation, and economic net worth, and provide a method to do so. Their approach, however, uses aggregates for net income, the return on equity, returns on assets, leverage ratios, and tax rates that provide little insight into the portfolio problems faced by large banks. Nevertheless, the estimation procedures, accounting constructs, and overall approach provide a basis for estimating both loss distributions and capital distributions essential for implementing both the Kupiec and O'Brien (1997) and the Taylor (2002) models.

How should the regulator decide on the level of CAR?

Taylor lists six factors that the regulator should consider in setting CAR:

1. The length of the income reporting period (generally quarterly)
2. Insolvency aversion (from a regulator's perspective)
3. Systemic importance of the bank
4. Government guarantee
5. Stage of business cycle
6. Local issues

Essentially, each of these factors can have a potential positive or negative affect on CAR. For example, CAR should increase with longer intervals of reporting income; CAR should also increase if the regulator postulates greater losses in the event of insolvency. Similarly, if a regulator considers one firm to represent a greater systemic threat, relatively higher CAR will force relatively greater capital precommitments. A regulator may require a CAR of .10 for a less systemically important institution and a CAR of .15 for a more important institution. Taylor argues that the more firms benefit from government guarantees, the less capital they need to hold other things being equal. This might lower regulatory CAR levels. In addition, CAR could be used to counter business cycles, raising CAR during expansions and lowering it during recessions. Regulators could consider local economic conditions in determining CAR, thereby providing individual banks greater or smaller incentives to raise or lower capital during rolling regional recessions and expansions.

Combining these factors requires considerable judgment, and barring an explicit regulatory objective function, the setting of CAR would depend on more qualitative information. One way to initiate the procedure is to consider a baseline CAR value. Call this CAR_b. Taylor suggests small increases and decreases about this value consistent with other information to connote more or less risky behavior.

Of course, the regulator need not be restricted in establishing CAR on a period-by-period basis. The regulator may choose a time path for CAR that satisfies an inter-temporal optimization consistent with a macroeconomic view and attention to systemic risks.

4. CONCLUSION

Financial regulators face a difficult challenge with capital adequacy. Their tools are crude and resources limited compared to the institutions they regulate. Over the last several decades they have tightened capital requirements during macroeconomic downswings and loosened requirements in upswings, effectively exacerbating economic cycles. The losses incurred by more than 2000 bank and thrift failures in the U.S. during the 1980s wiped out one deposit insurance fund and severely crippled another. Behind closed doors, regulators continue to lament the poor predictive accuracy of their off-site early warning systems.

This problem has grown beyond national boundaries to a point where regulators worldwide struggle to refine capital measurement, even as they embrace capital standards as their most important regulatory tool. Capital adequacy, minimum capital requirements, and risk-based capital requirements have become THE way for regulators to assure elected officials and society, at large, that financial institutions are safe and sound.

Reliance on historical financial statements, book value accounting, and "one size fits all" capital standards has finally begun to wear thin. "Yes/No" answers to the question, "Is this financial firm 'adequately capitalized'?" have been less comforting amid accounting scandals and megacorporation insolvencies.

Analysts have begun to ask whether book value assets today can actually buffer market losses incurred over a 10-year stress period. Is a firm with $1 of positive capital at the end of a 10-year stress period as adequately capitalized as a firm with $10 billion of positive capital? Shouldn't probability assessments come into play when dealing with capital adequacy?

From this turmoil, a solution has begun to emerge. Capital adequacy must be viewed in terms of economic net worth, and economic net worth is not known with certainty. Capital adequacy must be estimated as a conditional random variable. This is not new. It is, in fact, quite old, a back-to-basics story.

Cumbersome, assumption-laden regulatory models will give way to simpler models, more easily-estimated models, and models better designed for regulatory purposes. Models will lose their veneer of complexity and be viewed as simple ways to organize data. More importantly, multiple models will be incorporated into assessments of capital adequacy. Capital adequacy will no longer rely be based solely on off-site regulatory models. It will incorporate results from individual firm models, capital markets models, and academic models. It will be viewed in light of the current economic and business climate, and it will look to the future, not to last quarter's leverage ratio or capital level.

REFERENCES

Allen, L. and Saunders, A. (2002), *Credit Risk Measurement: New Approaches to Value at Risk and Other Paradigms*, New York, John Wiley and Sons.

Baer, H. and McElravey, J. (1992), "The Changing Impact of Capital Requirements on Bank Growth: 1975 to 1991," *Federal Reserve Bank of Chicago Working Paper*, Chicago.

Basel Committee (1999), "A New Capital Adequacy Framework," Consultative paper issued by the Basel Committee on Banking Supervision, Bank of International Settlements (BCBS), Basel, Switzerland.

Basel Committee (2001), "The New Basel Capital Accord, Basel II," BCBS, Basel, Switzerland.

Benninga, S. (2000), *Financial Modeling* (2nd Edition), MIT Press, Cambridge, Massachusetts.

Berger, A., Herring, R. and Szego, G. (1995), "*Finance and Economics Discussion Series* 95–23, Board of Governors of the Federal Reserve System (U.S.).

Borio, C. (2003), "Towards a Macro-prudential Framework for Financial Supervision and Regulation," *BIS Working Papers*, No. 128, February.

Calem, P. S. and Rob, R. (1996), "The impact of capital-based regulation on bank risk-taking: a dynamic model", *Federal Reserve Board Finance and Economics, Discussion Series*, pp. 96–12, February.

DeCamps, J., Rochet, J. and Roger, B. (2002), "The Three Pillars of Basel II: Optimizing the Mix in a Continuous-time Model." *Basel II: An Economic Assessment* (Basel, 17–18, May 2002), A workshop jointly organized by the Basel Committee on Banking Supervision, the Centre for Economic Policy Research, and the Journal of Financial Intermediation.

Federal Reserve Board of Governors (2003), "Differences in Capital and Accounting Standards among the Federal Banking and Thrift Agencies," Submitted to the Congress pursuant to section 121 of the Federal Deposit Insurance Corporation Improvement Act of 1991, Washington, D.C., July 24.

Froot, K. and Stein, J. (1998), "A New Approach to Capital Budgeting for Financial Institutions," *Journal of Financial Economics*, 47, pp. 55–82.

Furlong, F. and Keeley, N. (1990), "A Reexamination of Mean-Variance Analysis of Bank Capital Regulation," *Journal of Banking and Finance*, pp. 69–84.

Golub, B. and Tilman, L. (2000), *Risk Management: Approaches for Fixed Income Markets*, John Wiley & Sons, Inc., New York.

Gorton, G. and Winton, A. (1995), "Bank Capital Regulation in General Equilibrium," *National Bureau of Economic Research, Working Paper* 5244, Cambridge, Mass.

Karacadag, C. and Taylor, M. (2000), "The New Capital Adequacy Framework: Institutions Constraints and Incentive Structure," *IMF Working Paper Series* No. 00/93, June.

Kim, D. and Santomero, A. M. (1988), Risk in Banking and Capital Regulation," *Journal of Finance*, 43, pp. 1219–1233.

Koehn, M. and Santomero, A. (1980), "Regulation of Bank Capital and Portfolio Risk," *Journal of Finance*, 35, pp. 1235–1244.

Kupiec, P. and O'Brien, J. (1997), "Regulatory Capital Requirements for Market Risk and the Precommitment Approach," *Federal Reserve Board Working Paper.*

Lutton, T. (1999), "Peer Group Analysis and Risk Measurement," *OCC Draft Working Paper*, Office of the Comptroller of the Currency, December.

Morgan, G. (1992), "Capital Adequacy," *The New Pa grave Dictionary of Money and Finance*, Peter Newman, Murray Milgate, and John Eatwell, editors, Macmillan Press, New York.

Rochet, J. C. (1992), "Capital Requirements and the Behavior of Commercial Banks," *European Economic Review*, 43, pp. 981–990.

Santos, J. (2000), "Bank Capital Regulation in Contemporary Banking Theory: A Review on the Literature," *BIS Working Paper*, No. 90, Basel, Switzerland.

Saunders, A. (2000), *Financial Institutions Management: A Modern Perspective*, 3rd Edit., New York, Irwin/McGraw-Hill.

Saunders, A. and Wilson, B. (1995), "Bank Capital Structure: An Analysis of the Charter Value Hypothesis," Salomon Center, New York University, Working Paper.

Stein, J., Usher, S., La Gattuata, D. and Yourn, J. (2001), "A Comparable Method for Measuring Cashflow at Risk for Non-Financial Firms," *Journal of Applied Corporate Finance*, Vol. 13, No. 4.

Swamy, P.A.V.B, Lutton, T. and Bartholomew, P. (2001), "Improved Methods of Treating Critical Issues in Regulating and Supervising Bank Safety and Soundness," A. H. Chen, Ed., *Research in Finance*, New York: JAI, an Imprint of Elsevier Science.

Taylor, C. (2002), "New General Approach to Capital Adequacy: A Simple and Comprehensive Alternative to Basel II," CSFE Center for the Study of Financial Innovation.

Thakor, A. V. (1996), "Capital Requirements, Monetary Policy, and Aggregate Bank Lending," *Journal of Finance*, 51(1), pp. 279–324.

United States Congress Financial Institutions Reform, Recovery, and Enforcement Act of 1989(FIRREA).

United States Congress Federal Deposit Insurance Corporation Improvement Act of 1991 (FDICIA).

11

Bank Lending and the Effectiveness of Monetary Policy Under a Revised Basel Accord

Kevin T. Jacques[1] and David C. Schirm

I. INTRODUCTION

In the late 1980s, U.S. bank regulators, as part of the international Basel Committee on Banking Regulation and Supervisory Practices, adopted the risk-based capital standards (the Basel Accord), the primary purpose of which was to make bank capital requirements responsive to the credit risk in banks' portfolios of assets and off-balance-sheet activities. While capital ratios rose significantly in the years following the implementation of risk-based capital, the standards, because of their simplified approach, were not without problems, including that they failed to adequately differentiate between the credit risk of assets, in general, and commercial loans, in particular. Such weaknesses resulted in a variety of distortions, many of which were exacerbated by legal and financial engineering aimed at mitigating the requirements of the Basel Accord, thus making regulatory capital ratios less reliable as an indicator of financial strength.[2]

1. The views expressed are those of the authors and not necessarily those of the U.S. Department of the Treasury or John Carroll University. The authors thank Raj Aggarwal, Edward DeMarco, Cornelis Los, John Thornton, and seminar participants at Kent State University for their helpful comments. The idea for this paper came from discussions with David Nebhut of the Office of the Comptroller of the Currency.
2. Some of these distortions took the form of regulatory capital arbitrage. For a discussion of the problems of regulatory capital arbitrage as it pertains to the 1988 Accord, see Jones (2000).

Efforts are currently under way to revise the 1988 Basel Accord, with the revised standards to be applied to large, internationally active banks in both the U.S. and abroad.[3] Recognizing that the risk-based capital standards need to evolve, along with changes in financial markets and improvements in recent years in banks' risk measurement and management systems, one of the primary purposes of the revised Basel Accord is to more closely align regulatory capital requirements with the underlying credit risk in banks' activities, thereby reducing distortions existing in the current accord.[4] This is accomplished, in part, by incorporating credit ratings into the regulatory capital standards, and by allowing the risk-based capital requirements on certain assets to vary as the credit ratings of the underlying borrowing entities change. Given the proposed changes, Tanaka (2002), Van den Heuvel (2002b), and Kopecky and Van Hoose (2003b) note that little existing research has addressed the issue of how the revised Basel Accord affects the monetary transmission mechanism.

Theory suggests a number of possible ways regulatory capital standards may alter bank lending behavior and the effectiveness of monetary policy, often with conflicting results. Models such as those by Chami and Cosimano (2001) and Van den Heuvel (2002b) emphasize the relationship between monetary policy and bank capital, finding that changes in monetary policy alter bank profitability, which in turn changes bank capital and lending. Alternatively, under the bank lending channel hypothesis, monetary policy has a direct effect on the supply of bank loans as banks fund loans, at least in part, with reservable deposits. Van den Heuvel (2002a) notes that a binding regulatory capital requirement limits the ability of capital-constrained banks to increase lending in response to an expansionary monetary policy, thus making monetary policy less potent. In contrast, Stein (1998) and Van den Heuvel (2002a) note that bank capital may mitigate adverse selection problems. In the event of a contractionary monetary policy, capital-constrained banks are less likely to increase their issuance of reservable deposits and more likely to decrease lending, thus making monetary policy more potent if banks are

---

3. Ferguson (2003a) notes that approximately twenty large U.S. banks are likely to adopt the revised Accord at the outset, and while the number of banks to which the revised Accord will be applied is small, because these banks will be the largest, most internationally-active banks in the U.S., they account for over two-thirds of all assets in the U.S. banking system.
4. The revised Accord includes not only changes in regulatory capital requirements (Pillar 1) but also standards for supervisory review (Pillar 2) and enhanced disclosure requirements (Pillar 3). For more detail, see Basel Committee (2003).

capital-constrained. One possible explanation for these seemingly conflicting conclusions is that important cross-sectional differences exist in how banks respond to monetary policy shocks (Kashyap and Stein, 1994; Kishan and Opiela, 2000). However, common among all of these theories is the notion that monetary policy affects, either directly or indirectly, the supply of bank loans, and that the nature of this relationship can be influenced, at least in part, by regulatory capital standards.

An alternative way to address the issue of how regulatory capital standards influence bank lending and monetary policy is to examine empirical studies of the 1988 Basel Accord. Studies such as those by Hall (1993), Haubrich and Wachtel (1993), Jackson et al. (1999), Furfine (2000), and Aggarwal and Jacques (2001) suggest that banks altered the composition of their balance sheets in response to the 1988 risk-based capital standards, generally substituting low credit risk assets, such as securities, for assets with higher credit risk, such as commercial loans. If the composition of banks' assets has an influence on the effectiveness of monetary policy, as is true under the credit view of monetary policy, then asset substitution resulting from the revised Basel Accord may impact the transmission mechanism. Other studies, such as those by Kashyap and Stein (1994) and Thakor (1996), have shown that risk-based capital standards alter the relationship between money and bank lending, with implications for the effectiveness of monetary policy. In addition, Berger and Udell (1994), Hancock and Wilcox (1994), Brinkmann and Horvitz (1995), and Peek and Rosengren (1995b) have examined what role the standards played in the 1990 credit crunch, often with conflicting results. While prior research may suggest that the 1988 risk-based capital standards had a significant influence on bank portfolio composition and monetary policy, the existing research is limited in its applicability to the revised Basel Accord, as some key elements of the forthcoming revised standards differ significantly from the 1988 Basel Accord.

This study contributes to the literature on bank capital regulation by examining how the forthcoming revisions to the risk-based capital standards may alter bank lending and the effectiveness of monetary policy. Modifying recent work by Peek and Rosengren (1995a) and Kishan and Opiela (2000), an asymmetric response is shown in how banks react to monetary policy under the revised Basel Accord. Specifically, asymmetric differences exist in the effectiveness of monetary policy depending not only on whether banks are constrained by the revised risk-based capital standards but also the credit quality and relative liquidity of the assets held in the portfolios of capital-constrained banks. In addition, it is shown that under the revised Basel Accord, migrations in credit ratings also influence the effectiveness of monetary policy.

2. RISK-BASED CAPITAL

In June 1999, the Basel Committee issued a consultative paper that emphasized revising the 1988 Accord to more closely align the risk-based capital standards with the actual risk in banks' activities and to provide an incentive for banks to enhance their risk measurement and management systems. Under the proposed revisions, two general methods exist for calculating banks' regulatory capital requirements, one based on external credit ratings and the other based on the use of banks' internal credit risk models.[5]

Under the external ratings approach, the current reliance on risk weights and buckets is maintained, with modifications being made to remedy some of the existing Accord's flaws. In contrast to the 1988 Accord, which slotted assets and off-balance-sheet activities into one of four risk-weight categories based on the type and credit risk of the underlying asset, one of the major revisions to the Accord involves slotting bank claims and credit exposures, including commercial loans, into risk-weight categories on the basis of external credit agency ratings, and increasing the number of risk buckets to include a 150 percent risk-weight category.[6] As under the 1988 Accord, banks calculate their total risk-weighted assets as the sum of the dollar value of each asset or off-balance-sheet activity, multiplied by its corresponding risk weight. In order to meet minimum regulatory capital requirements, banks must hold

---

5. Under Pillar 1 of the revised Accord, the external credit ratings approach is also known as the standardized approach, while there are two internal ratings-based (IRB) approaches, the foundation IRB and the advanced IRB (A-IRB). The proposed changes to capital requirements under the revised Accord also incorporate capital charges for market and operational risk. Because the focus of this paper is on how changes to the credit risk portion of risk-based capital will influence bank lending and monetary policy, the issues of market and operational risk are not explored. For more information on capital charges under the revised Accord, see Basel Committee (2003).

6. For corporate loans rated AAA to AA- the 20 percent risk weight is applied. The 50 percent risk weight is applied to those loans rated A+ to A-, while the 100 percent risk weight is assigned to loans rated BBB+ to BB- and those loans that are unrated. Finally, corporate loans below BB- are assigned a 150% risk weight.

Tier 1 capital equal to at least 4% and total capital (Tier 1 + Tier 2) equal to at least 8% of its total risk-weighted assets.[7]

A second significant change in the revised standards is that a migration over time in the credit rating of a corporate borrower causes a loan to that borrower to be placed in a different risk-weight category. Under the proposed revisions, risk-based capital requirements on existing business loans are no longer invariant to changes in credit ratings. Rather, if the credit rating of the corporate borrowing entity deteriorates, the regulatory capital requirement on the loan increases. While the Basel Committee has proposed numerous changes to the original Basel Accord, none may be more important for bank portfolio composition and the effectiveness of monetary policy. Because migrating credit ratings introduce the possibility of increasing variability in regulatory capital requirements (Jokivoulle and Peura, 2001) and to the degree that credit ratings tend to be downgraded during recessions (Nickell et al., 2000; Bangia et al., 2002), regulatory capital standards may become increasingly procyclical (Lowe, 2002). This is in sharp contrast to the 1988 Accord where all commercial loans, regardless of credit rating, were slotted in the 100 percent risk-weight category. Given the existing research on the link between the stringency of regulatory capital requirements and monetary policy, the fact that credit ratings may migrate under the proposed standards raises additional issues as to the effectiveness of monetary policy under a revised Basel Accord.

3. THE MODEL

The preceding sections raise the issue of how the imposition of a revised risk-based capital standard, one where capital requirements are based on credit ratings and can migrate as the credit ratings on assets change, will influence bank lending and the transmission of monetary policy. To examine this issue, the one-period theoretical model of representative banks developed by Peek and Rosengren (1995a) and Kishan and Opiela (2000) is modified to incorporate the revised standards.[8] Specifically, banks

---

7. Under the risk-based capital standards, capital has two definitions. Tier 1 capital is comprised mainly of common equity, while Tier 2 capital includes cumulative perpetual preferred stock, term subordinated debt, and the allowance for loan and lease losses.

8. The one-period nature of the theoretical model is reflective of the short-run adjustment of banks to changes in monetary policy. Recent work by Kopecky and VanHoose (2003a,b) uses a multi-period model that differentiates between short-run and long-run effects of regulatory capital requirements, thus recognizing the endogeneity of capital.

are assumed to hold three assets, reserves (R), securities (S), and loans (L); two types of liabilities, demand deposits (DD) and large uninsured time deposits (TD); and capital (K), and as such, are subject to the traditional balance sheet constraint:

$$R + S + L = DD + TD + K \tag{1}$$

On the liability of the balance sheet, bank capital is assumed to be fixed in the short run, as theoretical (Stein, 1998) and empirical evidence (Cornett and Tehranian, 1994) suggests that raising capital is very costly, particularly for banks constrained by risk-based capital standards (Jacques and Nigro, 1997). Demand deposits are assumed to be inversely related to the federal funds rate, and the amount of time deposits depends on the spread between the rate banks pay on deposits (r_{TD}) and the mean rate on time deposits in the market (r_{TDM}), with a_0, a_1, f_0, and f_1 expected to be positive. Thus:

$$DD = a_0 - a_1 r_{FF} \tag{2}$$

$$TD = f_0 + f_1 (r_{TD} - r_{TDM}) \tag{3}$$

where r_{FF} is the federal funds rate.[9]

On the asset side of the balance sheet, banks hold reserves, securities, and commercial and industrial loans. Given the level of demand deposits, banks are required to hold reserves such that:

$$R = \alpha DD \tag{4}$$

with α being the reserve requirement ratio as set by the Federal Reserve, and banks being assumed to hold no excess reserves. In addition, banks are assumed to hold securities in fixed proportion to the level of demand deposits (h_1) net of reserves such that:

$$S = h_0 + h_1 DD - R \tag{5}$$

with h_0 and h_1 expected to be positive. In this model, securities serve as a buffer against liquidity problems arising from large withdrawals of transaction deposits.

---

9. For a discussion of using the federal funds rate as an indicator of the Federal Reserve's monetary policy, see Bernanke and Blinder (1992).

Furthermore, bank loan markets are assumed to be imperfectly competitive, with banks possessing some market power. Thus, banks' loans are influenced by the interest rate offered (r_L) relative to the mean rate in the market (r_{LM}) such that:

$$L = g_0 - g_1(r_L - r_{LM}) \tag{6}$$

The higher the interest rate a bank sets on its loans, relative to the market, the more loans decrease, with both g_0 and g_1 expected to be positive.

Finally, market interest rates on time deposits, loans, and securities are assumed to be related to the federal funds rate such that:

$$r_{TDM} = b_0 + \varphi r_{FF} \tag{7}$$

$$r_{LM} = c_0 + \varphi r_{FF} \tag{8}$$

$$r_S = e_0 + \varphi r_{FF} \tag{9}$$

For simplicity, Peek and Rosengren (1995a) and Kishan and Opiela (2000) make the assumption that all three interest rates respond equally to a change in the federal funds rate.

Given equations (1) through (9), banks are assumed to maximize profits (π) such that:

$$\pi = (r_L - \theta)L + r_S S - r_{DD}D - r_{TD}TD \tag{10}$$

where $r_L L$ is the interest income on loans, θL equals loan losses, $r_S S$ is the interest income on securities, and $r_{DD}D$ and $r_{TD}TD$ are the interest cost of demand and large time deposits, respectively. In attempting to maximize profits, banks face a potential regulatory capital constraint such that:

$$K \geq \gamma_S S + \gamma_L L \tag{11}$$

Equation (11) recognizes that banks are subject to risk-based capital requirements, where γ_S and γ_L measure the risk-based capital requirement for securities and loans, respectively.[10] To explicitly incorporate external credit ratings into the model, the risk-based capital requirement for banks' loans and securities can be rewritten:

$$\gamma_L = \bar{\rho}\tilde{\Omega}_L \tag{12a}$$

$$\gamma_S = \bar{\rho}\tilde{\Omega}_S \tag{12b}$$

where the risk weights on loans and securities, $\tilde{\Omega}_L$ and $\tilde{\Omega}_S$, are both variable and a function of the credit risk of the underlying entity such that:

$$\tilde{\Omega}_L = \tilde{\Omega}_L(c_L) \qquad \frac{d\tilde{\Omega}_L}{dc_L} < 0 \tag{12c}$$

$$\tilde{\Omega}_S = \tilde{\Omega}_S(c_S) \qquad \frac{d\tilde{\Omega}_S}{dc_S} < 0 \tag{12d}$$

In equations (12a) through (12d), $\bar{\rho}$ is the specified regulatory minimum capital ratio, currently fixed at 8% by the Basel Committee. Furthermore, under the external ratings approach, $\tilde{\Omega}_L$ varies inversely with the credit rating of the borrowing entity in the loan contract, c_L, and $\tilde{\Omega}_S$ varies inversely with the credit rating of the borrowing entity underlying the security, c_S, thus making $d\tilde{\Omega}_L / dc_L$ and $d\tilde{\Omega}_S / dc_S$ less than 0.[11]

By way of comparison, under the 1988 Accord, the risk-based capital requirements on loans and securities are invariant with respect to changes in credit ratings. In this case, equations (12a) and (12b) can be rewritten as:

---

10. Currently, banks are subject to both a leverage ratio requirement and a risk-based capital requirement. Including a leverage ratio requirement in this study would result in some banks being constrained by that requirement, but does not change the results for banks constrained by only the revised risk-based capital standards. Because the focus of this research is on how banks will respond to the revised Basel Accord, the question of the leverage ratio is ignored.

11. For commercial loans, $\tilde{\Omega}_L$ ranges between 20% and 150%, with the capital requirement, at the margin, on AAA-rated loans equal to 1.6% (.08 *20%) and for loans rated BB- or lower equal to 12% (.08 *150%). This occurs because, under the external ratings approach, while remains fixed at 8%, $\tilde{\Omega}_L$ varies inversely with the external credit rating of the borrowing entity, with $\tilde{\Omega}_L$ equaling 20%, 50%, 100%, or 150%.

$$\gamma_L = \bar{\rho}\bar{\Omega}_L \qquad \text{where} \quad \frac{d\bar{\Omega}_L}{dc_L} = 0 \qquad (13a)$$

$$\gamma_S = \bar{\rho}\bar{\Omega}_S \qquad \text{where} \quad \frac{d\bar{\Omega}_S}{dc_S} = 0 \qquad (13b)$$

where not only is $\bar{\rho}$ fixed, but because Ω_L and Ω_S are effectively independent of changes in credit risk, they too are fixed, thus making γ_L and γ_S fixed.

The model formed by equations (1) through (10) is identical to Peek and Rosengren (1995a) and Kishan and Opiela (2000), with one significant exception. This study explicitly recognizes that banks are subject to a risk-based capital requirement, and as such, adds equations (11) and (12a–12d). Peek and Rosengren (1995a) examine the model under the assumption that the leverage ratio is binding, with no role for risk-based capital, while Kishan and Opiela (2000) assume that regulatory capital standards are not binding. Comparisons with the Peek and Rosengren leverage ratio results and 1988 Basel Accord equations in (13a) and (13b) provide useful results for comparison purposes. But given the significant changes introduced by the revised Basel Accord, the results from those capital requirements provide limited insight into how monetary policy might be influenced by the revised Accord.

4. UNCONSTRAINED AND CONSTRAINED BANKS

Substituting equations (12a) through (12d) into (11), and using equations (1) through (9) to eliminate R, DD, TD, S, r_{TD}, r_L, r_{TDM}, r_S, and r_{LM}, the Lagrangian was formed and maximized with respect to loans. The first-order conditions were used to solve for L in the unconstrained case; by a similar method, other key variables, such as time deposits, were solved for.

Ceteris paribus, implementation of the revised Basel Accord may influence bank behavior in that some banks that were not constrained under the 1988 standards may become constrained under the revised standards. The opposite result is also possible. Given the existing research suggesting that bank behavior may differ depending on whether or not regulatory capital standards are binding, such an argument suggests the need to differentiate between unconstrained and constrained banks in examining the revised Accord.

Unconstrained Banks

Assuming banks are not constrained by the risk-based capital standards, a change in the federal funds rate can be shown to influence banks' portfolio composition such that:

$$\frac{dL}{dr_{FF}} = \frac{-g_1 a_1 (1-h_1)}{f_1 + g_1} < 0 \qquad \text{assuming } h_1 < 1 \tag{14}$$

$$\frac{dS}{dr_{FF}} = -a_1 (h_1 - \alpha) \; \begin{array}{c} < \\ > \end{array} \; 0 \tag{15}$$

$$\frac{dR}{dr_{FF}} = -a_1 \alpha < 0 \tag{16}$$

$$\frac{dTD}{dr_{FF}} = \frac{f_1 a_1 (1 - h_1)}{f_1 + g_1} > 0 \qquad \text{assuming } h_1 < 1 \tag{17}$$

$$\frac{dDD}{dr_{FF}} = -a_1 < 0 \tag{18}$$

$$\frac{d(deposits)}{dr_{FF}} = \frac{-a_1 (g_1 + f_1 h_1)}{f_1 + g_1} < 0 \tag{19}$$

The results of equations (14) through (19) show that an increase in the federal funds rate will increase banks' issuance of time deposits, as banks seek to replace funds lost as a result of a decrease in demand deposits, with equation (19) showing that collectively, the decrease in demand deposits is not fully offset by increasing time deposits, thus leading to a decrease in total deposits.[12] Given the contraction of liabilities, banks will reduce assets in response to the increase in the federal funds rate. Specifically, the decrease in demand deposits will lead to a contraction in reserves, with the impact on securities being uncertain. Kishan and Opiela (2000) argue that for banks that are unconstrained by regulatory capital standards or hold a large portfolio of securities relative to reserves, $(h_1 - \alpha)$ will be greater than zero, resulting in a decline in securities in response to an increase in the federal funds rate. Despite the change in securities, and the increase in time deposits, banks will reduce loans in response to a contractionary monetary policy, the magnitude of the decrease being determined by not only h_1 but also the interest rate sensitivities of

---

12. Because banks are not constrained by risk-based capital, the results of equations (14) through (19) are the same as those in Peek and Rosengren (1995a) and Kishan and Opiela (2000).

demand deposits (a_1), time deposits (f_1), and loans (g_1). For the purposes of this study, what is important to note is that for banks not constrained by the risk-based capital standards, the risk-based capital requirements on loans and securities, $\bar{\rho}\tilde{\Omega}_L$ and $\bar{\rho}\tilde{\Omega}_S$, do not influence either banks' portfolio composition or the response of their assets and liabilities to a change in the federal funds rate.[13]

Constrained Banks

Alternatively, banks may be constrained by the revised risk-based capital standards. Under this condition, differentiating the Lagrangian and using the first-order conditions to solve for key results yields:

$$\frac{dL}{dr_{FF}} = \frac{\bar{\rho}\tilde{\Omega}_S a_1 (h_1 - \alpha)}{\bar{\rho}\tilde{\Omega}_L} \;\; \begin{matrix}\leq\\>\end{matrix} \;\; 0 \tag{20}$$

$$\frac{dS}{dr_{FF}} = -a_1 (h_1 - \alpha) \;\; \begin{matrix}\leq\\>\end{matrix} \;\; 0 \tag{21}$$

$$\frac{dR}{dr_{FF}} = -a_1 \alpha \;\; < 0 \tag{22}$$

$$\frac{dDD}{dr_{FF}} = -a_1 \;\; < 0 \tag{23}$$

$$\frac{dTD}{dr_{FF}} = \frac{a_1 (1 - h_1)\bar{\rho}\tilde{\Omega}_L + a_1 (h_1 - \alpha)\bar{\rho}\tilde{\Omega}_S}{\bar{\rho}\tilde{\Omega}_L} \;\; \begin{matrix}\leq\\>\end{matrix} \;\; 0 \tag{24}$$

$$\frac{d(deposits)}{dr_{FF}} = \frac{a_1 (h_1 - \alpha)\bar{\rho}\tilde{\Omega}_S - a_1 h_1 \bar{\rho}\tilde{\Omega}_L}{\bar{\rho}\tilde{\Omega}_L} \;\; < 0 \text{ assuming } \tilde{\Omega}_S < \tilde{\Omega}_L \tag{25}$$

These results are fundamentally different from the unconstrained case in that the risk-based capital requirements on both loans and securities play a critical role in how assets and liabilities respond to changes in monetary policy. Specifically, not only do

---

13. As noted by Jacques and Nigro (1997), even banks that are not explicitly constrained by the risk-based capital standards may act as if the standards are binding. This may occur because banks desire to hold a buffer stock of capital above the regulatory minimum as insulation against a shock that would otherwise result in the bank becoming capital constrained, or because by holding capital above the regulatory minimum, banks may signal to the market and regulators that they are in compliance with the standards, thus leading to a reduction in costs.

$\bar{\rho}\tilde{\Omega}_L$ and $\bar{\rho}\tilde{\Omega}_S$ influence how loans, time deposits, and total deposits change as monetary policy changes, but the relative magnitude of the risk weights, $\dfrac{\bar{\rho}\tilde{\Omega}_S}{\bar{\rho}\tilde{\Omega}_L}$, is also an important factor.

As a point of comparison between the 1988 and revised Accords, recall from equations (13a) and (13b) that the capital requirements on loans and securities under the 1988 Accord are fixed. If banks are assumed to have a portfolio of assets comprised of securities slotted in the 20 percent risk-weight category ($\bar{\Omega}_S = 0.2$) and commercial loans ($\bar{\Omega}_L = 1.0$), then under the 1988 Accord, $\dfrac{\bar{\rho}\tilde{\Omega}_S}{\bar{\rho}\tilde{\Omega}_L} = 0.2$. In contrast, under the revised Accord, because of the dependence of the risk weights on credit ratings, $\dfrac{\bar{\rho}\tilde{\Omega}_S}{\bar{\rho}\tilde{\Omega}_L}$ varies according to the credit ratings on the underlying assets. Assuming that the credit rating of securities is such that the risk weight remains at 20 percent, then because not all commercial loans are slotted in the 100 percent risk-weight category under the revised Accord, but are instead weighted according to their credit rating, $\dfrac{\bar{\rho}\tilde{\Omega}_S}{\bar{\rho}\tilde{\Omega}_L}$ will vary, ranging between 0.13 and 1.0.[14] Given the greater granularity in risk weighting of commercial loans under the revised Accord, the effectiveness of monetary policy to change lending will differ depending on the credit quality of the borrowing entities. Assuming $(h_1 - \alpha) < 0$, if $\dfrac{\bar{\rho}\tilde{\Omega}_S}{\bar{\rho}\tilde{\Omega}_L} = 0.13$, as would occur if banks had portfolios comprised of commercial loans rated below BB-, then monetary policy would be less effective under the revised Accord than under the 1988 Accord. In this case, an increase in the federal funds rate would lead to a decrease in loans that is only 65 percent of the decrease that would have occurred under the 1988 Accord. Alternatively, if $\dfrac{\bar{\rho}\tilde{\Omega}_S}{\bar{\rho}\tilde{\Omega}_L} = 1.0$, as would occur if the portfolio is comprised of loans rated AA- or better, then monetary policy

---

14. To see this, note that if all loans are rated below BB- $\dfrac{\bar{\rho}\tilde{\Omega}_S}{\bar{\rho}\tilde{\Omega}_L} = \dfrac{.08*0.20}{.08*1.50} = 0.13$. For a portfolio comprised of commercial loans rated AA- or better, $\dfrac{\bar{\rho}\tilde{\Omega}_S}{\bar{\rho}\tilde{\Omega}_L} = \dfrac{.08*0.20}{.08*0.20} = 1.0$.

would be more effective under the revised Accord than under the 1988 Accord. In this case, the decrease in lending in response to an increase in the federal funds rate would be five times greater than under the 1988 Accord.

From the preceding example, and the results of equations (20) through (25), it can be seen that $(h_1 - \alpha)$ also differentiates the response of capital-constrained banks to changes in the federal funds rate. As such, three cases merit examination. One possibility is that banks have a large securities portfolio relative to their holdings of reserves, $(h_1 - \alpha) > 0$. This may be the case if securities are a substitute for external debt financing, and in the event of a contractionary monetary policy, banks can not frictionlessly switch between demand deposits and large uninsured time deposits, thus making external debt financing costly (Kashyap and Stein, 1997, James, 1995). These banks may be thought of as holding more liquid balance sheets. If $(h_1 - \alpha) > 0$, an increase in the federal funds rate increases time deposits but decreases demand deposits, thus leading to a decrease in total deposits. The fact that the change in total deposits is not equal to zero is in contrast to the findings of Peek and Rosengren (1995a) for banks constrained by the leverage ratio, but is consistent with the lending view of monetary policy in that banks do not fully insulate their lending activities from shocks by switching between types of deposits (Kashyap and Stein, 1994). The decrease in demand deposits results in a decrease in reserves with an accompanying decrease in securities. And given the fact that banks have decreased reserves and securities, similar to Peek and Rosengren (1995a), banks increase loans. While seemingly counterintuitive, this result is consistent with the empirical findings of Kashyap and Stein (1994) that contractionary monetary policy causes commercial lending at large banks to increase in the short run, as well as findings by Morgan (1998) that contractionary monetary policy causes loans under commitment to increase. More importantly, the fact that loans increase in response to a contractionary monetary policy means that if some significant subset of large banks are capital-constrained banks but possess more liquid balance sheets, monetary policy will be less potent.

A second case is where banks do not hold a large securities portfolio relative to their holdings of reserves, $(h_1 - \alpha) < 0$, thus implying less liquid balance sheets. In this case, the impact of a monetary policy shock on time deposits is indeterminate and depends on the relative magnitude of the parameters h_1, $\bar{\rho}\tilde{\Omega}_L$,

$\bar{\rho}\tilde{\Omega}_S$, and α. In the event of a contractionary monetary policy, while the sign of dTD/dr_{FF} is uncertain, the decrease in total deposits is greater and deposits are less available to support loans than in the preceding case of the more liquid bank, and consistent with the bank lending channel, the decrease in demand deposits is not fully offset by a change in time deposits. With liabilities again shrinking, total assets will also decrease. But unlike the case where banks have more liquid balance sheets, in this case, loans decrease and securities increase. Given the fact that these banks are constrained by the risk-based capital standards, and that the securities portfolio is relatively small, banks respond to the decline in total deposits by liquidating some loans. Because the risk-based capital standards place a capital requirement on both loans and securities, liquidating loans frees up some capital which banks can use to acquire interest-bearing securities. To the degree that large U.S. banks emphasize liability management in the management of their balance sheets, in general (Gardner, Mills, and Cooperman, 2000), and can more easily access markets for uninsured liabilities, in particular, this case may be more reflective of how U.S. banks that are likely to apply the revised Basel Accord will react. And in contrast to the preceding case, under these conditions, monetary policy is effective, as capital-constrained banks, like their unconstrained counterparts, decrease lending in response to a contractionary monetary policy.

Finally, the previous examples apply in cases where banks hold securities that carry nonzero risk weights under the risk-based capital standards. But as noted earlier, under the revised risk-based capital standards different amounts of capital are required against different types of assets based primarily on the credit rating of the underlying borrowers. With respect to securities, risk weights on AAA-rated sovereign securities, such as U.S. Treasury bonds, carry a 0 percent risk-based capital requirement at the margin, while the risk weights on other types of securities under the revised Accord may range between 20 and 150 percent, thus leading to capital requirements between 1.6 percent and 12 percent.[15] Examining the earlier results in this section, it can be seen that the effectiveness of monetary policy also depends on the credit rating of the securities in banks' portfolio. Equations (20) through (25) provide an analysis of the impact of changes in the federal funds rate on various components of the banks' balance sheets under the

---

15. Claims on sovereigns and their central banks carry a 0 percent risk weight if rated AAA to AA-. See Basel Committee (2003) for additional details.

assumption that banks hold securities with a nonzero risk weight. Alternatively, if all the securities in a banks' portfolios fall into the 0 percent risk-weight category ($\tilde{\Omega}_S = 0$), the results for time deposits, total deposits, and loans change significantly.[16] To see this, note that an expansionary monetary policy would lead to an increase in total deposits. On the asset side of the balance sheet, part of the increase in deposits would result in an increase in reserves, and depending on the sign of ($h_1 - \alpha$) securities may increase or decrease. But regardless of what happens to securities, banks will make no change in loans. This is the Kashyap and Stein (1994) and Kopecky and VanHoose (2003a) result, in that monetary policy is completely ineffective in changing bank lending. In the case where ($h_1 > \alpha$), banks choose to increase their securities and not their loans because, at the margin, an increase in loans would require already capital-constrained banks to add additional capital, while increasing AAA-rated government securities, which because of the 0 percent risk weight, requires no additional capital, yet allows banks to increase profits.

Collectively, the results for banks constrained by the forthcoming revised Accord concur with Kishan and Opiela (2000) in finding that bank capitalization is critical to explaining cross-sectional differences in the response of banks to changes in monetary policy. But by explicitly incorporating the revised risk-based capital standards into the model, it can be seen that the response of bank lending to monetary policy is asymmetric in that the relative liquidity of constrained banks' balance sheets and the credit quality of the banks' loans and securities are also critical components to understanding how banks respond to changes in monetary policy.

5. MONETARY POLICY AND CREDIT RATINGS MIGRATION

As noted earlier, two of the distinguishing features of the revised Basel Accord are the incorporation of credit ratings into the regulatory capital requirement and the possibility of capital requirements on certain assets changing as underlying credit ratings change. The previous section highlights the importance of the first of these two changes. To see the importance of credit ratings migration on the effectiveness of monetary policy, recall from equations (12a) through (12d) that, unlike the 1988 Accord,

---

16. A number of theoretical studies of the risk-based capital standards make this assumption, including Kashyap and Stein (1994) and Blum and Hellwig (1995).

under the revised Accord the risk-based capital requirements on loans and securities are a function of the credit ratings of the entities to which banks have credit exposures. The fact that loans migrate across risk-weight categories as credit ratings change, and that $(d\tilde{\Omega}_L / dc_L) < 0$, means that the banks' risk-based capital requirements change in response to fluctuations in credit ratings.[17]

In effect, changes in credit ratings can alter the effectiveness of monetary policy in two ways. First, a credit shock may cause banks to move between the unconstrained and risk-based capital constrained states. For example, if corporate credit ratings are positively correlated and change due to market-specific factors such as a recession (Saunders, 2000), then banks that were previously unconstrained may experience a significant number of credit rating downgrades in their portfolio of commercial loans, and as such, become constrained by risk-based capital. And as the preceding sections shows, the potency of monetary policy differs significantly depending not only on whether banks are constrained by the revised risk-based capital standards but also on other characteristics of banks' assets.

Second, using equations (20) through (25), changes in credit ratings will alter the responsiveness of the banks' assets and liabilities to changes in monetary policy. More specifically, the critical results for capital-constrained banks are:

$$\frac{d(\dfrac{dL}{dr_{FF}})}{dc_L} = \frac{d(\dfrac{dTD}{dr_{FF}})}{dc_L} = \frac{-a_1\,(h_1 - \alpha)\,\tilde{\Omega}_S}{\tilde{\Omega}_L^2} * \frac{d\tilde{\Omega}_L}{dc_L} \begin{matrix}<\\>\end{matrix} 0 \qquad (26)$$

Equation (26) is important in that it establishes that the transmission of monetary policy depends not only on the credit quality of the loans and securities comprising banks' assets but also on how banks' deposits and lending respond as credit ratings migrate. In contrast, under the 1988 Accord $(d\bar{\Omega}_L / dc_L) = 0$, thus making monetary policy effectively independent of migrations in the credit rating on banks' existing commercial loans. With regard to the revised Accord, as the credit rating of the borrowing entities deteriorates, the risk weight assigned to the loans increases with a corresponding increase in required capital on already capital-

---

17. Because the focus of much of the current discussion of the revised Accord involves changes in credit ratings on commercial loans, a simplifying assumption has been made that the loans and securities in banks' portfolios are from different corporate entities and that the credit rating of borrowing entities has been downgraded.

constrained banks. Ceteris paribus, given that the risk weight on loans is now greater in both an absolute sense and relative to the risk weight on securities, banks face a reconfigured profit maximization problem with a resulting change in how its loans and time deposits respond to monetary policy changes.

For banks with more liquid balance sheets ($h_1 > \alpha$), the change in the responsiveness of time deposits and loans to changes in the federal funds rate is positively related to changes in the credit rating of the underlying borrowing entity. Recognizing from equations (20) and (24) that $dTD/dr_{FF} > 0$ and $dL/dr_{FF} > 0$ when ($h_1 > \alpha$), the results suggest that as the credit ratings of the borrowing entities deteriorates, the responsiveness of loans and time deposits to changes in the federal funds rate becomes less positive (decreases). In effect, the higher risk weight means that the already capital-constrained banks face not only higher credit risk in their existing portfolios of loans but also increasingly stringent risk-based capital standards. As a result, raising external financing may become even more difficult, thus resulting in even less need for large time deposits and an even smaller increase in loans, with monetary policy becoming more effective in that the response of this cross section of banks is less positive than would otherwise be the case.

In contrast, for banks not holding a relatively large volume of securities ($h_1 < \alpha$), the responsiveness of time deposits and loans to changes in the federal funds rate is negatively related to the credit ratings of the borrowing entities. Thus, a deterioration in the credit ratings of borrowing entities causes the risk-based capital requirement on commercial loans to increase, with dL/dr_{FF} increasing (becoming less negative). For this group of banks, the results suggest that under the revised Accord monetary policy will be less effective in the face of deteriorating credit ratings than when credit ratings are improving. Combined with the findings for banks with more liquid balance sheets, the results provide further evidence of the asymmetric effectiveness of monetary policy under the revised Basel Accord.

6. RISK-BASED CAPITAL AND INTERNAL CREDIT RISK MODELS

Using a modification of the theoretical approach of Peek and Rosengren (1995a) and Kishan and Opiela (2000), we have compared the implications of the revised Basel capital standards on the effectiveness of monetary policy to influence bank lending. While our analysis assumes that banks' regulatory capital requirements are based on the external credit rating approach, as described in footnotes 4 and 5, the revised Accord also allows for the use of internal credit risk models to determine banks' credit risk exposure. In his recent Congressional testimony, Ferguson (2003b) notes that the twenty largest U.S. banking organizations most immediately impacted by the revised Accord will not use the external ratings approach, but instead will be required to implement the Advanced Internal Ratings-Based (A-IRB) approach and provide the critical inputs for supervisors to determine appropriate capital requirements, these inputs being the probability of default (PD), loss given default (LGD), and exposure at default (EAD). These inputs are then used in supervisory formulas to determine the minimum risk-based capital that must be held by banks. It is noteworthy that the inputs required by bank supervisors to determine the risk-based capital requirements under the revised Accord using the A-IRB approach are not unlike the inputs used by external credit rating agencies to evaluate default risk.

We hypothesize that our general conclusions about the effectiveness of Federal Reserve monetary policy to influence banks' lending behavior, using a modified version of our theoretical model to include the A-IRB approach, would be very similar to the conclusions drawn from our theoretical model using the external credit rating approach. Such further modification of our theoretical model could be accomplished by rewriting the risk-based capital requirement on banks' loans $\left(\bar{\rho}\tilde{\Omega}_L\right)$ in equation (12a) as a function of PD, LGD, and EAD, and incorporating the supervisory formulas as found in Basel Committee (2003). This is a topic for future research. Alternatively, recognizing that banks in many foreign countries will apply the external ratings approach rather than the A-IRB, substituting the relevant central bank interest rate for the federal funds rate in our model provides insights as to the effectiveness of monetary policy in those economies.

7. CONCLUSIONS

Existing research on the Basel Accord has raised the question of how revisions to the Accord are likely to influence the effectiveness of Federal Reserve monetary policy. In contrast to the 1988 Accord, the revised risk-based capital standards allow banks' capital requirements to be determined by credit ratings. Modifying recent work by Peek and Rosengren (1995a) and Kishan and Opiela (2000), this study finds that the effectiveness of monetary policy to influence bank lending differs depending on whether or not banks are constrained by the risk-based capital standards. In addition, the effectiveness of monetary policy to influence lending is also shown to depend on the credit quality of banks' loans and securities and the liquidity of banks' balance sheets. As such, the results are consistent with Kishan and Opiela (2000) in finding that differences in the response of banks' assets and liabilities to monetary policy depend on the capitalization of banks. But this study extends their results by also noting asymmetrical differences in the effectiveness of monetary policy to influence both the direction and magnitude of bank lending depending on banks' balance sheet liquidity and the credit quality of their assets. In contrast to the 1988 Accord, currently proposed revisions also allow regulatory capital requirements to migrate as the credit rating of the borrowing entity changes. The results of this study have also shown that the effectiveness of monetary policy is not invariant to migrating credit ratings. Rather, changes in the credit ratings of borrowing entities lead banks to have an asymmetric response to monetary policy changes depending on the relative liquidity of banks' balance sheets.

The results of this study have implications for the Federal Reserve's conduct of monetary policy, showing that whether monetary policy is made more or less effective in changing bank lending depends on more than just whether or not banks are constrained by the revised Basel Accord. Rather, if credit ratings change over business cycles, this study has shown the critical financial characteristics of banks and their assets that will determine the ability of monetary policy to influence both the direction and magnitude of bank commercial lending. The responsiveness of banks to monetary policy changes is asymmetric in that some characteristics will make monetary policy more potent, while others will make monetary policy less effective. But from a macroeconomic policy perspective, consistent with Bliss and Kaufman (2002), the implications of this study are that if the goal of the Federal Reserve is to simultaneously provide credit to the economy and manage interest rates, then the revised Basel Accord may complicate monetary policy.

REFERENCES

Aggarwal, Raj and KevinT. Jacques, (2001), The impact of FDICIA and prompt corrective action on bank capital and risk: Estimates using a simultaneous equations model, *Journal of Banking and Finance* 25, pp. 1139–1160.

Bangia, Anil, Francis X. Diebold, Andre Kronimus, Christian Schagen, and Til Schuermann, (2002), Ratings migration and the business cycle with application to credit portfolio stress testing, *Journal of Banking and Finance* 26, pp. 445–474.

Basel Committee on Banking Supervision, (2003), The New Basel Capital Accord: Consultative Document.

Berger, Allen N. and Gregory F. Udell, (1994), Did risk-based capital allocate bank credit and cause a 'credit crunch' in the United States? *Journal of Money, Credit, and Banking* 26, pp. 585–628.

Bernanke, Ben S. and Alan S. Blinder, (1992), The federal funds rate and the channels of monetary transmission, *American Economic Review* 82, pp. 901–921.

Bliss, Robert R. and George G. Kaufman, (2002), Bank procyclicality, credit crunches, and asymmetric monetary policy effects: A unifying model, *Federal Reserve Bank of Chicago Working Paper* 2002-18, pp. 1–15.

Blum, Jurg and Martin Hellwig, (1995), The macroeconomic implications of capital adequacy requirements for banks, *European Economic Review* 39, pp. 739–749.

Brinkmann, Emile J. and Paul M. Horvitz, (1995), Risk-based capital standards and the credit crunch, *Journal of Money, Credit and Banking* 27, pp. 848–863.

Chami, Ralph and Thomas F. Cosimano, (2001), Monetary policy with a touch of Basel, *International Monetary Fund Working Paper,* WP/01/151.

Cornett, Marcia M. and Hassan Tehranian, (1994), An examination of voluntary versus involuntary security issuances by commercial banks: the impact of capital regulations on common stock returns, *Journal of Financial Economics* 35, pp. 99–122.

Ferguson, Roger, (2003a), Comments before the Risk Management Association's Conference on Capital Management, Washington, D.C., April 9, 2003.

Ferguson, Roger, (2003b), Testimony before the Committee on Banking, Housing, and Urban Affairs, U.S. Senate, Washington, D.C., June 18.

Furfine, Craig, (2000), Evidence on the response of U.S. banks to changes in capital requirements, *Bank for International Settlements Working Paper,* No. 88.

Gardner, Mona, Dixie Mills, and Elizabeth Cooperman, (2000). *Managing Financial Institutions*, Fourth edition, New York: Dryden Press, pp. 740–746.

Hall, Brian, (1993), How has the Basle accord affected bank portfolios? *Journal of the Japanese and International Economies* 7, pp. 8–40.

Hancock, Diana and James Wilcox, (1994), Bank capital and the credit crunch: The roles of risk-weighted and unweighted capital regulations, *Journal of the American Real Estate and Urban Economics Association* 22, pp. 59–94.

Haubrich, Joseph and Paul Wachtel, (1993), Capital requirements and shifts in commercial bank portfolios, *Economic Review*, Federal Reserve Bank of Cleveland 3, pp. 2–15.

Jackson, Patricia, Craig Furfine, Hans Groeneveld, Diana Hancock, David Jones, William Perraudin, Lawrence Radecki, and Masao Yoneyama, (1999), Capital requirements and bank behaviour: The impact of the Basle Accord, Bank for International Settlements, *Basle Committee on Banking Supervision Working Papers*, No. 1.

Jacques, Kevin T. and Peter Nigro, (1997), Risk-based capital, portfolio risk, and bank capital: A simultaneous equations approach, *Journal of Economics and Business* 49, pp. 533–547.

James, Christopher, (1995), Discussion, *Federal Reserve Bank of Boston Conference Series, Is Bank Lending Important for the Transmission of Monetary Policy?* 39, pp. 76–79.

Jones, David, (2000), Emerging problems with the Basel Capital Accord: Regulatory capital arbitrage and related issues, *Journal of Banking and Finance* 24, pp. 35–58.

Jokivuolle, Esa and Samu Peura, (2001), A value-at-risk approach to banks' capital buffers: An application to the new Basel accord, *Bank of Finland Discussion Papers*, No. 15.

Kashyap, Anil K. and Jeremy C. Stein, (1994), Monetary policy and bank lending. In N.G. Mankiw, ed., *Monetary Policy*. Chicago: University of Chicago Press, pp. 221–256.

Kashyap, Anil K. and Jeremy C. Stein, (2000), What do a million observations on banks say about the transmission of monetary policy? *American Economic Review* 83, pp. 78–98.

Kishan, Ruby P. and Timothy P. Opiela, (2000), Bank Size, Bank Capital, and the Bank Lending Channel, *Journal of Money, Credit, and Banking* 32, pp. 121–41.

Kopecky, Kenneth J. and David VanHoose, (2003a), A Model of the Monetary Sector with and without Binding Capital Requirements, *Journal of Banking and Finance*, forthcoming.

Kopecky, Kenneth J. and David VanHoose, (2003b), Bank capital requirements and the monetary transmission mechanism, forthcoming, *Journal of Macroeconomics*, forthcoming.

Lowe, Phillip, (2002), Credit risk measurement and procyclicality, *Bank for International Settlements Working Paper*, No. 116.

Morgan, Donald P., (1998), The credit effects of monetary policy: evidence using loan commitments, *Journal of Money, Credit and Banking* 30, pp. 102–118.

Nickell, Pamela, William Perraudin, and Simone Varotto, (2000), Stability of ratings transitions, *Journal of Banking and Finance* 24, pp. 203–227.

Peek, Joe and Eric S. Rosengren, (1995a), Bank lending and the transmission of monetary policy, *Federal Reserve Bank of Boston Conference Series, Is Bank Lending Important for the Transmission of Monetary Policy?* 39, pp. 47–68.

Peek, Joe and Eric S. Rosengren, (1995b), The capital crunch: neither a borrower nor a lender be, *Journal of Money, Credit and Banking* 27, pp. 625–638.

Saunders, Anthony, (2000), *Financial Institutions Management: A Modern Perspective*. Third edition, Irwin McGraw-Hill Publishing Co.

Stein, Jeremy C., (1998), An adverse-selection model of bank asset and liability management with implications for the transmission of monetary policy, *RAND Journal of Economics* 29, pp. 466–486.

Tanaka, Misa, (2002), How do bank capital and capital adequacy regulation affect the monetary transmission mechanism? *Center for Economic Studies and the Ifo Institute for Economic Research Working Paper*, No. 799.

Thakor, Anjan V., (1996), Capital requirements, monetary policy, and aggregate bank lending: Theory and empirical evidence, *The Journal of Finance* 51, pp. 279–324.

Van den Heuvel, Skander J., (2002a), Does bank capital matter for monetary transmission? *Federal Reserve Bank of New York Economic Policy Review*, pp. 259–265.

Van den Heuvel, Skander J., (2002b), The bank capital channel of monetary policy, *University of Pennsylvania Working Paper*.

12

Is the New Basel Accord Incentive Compatible?

Paul H. Kupiec

I. INTRODUCTION

In the January 2001 consultative paper, "The New Basel Accord," the Basel Committee on Banking Supervision (BCBS) provides the rationale for a proposed revision to the 1988 Basel Capital Accord (the 1988 Accord). The proposed revisions are "intended to align capital adequacy assessment more closely with key elements of banking risks . . . and to secure the objective of prudentially sound, incentive-compatible and risk sensitive capital requirements."[1]

The New Basel Accord proposal, or so-called Basel II, departs from the format of the 1988 Accord and specifies credit risk weights that are linked either to internal loan classification schemes, as in the internal ratings-based (IRB) approaches, or to external credit ratings, as in the standardized approach. Both approaches set credit risk weights according to a credit's anticipated probability of default and are, at least in part, designed to mimic the techniques used internally by banks. The decision to base regulatory capital on credit risk measurement processes that are designed to be consistent with banks' internal risk measurement processes is a deliberate attempt to harmonize regulatory capital requirements with the best practices of internationally active banks.[2]

---

1. Basel Committee on Banking Supervisions, "Overview of The New Basel Capital Accord," January 2001, paragraphs 2 and 35.
2. Ibid., paragraphs 99 and 100.

The BCBS believes it has designed Basel II to "provide incentives for banks to enhance their risk measurement and management capabilities. . . ."[3] In particular, the committee reports that the capital proposals include incentives that are intended to encourage banks to evolve from the standardized approach, through the foundation IRB approach, and finally toward the advanced IRB approach for calculating capital. The BCBS's stated objective is to place "a greater emphasis on banks' own assessment of the risks to which they are exposed in the calculation of regulatory capital charges."[4] This objective reflects the committee's view that "ultimate responsibility for managing risks and ensuring that capital is held at a level consistent with a bank's risk profile remains with that bank's management."[5] It is in this context that the BCBS characterizes Basel II as an incentive-compatible approach for bank regulation.

Basel II may be designed to be compatible with banks' internal credit risk measurement practices, but is it really an incentive-compatible approach for bank regulation? Underlying this question is a deeper, unresolved issue concerning whether it is even possible to design an effective regulatory capital measure that is based on risk measures that banks themselves design for their own internal management purposes. If the need for bank regulation is based in part on the existence of externalities, it is important to understand if and how these externalities can be measured and controlled using the internal processes that banks have designed for their own profit maximization objectives.[6]

The goal of harmonizing regulatory capital guidelines with those used by banks in their internal risk management processes is appealing by virtue of the implicit promise of reduced regulatory burden. A priori, however, it is far from clear how such an approach will control the externalities that mandate bank regulation. While BCBS's consultative documents fully embrace the goal of harmonizing capital regulation with banks' internal processes, it is troubling that the BCBS fails to discuss the nature of the externalities that mandate capital regulation or provide any analysis that supports the claim that banks' internal processes can be harnessed to control the underlying market failure(s).

---

3. Ibid., paragraph 2.
4. Ibid., paragraph 5.
5. Ibid., paragraph 30.
6. See Kupiec (2002) for further discussion.

This paper provides a detailed analysis of the incentives that are created by the specific capital regulations that have been proposed for corporate credits in alternative versions of Basel II. Existing and proposed regulatory capital guidelines are analyzed in the context of a simple, but powerful, equilibrium model of a bank that benefits from subsidized insured deposits and endogenously selects its optimal level of credit risk exposure. The focus on deposit insurance provides modeling clarity and is not a limiting feature of the model. The qualitative aspects of the analysis will apply to any bank that receives a safety-net–related subsidy on its funding costs.

The analysis shows that, while all approaches proposed under Basel II will make regulatory capital requirements more sensitive to corporate credit risk, low-quality credits remain the most valuable to banks. The adoption of Basel II's standardized approach promises to have almost no effect on the incentives banks face regarding the choice of which loans to securitize and which loans to retain on their balance sheets. None of the approaches that have been proposed by the BCBS creates an incentive for banks to select loans with minimal expected loss given default. Even the advanced IRB approach does not encourage a bank to try to increase loan recovery rates. This feature of Basel II is particularly troubling as the loss given default characteristics of a bank's loans are the primary factor determining an insurer's cost of resolving a failed bank.[7] Moreover, in contrast to the BCBS's stated intentions, the analysis finds no economic incentive from the capital requirement framework in Basel II that will encourage banks to evolve from the standardized to the advanced IRB capital approach.

The findings in this study suggest that if only some banks are required by their national supervisors to adopt the IRB approaches, it is likely that natural banking clienteles will emerge from the incentives created by Basel II's alternative capital schemes. Differences in the regulatory capital treatment will allow banks that use the standardized approach to increase their share values by competing away lower-quality credit business from IRB banks. Large IRB banks have a regulatory capital induced competitive advantage in attracting relatively high-quality credits that may allow them to successfully attract these borrowers away from banks that use the standardized approach. As designed, Basel II may

---

7. The regulatory objective of least cost resolution is the basis for FDICIA's prompt corrective action supervisory guidelines (12 U.S.C. §1831o) and the guidelines that govern the U.S. FDIC's actions in insurance-related activities (12 U.S.C. §1823c(4)).

encourage segmentation in the credit qualities of internationally active banks and thereby abandon the "level playing field" objective of the 1988 Accord. The portfolio realignments encouraged under Basel II will likely strengthen the prudential solvency standards of sophisticated (IRB) money center banks. Overall financial market stability, however, may not be enhanced if poor quality credits are concentrated in standardized approach banks.

A final interesting result is the finding that Basel II's proposed capital schemes create incentives that will encourage banks to concentrate lending to counterparties that have an elevated probability of default in recessions. Capital requirements under the 1988 Accord do not depend on physical probabilities of loan default. Once regulatory capital is explicitly conditioned on a credit's physical probability of default, banks face incentives that encourage them to discriminate among credits on another basis. Among credits with a given probability of default, if investors are risk averse, the credits that default in recessions offer the largest ex ante risk premiums.[8] When capital requirements constrain bank insurance values, according to a credit's expected physical probability of default and loss given default, an important aspect of credit risk that remains unregulated is the timing of default. By choosing credits that are expected to default in recessions, shareholders benefit from the larger credit risk premium in nonrecession periods and thereby enhance the value of their deposit insurance guarantee. Because there are many ways to influence the deposit insurance value under the 1988 Accord, existing rules do not favor a particular phase of the business cycle when considering the timing of loan defaults.

The limitations of this study are recognized at the outset. The analysis is based on a single-period model with competitive lending markets and no corporate taxes, and so optimal loan selection is driven by the objective of maximizing deposit insurance values. If capital requirements are set sufficiently high so that the deposit insurance guarantee is valueless, the incentives discussed in this chapter will no longer exist. In a multiperiod setting that recognizes market power and taxes, bank franchise values and interest tax shields will become important determinants of bank behavior. Bank franchise values will, other things equal, lower insurance values from those calculated in this analysis, but recognition of

---

8. More formally, credits that default when the marginal utility of consumption is high (a recession, roughly speaking) offer the largest ex ante risk premia.

interest deductibility and taxes will offset this effect. While the model is specialized in many respects, it is designed to focus on the value of government-engendered safety nets and the direct effect they have on a bank's investment decisions. An outline of the paper follows.

Under the assumption of investor risk neutrality, Section II develops an equilibrium model in which banks fund themselves with insured deposits and endogenously select the risk characteristics of the single risky loan in which they invest. The single-loan and risk-neutrality assumptions greatly simplify the analysis with little cost, as a subsequent section establishes the generality of the results. The regulatory capital requirements under the Accord and the proposed alternative regulatory capital requirements of Basel II are discussed in Section III. Section IV analyzes optimal bank behavior when bank investment and financing decisions are constrained by the alternative regulatory capital regimes. Section V discusses the potential market equilibrium implications of Basel II. Section VI extends the simple risk-neutral banking model to a general equilibrium setting in which risk-averse investors are able to transact in complete Arrow-Debreu contingent claims markets. This extension establishes a link between optimal bank credit risk allocation and the macroeconomic environment. Section VII analyzes bank behavior in the risk-averse investor setting when banks are constrained by the alternative regulatory capital schemes. Section VIII discusses the extension of the single-loan model to a portfolio context. It is demonstrated that the results of the single-loan analysis immediately generalize once the credit risk parameters in the single-loan case are reinterpreted as measures of the insured bank's total portfolio credit risk—the bank's probability of default and the loss given default on its loan portfolio. A final section concludes the paper.

2. THE RISK NEUTRAL MODEL

For simplicity, we assume a two-state distribution of cash payoffs on the bank's loan: it either makes its entire payment of principle and interest, P, or it defaults. If the bond defaults, the bank's loss is assumed to be a fraction, LGD, of the promised principle and interest payment, P.[9] In this binomial setting, the bank selects the level of insured deposits to issue and the characteristics of its loan

---

9. In the analysis that follows, the par value of the loan, P, is fixed. The qualitative aspects of the analysis do not depend on this normalization.

portfolio (the loan's probability of default and its loss given default) to maximize the ex ante wealth of the bank's shareholders. The analysis does not consider information asymmetries that may arise in the context of the valuation of bank shares and assumes that the value of bank assets are transparent to equity market investors.[10]

Initially, the analysis assumes that investors behave as if they are risk neutral so that financial assets are valued as the discounted value of their expected future cash flows, where discounting takes place at the risk-free rate. A subsequent section relaxes this assumption and analyzes the bank incentive that arise when investors are risk averse.

Bank Loan Valuation

Under the risk neutral valuation assumption, the present value of the bank's loan is given by

$$L(pr_i, LGD_i) = \frac{P(1 - pr_i LGD_i)}{1 + r_f}, \tag{1}$$

where the index i is used to indicate that the loan characteristics selected by the bank, and r_f is the risk-free rate of interest. When a bank makes a loan, it lends the full fair present market value of the loan. The bank is not assumed to have any market power in lending markets.

The Valuation of the Claims of Bank Stakeholders

We assume the existence of a government agent, who insures the value of banks' transactions deposits at a fixed ex ante premium rate normalized to 0, and consider the present value of the claims of three bank stakeholders: equity, insured debt, and the deposit insurance authority.[11] All fixed income claims are modeled as discount instruments in this one-period, two-date model.

---

10. We assume away information issues, not because they are unimportant, but because the simplification allows for an analysis of the underlying operational incentives created by the proposed credit risks capital requirements under Basel II.
11. As a point of comparison, it should be noted that the U.S. deposit insurance premium rate is currently 0 for well-capitalized banks.

Let D be the terminal value of insured deposits. Assume $P > D$ to ensure that, in the high payoff state, deposits pay out their promised par value even in the absence of deposit insurance. Notice that deposit insurance is valuable provided that default probability is positive and $D > P(1 - LGD_i)$.

If the bank issues insured deposits with a terminal value of D, their present fair market value is $D(1 + r_f)^{-1}$. Assuming that deposit insurance is valuable, the present market value of the deposit insurer's stake, $INS(D, pr_i, LGD_i)$, depends on the level of the deposits issued by the bank, the probability of default, and loss given default characteristics of the loan selected by the bank,

$$INS(D, pr_i, LGD_i) = \frac{\left[D - P\left(1 - LGD_i\right)\right] pr_i}{1 + r_f}. \tag{2}$$

The market value of the bank's equity claims, $EQ(D, pr_i, LGD_i)$, depends on the level of insured deposits it issues, D, as well as on the probability of default, and loss given default risk characteristics selected by the bank,

$$EQ(D, pr_i, LGD_i) = \frac{Max\left(0, P\left(1 - LGD_i\right) - D\right) pr_i + \left(P - D\right)\left(1 - pr_i\right)}{1 + r_f}. \tag{3}$$

When deposit insurance is valuable, the present fair market value of equity simplifies

$$EQ(D, pr_i, LGD_i) = \frac{\left(P - D\right)\left(1 - pr_i\right)}{1 + r_f}. \tag{4}$$

Optimization and the Value of the Deposit Guarantee

Bank shareholder/managers decide on the level of insured deposits to be issued by the bank and select the credit risk characteristics (pr_i, LGD_i) of the bank's loan. Assuming that deposit insurance has value, the fair present market value of the profits that accrue to equity holders are given by expression (4). Given that the bank's deposits are subsidized, the initial investment that equity holders must commit, i.e., the shareholder's paid-in capital, is given by $L(D, pr_i, LGD_i) - D(1 + r_f)^{-1}$. The difference between the fair present market value of profits and shareholder's paid-in capital,

$$EQ(D, pr_i, LGD_i) - \left(L(pr_i, LGD_i) - \frac{D}{1 + r_f}\right) = INS(D, pr_i, LGD_i), \quad \text{is}$$

the value of the deposit insurance guarantee. The ex ante value of the deposit insurance guarantee, a wealth transfer from the deposit insurer to the bank shareholders, is pure profit from the shareholders' perspective. Bank shareholders maximize their ex ante wealth by maximizing the value of the deposit insurance guarantee.

3. REGULATORY CAPITAL REQUIREMENTS FOR CORPORATE LENDING

Regulatory capital requirements limit the degree to which a bank can use insured deposits to fund its loan portfolio. Under the 1988 Accord, a bank must have an amount of qualifying regulatory capital that is at least 8 percent of the value of its risk-weighted assets. A corporate loan has a 100 percent risk weight. Qualifying regulatory capital includes Tier 1 capital that is composed of paid-in shareholder equity capital and Tier 2 capital that includes qualifying subordinated debt (subject to regulatory limits) and a share of a bank's general loan loss provisions. For purposes of this analysis, qualifying regulatory capital is limited to paid-in equity capital and the 8 percent minimum regulatory capital require-ment imposes a limit on the insured deposit issuance that can be used to fund a loan,[12]

$$D \leq .92(1 + r_f)L(pr_i, LGD_i).\qquad(5)$$

If deposit insurance is valuable, the bank will, in this model setting, always maximize the use of insured deposit funding, and equation (5) will hold as an equality.

Basel II proposals recommend that regulatory capital require-ments for corporate credits be determined according to one of three methods: the so-called Standardized approach, or either a Foundation or Advanced IRB approach. The Standardized approach itself is not a single approach but two alternative approaches. One approach sets capital requirements according to the credit's sovereign external credit rating. The second approach bases the capital requirement on an issuer-specific external credit rating. The analysis that follows will consider only the second variant of the Standardized approach.

---

12. The restriction is made not only to simplify the analysis but also because a reasonable treatment analyzing the incentives generated when subordinated debt is included as qualifying equity capital requires that taxes and debt tax shields be included in the model.

The Standardized Approach

Table 1 reports the proposed risk weights and capital requirements for corporate credits under the Standardized approach, assuming that the regulatory minimum risk-weighted capital ratio is 8 percent. Define the correspondence $Cap(rating_i)$ to be a rule that assigns a capital requirement according to a credit's Standard & Poor's (S&P) rating ($rating_i$) using the rule in Table 1. Under the assumption that only paid-in equity qualifies as regulatory capital, the Standardized approach imposes an insured deposit limit,

$$D \leq \left(1 - Cap(rating_i)\right)(1 + r_f)L(pr_i, LGD_i). \tag{6}$$

If deposit insurance is valuable, the bank will maximize the use of insured deposit funding, and expression (6) will hold as an equality.

Table 1. The Standardized Approach

STANDARD & POOR'S RATING	STANDARDIZED RISK WEIGHT(PERCENT)	STANDARDIZED CAPITAL REQUIREMENT(PERCENT)
AAA to AA-	20	1.6
A+ to A-	50	4
BBB+ to BB-	100	8
Below BB-	150	12
Unrated	100	8

Source: Risk weights and capital requirements under the Standardized approach assume an 8 percent minimum regulatory risk-weighted capital ratio.

The IRB Approaches

Since the initial January 2001 consultative document, Basel II's IRB approaches have experienced substantial revisions, and the IRB capital functions have been expanded to include numerous specialized lending categories (retail, small- and medium-sized enterprises, residential mortgages, etc.). The analysis in this paper will focus on minimum capital requirements for corporate loans.

Under Basel II's IRB proposals, regulatory capital requirements for corporate loans will be determined by a risk-weighting function that depends on the ex ante risk characteristics of the credit. Under the Foundation IRB approach, the risk weight depends on the credit's ex ante probability of default. Under the Advanced IRB approach, the risk-weight depends on the credit's ex ante probability of default and loss given default.[13]

January 2001 IRB Corporate Capital Requirements

If qualifying capital is assumed to be limited to Tier 1 capital, the January 2001 Foundation IRB approach requires that the paid-in equity capital for a corporate loan be at least

$$.08\frac{Min\left[BRW_C(pr_i),625\right]}{100}L(pr_i,LGD_i),\text{where } BRW_C(pr_i),$$

the regulatory risk-weighting function for corporate credits is given by

$$BRW_C(pr_i)=976.5\left(1+.0470\frac{1-Max\left[pr_i,.0003\right]}{Max\left[pr_i,.0003\right]^{.44}}\right)\Phi\left(1.288+1.118\Phi^{-1}\left(Max\left[pr_i,.0003\right]\right)\right),$$

where $\Phi(.)$ represents the cumulative standard normal distribution function, and $\Phi^{-1}(.)$ represents the inverse of this function. Under the January 2001 Foundation IRB capital requirement, insured bank deposits must satisfy the inequality

$$D\leq\left(1+r_f\right)L\left(pr_i,LGD_i\right)\left(1-.08\frac{Min\left[BRW_C\left(pr_i\right),625\right]}{100}\right)\tag{7}$$

The use of insured deposits will be maximized (the equality in expression (7) will hold) when deposit insurance is valuable.

Ignoring the maturity adjustment and restricting qualifying capital to Tier 1 capital, the minimum paid-in equity capital requirement under the January 2001 Advanced IRB Approach is

$$.08\,Min\left[\frac{LGD_i}{.50}\frac{BRW_C(pr_i)}{100},12.5*LGD_i\right]L(pr_i,LGD_i),$$

and insured deposits must satisfy

$$D\leq\left(1+r_f\right)L\left(pr_i,LGD_i\right)\left(1-.08\left[\frac{LGD_i}{50}\frac{BRW_C(pr_i)}{100},12.5*LGD_i\right]\right).\tag{8}$$

Again, expression (8) will hold as an equality when deposit insurance is valuable.

---

13. The Advanced IRB approach also will include a maturity adjustment. The maturity adjustment is set to unity in this single-period model analysis.

April 2003 IRB Corporate Capital Requirements

The April 2003 consultative paper redefined the Foundation and Advanced IRB corporate risk-weighting functions in terms of "maturity" and "correlation" adjustment functions that enter into the risk-weighting formula. Under the April 2003 Basel II consultative paper formulations, the maturity and correlation functions are defined as

Maturity: $b(pr_i) = \left[.08451 - .058981n(pr_i)\right]^2$

Correlation: $R(pr_i) = .12\left(\dfrac{1-e^{-50pr_i}}{1-e^{-50}}\right) + .24\left(1-\dfrac{1-e^{-50pr_i}}{1-e^{-50}}\right).$

The April 2003 Advanced IRB regulatory capital requirement function, ignoring the effective maturity function adjustment, is defined as[14]

$$K(pr_i, LGD_i) = \left(\dfrac{LGD_i}{1-1.5b(pr_i)}\right)\Phi\left[\left(\dfrac{1}{1-R(pr_i)}\right)^{\frac{1}{2}}\Phi^{-1}(pr_i) + \left(\dfrac{R(pr_i)}{1-R(pr_i)}\right)^{\frac{1}{2}}\Phi^{-1}(.999)\right]. \tag{9}$$

The April 2003 Foundation IRB regulatory capital requirement is given by $K(pr_i,.45)$; that is, the foundation IRB risk weights are equivalent to the Advanced IRB risk weights, assuming $LGD_i = .045 \forall i$. Under the April 2003 revision to the Foundation IRB approach, when funding a corporate loan, deposits must satisfy

$$D \leq \left(1+r_f\right) L(pr_i, LGD_i)\left(1-K(pr_i, 0.45)\right). \tag{10}$$

Under the April 2003 Advanced IRB approach, when funding a corporate loan, deposits must satisfy

$$D \leq \left(1+r_f\right) L(pr_i, LGD_i)\left(1-K(pr_i, LGD_i)\right). \tag{11}$$

The April 2003 revisions to the IRB risk-weighting functions altered the shape of the January 2001 functions. Under the Foundation Approach, as the probability of default increases, the April 2003 capital requirements rise much more quickly for high-quality credits relative to the January 2001 function. For high-quality credits, for example credits with probability of default less than 2

---

14. Effective maturity is set equal to 2.5, and so the maturity adjustment factor is unity.

percent, the 2003 Foundation IRB capital requirements exceed those set by the January 2001 risk-weighting function. When the probability of default exceeds roughly 2 percent, the April 2003 capital function requires less capital than the January 2001 capital function. The change in the shape of the IRB minimum capital requirement functions were implemented to reduce the inherent "procyclicality" of minimum IRB capital requirements.

Procyclicality refers to the process by which a counterparty downgrade—either by an external credit rating agency or in an internal bank credit quality categorization process—results in higher minimum capital requirements. Because there is a natural tendency for credits to be downgraded in a recession, Basel II minimum capital requirements are expected to increase during business cycle downturns. Such behavior, more strongly manifest in the January 2001 capital functions, was deemed to be suboptimal because of its potential for limiting bank credit growth during recessions. Figure 1 plots the capital charges under the 2001 and 2003 Foundation IRB risk-weighting functions.

Figure 1. Alternative Foundation IRB Capital Functions

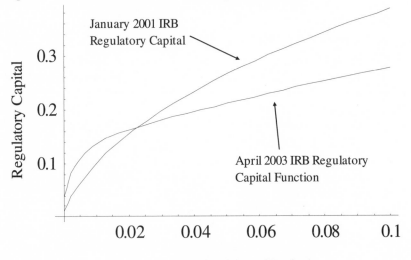

Probability of Default

Under the Advanced IRB approach, the capital charge is a three-dimensional surface defined over a credit's potential probability of default and loss given default. The April 2003 version of the Advanced IRB capital charge function was modified relative to the January 2001 parameterization with the intent to limit the

**Figure 2. Regulatory Capital Requirements Under the April 2003
Advanced IRB**

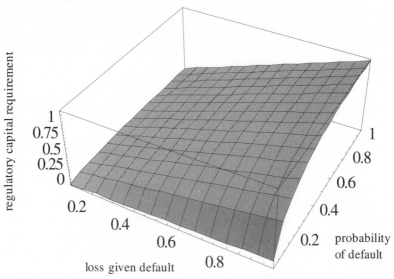

Figure 3. Insurance Value Under the 1988 Accord

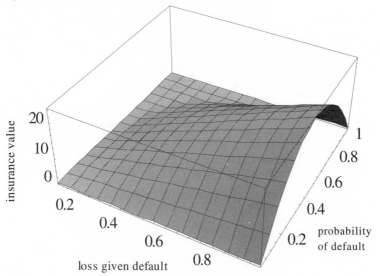

procyclicality of the Advanced IRB minimum capital requirements. The January 2001 and April 2003 capital surfaces have a cross section (for an LGD, fixed at 45 percent) identical to Figure 1. Figure 2 plots the Advance IRB minimum capital requirement surface for the April 2003 version of this function with effective maturity fixed at 2.5 years.

4. SHAREHOLDER VALUE MAXIMIZATION UNDER RISK NEUTRALITY

Shareholder-managers select the level of insured deposits and the loan risk characteristics to maximize the value of the deposit insurance guarantee, subject to any regulatory capital requirements that may constrain their admissible choice set. We consider bank optimization under six alternative capital requirement regimes: the Accord, the Standardized approach, and the January 2001 and April 2003 Foundation and Advanced IRB capital regimes assuming that the entire 8 percent capital requirement must be met with paid-in equity capital.

The 1988 Basel Accord

When paid-in equity capital is constrained by the rules of the 1988 Accord, shareholders attempt to maximize the deposit insurance value [equation (2)] subject to the deposit issuance constraint in equation (5). Figure 3 plots the constrained deposit insurance surface generated for a loan with $P = 110$ using $r_f = .05$. Notice that under the Accord, the deposit insurance value is maximized by selecting loans with a high probability of default and a large expected loss given default. Under the assumptions of this simple model, the loan characteristics $pr_i = .5$, $LGD_i = 1$ provide the global optimal for shareholder wealth. If the value of LGD_i is constrained by some upper bound, $LGD^U < 1$, the optimal solution is to set the loss given default to its upper bound and select the default probability to satisfy $pr_i^* = \dfrac{LGD^U - .08}{1.84 \ LGD^U}$.

The exact optimizing loan characteristics identified under this highly stylized model are less important than the qualitative predictions of the model. The model suggests that, under the 1988 Accord, banks face a strong incentive to hold relatively risky loans. The existing capital requirement framework creates no incentive for the bank to retain high-quality credits—credits with low probability of default and small expected losses given default. The model's predictions are consistent with the observed trend in bank behavior to securitize high-quality credits.

The Standardized Approach

Table 2 reports the insurance values associated with corporate credits rated under alternative Standard & Poor's categories. Insurance values are calculated under the 1988 Accord and under Basel II's revised Standardized approach for regulatory capital. The calculations in Table 2 assume that $P = 100$, $r_f = .05$, and $LGD_i = .50 \forall i$. The one-year rating-specific default probabilities are the Static Pools Average Cumulative Default Rates by Rating as reported by S&P, and the loss given default assumption corresponds closely with S&P's reported historical "all instruments" average recovery rate of 51.15 percent.[15] An S&P rating reportedly depends both on the probability of default and the loss given default. While there clearly are a range of ex ante default probabilities and recovery rates that could be consistent with a given S&P rating category, this information is not public, and so attention is restricted to the historical averages associated with each S&P credit rating category.

The calculations reported in Table 2 suggest that, for most ratings categories, the Standardized approach will have only a modest effect on insurance values relative to the values that can be attained under the Accord. For the group of intermediate-quality credits rated between BB+ and BB-, the Standardized approach is identical to the Accord. For more highly rated credits, the lower risk weights under the Standardized approach increase slightly the value of deposit insurance for these credits, but the higher insurance values are still tiny relative to the insurance values that can be generated by lending to more risky credits. For the lower-quality credits in the 150 percent risk weight category, the Standardized approach lowers insurance values relative to those attainable under the Accord, but not by much. Lower-quality credits are, by far, still the most profitable investment alternative for a bank that can fund them with subsidized insured deposits. Among the loans considered in Table 2, the CCC-rated credit maximizes shareholder wealth. Thus, notwithstanding increased sensitivity of regulatory capital requirements to credit risk, the Standardized

---

15. See "Ratings Performance 2000," Standard & Poor's, p. 16 (default probabilities) and p. 82 (recovery rates).

approach does not create incentives that will stem the trend of securitizing high-quality assets. The Standardized Approach is unlikely to encourage banks to retain high-quality credit on their balance sheets.

Table 2. Insurance Values Under Alternative Capital Regimes

STANDARD & POOR'S RATING	ONE-YEAR HISTORICAL PROBA-BILITY OF DEFAULT (PERCENT)	INSURANCE VALUE UNDER 1988 ACCORD	INSURANCE VALUE UNDER THE STANDARD-IZED APPROACH	INSURANCE VALUE UNDER THE 2001 FOUN-DATION IRB APPROACH	INSURANCE VALUE UNDER THE 2003 FOUN-DATION IRB APPROACH
AAA	0	0	0	0	0
AA+	0	0	0	0	0
AA	0	0	0	0	0
AA-	0.03	0.0132	0.0152	0.0149	0.1289
AA+	0.04*	0.0176	0.0193	0.0198	0.0171
A	0.05	0.0219	0.0241	0.0247	0.0212
A-	0.05	0.0219	0.0241	0.0247	0.0212
BB+	0.12	0.0527	0.0527	0.0578	0.0486
BBB	0.22	0.0966	0.0966	0.1032	0.0851
BBB-	0.35	0.1534	0.1534	0.1593	0.1294
BB+	0.44	0.1927	0.1927	0.1965	0.1587
BB	0.94	0.4093	0.4093	0.3826	0.3084
BB-	1.33	0.5767	0.5767	0.5074	0.4157
B+	2.91	1.2396	1.1194	0.8744	0.7946
B	8.38	3.3488	3.0123	1.0311	1.4459
B-	10.32	4.0276	3.6174	0.8040	1.4668
CCC	21.94	7.3339	6.5154	0	0.2038

Source: Deposit insurance values for selected Standard & Poor's ratings assuming a one-year probability of default equal to the historic S&P average, and a 50 percent loss given default. The calculations are based upon the assumption that investors are risk neutral, and $P=110, r_f=.05$.

*For credits rates AA+, the true historical one-year default rate average is 0.02 percent. The calculations use 0.04 percent to retain a monotonic relationship between rating quality and the expected default rate.

The Foundation IRB Approach

The value of the shareholder investment opportunity set under the January 2001 Foundation IRB can be calculated using equation (7) [as an equality] to substitute for D in equation (2).

The value of the shareholder investment opportunity set under the April 2003 Foundation IRB can be calculated using equation (10) [as an equality] to substitute for D in equation (2).

Figure 4. Insurance Value Under Alternative Foundation IRB Risk Weight Functions

Insurance Value Under April 2003 Foundation IRB

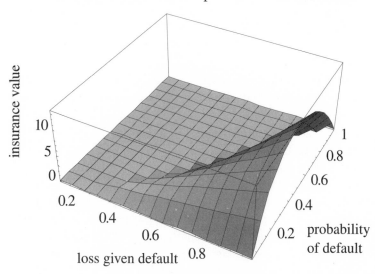

Figure 4 plots the value of the deposit insurance surface under the April 2003 Foundation IRB capital regime, assuming $P = 110$, and $r_f = .05$, and the change in the value of the deposit insurance surface that was engendered by the changes in this function relative to the January 2001 Foundation IRB function. A visual comparison of Figures 3 and 4 shows that the Foundation Approach IRB capital requirements will lower the value of the deposit insurance subsidy available to bank shareholders relative to the 1988 Accord. Under the model assumptions, the shareholder's global optimum under the January 2001 function is achieved by selecting a loan with $pr_i = .295$, and $LGD_i = 1$. Under the April 2003 specification, the local optimum is achieved at $pr_i = .44$ and $LGD_i = 1$. The move from the 1988 Accord to the April 2003 Foundation IRB approach will induce the bank to shift toward retaining assets with lower probabilities of default, but it will not create any incentive for banks to hold loans with small expected losses in default.

The second panel of Figure 4 shows that the changes made to the Foundation Approach IRB, in respect to procylicality concerns, have resulted in significantly higher deposit insurance values for a range of lower-quality credits relative to the insurance values conveyed under the January 2001 risk-weighting function. The increment in insurance value is a consequence of the reduced magnitude of the April 2003 minimum capital requirement for the high probability of default credits shown in Figure 1. In the interest of reducing procyclicality, the BCBS has changed the incentives created by the deposit insurance safety net, and, other things equal, banks face strong incentives to hold riskier loan portfolios than they would have under the January 2001 Foundation IRB risk-weighting function (Table 3).

While the Foundation IRB Approaches reduce the global maximum insurance value that can be generated relative to the 1988 Accord or the proposed Standardized approach, it does not reduce insurance values for all possible sets of loan characteristics. The last two columns of Table 2 report the value of the insurance guarantee under the alternative Foundation IRB approaches for alternative S&P-rated credits under the assumptions $P = 110$, $r_f = .05$, and $LGD_i = .50 \forall i$. Compared to capital requirements under the 1988 Accord and the Standardized approach, the Foundation IRB offers higher insurance values for all credits in the Standardized approach's 50 percent risk bucket and many in the 100 percent category (AA+ to BB+).

The Advanced IRB Approach

The deposit insurance values attainable under the January 2001 Advanced IRB risk-weighting function are calculated using equation (8) [as an equality] to substitute for D in equation (2).

The deposit insurance values attainable under the April 2003 Advanced IRB risk-weighting function are calculated using equation (11) [as an equality] to substitute for D in equation (2).

Figure 5 plots the deposit insurance value surface under the April 2003 Advanced IRB risk-weighting function, assuming $P = 110$, $r_f = .05$. The second panel of Figure 5 plots the change in the deposit insurance value surface that owe to the April 2003 changes made to the January 2001 IRB risk-weighting function. As is the case with the Foundation IRB Approach, the changes that were made to reduce procyclicality result in increased insurance value for a large set of credits.

Relative to the Foundation IRB approach, the Advanced IRB approach lowers the maximum value of the deposit insurance subsidy that can be generated by shareholders. Somewhat surprisingly, however, insurance values are not reduced by encouraging firms to select loans with smaller expected losses given default, as firms still gain insurance value from selecting loans with low recovery values. The global optimum loan under the January 2001 Advanced IRB risk weight function is a loan with $pr_i = 0.068$, and $LGD_i = 1$. The global optimum settings under the April 2003 formulation of the approach are $pr_i = 12.32$, and $LGD_i = 1$.

Figure 5. Insurance Values Under Alternative Advanced IRB Risk Weight Functions

Insurance Value Under April 2003 Advanced IRB

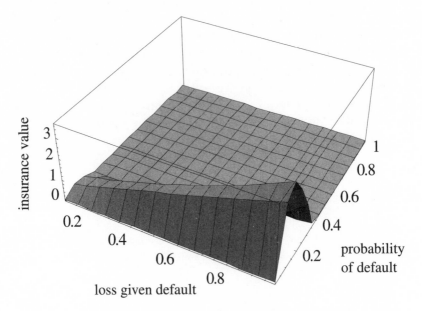

Insurance Value Difference Between 2003 and 2001 Advanced IRB

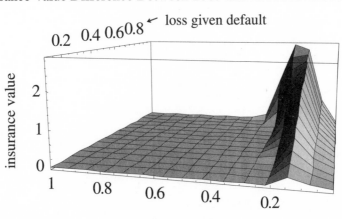

Table 3. Optimal Loan Characteristics Under IRB Approaches

FOUNDATION IRB CAPITAL

	January 2001		April 2003	
LGD (percent)	Optimal default probability (percent)	Optimal insurance value	Optimal default probability (percent)	Optimal insurance value
10	0.45	0.02	0.15	0.01
20	1.34	0.11	1.75	0.17
30	2.58	0.31	4.79	0.41
40	4.16	0.65	7.94	1.04
50	6.13	1.16	11.92	1.99
60	8.57	1.89	16.99	3.35
70	11.60	2.88	23.07	5.18
80	15.52	4.18	19.02	7.51
90	20.92	5.19	37.09	10.36
100	29.46	8.24	44.03	13.67

ADVANCED IRB

	January 2001		April 2003	
10	5.74	0.22	8.92	.31
20	5.83	0.45	9.14	.63
30	5.93	0.68	9.38	.95
40	6.03	0.92	9.65	1.29
50	6.13	1.16	9.95	1.65
60	6.25	1.41	10.28	2.02
70	6.37	1.66	10.67	2.40
80	6.50	1.92	11.11	2.81
90	6.64	2.19	11.65	3.24
100	6.80	2.46	12.32	3.70

Source: Optimal loan default probabilities and insurance values assuming $P = 110$, and $r_f = .05$.

While the Advanced IRB approach lowers the global maximum insurance value relative to the Foundation IRB (and all other approaches), insurance values are not reduced for all sets of loan characteristics. Table 3 reports the optimal insurance values and corresponding loan default probabilities associated with alternative LGD assumptions under both the Foundation and Advanced IRB approaches. The Table shows that when $LGD_i \leq .40$, the optimal insurance values and corresponding optimal probabilities of loan defaults are greater under the April 2003 Advanced IRB approach. When $LGD_i > .40$, the April 2003 Foundation IRB generates the largest insurance values and the largest corresponding optimal probabilities of loan default.

5. ASSESSING THE IMPLICATIONS OF THE NEW BASEL ACCORD

The results that have been derived thus far are based upon the assumption of investor risk neutrality, but they are not dependent on this assumption. Sections VI and VII demonstrate that investor risk aversion raises additional issues of importance for the regulatory debate, but it will not reverse any of the results that have been derived thus far. Given the increased level of complexity required to discuss the implications of risk aversion, it is useful to summarize the results that are most clearly apparent in the simpler risk-neutral setting.

A major goal of Basel II is to make regulatory capital requirements more sensitive to credit risk, in part at least, in order to remove incentives (under the 1988 Accord) that encourage banks to securitize high-quality credit and retain low-quality credits on their balance sheets. The analysis shows that, while all Basel 2 approaches make regulatory capital requirements more sensitive to credit risk, low quality credits remain the most valuable to banks. Indeed, the results suggest that a regulatory change from the 1988 Accord to the Standardized approach will have almost no effect on the incentives banks face when they decide which loans they choose to securitize and which loans they choose to retain on their balance sheets.

It is interesting to observe that none of the proposed approaches for regulatory capital creates an incentive for banks to select loans with minimal expected losses given default. Even the Advanced IRB approach—the only regulatory capital approach that specifically takes LGD into account—does not reduce a bank's incentive to try to select loans that are expected to experience substantial default losses. This feature of Basel 2 is particularly troubling, as the loss given default characteristics of a bank's loans are the primary factor determining the insurer's cost of resolving a failed bank.

Notwithstanding the BCBS's intentions, the regulatory capital "pillar" of Basel 2 does not include any economic incentive that will encourage a bank to evolve from the Standardized, to the Foundation IRB, to the Advanced IRB capital approaches. If banks are free to choose their loan characteristics, the Standardized approach offers the largest deposit insurance value. Insurance values that are attainable under the Foundation IRB approach are significantly smaller but remain larger than those that can be generated under the Advanced IRB approach. Absent other incentives from supervisors or from market discipline pressures, there is no reason to expect that banks will voluntarily evolve toward the more complex model-based capital regulations.

If some banks are required to adopt the IRB approaches, it is likely that natural banking clienteles will emerge from the incentives created by Basel 2's alternative capital schemes. To add clarity, we focus discussions around the S&P ratings. If a bank is forced to adopt one of the IRB approaches, given complete freedom, the bank would choose the Foundation IRB approach and focus on retaining low-quality loans (B- to B+, see Table 12), as these credits maximize the bank's insurance value. If however, other national regulators allow competitor banks to operate under the Standardized approach, the larger insurance values that can be generated by low-quality credits would allow Standardized approach banks to bid away the lower-quality credit business by underpricing their loans (subsidizing loan rates). Thus, differences in the regulatory capital treatments will allow the Standardized approach banks to gain business at the expense of the Foundation IRB banks and the insurer of the banks that use the Standardized approach. Notice that, should some authorities allow their banks to continue using the 1988 Accord's capital requirements, other things equal, these banks would be able to dominate the market for low-quality credits.

Under the proposed January 2001 formulation, Foundation IRB banks, however, have an advantage in retaining relatively high-quality credits. Under the assumptions of Table 2, this is true for example, for those loans rated BB+ to AA+ by S&P. The small insurance value advantage could have allowed the Foundation IRB banks to slightly under-price these credits to bid them away from the banks using the Standardized approach, or indeed even banks remaining under the 1988 Accord's capital requirements. The April 2003 reformulation, however, removes these benefits, and the Standardized Approach produces dominate insurance values for all credits examined in Table 2.

The final segmentation of the market is related to sorting highly rated loans (BB+ to AA+) according to loss given default. Expected loss given default can vary widely among loans in a given S&P rating category. For any subset of loans with $LGD_i > .40$,

Table 3 shows that a bank can increase its insurance value by moving from the April 2003 version of the Foundation IRB to the Advanced IRB approach. Advanced IRB banks may use part of the gain in insurance value to attract the set of high-quality credits that also have below average expected losses in default.

In the resulting banking market equilibrium, simple absolute advantage arguments could be employed to suggest that banks using the Standardized approach will choose to compete for the lowest-quality loans; banks using the Foundation IRB approach will choose to compete for loans similar to those that would receive an S&P rating of between BB+ and AA+ but have above average expected loss given default $(LGD_i > .40)$; and banks using the Advanced IRB would compete for the loans that would receive an S&P rating of between BB+ and AA+ but also have below average expected loss given default $(LGD_i \leq .40.)$. In this equilibrium, the banks using the most sophisticated approach for internal credit risk measurement (a necessary condition to qualify for using the Advanced IRB approach) retain the highest-quality credits, whereas the banks least capable of quantifying their credit risk retain the lowest-quality loans on their balance sheets. Thus, the three-option approach of Basel 2 could encourage segmentation in the credit qualities of internationally active banks according to their regulatory capital scheme. The "level playing field" objective of the 1988 Accord is abandoned.

While the BCBS has been studying the potential regulatory capital implications of Basel 2 by having cooperating banks estimate their potential capital requirements under the proposed IRB approaches, these estimates are based on banks' current portfolio compositions. Given the incentives created under Basel 2, it is likely that the composition of banks' credit portfolios will change, perhaps markedly, following the implementation of the regulatory capital regime. Ultimately then, after banks rebalance their portfolios, it is unclear whether Basel 2 will improve the stability of the international banking system. While the prudential solvency standards of sophisticated money center banks may be strengthened, the incentives that encourage a concentration of lower-quality credits in Standardized approach banks (of which there are expected to be many) may not result in enhanced financial market stability.

6. MODELING INVESTOR RISK AVERSION

Introducing the assumption that shareholders are risk averse significantly enriches the analysis. In order to gauge the effects of risk aversion in this simple model setting, it is necessary to establish the theoretical link between the physical probability of default and the equivalent martingale (or risk-neutral) probability of default that is used by risk-averse investors to value claims on future cash flows. This section will introduce an explicit general equilibrium model with risk-averse investors that elicits a transparent and intuitive link between the physical and equivalent martingale probabilities of loan default.

Assume that the nominal value of aggregate output in the economy evolves according to a discrete probability distribution with S possible outcomes. Without any loss of generality, we index the possible states of aggregate output values in order of increasing magnitude and let y_i represent the physical probability that the ith output state is realized.

Assume that there are N representative investors, each with an initial wealth level W_0, who invest their entire wealth in a portfolio of S Arrow-Debreu securities with the objective of maximizing the value of a mean-variance expected utility function over end of period wealth,

$$E\left(U\left(\tilde{W}\right)\right)=\alpha E\left(\tilde{W}\right)-\Gamma Var\left(\tilde{W}\right), \text{ where } E\left(\tilde{W}\right)=\sum_{i=1}^{S} y_i x_i, \text{ and } Var\left(\tilde{W}\right)=\sum_{i=1}^{S} y_i x_i^2-\left(\sum_{i=1}^{S} y_i x_i\right)^2,$$

and x_i is the number of Arrow-Debreu securities held by the agent. Each of these securities pays one unit of value (henceforth referred to as dollars) when state i is realized and nothing in any other state of nature. We assume that investors behave as if they are price takers.

If p_i represents the price of an Arrow-Debreu security that pays a dollar in state, it is straightforward to show that the representative agent's utility maximizing share demands are given by

$$x_i^* = \frac{1}{\sum_{i=1}^{S} p_i}\left[W+\frac{a}{2\Gamma}\left[\left(\sum_{i=1}^{S} \frac{p_i^2}{y_i}\right)-\frac{p_i}{y_i}\right]\right], i=1,2,3,\ldots,S.$$

(12)

Equilibrium market clearing prices are determined by setting aggregate supply equal to aggregate demand and solving for the individual Arrow-Debreu security prices. If X_i^Q represents aggregate output in state i, equilibrium requires $N x_i^* = X_i^Q, \forall i,$ or in terms of per capital output, $x_i^* = \dfrac{X_i^Q}{N}, \forall i.$ The second condition implies that in this representative agent setting, N can be eliminated by solving for equilibrium in terms of per capita aggregate output. To simplify notation, reinterpret X_i^Q as per capita output in state i and drop any subsequent reference to the number of investors in the economy.

Define the expected value of per capita output, $E\left(X^Q\right) = \displaystyle\sum_{i=1}^{S} y_i X_i^Q$, the variance of per capita output,

$$Var\left(X^Q\right) = \sum_{i=1}^{S} y_i \left(X_i^Q\right)^2 - \left(\sum_{i=1}^{S} y_i X_i^Q\right)^2,$$

and a constant, $K = \dfrac{aW_0}{aE\left(X^Q\right) - 2\Gamma Var\left(X^Q\right)}.$

The equilibrium market clearing Arrow-Debreu security prices can be written as

$$p_i = y_i K\left[1 + \frac{2\Gamma}{a}\left(E\left(X^Q\right) - X_i^Q\right)\right], \quad i = 1, 2, 3, \ldots, S. \tag{13}$$

A fundamental risk-free claim is a portfolio comprised of one Arrow-Debreu security from each state. The equilibrium price of a risk-free claim, $\displaystyle\sum_{i=1}^{S} p_i = K,$ implies an equilibrium risk-free rate of

$$r_f = \frac{1}{K} - 1.$$

Security Valuation and the Risk-Neutral Probability Measure

In this model setting, it is well known that the equilibrium value of a security or contingent claim can be determined by valuing a portfolio of Arrow-Debreu securities that replicate the state payoffs on the contingent claim contract that is being priced. The equilibrium absence of arbitrage condition requires that the value of the claim must equal the equilibrium price of the replicating portfolio of Arrow-Debreu securities. In addition to the traditional Arrow-Debreu portfolio pricing solution, Harrison and Pliska (1981) establish that the absence of arbitrage in a state space model implies the existence of the risk-neutral pseudo probability measure and the equivalent martingale market valuation condition. The pseudo probability measure is unique if markets are complete (as they are assumed to be in this model).

The equivalent martingale market valuation condition requires that the equilibrium price of a security equal the present value of the securities' expected future payoffs, where the expectation is taken with respect to the equivalent martingale (risk-neutral) measure, and the present value discounting occurs at the risk-free rate of interest. In the case of a simple Arrow-Debreu security, the equivalent martingale valuation condition requires

$$p_i = \frac{y_i^E}{\left(1 + r_f\right)},$$

(14)

where y_i^E represents the equivalent martingale probability of a realization of state i. Using expressions (10), (11), and i, the physical and risk-neutral probabilities relationship is given by

$$y_i^E = y_i \left[1 + \frac{2\Gamma}{a} \left(E\left(X^Q \right) - X_i^Q \right) \right], \text{ for } i = 1,2,3,.....,S.$$

(15)

Parameters "a" and "Γ" are both required to be positive. Equation (15) requires that the risk-neutral probability associated with state i is greater than the state's physical probability if the level of per capita output in state i is below the expected value of per capital output. Conversely, the risk-neutral probability associated with state i is less than the physical probability of state i if per capita output in state i exceeds average per capita output. Other things equal, the differences between the risk-neutral and physical probabilities are greater the larger are investors' aversions to taking risk (the larger is Γ).

Loan Valuation Under the Risk-Neutral Measure

Consistent with the simple two-state model of a bank loan developed in section two, consider a loan that has two possible cash flow states: a good state in which it pays off its promised maturity value, P, and a default state in which it pays off $P(1-LGD_i)$. Given P, and a bank selected LGD_i, when investors are risk averse, the fair market value of this bank loan depends not only on the probability that the bank defaults, but also on the economic states in which the bank defaults. Let Ω_i represent the set of states in which loan i defaults. Let $pr_i^E = \sum_{\forall i \in \Omega_i} y_i^E$ represent the probability of default under the equivalent martingale measure.

When investors are risk averse, the equilibrium value of the bank loan is given by

$$L\left(LGD_i, pr_i^E\right) = \frac{P\left(1 - LGD\ pr_i^E\right)}{1 + r_f}, \tag{16}$$

which is identical to expression (1) after replacing the physical probability of default with the equivalent martingale probability of default. Using expression (12), it is straightforward to show that

$$pr_i^E = pr_i \left[1 + \frac{2\Gamma}{a}\left(E\left(X^Q\right) - \sum_{\forall i \in \Omega_i}\left(\frac{y_i}{pr_i}\right)X_i^Q\right)\right], \tag{17}$$

where $pr_i = \sum_{\forall i \in \Omega_i} y_i$. Expression (14) shows that a loan's equivalent martingale probability of default will exceed its physical probability of default if the physical expected per capital output in loan default states is less than the physical unconditional expected per capital output. Thus, the risk-neutral probability of default exceeds the physical probability of default when the loan default occurs in states that have a conditional average GDP per capita that is below the unconditional expected GDP per capita for the economy. Conversely, if the average level of output per capita in default states exceeds the economy's unconditional expected output per capita, $pr_i^E < pr_i$.

The Value of Deposit Insurance Under Risk Aversion

The introduction of risk aversion complicates the expression for deposit insurance valuation because, while the loan pricing condition requires only the substitution of the risk neutral for the physical probability measure, the regulatory capital restrictions on the level of insured deposits may depend on both the physical and the risk-neutral probability measures. Let

$$INS\left(pr_i, pr_i^E, LGD_i\right) = \frac{\left[D\left(pr_i, pr_i^E, LGD_i\right) - P\left(1 - LGD_i\right)\right]pr_i^E}{1 + r_f} \tag{18}$$

represent the generic expression for deposit insurance value, where the notation $D(pr_i, pr_i^E, LGD_i)$ indicates that the level of insured deposits may be a function of a credit's physical probability of default, its risk-neutral probability of default, and its loss given default.

Under the Accord, qualifying capital must be at least 8 percent of a loan's value. If qualifying capital is restricted to paid-in equity capital, this condition requires that

$$D \leq .92\left(1 + r_f\right)L\left(pr_i^E, LGD_i\right).$$
(19)

Similarly, under the Standardized approach, the use of insured deposit funding must satisfy the inequality

$$D \leq \left(1 - Cap\left(rating_i\right)\right)\left(1 + r_f\right)L\left(pr_i^E, LGD_i\right).$$
(20)

Under the Foundation IRB, a credit's risk weight is set according to a loan's physical probability of default. The risk weight determines what proportion of the value of the loan must be financed with paid-in equity capital, but the fair value of the loan itself is determined by the equivalent martingale probability of default. Thus, under the Foundation IRB, the regulatory capital requirement restricts insured deposits according to

$$D \leq \left(1 + r_f\right)L\left(pr_i^E, LGD_i\right)\left(1 - .08\frac{BRW_C\left(pr_i\right)}{100}\right).$$
(21)

Similarly, under the Advanced IRB approach, insured deposit financing will be restricted by the relationship

$$D \leq \left(1 + r_f\right)L\left(pr_i^E, LGD_i\right)\left(1 - .08\frac{LGD_i}{.50}\frac{BRW_C\left(pr_i\right)}{100}\right).$$
(22)

Under any of these capital rules, shareholders maximize the use of insured deposit financing (the equality will hold) when the insurance guarantee is valuable.

7. OPTIMAL BANK BEHAVIOR WHEN SHAREHOLDERS ARE RISK AVERSE

The risk characteristics of a bank's optimal loan portfolio depend on both the risk aversion of equity investors and the regulatory capital scheme under which banks operate. Under some of the regulatory capital schemes, deposit insurance values can be enhanced by concentrating bank loan defaults so that they occur in states of nature that are characterized by below average output per capita. The alternative capital regimes are considered in turn. Deposit insurance values are determined by substituting a regulatory capital requirement's insured deposit issuance restriction (as an equality) into expression (18).

Figure 6 plots the deposit insurance value surface under the Accord when investors are risk averse. The figure includes surfaces for alternative assumptions about per capita output in the states of nature in which a loan defaults. The surface in Figure 6 is generated under the assumptions: $a = 45, \Gamma = 1$, and the representative investor's wealth, W, has been normalized to be consistent with $r_f = .05$ when the aggregate output per capita satisfies the implicit assumption $E(X^Q) = 30, Var(X^Q) = 60.5.$[16] The qualitative results are independent of the parameter values assumed.

Figure 6. Deposit insurance value surface under the Accord when investors are risk averse

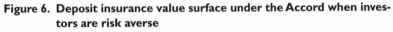

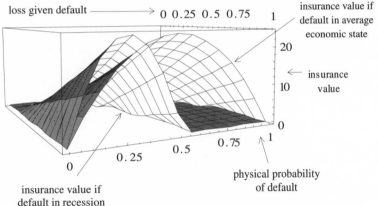

If a loan is expected to default in a state in which aggregate per capita output is equal to the unconditional average aggregate output per capita, the deposit insurance value surface is identical to the surface that prevails when investors are risk neutral. In this instance, the global optimal corresponds to $pr_i = .50, LGD_i = 1$. If the loan defaults in states of nature in which aggregate per capita output is less than the unconditional output per capita, Figure 4 shows that the optimal insurance and loss given default values are unchanged, but the optimal physical probability of default is

---

16. These specific parameter values underlie Figures 6 and 7, and Tables 4–6.

reduced from 50 percent. The converse is true if the loan is expected to default in states in which per capita output exceeds its unconditional average.

Table 4 provides additional details about the relationship between insurance values, physical probabilities of default, and recovery rates under the assumption that the loan defaults in states of nature in which output per capita deviates from its unconditional average value. The characteristics of the aggregate output per capita distribution restricts a bank's ability to choose the probability of default and the state of default. Loans that have very large physical probabilities of default cannot also default in states of nature that have a conditional expected output per capita that is significantly below average.[17] To account for this technical limitation, without imposing any distributional restrictions that are otherwise unnecessary, default rates greater than 60 percent are arbitrarily considered to be infeasible for loans that default in states of nature in which conditional expected per capita output is significantly below average.

The results reported in Table 4 show that, under the Accord, provided that a bank is able to freely select a loan's physical probability of default, there is no incentive for the bank to prefer that a loan default in any particular state of nature. While the optimal physical probability of default will depend on the macroeconomic conditions that are expected to prevail when loan default occurs, there is nothing in the regulatory capital requirement that makes a bank prefer that default occur in any particular macroeconomic state. To the extent that supplemental supervisory actions (for example CAMEL bank ratings systems) may create incentives for banks to select loans with low physical probabilities of default, banks under the Accord may prefer loans that default under recessionary or slow-growth conditions, but the capital regulations of the Accord itself do not create a bank preference for loans that are expected to default when macroeconomic output is below average.

---

17. Assume that the states of nature are ranked in order of increasing output per capita. For any given probability of default, assume default occurs in the states of nature with the smallest output per capita (this is an optimal ordering under all approaches other than the Accord, and it is equivalent to any other optimal ordering under the Accord). As the physical probability of default increases, the conditional expected output per capita is always less than the unconditional expected output per capita, but the difference between the expectations must converge to zero as the probability of default approaches unity. For any given probability of default, the difference between the conditional and unconditional expected output per capita will depend on the specific characteristics of the output per capita probability density function.

Table 12-4. Optimal Loan Characteristics Under the 1988 Basel Accord

LGD_i	$E(X^s) - \sum_{Y_i \in D}\left(\frac{Y_i}{pr_i}\right)X_i^s = -20$		$E(X^s) - \sum_{Y_i \in D}\left(\frac{Y_i}{pr_i}\right)X_i^s = -10$		$E(X^s) - \sum_{Y_i \in D}\left(\frac{Y_i}{pr_i}\right)X_i^s = 0$		$E(X^s) - \sum_{Y_i \in D}\left(\frac{Y_i}{pr_i}\right)X_i^s = 10$		$E(X^s) - \sum_{Y_i \in D}\left(\frac{Y_i}{pr_i}\right)X_i^s = 20$	
	pr_i^* percent	$INS(pr_i^*, LGD_i)$	pr_i^* percent	$INS(pr_i^*, LGD_i)$	pr_i^* percent	$INS(pr_i^*, LGD_i)$	pr_i^* percent	$INS(pr_i^*, LGD_i)$	pr_i^* percent	$INS(pr_i^*, LGD_i)$
0.1	> 60	–	19.56	0.11	10.87	0.11	7.52	0.11	5.75	0.11
0.2	> 60	–	58.69	2.05	32.61	2.05	22.58	2.05	17.26	2.05
0.3	> 60	–	> 60	–	39.86	4.59	27.59	4.59	21.10	4.59
0.4	> 60	–	> 60	–	43.47	7.29	30.10	7.29	23.02	7.29
0.5	> 60	–	> 60	–	45.65	10.04	31.61	10.04	24.17	10.04
0.6	> 60	–	> 60	–	47.10	12.83	32.61	12.83	24.94	12.83
0.7	> 60	–	> 60	–	48.13	15.63	33.32	15.63	25.48	15.63
0.8	> 60	–	> 60	–	48.91	18.45	33.86	18.45	25.90	18.45
0.9	> 60	–	> 60	–	49.52	21.27	34.28	21.27	26.21	21.27
1.0	> 60	–	> 60	–	50.00	24.10	34.62	24.10	26.47	24.10

Source: Optimal physical probability of default and insurance values under the Accord. The entries correspond to optimal loan default probabilities and a corresponding insurance value conditional on a loss given default value and an assumption about the conditional expected output per capita in default states. The calculations are based upon the assumptions $a = 45$, $\Gamma = 1$, $E(X^Q) = 30$, $Var(X^Q) = 60.5$, and $r_f = .05$.

While the capital regulations of the Accord may not create incentives for banks to concentrate their lending to counterparties that are expected to default when per capita output is below average, all of the approaches proposed in Basel II include this feature. Table 5 reports the optimal equivalent martingale probability of default that is associated with each risk weight category of the Standardized approach assuming a 50 percent loss given default. Recall that each rating class has an associated (publicly) unknown expected probability of default that is determined by S&P. Historical default rate data by S&P rating suggest that the physical default rates associated with each regulatory "bucket" in the Standardized approach are significantly less than the optimal risk-neutral default rates associated with that bucket Table 5. Banks using the Standardized approach face an incentive to choose loans with risk-neutral default rates that exceed (likely by as much as possible) the physical default rate S&P uses to determine a rating grade. Banks accomplish this by selecting among credits with a given S&P rating those credits that are expected to default when aggregate per capita output is the smallest.[18]

Table 5. Optimal Default Rates Under the Equivalent Martingale Measure

STANDARDIZED APPROACH CAPITAL REQUIREMENT (PERCENT)	LGD	APPROXIMATE AVERAGE S&P PHYSICAL DEFAULT PROBABILITY (PERCENT)	OPTIMAL RISK - NEUTRAL DEFAULT PROBABILITY (PERCENT)
1.6	0.5	0.03	49.19
4.0	0.5	0.05	47.97
8.0	0.5	0.50	45.65
12.0	0.5	10.00	43.18

Source: Insurance value-maximizing risk-neutral probabilities of default for the Standardized approach risk buckets under representative loss given default and physical probabilities of default for each risk weight category.

Similar to the Standardized approach, when investors are risk averse, both IRB approaches create an incentive for a bank to prefer loans that are expected to default when per capita output is

---

18.   In the real-world setting, this is accomplished, for example, by selecting among credit with a given rating, those that offer the greatest interest margins.

below average. Figure 7 provides a visual guide to the implications of risk aversion for the IRB approaches. Figure 7 plots the deposit insurance value surface under the January 2001 Advanced IRB approach when investors are risk averse, and the bank can select the macroeconomic conditions that prevail when its loan defaults. Figure 7 shows that the introduction of investor risk aversion does not affect the optimal loss given default setting (it remains 100 percent), but the bank can, however, increase the value of its deposit insurance by selecting a loan that is expected to default when output per capita is below average. Similar effects are generated under the Foundation IRB approach (not pictured).

Figure 7. Illustration of the implications of risk aversion for the deposit insurance value function under the January 2001 Advanced IRB capital requirement

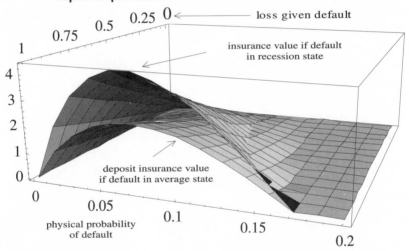

Table 6 provides more detail regarding the implications of investor risk aversion for the IRB regulatory capital approaches. Table 6 reports optimal physical probabilities of default and corresponding insurance values for alternative combinations of assumptions regarding loss given default and the average per capita output in default states under the January 2001 Foundation IRB approach. The results show that for any loss given default assumption, deposit insurance values under the Foundation IRB approach increases as the average value of per capita output in default states decreases. In other words, ex ante insurance values are enhanced if loan defaults are expected to occur when macroeconomic activity is depressed. The results are qualitatively similar for the Advanced IRB approach and for the April 2003 reformulations of both the Foundation and Advanced risk-weighting functions.

Under either IRB approach, for any loss given default, the optimal physical probability of default is a decreasing function of the conditional average per capital output in default states. Thus, to the extent that investor risk aversion creates incentives for banks to select loans with smaller physical probabilities of default, it is because banks can identify loans that are expected to default in states of nature where aggregate output is below average. In such an instance, even though the bank loans appear to be safer when measured according to their physical probability of default, the banks' deposit insurance guarantee will actually have greater value.

Table 6. Optimal Loan Characteristics Under the January 2001 Foundation IRB Approach

	$E(X^s) - \sum \left(\frac{y_i}{pr_i}\right) X_i^s = -20$		$E(X^s) - \sum \left(\frac{y_i}{pr_i}\right) X_i^s = -10$		$E(X^s) - \sum \left(\frac{y_i}{pr_i}\right) X_i^s = -0$		$E(X^s) - \sum \left(\frac{y_i}{pr_i}\right) X_i^s = 10$		$E(X^s) - \sum \left(\frac{y_i}{pr_i}\right) X_i^s = 20$	
	%	$INS(pr_i{*}, LGD_i)$	%	$INS(pr_i{*}, LGD_i)$	%	$INS(pr_i{*}, LGD_i)$	%	$INS(pr_i{*}, LGD_i)$	%	$INS(pr_i{*}, LGD_i)$
0.1	0.46	0.005	0.46	0.01	0.45	0.02	0.45	0.03	0.45	0.035
0.2	1.39	0.01	1.37	0.06	1.34	0.11	1.30	0.16	1.30	0.20
0.3	2.74	0.04	2.66	0.18	2.58	0.31	2.50	0.43	2.43	0.55
0.4	4.58	0.08	4.36	0.38	4.16	0.65	3.97	0.90	3.81	1.14
0.5	7.06	0.14	6.56	0.68	6.13	1.16	5.76	1.60	5.43	1.99
0.6	10.39	0.24	9.39	1.13	8.57	1.89	7.88	2.55	7.29	3.14
0.7	15.08	0.39	13.11	1.76	11.60	2.88	10.41	3.82	9.44	4.62
0.8	22.41	0.60	18.31	2.62	15.52	4.18	13.49	5.44	11.92	6.47
0.9	40.26	0.94	26.60	3.83	20.92	5.91	17.36	7.49	14.87	8.47
1.0	> 60	-	53.37	5.75	29.46	8.24	22.54	10.08	18.46	11.50

Source: Optimal physical probability of default and insurance values under the January 2001 proposed Foundation IRB approach. The entries correspond to optimal loan default probabilities and a corresponding insurance value conditional on a loss given default value and an assumption about the conditional expected output per capita in default states. The calculations are based upon the assumptions $a = 45$, $\Gamma = 1$, $E(X^Q) = 30$, $Var(X^Q) = 60.5$, and $r_f = .05$.

Loan Portfolios

Thus far, the discussion has focused on a bank's choice of the risk characteristics of a single loan and has excluded consideration of issues related to credit risk diversification and the construction and characteristics of optimal bank loan portfolios. This section considers the characteristics of an optimal credit portfolio when deposit insurance is valuable. It develops a formal argument that justifies the emphasis on the profitability of a single-loan investment. The analysis will show that, if a bank is maximizing the value of its insurance guarantee, only loans that have a positive ex ante insurance value will be included in an optimal bank loan portfolio.

In the single loan setting, if deposit insurance is valuable, when the bank's loan defaults, the bank defaults on its insured deposits. When the bank has a portfolio of loans, this one-to-one default correspondence no longer holds. In a one-period model, the bank defaults on its deposits when the end-of-period value of its loan portfolio falls short of the value of its insured deposits.

Let P_{Bnk} represent the promised terminal payoff on a bank's entire loan portfolio. Let pr_{Bnk} and pr_{Bnk}^{E} represent the physical and risk-neutral probabilities that the bank defaults on its loan portfolio, and LGD_{Bnk} represent the fractional loss on the bank's loan portfolio that is expected to occur if the bank defaults on its deposits. Notice that loss given default is measured relative to the loan portfolio's promised payoff. If D_{Bnk} represents the promised terminal payment on the bank's entire base of insured deposits which is restricted in magnitude if the bank is under a regulatory capital constraint. The value of the bank's deposit insurance guarantee can be written

$$INS(D_{Bnk}, P_{Bnk}, LGD_{Bnk}, pr_{Bnk}^{E}) = \frac{\left(D_{Bnk} - P_{Bnk}(1 - LGD_{Bnk})\right) pr_{Bnk}^{E}}{1 + r_{f}}. \quad (23)$$

The similarities between the expression for the value of the deposit guarantee in the portfolio case and the value of the guarantee in the context of a single loan (expression (18)) are transparent. In a portfolio context, the bank will select loans so that the implied values for P_{Bnk}, D_{Bnk}, LGD_{Bnk}, and pr_{Bnk}^{E} maximize the ex ante value of the bank's insurance guarantee subject to any constraints imposed by regulatory capital requirements.

Section 1 in the Appendix derives the relationship between specific loan characteristics and P_{Bnk}, D_{Bnk}, LGD_{Bnk}, and pr_{Bnk}^{E} in expression (23) for a two-loan portfolio under regulatory capital requirements specified by the Accord. Arguments similar to those in the Appendix can be used to derive expression (23) for any bank portfolio under any of the alternative capital regimes.

Optimal Portfolio Construction

While expression (23) is a general expression for calculating the ex ante value of a bank deposit insurance guarantee, the expression itself is not very revealing as to the characteristics of the loans that are included in an optimal bank loan portfolio. This section addresses this issue.

Consider a bank that is considering adding an additional loan, loan i, to an existing portfolio that generates a positive ex ante insurance value for the bank. Let the insurance value of the existing portfolio be represented by $\dfrac{\left[D_{Bnk} - P_{Bnk}(1 - LGD_{Bnk})\right] pr_{Bnk}^{E}}{1 + r_f}$, where the magnitude of D_{Bnk} depends on the regulatory capital scheme in force as well as the characteristics of the individual loans in the banks portfolio. If loans are fairly priced and the bank's objective is to maximize the value of its insurance guarantee, Section 2, in the Appendix proves the following:

THEOREM 1: *If a bank is attempting to maximize the value of its deposit insurance guarantee, a loan must have positive insurance value when it is evaluated as a stand-alone investment if it is included in a bank's optimal loan portfolio.*

A necessary condition for a loan to be included in an optimal bank loan portfolio is that the loan have a positive ex ante deposit insurance value when it is evaluated on a stand-alone basis investment. If the loan does not have a positive insurance value as a stand-alone investment, the addition of the loan to the portfolio will reduce the maximum attainable deposit insurance value that can be generated by the bank. This theorem provides a justification for focusing attention on the single-loan model of a bank that has guided the analysis of the alternative Basel II capital proposals.

Under any of the capital proposals, profit-maximizing banks will only consider loans that generate positive insurance values, and they will select the combination of loans that generates implied values for P_{Bnk}, D_{Bnk}, LGD_{Bnk}, and pr_{Bnk}^{E} and that maximizes expression (23). If banks attempt to maximize the value of their insurance guarantee, they will select loans to achieve target values for P_{Bnk}, D_{Bnk}, LGD_{Bnk}, and pr_{Bnk}^E that depend on the regulatory capital scheme in force.

8. CONCLUSION

The proposals in pillar 1 of the New Basel Accord will create regulatory capital requirements that are sensitive to credit risk. Banks following the Standardized approach will face reduced insurance values for credits in the 150 percent risk category; however, this category will remain the most attractive category for bank lending. Bank's that are forced to adopt an IRB approach for capital stand to bear significant reductions in the values of their deposit insurance guarantees should they continue to hold the loan portfolios that were optimal under the 1988 Accord. There is, however, little likelihood that the latter condition will prevail. Basel II proposals will generate strong incentives for banks to modify their existing loan portfolios. The proposals may encourage the formation of stable bank clienteles in which a bank's customer base and risk profile are determined by the regulatory capital regime.

While Basel may reduce deposit insurance values in some institutions, the incentives it engenders ultimately are not compatible with existing bank regulatory objectives or the stated goals of the BCBS. The Standardized approach promises to have little effect on bank securitization activities. The proposals do not foster incentives that will encourage banks to voluntarily evolve from the Standardized to the Advanced IRB approach. The proposals encourage market segmentation among internationally active banks that is completely at odds with the "level playing field" objective of the 1988 Accord. None of the proposed approaches for regulatory capital create an incentive for banks to control their potential loss given default, and indeed even the "sophisticated" IRB approaches encourage bank behavior that is at odds with the regulatory objective of least-cost resolution.

A final issue relates to macroeconomic stability. In contrast to the 1988 Accord, all of the Basel II proposed capital schemes contain incentives that may encourage banks to purposely concentrate lending to credits that are expected to default in recessions. When investors are risk averse and capital requirements focus on the physical probability of default as they do under the Basel II, banks may be able to select the timing of default (relative to the business cycle) to enhance the value of their deposit insurance guarantee.

APPENDIX

I. Derivation of Expression (23)

This appendix demonstrates the mechanics of expressing a bank's deposit insurance value in a form equivalent to expression (23). To simplify the analysis, assume that the promised terminal payment on all loans are normalized to P. Loans differ according to their expected macroeconomic state of default, their expected loss given default, and their probability of default. To facilitate the analysis, we utilize the Arrow-Debreu state space representation of capital market equilibrium. To add clarity, we illustrate the derivation of expression (20) under the capital requirements of the Accord.

Under the capital requirements of the Accord, the general expression for deposit insurance value for a portfolio of two loans is given by $\dfrac{\left[D_{Bnk}^A - P_{Bnk}(1 - LGD_{Bnk})\right]pr_{Bnk}^E}{1 + r_f}$, where

$$P_{Bnk} = 2P, D_{Bnk}^A = \left[.92\left(P\left(2 - LGD_i pr_i^E - LGD_j pr_j^E\right)\right)\right], \text{ and } pr_{Bnk}^E \text{ and } LGD_{Bnk}$$

depend on the characteristics of the loans included in the portfolio, which, aside from the extent to which the bank uses insured deposit funding, are the only choice variables of the bank. The superscript A has been appended to D_{Bnk} to denote capital requirements under the Accord.

We remark that the deposit insurance values associated with individual loans are not additive unless specific conditions are satisfied,

$$\frac{\left[D_{Bnk}^A - P_{Bnk}\left(1 - LGD_{Bnk}\right)\right]pr_{Bnk}^E}{1 + r_f} \neq \frac{\left[D_i^A - P\left(1 - LGD_i\right)\right]pr_i^E}{1 + r_f} + \frac{\left[D_j^A - P_j\left(1 - LGD_j\right)\right]pr_j^E}{1 + r_f},$$

where $D_i^A = .92\left(P\left(1 - LGD_i pr_i^E\right)\right)$, $D_j^A = .92\left(P\left(1 - LGD_j pr_j^E\right)\right)$.

Recall that pr_i and pr_j represent the physical probabilities that loan i and j default. Let Ω_i and Ω_j represent the set of economic states in which these respective loans default. Let $\Omega_{ij} = \Omega_i \cap \Omega_j$ represent the intersection of the set of states in which loan i and loan j default, and $pr(\Omega_{ij})\left[pr^E(\Omega_{ij})\right]$ represent, respectively, the physical [equivalent martingale] probability associated with the intersection of default states.[19]

In the two-loan portfolio cases, we consider four alternative conditions under which the bank may default. In all cases, the prior definitions of D_{Bnk}^A and P_{Bnk} apply. It is straightforward to show that the bank will default if a single loan, loan i, defaults,

provided $LGD_i > \left[\dfrac{.16 - 1.84\left(1 + r_f\right) + .92\left(1 + r_f\right)LGD_j\,pr_j^E}{1 - .92\left(1 + r_f\right)pr_i^E}\right]$

In this case, if the bank maximizes the use of insured deposits, the deposit bank's deposit insurance value under the Accord is given by $\dfrac{\left[D_{Bnk}^A - P_{Bnk}\left(1 - LGD_{Bnk}\right)\right]pr_{Bnk}^E}{1 + r_f}$, where $LGD_{Bnk} = \dfrac{LGD_i}{2}$, and $pr_{Bnk}^E = pr_i^E$.

Consider as the second alternative, the case in which the bank defaults if, and only if, both of its loans default. In this case, the physical [equivalent martingale] probability that both loans default is $pr(\Omega_{ij})\left[pr^E(\Omega_{ij})\right]$. If a bank maximizes its use of insured deposits, the ex ante value of the bank's deposit insurance guarantee can be written in terms of loan specific characteristics as $\left[D_{Bnk}^A - P_{Bnk}\left(1 - LGD_{Bnk}\right)\right]pr_{Bnk}^E$ where

$$LGD_{Bnk} = \frac{LGD_i + LGD_j}{2}, \text{ and } pr_{Bnk}^E = pr^E\left(\Omega_{ij}\right).$$

A third alternative is the case in which the bank will default if: (i) loan i defaults; or (ii) if both loans default. In this instance, the physical probability of default in this instance is $pr_{Bnk} = pr_i$, but the ex ante loss given default has two potential values depending on the states in which the bank defaults. In this case, the deposit insurance value can be written

---

19. $pr^E\left(\Omega_{ij}\right) > 0 \Leftrightarrow pr\left(\Omega_{ij}\right) > 0$.

$$\left[D_{Bnk}^{A} - P(2 - LGD_{i}) \right]\left(pr_{i}^{E} - pr^{E}(\Omega_{ij}) \right) + \left[D_{Bnk}^{A} - P(2 - LGD_{i} - LGD_{j}) \right]\left(pr^{E}(\Omega_{ij}) \right)$$

$$= \left[D_{Bnk}^{A} - P_{Bnk}(1 - LGD_{Bnk}) \right] pr_{Bnk}^{E},$$

where $LGD_{Bnk} = \dfrac{1}{2 pr_{i}^{E}}\left(pr_{i}^{E} LGD_{i} + pr^{E}(\Omega_{ij}) LGD_{j} \right)$, and $pr_{Bnk}^{E} = pr_{i}^{E}$.

A final alternative is the case in which the bank will default if: (i) loan i defaults; (ii) loan j defaults, or (iii) if both of its loans default. In this instance, the equivalent martingale probability of default is $pr_{Bnk}^{E} = pr_{i}^{E} + pr_{j}^{E} - pr^{E}(\Omega_{ij})$, and the ex ante loss given default has three potential values. If the bank maximizes the use of insured deposits, its insurance value can be written

$$\left[D_{Bnk}^{A} - P(2 - LGD_{i}) \right]\left(pr_{i}^{E} - pr^{E}(\Omega_{ij}) \right) + \left[D_{B}^{A} - P(2 - LGD_{j}) \right]\left(pr_{j}^{E} - pr^{E}(\Omega_{ij}) \right)$$

$$+ \left[D_{Bnk}^{A} - P(2 - LGD_{i} - LGD_{j}) \right]\left(pr^{E}(\Omega_{ij}) \right)$$

$$= \left[D_{Bnk}^{A} - P_{Bnk}(1 - LGD) \right] pr_{Bnk}^{E},$$

where $LGD_{Bnk} = \dfrac{1}{2\left(pr_{i}^{E} + pr_{j}^{E} - pr^{E}(\Omega_{ij}) \right)}\left(pr_{i}^{E} LGD_{i} = + pr_{j}^{E} LGD_{j} \right)$.

This two-loan example formally establishes the link between the risk characteristics of the individual loans in a bank's loan portfolio and the probability of bank default $\left(pr_{Bnk}, pr_{Bnk}^{E} \right)$, and loss given bank default $\left(LGD_{Bnk} \right)$ values that determine a bank's insurance value in expression (23). While the algebra gets more complicated as the number of loans in a portfolio increases, the same algorithm can be used to express the ex ante value of the bank's deposit insurance guarantee in terms of individual loan characteristics in these cases, as well. Similar arguments can be used to construct the insurance value expression for the bank in terms of the portfolio's individual loan characteristics under any of the regulatory capital rules.

2. Proof of Theorem I

Recall that loan i has a zero insurance value when funded using the maximum permitted share of insured deposits, D_{i}, if its loss given default is sufficiently small so that the loan's proceeds in default are sufficient to pay principle and interest on the insured deposits that were used to fund it, $D_{i} < P(1 - LGD_{i})$.

Let Ω_{Bnk} represent the set of states of nature in which the bank defaults on its deposits, given its exiting loan portfolio. Let $\Omega_{Bnk,i} = \Omega_{Bnk} \cap \Omega_i$.

In the first part of the proof, we consider the case when the new loan is small relative to the bank's existing portfolio. In particular, we assume $D_{Bnk} > P_{Bnk}(1 - LGD_{Bnk}) - (P - D_i)$ so that even if the new loan does not default, the bank will still default on its insured deposit obligations. In this case, the addition of the new loan does not change the probability that the bank defaults; it only changes the bank's default severity.

Case 1: The bank portfolio and the additional loan default in exactly the same states, $\Omega_{Bnk,i} = \Omega_{Bnk}$. Define $P(1 - LGD_i) - D_i = \varepsilon$, and note that $\varepsilon \geq 0$ when the new loan has a nonpositive insurance value. After the addition of the new loan, the bank's new deposit insurance value can be written

$$\frac{\left[D_{Bnk} + D_i - P_{Bnk}(1 - LGD_{Bnk}) - P(1 - LGD_i) \right] pr_{Bnk}^E}{1 + r_f} =$$

$$\frac{\left[D_{Bnk} - P_{Bnk}(1 - LGD_{Bnk}) - \varepsilon \right] pr_{Bnk}^E}{1 + r_f} < \frac{\left[D_{Bnk} - P_{Bnk}(1 - LGD_{Bnk}) \right] pr_{Bnk}^E}{1 + r_f}.$$

Case 2: The intersection of the set of default states for the new loan and the bank under the existing portfolio of loans is the null set $\Omega_{Bnk,i} = \varnothing$. In this case, in the states when the bank defaults on its existing portfolio, the new loan is worth $P - D_i > 0$. In this instance, the bank's new deposit insurance value can be written

$$\frac{\left[D_{Bnk} + D_i - P_{Bnk}(1 - LGD_{Bnk}) - P \right] pr_{Bnk}^E}{1 + r_f} =$$

$$\frac{\left[D_{Bnk} - P_{Bnk}(1 - LGD_{Bnk}) - (P - D_i) \right] pr_{Bnk}^E}{1 + r_f} < \frac{\left[D_{Bnk} - P_{Bnk}(1 - LGD_{Bnk}) \right] pr_{Bnk}^E}{1 + r_f}.$$

Case 3: The intersection between the set of states in which the loan defaults and the bank defaults under its existing portfolio is nonempty, but not identical. There are some states, $0 < pr(\Omega_{Bnk,i}) < pr(\Omega_{Bnk})$. Under these conditions, the new portfolio's deposit insurance value can be written

$$\frac{\left[D_{Bnk} + D_i - P_{Bnk}\left(1 - LGD_{Bnk}\right) - P\left(1 - LGD_i\right)\right] pr^E\left(\Omega_{Bnk,i}\right)}{1 + r_f} +$$

$$\frac{\left[D_{Bnk} - P_{Bnk}\left(1 - LGD_{Bnk}\right) - \left(P - D_i\right)\right]\left(pr^E\left(\Omega_{Bnk}\right) - pr^E\left(\Omega_{Bnk,i}\right)\right)}{1 + r_f},$$

which can be written

$$\frac{\left[D_{Bnk} - P_{Bnk}\left(1 - LGD_{Bnk}\right)\right] pr^E\left(\Omega_{Bnk}\right)}{1 + r_f} - \frac{\left[D_{Bnk} - P_{Bnk}\left(1 - LGD_{Bnk} - \dfrac{P}{P_B} LGD_i\right)\right] pr^E\left(\Omega_{Bnk,i}\right)}{1 + r_f},$$

where $\dfrac{\left[D_{Bnk} - P_{Bnk}\left(1 - LGD_{Bnk} - \dfrac{P}{P_{Bnk}} LGD_i\right)\right] pr^E\left(\Omega_{Bnk,i}\right)}{1 + r_f} > 0.$

Clearly, if the loan is small relative to the bank's existing portfolio, the addition of the loan to the bank's existing portfolio will reduce the ex ante value of the bank's insurance guarantee unless the loan has positive insurance value as a stand-alone investment.

A trivial case occurs when the new loan is very large relative to the bank's existing portfolio $\left(P\left(1 - LGD_i\right) - D_i\right) - \left(D_{Bnk} - P_{Bnk}\left(1 - LGD_{Bnk}\right)\right) > 0$. In this case, the loan is sufficiently large so that even if the loan defaults, the proceeds it generates (in excess of the maximum insured deposits used to fund the loan) are large enough to ensure that the bank can repay all of the insured deposits used to fund its existing portfolio. In this instance, the ex ante value of the insurance guarantee is 0.

Alternatively, if $\left(P\left(1 - LGD_i\right) - D_i\right) - \left(D_{Bnk} - P_{Bnk}\left(1 - LGD_{Bnk}\right)\right) < 0 < \left(P - D_i\right) - \left(D_{Bnk} - P_{Bnk}\left(1 - LGD_{Bnk}\right)\right)$, three cases must be considered. If $\Omega_{Bnk,i} = \Omega_{Bnk}$, the details are analogous to Case 1 above, and the addition of the new loan unambiguously lowers the bank's insurance value. Alternatively, if $\Omega_{Bnk,i} = \varnothing$, the new loan always performs when the bank would otherwise default, given its existing loan portfolio, and the proceeds from the new loan are more than sufficient to forestall a bank default. In this case then, the ex ante value of the deposit insurance guarantee is 0 if the new loan is added to the bank's existing loan portfolio. The final case to consider is when there is some overlap in the states in which the new loan and the bank's existing loan portfolio generate a default, $\emptyset < pr(\Omega_{Bnk,i}) < pr(\Omega_{Bnk})$. When the new loan is included, the bank's new deposit insurance value can be written

$$\frac{\left[D_{Bnk} + D_i - P_{Bnk}(1 - LGD_{Bnk}) - P(1 - LGD_i)\right]pr^E(\Omega_{Bnk,i})}{1 + r_f}$$

$$+ \frac{\left[Max(D_{Bnk} - P_{Bnk}(1 - LGD_{Bnk}) - (P - D_i), 0)\right]\left(pr^E(\Omega_{Bnk}) - pr^E(\Omega_{Bnk,i})\right)}{1 + r_f}$$

$$\left(P(1 - LGD_i) - D_i\right) - \left(D_{Bnk} - P_{Bnk}(1 - LGD_{Bnk})\right) < 0 < (P - D_i) - \left(D_{Bnk} - P_{Bnk}(1 - LGD_{Bnk})\right),$$

which implies that the second term is zero. Using the notation, $P(1 - LGD_i) - D_i = \varepsilon \geq 0$, the bank's new deposit insurance value can be written

$$\frac{\left[D_{Bnk} + D_i - P_{Bnk}(1 - LGD_{Bnk}) - \varepsilon\right]pr^E(\Omega_{Bnk,i})}{1 + r_f} < \frac{\left[D_{Bnk} + D_i - P_{Bnk}(1 - LGD_{Bnk})\right]pr^E(\Omega_{Bnk})}{1 + r_f}.$$

Q.E.D.

REFERENCES

Arrow, K. J., (1953), "Le rôle des valeurs boursières pour la répartition la meilleure des risques," *Économétrie*, Paris, Centre National de la Recherche Scientifique, pp. 41–48.

Debreu, G., (1959), *Theory of Value*, Cowles Foundation Monograph 17. New Haven: Yale University Press.

Bank for International Settlements, (1988), *International Convergence of Capital Measurement and Capital Standards*, Basel Committee on Banking Supervision, Basel, Switzerland.

———, (1999b), *A New Capital Adequacy Framework*, Basel Committee on Banking Supervision, Basel, Switzerland.

———, (2001), *The New Basel Accord*, Basel Committee on Banking Supervision, Basel, Switzerland.

———, (2003), *Third Consultative Paper of the New Basel Capital Accord*, Basel Committee on Banking Supervision, Basel, Switzerland.

Harrison, J., and S. Pliska, (1981), "Martingales and stochastic integrals in the theory of continuous trading," *Stochastic Process and Their Applications*, Vol. 11, pp. 215-260.

Kupiec, P. H., (2002), "Internal Models-Based Capital Regulation and Bank Risk-Taking Incentives," IMF Working Paper No. WP/02/125, Washington, D.C.

Standard & Poor's, (2001), "Ratings Performance 2000: Default Transition, Recovery, and Spreads," January.

13

Optionality and Basel II[1]

Robert Brooks and Benton E. Gup

INTRODUCTION

The new Basel Capital Accord (Basel II) is set to replace the 1988 Basel Capital Accord. Expected to take effect in 2006, Basel II contains three "pillars" to deal with capital, supervisory reviews, and market discipline. We focus on Pillar 2, which is called the "Supervisory Review Process." It requires bank supervisors to assess bank capital adequacy in relation to a bank's risk profile and to intervene to prevent capital from falling below minimum levels. The minimum levels are 4% each for Tier 1 and Tier 2 capital.[2]

Part of the supervisory process involves assessing the various risks associated with banks, including interest rate risk (IRR). The Basel Committee on Banking Supervision defines IRR as the exposure of a bank's financial condition to adverse movements in interest rates that can affect a bank's income as well as the value of a bank's assets, liabilities, and off-balance-sheet positions.[3] The primary sources of IRR come from repricing risk, yield curve risk, basis risk, and optionality. The Basel Committee defines "optionality" as options embedded in bank assets, liabilities, and off-balance-sheet positions.

The new Basel Capital Accord does not have a mandatory capital charge for IRR risk, and we are not proposing one. Nevertheless, we show that optionality can have a significant effect on a bank's economic value and capital adequacy when there are inter-

---

1. The authors gratefully acknowledge the helpful comments of George Kaufman and Gerald Bierwag for earlier drafts of this article.
2. "Pillar 2 (Supervisory Review Process)," Basel Committee on Banking Supervision, Bank for International Settlements, Consultative Document, January 2001.
3. "Principles for the Management and Supervision of Interest Rate Risk," Basel Committee on Banking Supervision, Bank for International Settlements, Consultative Document, January 2001, p. 5.

est rate shocks, and it may cause banks to become significantly undercapitalized. The optionality is linked to duration—the change in a bank's economic value associated with a change in interest rates.[4] The standardized interest rate shock recommended by the Basel Committee for stress testing is a 200-basis-point parallel shock.

The current and past Consultative Documents on Basel II do not deal adequately with option-adjusted durations, or with the impact on IRR of put and call options embedded in fixed-rate loans and deposits with known maturities.[5] Fixed-rate loans with a prepayment option and certificates of deposit (CDs) that can be liquidated before maturity with no interest rate penalty for early withdrawal are examples of such products with embedded options.[6] With respect to the loan, the bank is short a put option on rates. If interest rates decline, the borrower will refinance the loan at a lower rate. In the case of the CD, the bank is short a call option on rates. If interest rates increase, depositors will withdraw their CDs and pursue higher rates. Thus, the exercise of options embedded in bank assets and liabilities undermines the structure of the bank regulators. Basel Committee suggests that banks report their assets, liabilities, and off-balance-sheet positions in time bands based upon their remaining maturities or nearest repricing dates.[7] Each position will be multiplied by IRR "risk weights," and then summed to produce a net risk-weighted position. The net position represents the estimated change in the bank's net economic value.

In essence, we point out the danger of not using option-adjusted durations when the embedded options are contained in a bank's assets or liabilities. Measuring option-adjusted durations is a difficult task and beyond the scope of this chapter. Some work on option-adjusted duration has been done. The Office of Thrift Supervision (1994) suggested the use of a net present value model and a Monte Carlo simulation approach to value assets with

---

4. The testing of IRR using duration is discussed in "Principles for the Management and Supervision of Interest Rate Risk," (2001), 28–29. Economic value is defined as the net present value of assets less the net present value of liabilities plus the net present value of off-balance sheet instruments. ("Principles for the Management and Supervision of Interest Rate Risk," 2001, p. 6) It should not be confused with "market value or market capitalization" of a bank that is determined by multiplying the stock price times the number of shares outstanding. The "embedded losses" were barely mentioned in "Principles for the Management of Interest Rate Risk (1997).

5. It is noteworthy that Basle Committee overlooked optionality in its *Framework for Supervisory Information about the Derivatives Activities of Banks and Securities Firms*, (May 1995).

6. Chance and Broughton (1988) examine indexed CDs.

7. "Principles for the Management and Supervision of Interest Rate Risk," (2001), Annex 2 and 3.

embedded options that have a significant impact on assets' price sensitivity. They also considered assets' effective duration. The OTS was particularly concerned about mortgage products with options, such as interest rate caps and floors. Options embedded in liabilities are not dealt with extensively by the OTS. Fabozzi and Modigliani (1992) used Monte Carlo simulations to estimate option-adjusted spreads for mortgage-backed securities. Anderson, Barber, and Chang (1993) and DeRosa, Goodman, and Zazzarino (1993) estimated a modified duration for mortgage-backed securities, which accounts for interest rate sensitivity. Carlson and Lawler (1987) examined closed form formulas for mortgage-backed securities. Bierwag (1987) examined the experience of callable bonds from January to May 1986, when interest rates declined sharply. The behavior of callable bonds and mortgage-backed securities are analogous during periods of declining rates. Investment managers who failed to properly account for the duration shift on the callable bonds suffered large losses in their portfolios during the period under consideration. The extent of losses depended on their ability to forecast interest rate changes correctly. The use of option-adjusted durations may have mitigated some of the effects of the interest rate risk. Bierwag suggested that the prudent use of duration models requires that the callability options either be evaluated or avoided. The widespread use of embedded options in both asset and liability products suggests that they are not being avoided. Furthermore, it does not appear that all of the options are being evaluated. Simons (1995) examined banks' use of derivatives for commercial bank asset/liability management, but said nothing about embedded options.

The effect of duration on interest rate risk has been examined by Hanweck and Shull (1994), O'Keefe (1993), and Cohen (1993).[8] In general, the articles concluded that the duration standard for capital adequacy is more sensitive to interest rate changes than the former flat-rate capital standards. However, the duration standard can be misleading at times, and it may result in significant errors with respect to measuring capital adequacy. This chapter adds to the growing body of literature by examining the effects on

---

8. Gilkeson and Ruff (1992) examined the effect on interest rate changes on CDs with withdrawal penalties for early redemption. They did not, however, deal with the duration of CDs. Nevertheless, they do show that CDs should not be treated as standard fixed-income securities because it fails to account for early withdrawal options embedded in CDs.

capital adequacy of changes in interest rates on the value of options embedded in bank loans and deposits. Cohen (1991) examined embedded options, but not in connection with capital standards.

In Section I we examine the impact of embedded options on a bank's balance sheet that is fully immunized by traditional measures. In addition, we examine the bank's risk-based capital to asset ratios. In Section II we examine the impact of embedded options on banks that are not immunized. First, we analyze the case where the equity duration is positive, and then we analyze the case where the equity duration is negative. Concluding comments are given in Section III.

I. THE EFFECT OF INTEREST RATE CHANGES ON A FULLY IMMUNIZED BANK

To illustrate the nature of the problem of measuring interest rate risk, consider the following example. Suppose that a hypothetical bank financed $100 million in assets with $90 million in non-core rate-sensitive liabilities and with $10 million in equity. The results presented here are scale invariant, so the bank size does not matter. The bank has no off-balance-sheet liabilities. By FDIC risk-based capital standards, this position of the bank is consistent with a risk-based capital ratio of 10%.[9] For simplicity, the bank's sole assets is a 6% fixed rate, non-amortizing loan with 2.86 years to maturity, and its sole liability is a 3% CD with 3 years to maturity. Interest payments on both the loan and the CD are annual.

As we will show below, this maturity structure was selected to achieve an equity duration of zero. Recall modified duration can be computed as

$$D = \frac{dP/P}{dy} = \frac{1}{1+y}\sum_{t=1}^{n}(i-f)\frac{CF_i/(1+y)^{i-f}}{P} \tag{1}$$

---

9. The capital category distribution is defined as follows:
Total risk-based capital

Well capitalized	≥10%
Adequately capitalized	≥8%
Undercapitalized	<8%
Significantly undercapitalized	<6%
Critically undercapitalized	—— (tangible equity of ≤2%)

Undercapitalized banks are required by bank regulators to take Prompt Corrective Action (PCA) to restore their capital to adequate levels. Failure to comply with the PCA may result in the closure of the bank by the regulators.

where n is the number of remaining cash flows, CF_i is the cash flow at time i, f is the fraction of the period elapsed since the last cash flow, y is the periodic yield to maturity, and P is the current market value of the security. In this case, the duration of assets is 2.545 years, and the duration of liabilities is 2.829 years. The duration of the bank's assets and liabilities are fully immunized, resulting in an equity duration of zero.

The duration of the assets in this financed position can be written as

$$D_A = \frac{L}{A}D_L + \frac{E}{A}D_E \qquad (2)$$

where the duration of the assets is the value-weighted duration of liabilities and the equity used in financing the position. Solving for the duration of equity, we have

$$D_E = \left(D_A - \frac{L}{A}D_L \right)\frac{A}{E}. \qquad (3)$$

Thus, with the data given above, we see

$$D_E = \left(2.545 - \frac{90}{100}\, 2.829 \right)\frac{100}{10} \cong 0.$$

With this capital structure and interest rate sensitivity, the market value and the equity position should be relatively insensitive to changes in interest rates. Thus, there is no change in the $10 million net economic value or market value of the bank's equity when the loan rate is 6% and the CD rate is 3%. We assume a constant 3% net interest spread on new assets and liabilities. For details on computing duration for securities with embedded options, see Choi [1996].

Before we consider the embedded options, let's examine the effects of an instantaneous 200 basis point parallel increase in the yield curve from 6% to 8%. As shown in Exhibit 1, the market value of the bank's assets will decline $4.91 million to $95.09 million. The market value of the liabilities will decline $4.90 million to $85.10, and the market value of the equity will fall only $0.01 million to $9.99. Although the market value of the equity declined, the total risk-based capital to asset ratio improved from 10% ($10/$100) to 10.5% ($9.99/$95.09).

Exhibit 1. Bank Market Values–Fully Immunized ($ millions)

Panel A: No Embedded Options

INTEREST RATES	ASSETS	LIABILITIES	EQUITY	CAPITAL TO ASSET RATIO
4.0%	$105.28	$95.29	$9.98	9.48%
6.0%	$100.00	$90.00	$10.00	10.00%
8.0%	$95.09	$85.10	$9.99	10.50%

Panel B: Embedded Liability Options

INTEREST RATES	ASSETS	LIABILITIES	EQUITY	CAPITAL TO ASSET RATIO
4.0%	$105.28	$95.29	$9.98	9.48%
6.0%	$100.00	$90.00	$10.00	10.00%
8.0%	$95.09	$90.00	$5.09	5.35%

Panel C: Embedded Asset Options

INTEREST RATES	ASSETS	LIABILITIES	EQUITY	CAPITAL TO ASSET RATIO
4.0%	$100.00	$95.29	$4.71	4.71%
6.0%	$100.00	$90.00	$10.00	10.00%
8.0%	$95.09	$85.10	$9.99	10.50%

Panel D: Embedded Asset and Liability Options

INTEREST RATES	ASSETS	LIABILITIES	EQUITY	CAPITAL TO ASSET RATIO
4.0%	$100.00	$95.29	$4.71	4.71%
6.0%	$100.00	$90.00	$10.00	10.00%
8.0%	$95.09	$90.00	$5.09	5.35%

Similarly, an instantaneous 200 basis point parallel decrease in the yield curve will increase the value of the assets to $105.28 million, the liabilities to $95.29 million, and the equity to $9.98. The capital ratio declined to 9.48%. The slight differences in sensitivity to interest rate changes between assets and liabilities result in slight losses in equity when interest rates rise or fall. From all appearances, this bank position does not contribute much interest rate risk to the bank. Asset and liability market value changes are roughly equivalent; hence interest rate losses for assets are offset by declining values of liabilities. The capital to asset ratio increases slightly as loan rates increase primarily because asset values have fallen. This bank is essentially fully immunized. We turn now to examine the impact of embedded options on the equity value of the bank. We first examine the impact of embedded liability options and then to embedded asset options.

Exhibit 2. Fully Immunized Bank Capital to Asset Ratio Constant Interest Rate Spread

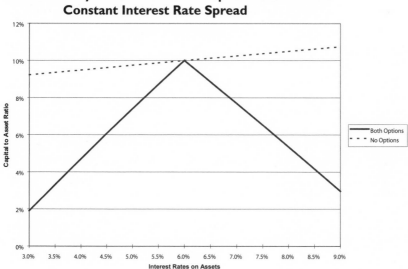

Exhibit 3. Bank Market Values – Positive Duration ($ millions)

Panel A: No Embedded Options

INTEREST RATES	ASSETS	LIABILITIES	EQUITY	CAPITAL TO ASSET RATIO
4.0%	$108.62	$95.29	$13.33	12.27%
6.0%	$100.00	$90.00	$10.00	10.00%
8.0%	$92.25	$85.10	$7.15	7.75%

Panel B: Embedded Liability Options

INTEREST RATES	ASSETS	LIABILITIES	EQUITY	CAPITAL TO ASSET RATIO
4.0%	$108.62	$95.29	$13.33	12.27%
6.0%	$100.00	$90.00	$10.00	10.00%
8.0%	$92.25	$90.00	$2.25	2.44%

Panel C: Embedded Asset Options

INTEREST RATES	ASSETS	LIABILITIES	EQUITY	CAPITAL TO ASSET RATIO
4.0%	$100.00	$95.29	$4.71	4.71%
6.0%	$100.00	$90.00	$10.00	10.00%
8.0%	$92.25	$85.10	$7.15	7.75%

Panel D: Embedded Asset and Liability Options

INTEREST RATES	ASSETS	LIABILITIES	EQUITY	CAPITAL TO ASSET RATIO
4.0%	$100.00	$95.29	$4.71	4.71%
6.0%	$100.00	$90.00	$10.00	10.00%
8.0%	$92.25	$90.00	$2.25	2.44%

Embedded Liability Options

Assume that this bank has embedded options on its liabilities but not its assets. Specifically, this bank's CDs allow for early withdrawal of funds at no penalty. When interest rates rise, depositors will exercise their right to withdraw funds and reinvest them at another bank or even at the same bank at a higher rate. Essentially, depositors have a put option on the CD. They can "sell" the CD back to the bank at par. Alternatively, they have a CD plus a call option on interest rates. Either way, the bank's liabilities will never be worth less than par; otherwise, the depositor is not behaving rationally.

When incorporating this type of analysis, one consideration is the likelihood of suboptimal behavior on the part of bank customers if they do not behave rationally. The suboptimal behavior will reduce, but not eliminate, the harmful effects of banks being short embedded options.

The effect of embedded liability options is to have liabilities whose market value never falls below par because of the rational actions of depositors. This is unfortunate for banks because, ceteris paribus, they would like to have their liabilities decline in value, which would increase the value of their equity. Exhibit 1, Panel B, illustrates the change in the market value of equity of this bank when it offers CD's with no early withdrawal penalty and when depositors behave rationally. The exhibit reveals that this bank has considerable interest rate risk exposure when loan rates rise. Recall that we assumed a constant 3% net interest spread.

When loan rates increase by 200 basis points, the market value of the bank's assets declines $4.91 million to a level of $95.09 million. However, its liabilities remain at par. Thus, the market value of equity declines $4.91 million to a level of $5.09 ($95.09–$90.00) million. Now the capital to asset ratio is 5.35% ($5.09/$95.09). Next we examine the impact of embedded asset options.

Embedded Asset Options

Assume that this bank has embedded options on its assets, but not on its liabilities. When interest rates fall, borrowers will exercise their right to refinance their loans at a lower rate and they will prepay their loans. Essentially, borrowers have a call option on their loans; they can exercise their right and buy their loans back at par. Alternatively, the borrower has a loan plus a put option on interest rates. Either way, the bank's assets will never be worth more than par when borrowers behave rationally.

The effect of embedded asset options is to have assets whose market value never rises above par. Obviously, banks would like to have assets rise in value because, other things being equal, this will increase the value of its equity. Exhibit 1, Panel C, illustrates the change in the market value of equity of this bank when it makes loans with no prepayment penalty and when bank customers all behave rationally. The bank has considerable interest rate risk exposure when loan rates fall.

If interest rates decline by 200 basis points, the market value of the bank's assets would increase by $5.28 million if the borrowers had no options on their loans. However, because these loans can be prepaid, the market value of the assets remains at $100 million. Unfortunately for the bank, the market value of the liabilities will increase $5.28 million for a market value of $95.29 million. Thus, the market value of equity will fall to $4.71 ($100–$95.29) million. The capital to asset ratio would be 4.71%, which is significantly undercapitalized. Once loan rates decline below 6 percent, the capital to asset ratio declines precipitously.

Many banks are short embedded options on both sides of the balance sheet. That is, they have loans that can be prepaid and deposits that have no early withdrawal penalty. If interest rates rise sharply, depositors will withdraw funds, and borrowers will hold off on any prepayments. If interest rates fall sharply, depositors will hold no incentive to withdraw funds, and borrowers will prepay their loans. The best the bank can hope for is stable interest rates. As shown in Exhibit 1, Panel D, if interest rates move in either direction, the market value of equity and the capital to asset ratios will decline. Equally important, only a modest change in rates is required before the bank will be undercapitalized.

One can say with absolute certainty that interest rates will change. History reveals that market-determined and bank-administered interest rates do not remain stable for long periods. For example, the prime rate charged by banks increased from an average of 7.86 percent in 1975 to 18.87 percent in 1981. Then the prime rate declined to 4.25 percent in 2003. Exhibit 2 illustrates the impact of embedded options on the capital to asset ratio. Comparing no options with both options, we observed that ignoring embedded options significantly overstates the capital to assets ratio.

The prices of embedded options should be reflected in the price of the products offered by the bank. A fixed-rate loan with the prepayment option should have a higher rate than the same loan with no prepayment option. Similarly, a CD with no early withdrawal penalty should have a rate lower than a CD with an early withdrawal penalty. The differences in the rates represents the amortized cost of the options. For example, if each option were priced at 50 basis points per year, then the 3% net interest spread (interest income less interest expense) of our hypothetical fully immunized bank overstates the true interest rate spread by 100 basis points. Thus, the narrower spread of 2% is a much more

Exhibit 2. Fully Immunized Bank Capital to Asset Ratio
Constant Interest Rate Spread

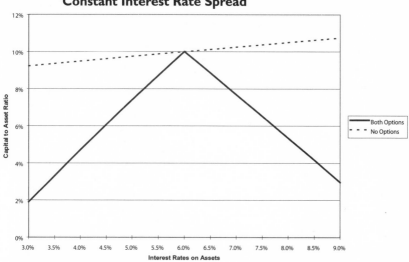

accurate estimate of the realized future net interest spread. Banks with embedded options are exposed to significant interest rate risk if rates move suddenly. As noted previously, such shifts did occur in the late 1970s and early 1980s as well as the sharp fall in rates in the early 2000s.

II. INTEREST RATE CHANGES – POSITIVE AND NEGATIVE DURATION

Positive Duration

The previous examples focus on a hypothetical bank with a fully immunized portfolio of assets and liabilities. Now we examine the effects of interest rate changes on a bank with positive duration, which means that it is "asset sensitive." Exhibit 3, Panel A, illustrates the effects of interest rate changes on the market value of a bank with no embedded options and positive duration. Specifically, we assume the bank an has asset duration of 4.08, liability duration of 2.83, and hence, an equity duration of 1.71. If interest rates increase, the data reveal that the market value of the assets will decline more than the market value of the liabilities, thereby decreasing the value of the equity. If interest rates increase, the reverse is true, and the capital to asset ratio declines as interest rates increase.

Exhibit 3. Bank Market Values – Positive Duration ($ millions)

Panel A: No Embedded Options

INTEREST RATES	ASSETS	LIABILITIES	EQUITY	CAPITAL TO ASSET RATIO
4.0%	$108.62	$95.29	$13.33	12.27%
6.0%	$100.00	$90.00	$10.00	10.00%
8.0%	$92.25	$85.10	$7.15	7.75%

Panel B: Embedded Liability Options

INTEREST RATES	ASSETS	LIABILITIES	EQUITY	CAPITAL TO ASSET RATIO
4.0%	$108.62	$95.29	$13.33	12.27%
6.0%	$100.00	$90.00	$10.00	10.00%
8.0%	$92.25	$90.00	$2.25	2.44%

Panel C: Embedded Asset Options

INTEREST RATES	ASSETS	LIABILITIES	EQUITY	CAPITAL TO ASSET RATIO
4.0%	$100.00	$95.29	$4.71	4.71%
6.0%	$100.00	$90.00	$10.00	10.00%
8.0%	$92.25	$85.10	$7.15	7.75%

Panel D: Embedded Asset and Liability Options

INTEREST RATES	ASSETS	LIABILITIES	EQUITY	CAPITAL TO ASSET RATIO
4.0%	$100.00	$95.29	$4.71	4.71%
6.0%	$100.00	$90.00	$10.00	10.00%
8.0%	$92.25	$90.00	$2.25	2.44%

Positive Duration and Embedded Liability Options

Assume that the bank with positive duration has embedded liability options but no embedded asset options. Rational depositors will exercise their options in the manner described previously if interest rates increase, and they will do nothing if interest rates decline. The results of their actions on the market value of the bank's equity are shown in Exhibit 3, Panel B. If interest rates increase, the market value of the equity declines as before. Conversely, a decline in interest rates results in higher market value of equity, but not as high as in the case with no embedded liability options. The capital to asset ratio follows the same pattern.

Positive Duration and Embedded Asset Options

In this example, the bank has embedded asset options but no embedded liability options. Because the bank has positive duration, any change in interest rates will result in a decline in the market value of its equity and its capital to asset ratio (See Exhibit 3, Panel C). Equally important, a decline in interest rates will have a greater negative effect on the value of the equity and the capital to asset ratio than an equal increase in interest rates.

Positive Duration and Embedded Asset and Liability Options

When the bank with positive duration has embedded options in both its assets and liabilities, any change in interest rates will result in a lower market value of its equity and lower capital to asset ratios. However, an increase in interest rates will have a greater negative change on the market value of its equity (and capital to asset ratio) than an equal decrease in interest rates.

Exhibit 4 illustrates the capital to asset ratio for an asset-sensitive bank. Comparing Exhibit 4 with Exhibit 2 we observe the same results for rates declining because the positive duration was introduced as a longer asset duration. There is a much more dramatic effect when rates rise. The positive duration is particularly painful because the assets are more rate sensitive and the liabilities have no rate sensitivity.

Negative Duration

The term negative duration means that the duration of the bank's liabilities are longer than the duration of its assets. We introduce negative duration by shortening the asset duration to 0.82. Hence, the equity duration is −1.92. The bank is said to be "liability sensitive" to changes in interest rates. As shown in Exhibit 5, Panel A, if interest rates increase, the market value of the liability declines more than the market value of the assets, and the market value of the equity increases. If rates fall, the reverse occurs. As shown in Panel A, the capital to asset ratio is positively associated with the level of interest rates.

Exhibit 4. Positive Duration Bank Capital to Asset Ratio Embedded Asset and Liability Options Constant Interest Rate Spread

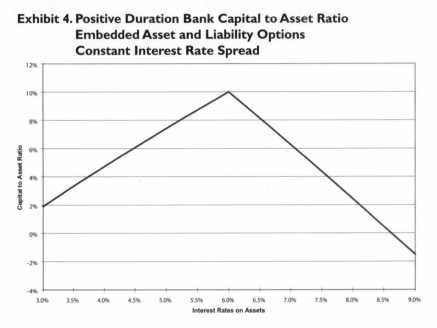

Exhibit 5. Bank Market Values – Negative Duration ($ millions)

Panel A: No Embedded Options

INTEREST RATES	ASSETS	LIABILITIES	EQUITY	CAPITAL TO ASSET RATIO
4.0%	$101.66	$95.29	$6.37	6.26%
6.0%	$100.00	$90.00	$10.00	10.00%
8.0%	$98.40	$85.10	$13.30	13.52%

Panel B: Embedded Liability Options

INTEREST RATES	ASSETS	LIABILITIES	EQUITY	CAPITAL TO ASSET RATIO
4.0%	$101.66	$95.29	$6.37	6.26%
6.0%	$100.00	$90.00	$10.00	10.00%
8.0%	$98.40	$90.00	$8.40	8.53%

Exhibit 5. Bank Market Values – Negative Duration ($ millions) *(cont.)*

Panel C : Embedded Asset Options

INTEREST RATES	ASSETS	LIABILITIES	EQUITY	CAPITAL TO ASSET RATIO
4.0%	$100.00	$95.29	$4.71	4.71%
6.0%	$100.00	$90.00	$10.00	10.00%
8.0%	$98.40	$85.10	$13.30	13.52%

Panel D : Embedded Asset and Liability Options

INTEREST RATES	ASSETS	LIABILITIES	EQUITY	CAPITAL TO ASSET RATIO
4.0%	$100.00	$95.29	$4.71	4.71%
6.0%	$100.00	$90.00	$10.00	10.00%
8.0%	$98.40	$90.00	$8.40	8.53%

Negative Duration and Embedded Liability Options

If our hypothetical bank has only embedded liability options, any change in interest rates results in lower equity values and capital to asset ratios. Increases in interest rates have a greater negative effect than decreases (see Exhibit 5, Panel B).

Negative Duration and Embedded Asset Options

If our hypothetical bank has only embedded asset options, an increase in interest rates results in an increase in both the market value of the equity and the capital to asset ratio. However, an equivalent decrease in interest rates results in a greater than proportional decrease in the market value of the equity and the capital to asset ratio (see Exhibit 5, Panel C).

Negative Duration and Embedded Asset and Liability Options

If the bank with negative duration has embedded options in both its assets and liabilities, any change in interest rates will result in lower market values of its equity and lower capital to asset ratios.

Exhibit 6 illustrates the capital to asset ratio for a liability sensitive bank. Comparing Exhibit 6 with Exhibit 5 we observe again the same results for rates declining because the negative duration was introduced as a longer asset duration. There is a less of an effect when rates rise. The negative duration is beneficial because the liabilities are more rate, partially offsetting the adverse impact of the embedded options.

Exhibit 6. Positive Duration Bank Capital to Asset Ratio Embedded Asset and Liability Options Constant Interest Rate Spread

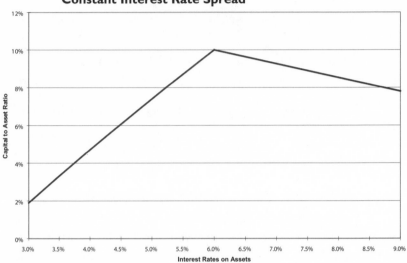

III. CONCLUSION

This article examined the effect of optionality/embedded options on the IRR and capital adequacy. The issue is important because Basel II mandated that regulators consider IRR in their risk-based capital guidelines. However, the guidelines do give sufficient weight to embedded options, nor do they consider option adjusted durations. For purposes of illustration, we only considered corner solutions of embedded options. Thus, this article demonstrated that a hypothetical bank, which is fully immunized in terms of equity duration, has significant interest rate risk due to embedded options in assets and liabilities. Because of the embedded options, the net interest spread is overstated. Accordingly, changes in interest rates have a greater effect on net interest income than was previously thought. It also affects the bank's capital adequacy but to a lesser degree.

In banks that have positive or negative duration with embedded asset and liability options, any change in interest rates will have a detrimental effect on the market value and capital to asset ratios of the banks' equity if borrowers and depositors behave rationally.

Our example takes a simple and extreme case to illustrate our points. We recognize that, in reality, banks have a variety of embedded options on both the asset and liability sides of their balance sheets. Moreover, not all of the bank's customers will exercise their options at the optimal times, or at the same time. Nevertheless, the changes in the market value of the equity will be in the same directions but not necessarily in the same magnitudes as those presented here. Therefore, the effects on capital adequacy and interest margins may be overstated.

It is important for bank managers to recognize the economic value and resultant risks related to offering loans and deposits with embedded options. It is equally important for regulators to correctly measure interest rate risk. To date, Chateau (1990) used quadratic approximation methods to examine the early exercise of capped variable rate loan commitments. In addition, the previously cited works involving mortgage-backed securities, combined with the current use of Monte Carlo simulations for measuring option adjusted spreads, provides a foundation for additional research dealing with option adjusted durations.

REFERENCES

Anderson, Gary A., (1993), Joel R. Barber, and Chun-Hao Chang, "Prepayment Risk and the Duration of Default-Free Mortgage-Backed Securities," pp. 1–9, *The Journal of Financial Research*, Spring.

Basle Committee on Banking Supervision and the Technical Committee of the International Organisation of Securities Commissions (IOSCO), (1995), *Framework for Supervisory Information about the Derivatives Activities of Banks and Securities Firms*, May.

Bierwag, Gerald O., (1987), *Duration Analysis: Managing Interest Rate Risk*, Cambridge, Mass.: Ballinger Publishing Co., Chapter 13.

Carlson, Steven J., and Thomas A. Lawler, (1987), "Closed Form Formulas: A More Efficient Way of Computing the Price, Duration, and Weighted Average Life of Mortgage Pools," appears in *Mortgage-Backed Securities: New Strategies, Applications and Research*, Frank J. Fabozzi, ed., Chicago, IL, Probus Publishing.

Chance, Don M., and John C. Broughton, (1998), "Market Index Depository Liabilities: Analysis, Interpretation, and Performance," *Journal of Financial Services Research*, December, pp. 335–352.

Choi, Sam, (1996), "Effective Durations for Mortgage-Backed Securities: Recipes for Improvement," *Journal of Fixed Income*, March, pp. 23–30.

Cohen, Hugh, (1993), "Beyond Duration: Measuring Interest Rate Exposure," *Economic Review*, Federal Reserve Bank of Atlanta, March/April, pp. 23–31.

Cohen, Hugh, (1991), "Evaluating Embedded Options," *Economic Review*, Federal Reserve Bank of Atlanta, November/December, pp. 9–16.

DeRosa, Paul, Laurie Goodman, and Mike Zazzarino, (1993), "Duration Estimates on Mortgage Backed Securities," *Financial Analysts Journal*, Winter, pp. 32–38.

Fabozzi, Frank, and Franco Modigliani, (1992), *Mortgage and Mortgage-Backed Securities Markets*, Boston: Harvard Business School Press, Chapter 13.

Federal Reserve Press Release, September 14, 1993, dealing with Interest Rate Risk, 1–155.

Gilkeson, James H., and Craig K. Ruff, (1992), "The Valuation of Retail CD Portfolios," Unpublished paper, October 1.

Hanweck, Gerald A., and Bernard Shull, (1994), "Bank's Exposure to Interest Rate Risk and Capital Adequacy: An Appraisal of the Federal Agencies' Approach," Presented at the 30th Annual Conference on Bank Structure and Competition, Federal Reserve Bank of Chicago, May.

O'Keefe, John P., (1993), "Risk-Based Capital Standards for Commercial Banks: Improved Capital Adequacy Standards?" pp. 1–15, *FDIC Banking Review*, Spring/Summer.

"Pillar 2 (Supervisory Review Process)," (2001), Basel Committee on Banking Supervision, Bank for International Settlements, Consultative Document, January.

"Principles for the Management and Supervision of Interest Rate Risk," (2001), Basel Committee on Banking Supervision, Bank for International Settlements, Consultative Document, January.

"Principles for the Management of Interest Rate Risk," (1997), Basel Committee on Banking Supervision, Bank for International Settlements, Consultative Proposal, January.

Simons, Katerina, (1995), "Interest Rate Derivatives and Asset-Liability Management by Commercial Banks," *New England Economic Review*, Federal Reserve Bank of Boston, Jan./Feb., pp. 17–28.

The OTS Net Portfolio Value Model, (1994), Office of Thrift Supervision, Risk Management Division, November.

14

The Impact of the Basel II Capital Accord on Australian Banks

Peter Docherty, Chris Terry, and Rowan Trayler

I. INTRODUCTION

The impact of the new Basel Capital Accord (Basel II) on the Australian banking system must be understood in terms of the system's particular structure and against the background of developments in the Australian financial system, generally, across the 1990s. These developments interacted with the 1988 Basel Capital Accord (Basel I) in ways that, it will be argued, place Australian banking in a relatively good position to adopt the new guidelines, although some adjustments may be necessary if they are to most effectively achieve their intended goals in the Australian context.

This article briefly reviews the logic of prudential regulation before outlining the structure of Australian banking and regulatory systems. The impact of Basel I on Australian banks is then examined in conjunction with a number of other important developments in the Australian financial system during the 1980s and 1990s. This sets the background for a focused consideration of Basel II's potential impact on Australian banking. The issues considered include: the risk-rating methodology of local banks; the role of securitization in the local market; the significant role played by mortgage lending in Australia; the potential for Australian banks to undertake credit risk mitigation; and questions of competitive neutrality and incentives for economic growth.

2. THE RATIONALE FOR PRUDENTIAL REGULATION

Basel II is designed to enhance prudential regulation in adopting countries by strengthening its approach to capital adequacy and increasing the risk-sensitivity of bank capital regulation (Basel Committee 2001a, page 6). Other explicit objectives of Basel II include: maintenance of the existing levels of capital in adopting banking systems, and enhancement of competitive equality. These features of the new system are intended to strengthen the positive features of Basel I at the same time as overcoming its weaknesses.

Prudential regulation generally arises as a by-product of the public policy objective of minimising the possibility of systemic failure in the financial system, which the existence of asymmetric information generates (Hogan & Sharpe 1997, pages 15–20; Mishkin 2001, page 5). Credit risk is inherent to banking, but one of the chief functions of banks is to overcome informational asymmetries between potential borrower and potential lender that exacerbate this risk. Banks, it is argued, are better placed than unsophisticated depositors to perform this function so that delegation of credit risk evaluation and monitoring to banks is in the interests of depositors (Diamond 1984, cf. Chant 1992).

Informational asymmetry, however, also applies to the bank-depositor relationship, and this generates problems when credit risk is realised, and banks begin to suffer losses, especially if those losses are significant. Depositors are able to observe the losses experienced by their bank but, due to information asymmetries, cannot tell whether those losses are large enough to affect the bank's ability to repay all deposits. Given that the nominal value of bank deposits is fixed, the operation of a sequential service constraint for withdrawal of deposits in full, creates an incentive for individual depositors to withdraw their funds and to be as close to the front of the withdrawal queue as possible (Greenbaum & Thakor 1995, page 455). The existence of asymmetric information thus creates the conditions for credit losses to generate runs on troubled banks. But it also creates the conditions for a run at a single, potentially troubled bank to spread to other, healthy institutions. When a single institution begins to experience problem loans and defaults, depositors at other institutions may have difficulty assessing whether these problems apply to their own bank. The same conditions that led depositors to run on the problem bank can now lead depositors to run on a perfectly healthy institution. Contagion of this kind has the potential to destabilise entire banking and financial systems, and the possibility of contagion is underscored when interbank exposures through the payments system, are taken into account.

It is to protect unsophisticated depositors, the integrity of the payments system, and to prevent contagion and systemic risk that some kind of safety net is frequently provided by public institutions (Mishkin 2001, page 5). Safety nets may take a range of forms, including deposit insurance, explicit or implicit deposit guarantees, and lender-of-last-resort facilities. All forms of safety net, however, have the potential to generate moral hazard problems, reducing incentives for bank managers, on the one hand, to avoid making risky lending decisions, and for depositors, on the other hand, to monitor bank manager behaviour and to withdraw funds when risks are excessive. The significant financial and economic externalities associated with systemic risk thus warrant the provision of some form of safety net, but the net's very existence increases the probability that it will be needed.

Prudential regulation is usually offered as the solution to these moral hazard problems (Hogan & Sharpe 1997, page 18). It may take one of two potential forms. Firstly, it may prohibit risk-taking behaviour and/or mandate risk-reducing, or prudent, behaviour. Limiting concentrations of lending to particular borrowers, minimum liquidity ratios, and reserve requirements are examples of this kind of regulation. Secondly, regulation may attempt to realign the incentive structure faced by bank managers, which is distorted by the existence of the safety net. Under this kind of regulation, risk-taking behaviour is not prohibited but penalised, while risk-reducing behaviour is rewarded. Basel I that required banks to hold additional capital against activities, which exposed them to additional risk, represented an example of this kind of regulation. The proposed Basel II is designed to enhance this dimension of Basel I and to increase the risk-sensitivity of bank capital regulation, further realigning bank management incentives.

The following sections consider the structure of the Australian banking system, how the above principles have been applied to this system, and in particular, the impact on the system of the Basel I.

3. THE STRUCTURE OF THE AUSTRALIAN BANKING INDUSTRY

Australian banking has traditionally been characterised by a high level of market concentration. This continues to be the case, although increased competition and market contestability was generated from the mid-1980s with a significant expansion in the number of banking licences granted under the *Banking Act*. This was undertaken as part of a general process of financial system deregulation begun a few years earlier.

There are currently thirteen Australian-owned banks consisting of what are referred to as the big four banks (that collectively dominate both the retail and wholesale markets[1]), a well-established wholesale bank, plus six smaller banks with almost exclusively retail exposures. Subsidiaries of twelve foreign-owned banks are free to participate in the retail market, but their retail operations are relatively small. Another twenty-six foreign banks have Australian branches, which mainly engage in wholesale banking activities. In addition, there are two groups of nonbank thrift institutions (building societies and credit unions), which concentrate on the retail market but, individually and collectively, play a small role in this market. Collectively, all of these institutions are referred to in Australia as authorised deposit-taking institutions *(ADIs)*.

The dominance of the big four in the retail-banking sector is facilitated nationally through networks of branches, agencies, *ATMs* and *EFTPOS* terminals, as well as through their electronic banking facilities. Moreover, the big four are financial conglomerates that have insurance and fund management subsidiaries as well as significant overseas operations. The National Australia Bank *(NAB)*, for example, has overseas operations almost as large as its domestic banking business.

The retail-banking sector is supplied by the big four and by a small group of so-called *regional* banks (i.e., banks that operate mainly in one or a few of the eight states and territories), and by the 14 building societies and 187 credit unions. As suggested above, foreign bank subsidiaries also operate in the retail markets, but

---

1. These are the Australia and New Zealand Banking Group (ANZ), the Commonwealth Bank of Australia (CBA), the National Australia Bank (NAB), and Westpac Banking Corporation (WBC).

none has an established national branch network. The wholesale-banking sector is supplied by the big four and many of the world's leading international banks, along with domestic and international securities companies.

An overview of the structure of Australian *ADIs* (as at March 2003) is provided by the data in Table 1. Observe the relative unimportance of the nonbank *ADIs*. Nonbank deposits represented about 6% of total deposits, and nonbank assets represented less than 4% of total assets. Note, also, the important role housing loans play in nonbank *ADI* lending. Personal loans make up most of the balance of their loans.

Table 1. Liabilities and assets of ADIs, March 2003, ($AUDm)

ADI	DEPOSITS	TOTAL LIABILITIES	HOUSING LOANS	TOTAL ASSETS
Banks	536,659	940,956	358,960	1,011,901
Building societies	11,338	11,747	8,483	12,765
Credit unions	23,817	25,366	15,207	27,801
Totals	571,814	978,069	382,650	1,052,467

Source: *Australian Prudential Regulation Authority.*

A slightly more detailed picture of the assets of nonbank *ADIs* is provided by the data in Table 2. Given the small size of these institutions, the domestic nature of their activities, and the concentration of their lending, it is expected that they would use the standard risk assessment models in Basel II.

Table 2. Nonbank ADI assets, March 2003, ($AUDm)

ASSETS	ALL CREDIT UNIONS	ALL BUILDING SOCIETIES
Notes and coins	211.1	66.6
Deposits at call	983.6	177.3
All other deposits	2,626.2	168.0
Investment securities	1,034.4	1,888.9
Housing loans	15,206.8	8,482.5
Other loans and advances	7,047.4	1,547.3
(Provisions for impairment)	(152.5)	(16.2)
Total assets	27,801.1	12,674.5

Source: *Australian Prudential Regulation Authority.*

The liabilities of the major banks (the big four, plus St George Bank) are shown by the data in Table 3 relative to the other banks, as at March 2002. The majors held almost 75% of total deposits.

Table 3. Liabilities of bank ADIs, March 2002, ($AUDm)

BANK	TOTAL DEPOSITS	TOTAL LIABILITIES	TOTAL ASSETS
ANZ	59,254	104,874	119,547
CBA	110,225	151,363	164,151
NAB	75,770	129,751	165,997
WBC	76,818	112,968	131,364
St George	37,265	48,717	52,285
The majors	359,332	547,673	633,344
Other Australian	56,299	69,816	74,410
Foreign banks	66,894	141,460	148,636
Total banks	482,525	758,949	856,390
Building societies	10,674	11,670	12,661
Credit unions	21,590	23,161	25,415
Totals, all ADIs	514,789	793,780	894,466

Sources: *www.apra.gov.au/ADIs/statistics*

The data in Table 4 show that the majors were less dominant in the wholesale deposit market where they held 55% of certificate of deposits. In the bill acceptance market, though, the big four are particularly dominant holding over 97% of bill acceptances.

Table 4. Selected Liabilities of bank ADIs, March 2002, ($AUDm)

ADI	CERTIFICATES OF DEPOSIT	BORROWINGS	BILL ACCEPTANCE LIABILITIES	TOTAL LIABILITIES
ANZ	8,916	718	14,366	104,874
CBA	15,743	5,452	11,961	151,363
NAB	8,906	5,986	22,704	129,751
WBC	16,885	3,698	5,051	112,968
St George	7,415	805	1,454	48,717
Majors	57,865	16,659	55,536	547,673
Other Aust.	15,279	2,757	21	90,237
Foreign	18,409	2,755	57	121,039
Total	91,553	22,171	55,614	758,949

Source: *www.apra.gov.au/ADIs/statistics*

An indication of the credit risk exposure of the assets of major banks is provided by the data in Table 5 that show assets according to capital adequacy risk categories. Note that the data refer to the unadjusted value of balance sheet assets, although data for the *ANZ* bank include the credit equivalent of off-balance-sheet contracts.

Table 5. Assets by risk category, Major Banks, September[1] 2002, ($AUDm)

CATEGORY BANK	0%	20%	50%	100%	TOTAL
ANZ	21 188	10 827	65 575	82 697	180 287
CBA	22 315	13 401	86 378	77 474	199 568
NAB	25 191	45 053	88 212	163 854	322 310
WBC	30,610	10,090	79,690	62,101	182,491
St George	7 099	485	32 730	14 440	54 754

Note: [1] 30 June 2002 for the Commonwealth Bank.
Source: 2002 Annual Reports of each bank.

Data on the impaired assets of banks, as at June 2002, provided by *APRA* show that they represented 0.5 percent of the global consolidated group assets of all locally incorporated banks, the absolute amounts being impaired assets of $AUD6b, and total assets being $AUD1175.8b. Not all banks achieved this average impaired assets experience, with the Australian-owned banks performing better than the foreign-owned banks on this date.

Over recent years, the majors have engaged in credit-risk transfer strategies, such as the securitisation of both personal and commercial loans and arranging finance for borrowers through special purpose entities. This issue is given further consideration later, but as at the end of March 2003, the total value of assets that have been securitised by special purpose entities is $AUD123b, of which $AUD87b are mortgaged-backed assets.

The other driving forces in Australia on asset/liability management by *ADIs* are not as great as, for example, in the *USA*. Loans by *ADIs* are mostly on a floating rate as are their funding sources. There is a serious maturity mismatch between deposits (the average maturity is less than three months) and loans (the average maturity is more than five years), but this has not posed a serious funding risk, especially for the major banks that can (and do) access wholesale capital markets both domestically and overseas.

4. PRUDENTIAL REGULATION IN AUSTRALIA

The application of Basel II in Australia will be the responsibility of the *Australian Prudential Regulation Authority (APRA)*, which was established in July 1998 as a single regulator for all of Australia's financial institutions, including banks and other deposit-taking institutions. Prior to the establishment of *APRA*, financial regulation in Australia was institution-specific, with four different regulators for federally licensed banks, nonbank deposit-takers, insurance and pension funds, and securities markets. The most prominent of these was the *Reserve Bank of Australia (RBA)*, which had firmly established the approach to bank supervision in Australia, and which was also (and continues to be) responsible for the formulation and implementation of monetary policy.

For most of the postwar years in Australia, bank regulation fell into the first of the two categories identified in Section 2. Banks were required to hold a significant proportion of their assets in the form of liquid government securities, a requirement that served both a prudential and a monetary policy function.[2] While the precise philosophy and structure of this liquidity requirement varied periodically, the *RBA* began to refine its approach to regulation in January 1985 when it issued its first *Prudential Statement* (Reserve Bank of Australia, 1985), following a period of consultation with the banking industry. The four-page statement *(PSA1)* set out the need for supervision, the *RBA*'s approach to supervision, and outlined its initial guidelines, including a capital adequacy requirement. According to *PSA1*, the *RBA*'s approach to supervision was:

"predicated on the view that the prime responsibility for the prudential management of a bank's business lies with the bank itself. The *[RBA's]* system of supervision is directed toward satisfying itself that individual banks are following management practices which limit risks to prudent levels; and that banks' prudential standards are being observed and kept under review to take account of changing circumstances."

The major areas of risk management considered by the *RBA* in its supervisory role included "capital and liquidity adequacy, earnings, loan loss experience, concentration of risks, the maturity structures of assets and liabilities, potential exposures through

---

2. This requirement was partly an explicit requirement and partly a matter of convention with incentives for compliance. The combined value of so-called *Liquid Government Securities (LGS)* convention and the *Statutory Reserve Deposit (SRD)* requirement averaged around 20% of deposits during the 1960s (Davis & Wallace 1971, pages 238 ff).

equity associations and international banking operations." It also stated that it "look[ed] for timely information from individual banks" and conducted regular meetings to discuss operations from a prudential viewpoint.

The *RBA* argued that capital was required to provide a cushion to absorb losses and to demonstrate shareholder commitment to a bank's ongoing operations. Its concept of "adequate capital" was expressed in terms of a "cushion of free capital resources (i.e., shareholders' funds less investments in premises, subsidiaries, and associated companies) to support deposits."

The relatively small number of banks in Australia was an important factor in determining the *RBA*'s approach to supervision. It stated that its preferred approach was to develop a prudential supervision regime in consultation with banks. It also stated the expectation that the arrangements would become more formal over time as a result of financial innovation and the developing need to coordinate with overseas supervisors, as new banks entered Australia and Australian banks expanded into overseas markets.

In 1988 the *RBA* adopted Basel I in full. It applied the capital adequacy requirement *(CAR)* on the basis of the five credit-risk factors and the conversion factors for off-balance-sheet, credit-risk exposure for inclusion in the five risk categories. In 1989 the *Banking Act* was amended to provide a legislative basis for prudential supervision, and in 1996 the *RBA* incorporated market risk into its *CAR* in line with Bank for International Settlements recommendations. The adoption of Basel I and its subsequent refinements represented a formalisation of the shift in Australian regulatory philosophy away from the first kind of approach, identified in Section 2, toward the second, incentive-based approach.

Prior to 1992 the *RBA*'s prudential supervision framework did not cover nonbank deposit-taking and other nonbank financial institutions *(NBFIs)* unless they were bank subsidiaries. Building societies and credit unions were, however, subject to the control of one of Australia's seven state or territory governments. In 1992 an intergovernmental agreement established the *Australian Financial Institutions Commission (AFIC)* to supervise these deposit-taking institutions. The *RBA*'s prudential regime was clearly defined by this time, and *AFIC* essentially applied this regime to the smaller deposit-taking institutions with some relatively minor modifications.[3]

---

3. The main modification was the application of a 12% capital adequacy requirement rather than the *RBA*'s 8% requirement.

Another complication in the regulatory framework centred around banks that operated solely within state boundaries. These so-called *state banks* had been established mainly to offer thrift services to households, particularly in regional areas, but during the 1980s they became more active as financiers of business through their investment bank subsidiaries. They were not subject to *RBA* supervision (which was created and authorised under federal legislation), and most were directly owned by state governments. Supervision of these institutions was theoretically the responsibility of state finance departments who also acted as agents for the banks' owners, but the banks entered a voluntary agreement to comply with *RBA* prudential supervision without being subject to the *Banking Act.*

In 1996 a newly elected conservative Government established the *Financial System Inquiry (FSI),* known more popularly as the Wallis Inquiry, to make recommendations for a new regulatory system. In essence, the Wallis Inquiry (*FSI*, 1997, page 317) recommended that a single regulator be established to replace the institution-based system of regulators.

The Council of Supervisors had been established in 1992 to coordinate the activities of the *RBA* (supervising banks), *AFIC* (supervising deposit-taking *NBFIs*), the Insurance and Superannuation Commission *(ISC)*, and the Australian Securities Commission *(ASC)*. Only the first of these two bodies had established a coherent prudential supervision regime. Even by the end of the decade, coherent supervision arrangements had not been established to protect policyholders and members of superannuation schemes (pension funds). The thrust of the Wallis Inquiry's chief recommendation was, therefore, to consolidate the prudential supervision roles of the *RBA* and *AFIC,* and to establish more formal supervision arrangements for the other types of institutions.

The Government implemented recommendation 31 of the Wallis Committee by establishing *APRA* in July 1998 as the single regulator of deposit-taking institutions, insurance companies, and superannuation funds in Australia. The *RBA* continues to operate as Australia's central bank, whereas *AFIC* was disbanded, and the activities of the Australian Securities and Investment Commission *(ASIC)* were focused on resolving problems for investors, arising from information asymmetry and the conduct of financial advisors and planners taking over from the *ASC* (Carmichael, 2002).

The establishment of *APRA* has not brought radical changes to the prudential supervision of *ADIs*. This should not be surprising, since the Prudential Supervision Division of the *RBA* was transferred to *APRA*, and the Deputy Governor of the *RBA*, responsible for prudential supervision, became *APRA*'s Chief Executive Officer.

5. THE IMPACT OF BASEL I ON THE AUSTRALIAN BANKING SYSTEM

We explain the impact of Basel I on the Australian banking system in the context of a number of other developments that characterised the financial system in the late 1980s. These developments included: increased competition in the banking sector, following deregulation of interest rates, and liberalisation of entry into banking; the widening current account deficit in the Australian balance of payments and the monetary policy response to this problem; and the property boom of the late 1980s.

Strong economic growth and deregulation of the Australian banking sector in the mid-1980s combined to produce significant credit growth for both corporate and housing finance between 1985 and 1990 (Simon 2003, page 23). Growth in business credit was associated with increased demand, which may be divided into two stages (Simon 2003, pages 24 & 27). Initially, demand was fuelled by an increase in takeover activity associated with rising stock prices, and loans from financial institutions were frequently secured against stock in highly leveraged companies. The 1987 stock market crash resulted in a number of defaults on this lending and caused distress for several Australian investment banks. In the second stage, demand was fuelled by a boom in commercial property prices. On the supply side, intense competition between the increased number of banks in the industry, following deregulation, generated a significant decline in credit standards (Gizycki & Lowe 2000, page 183).

These developments left borrowers and the banking system vulnerable to the large increases in interest rates, which began in late 1988. Monetary policy was progressively tightened from that time in response to a deterioration in Australia's current account balance associated with the strong level of economic activity. The cash rate[4] peaked at 18% in 1989–90, and benchmark overdraft

---

4. Australia's equivalent of the federal funds rate.

rates exceeded 20%. Property prices subsequently peaked in 1990, and the resulting burst of the property price bubble, combined with other effects of the high interest rates, generated the 1990–92 recession.

A number of Australian banks, including two of the largest institutions, suffered considerable losses during this period. Gizycki and Lowe (2000, page 83) report nonperforming loans of 6 percent by mid-1992. The banking system also suffered a number of runs and a degree of contagion, which required liquidity support for some institutions, assurances from public bodies about the health of others, and a number of organised takeovers or publicly assisted balance sheet reorganisations. The conditions for significant systemic risk were thus present in the Australian financial system between 1990–92, but realisation of this risk was arguably prevented by the active involvement of public authorities at both state and federal levels.

While the Australian banking system experienced significant losses during this recession, both aggregate, regulatory capital and the capital ratios of the majors remained above the 8 per cent minimum capital requirement. The banks subsequently responded in a number of related ways to the crisis, conditioned to some degree by the structure of Basel I. Firstly, banks restricted lending to the corporate sector and tightened credit standards. This was an obvious response to the realisation of risk resulting from poor credit evaluation and management during the boom conditions of the late 1980s. Secondly, related to this was an effective rebuilding of capital ratios, which increased in aggregate terms from below 10 percent at the beginning of the recession to above 12 percent by the end of 1995 (See Chart 1). Thirdly, as a logical corollary to the first and second responses, banks gave greater emphasis to housing in their lending decisions. This response was also encouraged by the lower capital provision under Basel I for housing lending as opposed to commercial lending. Lastly, banks successfully attempted to increase profitability by cutting operating expenses and increasing noninterest income, despite interest margin compression resulting from increased competition. These measures restored the after-tax return on equity in the Australian banking sector to around 15 percent by 1995, after falling to as low as 9.71 percent in 1990 (Gizycki and Lowe 2000, page 197).

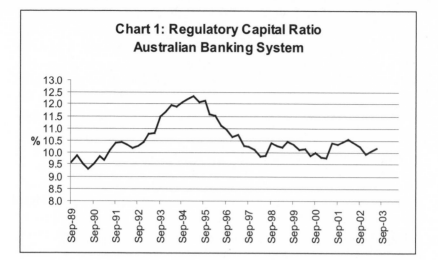

Chart 1: Regulatory Capital Ratio
Australian Banking System

A further development noted by Gizycki and Lowe (2000, page 198 ff) was the increased commoditisation of risk in the Australian financial system during the 1990s. This revolved largely around growth of markets in asset-backed securities, which banks employed partly as a result of their capital-management strategies, but developments in derivative markets, including credit derivatives, must also be noted (Reserve Bank of Australia 2003a). Against this background of developments in the 1980s, Basel I can be argued to have contributed to a bias in Australian bank lending towards housing finance and to the development of securitisation. This occurred, however, only after an initial, negative experience with credit risk, and the growth of securitisation has been focused on mortgage-backed securities rather than more heterogeneous corporate loans. Corporate loan-backed securities have been difficult to issue into the small Australian market, whereas the appetite for lower risk mortgage-backed securities has been more substantial given an increasing trend in household balance sheets toward market-related investments and away from bank-intermediated deposits.[5] Banks have therefore made use of the mortgage-backed market, reducing the volume of housing on their books and freeing capital for allocation against corporate lending, which was proportionately less significant than it had been prior to the credit problems of the 1990–92 period.

---

5. Increased holdings of market-related investments resulted from of a number of privatisations of previously public companies and demutualisations of financial cooperatives on the supply side, and from the 1991 federal government policy of extending compulsory membership of pension schemes on the demand side (Gizycki & Lowe 2000, page 188).

A further development in the Australian banking sector during the 1990s, reflecting a worldwide trend, serves to underscore some important problems with Basel I. Australian Banks invested an increasing amount of resources in developing economic capital allocation models as the 1990s progressed, rather than relying simply on the capital mandates of Basel I. It was argued above that part of the bank response to the 1990–92 credit quality problems was to significantly increase capital provisions above regulatory mandates. This was designed partly as a safety precaution against the possibility of further losses and partly as a signal to the markets that prudential behaviour at Australian banks had been restored. Either interpretation suggests that the 1990–92 credit quality problems demonstrated that simply maintaining the regulatory minimum was an inadequate approach to bank capital management.

Even if the Basel I guidelines had been in place for a longer period, prior to the boom conditions of the late 1980s,[6] it is doubtful that they would have assisted to any significant degree in avoiding the subsequent credit problems. Gup (2003, page 74) highlights the lack of risk-sensitivity in Basel I. Hogan & Sharpe (1990) criticise Basel I's tendency to work against the objective of discouraging bank risk-taking behaviour by attaching a risk weight of 100% to the value of *all* commercial loans, irrespective of counterparty. The resulting indiscriminate capital requirement of 8 percent against corporate lending generally created an incentive under Basel I for banks to pursue a larger proportion of riskier, higher return loans in order to more easily finance the required capital provision of 8 percent. Longer operation of Basel I may simply, therefore, have reinforced the observed risk-taking behaviour of the late 1980s, according to this interpretation.

When banks suffered the consequences of poor credit evaluation during the 1990–92 recession, they subsequently moved away from the regulatory model, significantly increasing capital in the two-year period following the 1990–92 recession. This response, however, had the potential to impose significant and possibly unnecessary capital costs and raised afresh the question about the appropriate amount of capital that banks should hold against corporate lending. Australian banks thus faced an incentive to significantly improve their techniques for credit-risk evaluation, and to link credit assessment outcomes to capital management. A

---

6. The 1988 Basel Capital Accord was introduced almost immediately in Australia. Lending decisions subject to Basel I were being made therefore for around twelve months before the onset of the recession in 1990.

divergence consequently emerged in the Australian context between regulatory and economic capital that reflected the weakness of Basel I and the experience of Australian banks with credit risk.

6. THE POTENTIAL IMPACT OF BASEL II ON THE AUSTRALIAN BANKING SYSTEM

A fundamental objective of Basel II is to increase the risk sensitivity of capital requirements in a way which more closely aligns regulatory capital with economic capital (Evans 2003, page 78). In the Australian context, such an approach would have provided banks with a disincentive to have financed either the degree of takeover activity that they did or speculative purchasing during the commercial property boom. To the extent that increased granularity of commercial credit risk and capital offsets for credit-risk mitigation are possible under Basel II, banks have an incentive to improve the measurement and management of credit risk. This has the potential to significantly reduce the bias in the Australian system in favour of housing finance with the concomitant effects of potential increased economic growth.

On the basis of quantitative impact studies carried on with the cooperation of Australian banks, *APRA* has identified a number of potential implications of Basel II features. Chief among these is the differential impact of the Basel II on institutions of different sizes. Smaller institutions are likely to face an increase in their overall capital requirement, while larger institutions are likely to face significant reductions (*APRA* 2002, pages 3–4).

The source of this differential for Australian institutions is threefold. Firstly, a significant source of capital reduction is the possibility under either of the *Internal Ratings-Based (IRB)* approaches (Basel Committee 2003a, page 4) to use external credit ratings to identify corporate lending of higher credit quality against which a lower capital charge will apply. Smaller institutions are less likely to lend to corporates, which are externally rated, and are more likely to use the *Standardised* approach, which is not subject to the saving.

Secondly, the *IRB* approaches allow the *Standardised* risk weights for housing to be varied depending on banks' own estimates of *loss given default (LGD)* on this kind of lending. *APRA* (2002, page 4) estimates that the weights on the housing portfolio of Australian Banks are likely to be as low as 15 percent, compared with the initial *Standardised* weight of 50 percent or its most recently revised value of 35% (Basel Committee 2003b, page 11; Trinephi, 2003, page 4). Smaller institutions utilising the standard weights will not benefit from these potential savings.

Thirdly, the new guidelines allow increased capital relief from securitisation and various forms of credit-risk mitigation, which larger institutions are likely to utilise more effectively. This particularly applies to credit-risk mitigation techniques.

While these three features of Basel II are sources of potential competitive inequality for the Australian system, closer examination of them indicates that Australian banks and regulatory structures are well-placed to adopt the new guidelines. It may also be argued that the possibility of competitive inequality itself comes with potential benefits that suggest Basel II may result in an overall improvement in the regulatory structure for bank capital management. The following subsections, therefore, examine the dimensions of these three features in more detail to further explore this argument.

(i) Risk Rating Methodology

The most significant capital savings available under Basel II are associated with risk weightings generated by banks' internal risk rating systems. McDonald & Eastwood (2000) survey risk-rating systems at 10 Australian banks, including a number of large institutions, to evaluate the impact of the proposed new guidelines on bank risk management practices.

Four aspects of McDonald's and Eastwood's results stand out. Firstly, all 10 of the institutions surveyed used what McDonald & Eastwood (2000, page 9) refer to as two-dimensional ratings methodologies. Rating systems at surveyed banks generated numerics for a range of credit exposure features, including probability of default *(PD)*, loss-given default *(LGD)*, and expected loss *(EL)*, rather than simply focusing on a single rating measure of *PD* or *EL* for each exposure. This compared to a Basel Committee on Banking Supervision (2000) survey of 30 G-10 banks in which only one third of institutions used two-dimensional ratings methodologies.

Secondly, the surveyed Australian banks used a number of *PD* grades comparable with institutions overseas. The majority of banks surveyed used either 9 or 10 customer *PD* grades, which falls in the middle of the distribution for banks in the Basel survey

(McDonald & Eastwood 2000, pages 12–13). One local institution utilised 22 *PD* grades. On the surface, this result suggests that Australian banks' systems are characterised by sufficient risk identification granularity to allow them to take advantage of the broader risk-weight classifications in Basel II. Not only does this imply the potential for increased risk-sensitivity of capital allocation at Australian banks but also the possibility of the capital reductions identified by *APRA*. This conclusion must, however, be tempered to a degree because of the clustering of actual credit-risk assessments within a small number of the available risk grades. The extent of this clustering is in line with practices at overseas institutions, and according to McDonald & Eastwood (2000, page 14), is partially an artefact of the developing nature of risk management practices at some of the small to medium institutions in the Australian banking industry. These smaller institutions have traditionally utilised relatively fewer risk grades within which recently observed actual assessments are clustered. But as part of the process of improving risk management practices, a greater number of classifications have been introduced so that the variance of observed assessment distributions should increase over the next few years.

The third important result from McDonald's & Eastwood's survey is the role played by the judgment of credit assessors' versus outcomes from quantitative models in assigning risk ratings. They use a threefold classification to capture the role played by assessor judgment (McDonald & Eastwood 2000, pages 16–17): statistical model-based approaches with no judgment overrides; constrained judgment-based processes where ratings are quantitatively generated but the results feed into a judgment-based assigning process; and judgment-based processes where traditional credit evaluation based on assessor judgment drives rating determination. Most Australian banks use assessor-based approaches, although there appears to be a clear difference between the approaches of larger and smaller institutions. Larger institutions make greater use of statistical models and have greater capacity to generate the loan-loss statistics required to drive quantitative risk-rating determination. These institutions tend to allow significantly less judgment overriding of model ratings than do smaller institutions, which are more likely to utilise judgment-based methodologies (McDonald & Eastwood 2000, page 17).

The fourth aspect of the Australian survey results to be high-lighted regards the different applications of internal ratings pro-cesses by Australian banks. The smaller banks utilise ratings solely for stand-alone, credit-risk assessment and indirectly for loan pricing. The larger institutions make broader use of internal rat-ings for loan pricing, capital management, and employee compen-sation purposes. These differences clearly reflect the ability of the larger institutions to run statistical-quantitative models, which gen-erate more precise rather than generally qualitative ratings that are more conducive as inputs into other quantitative processes such as capital allocation models.

Two broad conclusions are suggested by McDonald's and East-wood's analysis. The first is that Australian banks are reasonably well-placed to cope with the adoption of the credit-risk guidelines of Basel II. The large Australian banks, in particular, have been developing relatively sophisticated credit-rating systems on both stand-alone and portfolio bases in recent years. Their use of two-dimensional ratings systems, wide ranges of customer risk catego-ries, and extensive quantitative applications of rating methodolo-gies places these banks in a good position to adopt the *Advanced IRB Approach* to credit-risk capital allocation. This will allow them to enjoy potentially significant capital savings from adoption of Basel II.

The second conclusion is that, as in other parts of the world, including the United States, a differential impact on large versus small Australian banks can be expected. This differential impact may *not*, however, be as accentuated as in other parts of the world. Like their larger counterparts, smaller Australian banks have been improving credit-risk management practices in recent years. This is reflected in their use of two-dimensional rating methodologies, a broadening set of customer risk categories, and increasing use of quantitative models, even if the results of these models are supple-mented by assessor judgment and more limited in application than at the larger banks. These developments in risk management practices to some extent place smaller institutions in a position to consider use of the *Foundation IRB approach* and possibly the *Advanced IRB approach* down the track. The main limitation on the use of these methodologies will be access to historical loan loss data and the cost of implementing quantitative credit-risk modelling on a wider scale, relative to the limited potential capital savings asso-ciated with a lack of diversity in their corporate loan books. How-ever, as these institutions continue to grow and expand their corporate exposures, the case for migration to more sophisticated approaches will become stronger. For the time being, it is expected that such institutions will use the *Standardised approach.*

(ii) Housing Risk Weights

Basel II guidelines initially maintained the existing 50 percent risk weight for housing loans under the *Standardised approach* (Basel Committee 2001b, page 11) but subsequently amended this weight down to 35% (Basel Committee 2003b, page 11). The 50% weight originally represented a concession on the standard 100 per cent risk-weighting in recognition of the higher average credit quality of mortgage-related finance. *APRA* (2000, page 15), however, points out that such a capital charge is excessive when compared to the loan loss experience of the Australian mortgage lending market, an experience shared by mortgage loan markets in other countries. They cite Australian data, which demonstrates average loan loss rates between 1965 and 2000 for insured mortgage loans of 0.17 percent of asset values, with a peak loss rate of 0.70 percent. The average rate falls for bank mortgage lending, which includes some higher quality lending without mortgage insurance, to around 0.10 to 0.30 percent. *APRA* estimates that a capital charge of one percent, as opposed to four percent under the current and initially proposed new Accord guidelines, would be adequate to cover the credit risk associated with Australian bank mortgage lending portfolios.

This assessment is confirmed by Esho & Liaw (2002) who estimate overall loan quality at Australian banks between 1991 and 2001. They explain two measures of loan quality, the ratio of impaired to total assets and credit losses,[2] as a function of portfolio composition, loan growth, cost efficiency, a moral hazard proxy, and general macroeconomic conditions. They find that a 10 percent portfolio switch of assets from the 50 percent housing loan risk class to the 100 percent commercial loan risk class has the potential in the Australian context to lead to an approximately 30 percent increase in the ratio of impaired to total assets and an approximately 25 percent increase in credit losses. A similar switch from the 50 percent class to the 20 percent class has a negligible effect on either measure of credit quality (Esho & Liaw 2002, page 16). Esho & Liaw conclude that the small risk associated with

---

2. Defined as net asset write-offs and specific provisions divided by total assets (Esho & Liaw 2002, page 4).

housing loans in Australia relative to loans in the 100 percent risk class warrants a smaller capital charge against housing loans, although they argue for a slightly smaller reduction than *APRA*'s (2001b, page 7) suggestion that the housing weight in the *Standardised approach* be reduced to 20 percent.

The usual reasons offered for such low losses in the Australian mortgage lending market include: the relatively high level of Australian home ownership; favourable bankruptcy laws, which allow appropriation of compensating bank balances where the value of realised collateral is insufficient to extinguish the value of defaults; and the nontax deductibility of interest payments on housing loans, which encourages more rapid debt retirement (*APRA* 2000, pages 15–16; Esho & Liaw 2002, pages 15–16).

The housing loan guidelines were therefore at one stage likely to be one of the more controversial aspects of Basel II in the Australian context. *APRA* (2002, page 4) argued that the discrepancy between the 50 percent weight for housing loans under the original *Standardised approach* and the 5–10 percent weight generated by the *IRB* approaches in the Australian context (cf. *APRA* 2001b, page 7) would have lead to a significant competitive inequality in Australia. According to Table 1 above, housing loans account for around 58 percent of nonbank *ADI* assets as opposed to about 36 percent of bank assets. Smaller *ADIs* using the *Standardised approach* would thus be at a significant capital disadvantage for a large proportion of their business, and we would expect to see these institutions involvement in securitisation programs increase significantly were Basel II measures to be implemented as they stood at that stage. *APRA* (2002, page 4) therefore suggested that it was likely to exercise "a degree of national discretion when implementing the new framework for Australian *ADIs*." This implied that it would have varied the risk weight on housing loans to 20 percent, in line with its recommendations to the Basel Committee (*APRA* 2000, pages 15–17; 2001b, page 7). With the subsequent revision in the proposed risk-weighting down to 35%, *APRA* has suggested it is now likely to adopt the proposed guidelines without significant adjustment (Trinephi 2003, pages 4–5).

(iii) Securitisation

The process of moving assets off the balance sheet via securitisation has been an important feature of bank asset-liability management in Australia over the last ten years, or so. As argued above, this has largely been driven by the impact of competitive pressures on interest rate margins from mortgage loan originators. Banks have increasingly sought to locate funding sources as alternatives to deposit funds because of this competitive pressure and to replace interest income with fee income as interest margins have been squeezed.

Between 1993, at the end of the last recession in Australia, and 2000, asset-backed securities on issue grew by an average of approximately 530 percent. In 2000, total securitised assets outstanding were in excess of $AUD60b, of which the vast majority were backed by mortgages. By March 2003, this had grown to $AUD123b, of which $AUD87b were backed by mortgages. In 2000, credit card, lease and trade receivables made up approximately 17 percent of assets outstanding and repackaged securities just under 20 percent. It is not surprising then that close to 90 percent of securities issued against these asset pools were rated AAA or A1+ (Liaw & Eastwood 2000, page 9). Securitisation of commercial loans has been very unsuccessful in the Australian market with less than one percent of noninvestment grade securities on issue.

Securitisation of mortgage lending has thus been used increasingly by Australian banks, which account for about 30 percent of asset-backed securities on issue, although it remains a relatively marginal source of funding for these institutions. Securitisation does, however, alter the risk profile of an institution's loan book and exposes the institution to risks, which are frequently less transparent than loans left on the balance sheet. In Australia, *APRA* has been particularly concerned with risks arising from credit enhancement features of securitisation programs such as *first-loss* or *spread accounts* and from so-called *moral hazard* risk. Structural credit enhancements such as first-loss accounts designed to absorb defaults on the underlying asset portfolio ahead of securities issued against the portfolio are frequently funded by the originating institution. This exposes the institution to a residual risk despite having moved the underlying assets off the balance sheet (Gup 2003, page 74). Any capital relief afforded the institution by securitisation of the assets should therefore be reduced where there is an exposure under credit enhancement facilities designed to increase the rating and marketability of the securities issued against the portfolio.

Since 1995 the value of first-loss exposures has been required to be deducted from an *ADI*'s capital base. Other exposures, whether through credit enhancement arrangements or other support features such as provision of liquidity facilities, attract a capital charge that depends upon the degree of separation between the *ADI* and the securitisation program as defined by a clear set of criteria (*APRA* 2000, page 20). Basel II essentially brings the international standard closer to current Australian practice (Liaw & Eastwood 2000, page 15). The proposed guidelines incorporate a link between the rating of the securities associated with a bank's exposure and the capital charge so that holdings of highly rated asset-backed securities attract a small charge while unrated exposures including first-loss accounts, must be deducted from the capital base (Basel Committee 2001b, page 88).

Given the existing prudential standard imposed by *APRA*, Basel II's securitisation guidelines can be expected to have a relatively small impact on the operation of Australian banks and *ADIs*. The significance of this result is that the securitisation of nonmortgage lending in the Australian market is likely to develop at a slow pace. Credit enhancement facilities such as first-loss accounts are likely to be much more important features for investors in securities backed by higher risk corporate loans. However, given the relatively low loss-given-default rates on Australian mortgage lending, first-loss exposures on securitised corporate loans could be expected to represent a much more serious risk than first-loss exposures to mortgage-backed programs. Were *APRA* to consider additional capital charges under Pillar II for such exposures, the attractiveness of securitisation programs for any but the most highly rated corporate loans would be low, and banks could be expected to look elsewhere for avenues to offset risk exposures associated with corporate lending.

This suggests that the impact of securitisation programs on Australian banks will largely continue to be associated with moving mortgage lending off the balance sheet. This may have the impact of increasing the average riskiness of bank loan books, which could be expected to indirectly increase the average capital that must be held by these institutions depending on the relative growth rates of mortgage versus corporate lending. A continued bias toward increasing the growth rate of mortgage lending could be expected. This effect may to some degree be mitigated by proposed changes to the risk weight for mortgage loans discussed in the previous section.

(iv) Credit Risk Mitigation

An important dimension of Basel II designed to increase the risk-sensitivity of bank capital regulation is its treatment of credit-risk mitigation techniques. Use of collateral, guarantees, and other credit-risk reduction measures such as credit derivatives, which reduce the size of losses in cases of default, imply lower levels of economic capital provisioning. Basel II more carefully reflects the role of credit-risk mitigation techniques in at least two important ways. Firstly, it allows a wider definition of collateral types that may be used to reduce regulatory capital, given a bank's underlying credit-risk profile. Secondly, it explicitly recognises the role of banks' increasing use of instruments such as credit derivatives.

The potential impact that this dimension of Basel II will have on Australian banking is quite important. The big four banks have increasingly made use of credit derivatives to hedge credit risk, but markets for these instruments in Australia continue to be small and relatively illiquid. Three primary instruments are used in the Australian market (*APRA* 1999, pages 4–6): credit-default swaps *(CDS)*, total-rate-of-return swaps *(TROR)*, and credit-linked notes *(CLNs)*. Of these, the most significant is the *CDS* market. At June 2002 there were publicly quoted prices for about 30 companies in the *CDS* market, with approximately $AUD20b outstanding (Reserve Bank of Australia 2003a, page 57).[2]

Two issues are likely to be important for assessing the impact of Basel II on the local industry. The first is where regulatory guidelines require derivatives to be recorded in the bank's balance sheet. Under adjustments to the Basel I, offsets for hedging-contracts are treated differently depending whether they are found in the banking book, or the trading book (*APRA* 1999, page 7). In the banking book, capital charges apply to the overall hedged position, while in the trading book, the hedged position is substituted for the underlying position, at least for perfect hedges. For imperfect hedges, the two positions are subject to separate capital charges. Imperfect hedges may thus result in a higher capital charge compared with completely unhedged positions when recorded in the trading book. Since perfect hedges are unlikely in the *CDS* market, prudent banks could be subject to higher capital charges under these arrangements (*APRA* 1999, page 7).

---

2. Basel II excludes *CLNs* as credit-risk mitigants (Basel Committee 2001b, page 28 fn25).

APRA currently treats credit derivatives in the banking book as direct credit substitutes (*APRA* 1999, page 10). Thus, *CDSs* are translated onto the balance sheet using a 100 percent credit conversion factor. For adequately documented matching protection *purchased*, risk-weighted assets are adjusted using a risk weight appropriate to the risk class of the protection seller. For protection *sold* under the *CDS*, the same process is followed, but the risk weight applied is that appropriate to the *reference credit* being protected. Under Basel II, credit-risk mitigation is recognised within the banking book in a manner similar to the approach taken by *APRA* (Basel Committee 2001b, page 15), but the relevant risk weight is determined for full protection *purchased* as the weighted average of the risk weight for the underlying credit exposure and the risk weight of the protection seller.[9]

Given that most Australian *CDS* contracts are traded between financial institutions with risk weightings lower than the weighting of underlying credit exposures, Basel II may result in slightly lower levels of capital relief than the existing Australian arrangements. As *APRA* (2000, page 22) points out, however, the exact extent of mitigation for particular circumstances requires detailed modelling.

The second issue is the impact that mitigation is likely to have on the development of the credit derivatives market in Australia. *APRA* (2000, page 22) argues that expanding the role of mitigation will increase demand for services from the credit derivatives market. This is most likely to affect the *CDS* market, not only increasing the volume of activity but also generating improvements in documentation to minimise regulatory relief reductions under Basel II. Developments in this market potentially increase the efficiency of the financial system by enabling the shifting of risk to those most prepared to bear it.

In the Australian context, however, a number of factors will affect the development of the *CDS* and related markets. The first is the extent of demand for the credit risks, which banks will be hedging in these markets. It was argued above that Australian investors became more sophisticated over the course of the 1990s, increasing their appetite for higher returns and associated risks.

---

9. The weight applied to the underlying exposure is set at 0.15 percent (Basel Committee 2001b, page 30). This is designed to account for ambiguities in documentation and imperfectly hedged positions, which tend to characterise operations in these markets.

The growth of pension funds and other types of managed funds over this period may thus be taken as a signal that sufficient demand exists to facilitate growth in credit derivative markets.

However, the existence of this demand is less certain when two additional features of the Australian context are recognised. On the one hand, banks are likely to hedge the most extreme of the risks faced in their banking books. On the other, a large proportion of the stocks held by pension and managed funds are those of highly rated companies. Managed funds are likely to absorb some of the credit risks, which banks wish to offload for the additional return that *CDS* premiums will generate, but whether they will be able to absorb significant quantities of risk remains to be seen. This question is underscored when the theoretical function of banks in assessing idiosyncratic risk is recalled. If credit risk is to be increasingly transferred from banks to various forms of managed funds by the development of markets in credit derivatives, managed funds or ratings agencies, on their behalf, must extend their abilities to evaluate and monitor the associated risks. This is, however, precisely the area in which banks are argued to possess a comparative advantage over markets. Banks develop relationships with their clients, which extend over significant periods of time and extend a range of services, including both payments and credit facilities. The information made available to banks by both the long-term relationships they have with clients and the combination of services provided to those clients is significant in reducing informational asymmetries, which generally exacerbate credit risk. It is difficult to see that this function will change significantly in the Australian context given the large volume of idiosyncratic loans to small-and medium-sized businesses supplied by the banking sector. Recent failed attempts to securities corporate loans reflect to some extent this set of forces.

The Reserve Bank of Australia (2003a, page 60) has recently argued that the development of credit-risk transfer *(CRT)* markets has the potential to *increase* the extent of credit risk in the financial system rather than simply to facilitate a better allocation of that risk among market participants. Two reasons are offered to support this conclusion. Firstly, less care will be taken by banks in initially assessing and then providing ongoing monitoring of credit risk than currently, because *CRT* markets enable this risk to be hedged. That is, banks will have an incentive to *reduce* their theoretical evaluation and monitoring functions over time, leading to acceptance of higher levels of credit risk and an overall reduction in credit quality. Secondly, as suggested above, banks will use *CRT* markets to offload their greatest risks. As they receive signals that the credit quality of particular loans is declining, *CRT* markets will be used to purchase protection, and losses will be absorbed by other parties who may be subject to less stringent capital regulation than banks.

Only the second of these conclusions appears to have any validity in the Australian context. The two effects identified by the Reserve Bank require different assumptions about bank evaluation and monitoring. If banks are to offload their highest risks before losses are incurred, they have an incentive to evaluate and monitor credit quality. The first issue, of a type of bank-moral-hazard problem, is thus unlikely to emerge. In fact, the probability that banks will prefer to hedge their worst credit risks, predicated on both an ability and an incentive to evaluate and monitor idiosyncratic credit risk more effectively than other market participants, should be interpreted as a factor that will retard the development of *CRT* markets in Australia. A market in which significant credit risks are traded is likely to be a treacherous one for investors without adequate credit evaluation skills. The credit-risk evaluation capability of ratings agencies may, however, alleviate this result to some extent for the debt of highly rated public companies.

(v) Additional Issues

APRA (2000, 2001b, 2002) has identified a number of further issues it regards as important with respect to implementation of Basel II in the Australian context. In addition to those considered above, these include interest rate risk in the banking book, provision for large exposures, and Pillar 3 implementation.

Under Basel II, interest rate risk in the banking book *(IRRB)* is to apply only to "outlier" institutions with excessive exposures in this area, and capital provisions are to be determined for this risk under Pillar 2. *APRA* (2002, page 4) has argued that repricing mismatch in the banking books of Australian banks is of the order of five times that for interest rate risk in their trading books. Consequently, *APRA*'s submissions to the Basel Committee recommend that capital provisions for *IRRB* apply to all banks and be calculated as part of Pillar 1 (*APRA* 2000, page 26; 2001b, page 41). Such an approach would remove potential incentives for banks to shift interest rate risk from the trading to the banking book and would more reasonably justify the expense to which banks must go under Basel II to calculate *IRRB* by rewarding them with potential capital savings. *APRA* (2002, page 4) is " giving serious consideration to mandating a capital charge for *IRRB* as part of the Pillar 1 framework, at least for Australian *ADIs* electing to use the more advanced approaches."

APRA is also concerned about the issue of large credit exposures. It argues that the lack of distinction between small and large exposures in Basel II ignores the increased risk faced by a portfolio with a large exposure to a single obliger and that significantly concentrated exposures should attract an additional capital charge (*APRA 2001b*, pages 17–18; 2002, page 4). While the Basel Committee considered a possible adjustment to take account of larger concentrations, it appears unlikely that this will be adopted in the final guidelines (*APRA* 2002, page 4). *APRA*'s concern with this issue reflects, to some extent, the Australian experience of the late 1980s considered above and the potential impact that single borrowers can have within a financial system of Australia's size. Once again *APRA* may consider its own adjustment under Pillar 2 to deal with this issue.

An increased risk-sensitivity of regulatory capital requirements is clearly enhanced by the disclosure requirements of Pillar 3 and the impact of market reaction via its share price on the risk-taking behaviour of bank managers. Ratings agency evaluations of bank debt and share price reactions to variations in the rate of return on bank equity clearly sharpen the consequences of risk management decisions, which affect the amount of capital in a bank's balance sheet. *APRA* has expressed its full support of Pillar 3 provisions under Basel II and has even indicated its intention to encourage Australian banks to increase public disclosure of key credit risk and capital allocation indicators ahead of the 2006 implementation date (*APRA* 2002, page 5).[3]

---

3. Gup (2003, page 75) argues that Pillar 3 simply constitutes "wishful thinking" on the part of regulatory authorities that markets will perform part of their function. Rich (2003, page 82) argues the contrary view that Pillar 3 provides an important complementarity to Pillar 1, especially given the range of possible outcomes for different banks under the *Advanced IRB* approach.

7. CONCLUSION

In principle, the chief objective of the Basel II Capital Accord to increase the risk-sensitivity of regulatory capital requirements for banks should help to overcome some of the problems with the Basel I Capital Accord and further realign bank management incentives to reduce the moral-hazard problems generated by the existence of public safety nets.

Basel II's attempt to cater for the diversity of bank sizes, however, by offering the *Standardised* as well as the more sophisticated *IRB* approaches to credit-risk provisions, generates the potential problem of competitive inequality between large and small banks. This may, however, represent a structural inevitability rather than a flaw in Basel II's design. The existence of bank-size differentials in markets already suggests the need for the range of regulatory options contained in the new guidelines. If the guidelines are to encourage small institutions to develop and strengthen their risk management systems over time, it seems reasonable to offer modest capital reductions as an incentive for migration to more sophisticated systems. The question must be whether the size of potential capital savings under the more advanced approaches creates such a competitive disadvantage for small institutions that migration to better systems over time is pointless or impossible. The Australian bank regulator, *APRA*, has argued that the competitive disadvantage is too large in the Australian context and that it may use its discretion under Pillar 2 to reduce the extent of this disadvantage, although reduction of the housing risk weight to 35% has moderated this stance.

In other respects, however, Australian banks appear to be well-placed to adopt the guidelines of Basel II (cf. Trinephi 2003, page 4). Recent research on the internal-ratings systems employed by Australian banks, increased use of securitisation, and the development of credit-risk mitigation techniques and markets indicates that Australian banks have devoted considerable resources to improving credit-risk management systems over the last ten years. *APRA*, and its predecessor, the Reserve Bank of Australia, have also attempted to develop a regulatory framework that employs and takes account of the latest developments in risk management methodology. In some respects, elements of Basel II bring the international standard closer to current practice in the Australian system.

It has been argued that the driving force behind these developments in the Australian banking industry and regulatory system was the experience of credit quality-related losses suffered during the 1990–92 recession. The impact of poor lending decisions following deregulation in the late 1980s signalled to all participants in the financial system the importance of improving credit-risk management systems in the banking industry. The increased convergence of regulatory and economic capital embodied in Basel II thus both reflects and enhances the state of bank capital regulation in Australia, issues of potential competitive inequality not-withstanding.

REFERENCES

Australian Prudential Regulation Authority (1999), *Capital Adequacy Treatment of Credit Derivatives*, April.

Australian Prudential Regulation Authority (2000), *A New Capital Adequacy Framework: Submission to the Basel Committee on Banking Supervision.*

Australian Prudential Regulation Authority (2001a), *The New Basel Capital Accord: Submission to the Basel Committee on Banking Supervision*, May.

Australian Prudential Regulation Authority (2001b), "Basel Committee on Banking Supervision: Proposed Changes to the Basel Accord," *APRA Insight*, 3rd Quarter, pp.4–8.

Australian Prudential Regulation Authority (2002), "APRA's Views on Basel II: Managing the Transition," *APRA Insight*, 2nd Quarter, pp.3–6.

Basel Committee on Banking Supervision (2000), *Range of Practice in Banks' Internal Rating Systems*, January, (*http://www.bis.org*).

Basel Committee on Banking Supervision (2001a), *Consultative Document: Overview of the New Basel Capital Accord*, January, Bank for International Settlements.

Basel Committee on Banking Supervision (2001b), *Consultative Document: The New Basel Capital Accord*, January, Bank for International Settlements.

Basel Committee on Banking Supervision (2003a), *Consultative Document: Overview of the New Basel Capital Accord*, April, Bank for International Settlements.

Basel Committee on Banking Supervision (2003b), *Consultative Document: The New Basel Capital Accord*, April, Bank for International Settlements.

Carmichael, J. (2002), "Experiences with Integrated Regulation," *APRA Insight*, 1st Quarter, pp. 3–7.

Chant, J. (1992), "The New Theory of Financial Intermediation," in Dowd, K. and Lewis, M. K. (eds), *Current Issues in Financial and Monetary Economics*, London: Macmillan.

Davis, R. W. & Wallace, R. H. (1971), "Lessons of the 1960 Bank Credit Squeeze," in Runcie N. (ed.), *Australian Monetary and Fiscal Policy*, London: University of London Press, pp. 237–261.

Diamond, D. (1984), "Financial Intermediation and Delegated Monitoring," *Review of Economic Studies*, 51, pp. 393–414.

Esho, N. & Liaw, A. (2002), "Should the Capital Requirement on Housing Lending be Reduced? Evidence from Australian Banks," *Australian Prudential Regulation Authority Working Paper 2002-02*, June.

Evans, C. (2003), "Pillar One Requirements and Approaches," *Journal of Banking and Financial Services*, 117 (5), pp. 78–79.

Financial System Inquiry (1997), *Final Report*, Canberra: Australian Government Publishing Service.

Gizycki, M. & Lowe, P. (2000), "The Australian Financial System in the 1990s," in Gruen, D. & Shrestha, S. (eds), *The Australian Economy in the 1990s*, Sydney: Reserve Bank of Australia, pp. 180–215.

Greenbaum, S. & Thakor, A. V. (1995), *Contemporary Financial Intermediation*, Fort Worth: Dryden Press.

Gup, B. (2003), "A Brief History of Basel," *Journal of Banking and Financial Services*, 117 (5), pp. 74–75.

Hogan, W. & Sharpe, I. G. (1990), "Prudential Regulation of Australian Banks," *Economic Record*, 66, pp. 127–45.

Hogan, W. & Sharpe, I. G. (1997), "Prudential Regulation of the Financial System: A Functional Approach," *Agenda*, 4, pp. 15–28.

Liaw, A. & Eastwood, G. (2000), "The Australian Securitisation Market," *Australian Prudential Regulation Authority Working Paper No. 6*, October.

McDonald, A. & Eastwood, G. (2000), "Credit Risk Rating at Australian Banks," *Australian Prudential Regulation Authority Working Paper No. 7*, December.

Mishkin, F. S. (2001), "Prudential Supervision: Why Is It Important and What Are the Issues?" in Mishkin, F. S. (ed.), *Prudential Supervision*, New York: National Bureau of Economic Research, pp. 1–29.

Reserve Bank of Australia (1985), *Prudential Supervision of Banks, Prudential Statement No. A1*, Sydney.

Reserve Bank of Australia (1988), *Capital Adequacy of Banks, Prudential Statement No. C1*, Sydney.

Reserve Bank of Australia (1991), "Directions for Prudential Supervision in the 1990s," *Bulletin*, May, pp. 6–13.

Reserve Bank of Australia (1995), "Supervisory Developments: The Reserve Bank's Perspective," *Bulletin*, April, pp. 28–33.

Reserve Bank of Australia (2003a), "Credit Risk Transfer Markets: An Australian Perspective," *Bulletin*, May, pp. 55–62.

Simon, J. (2003), "Three Australian Asset Price Bubbles", Paper presented at the *Reserve Bank of Australia Annual Conference: Asset Prices and Monetary Policy*, August 18–19.

Trinephi, N. (2003), "Basel Accord: Ready and Waiting," *Australia Risk*, August, pp. 4–5.

15

Basel Skepticism—From a Hungarian Perspective

Júlia Király and Katalin Mérő[1]

I. INTRODUCTION

Basel II is a natural, but not necessarily the most successful, answer to the deficiencies of Basel I. It is generally accepted that Basel I was a kind of "rule of thumb," which lacked theoretical underpinning. Peter Cook[2] and his team's highly appreciated contribution was twofold. Firstly, they made the banking world accept that it is not necessarily the notion of "equity," which expresses the solidness of a bank, and prompted the introduction of the notion of "regulatory capital" or "broad capital." Secondly, they initiated the recognition that the total risk of a bank is not necessarily a linear function of total assets—it is recognized by the highly nonlinear risk-weight function. (The "risk-weighted asset" function has a lot of breaking points.) The Cook-construction was simple—that is one of the greatest merits of Basel I: it is easy to understand and apply. However, academic circles have warned the banking community from the very beginning that the applied risk-weight function is as "dubious" as it is simple.

In recent years, there has been a significant development in determining economic capital based first of all on the value-at-risk (VAR) philosophy. Many academic people argue that the VAR is far from being the best risk measure, since it is not a coherent measure of risk, but the "principle of simplicity" won again—and the new regulatory approach is based on the VAR principle.

---

1. The views expressed in this chapter are the personal views of the authors and not that of the National Bank of Hungary.
2. Cook was the leader of the committee that worked out the original Basel I capital rules.

The New Basel Capital Accord—or Basel II, in its colloquial name—was a simple and brilliant framework in its original form, in 1999, when the first consultative paper was released by the Basel Committee on Banking Supervision (BCBS). Academic circles and professionals both applauded and welcomed the new idea with hope and enthusiasm. The banking community as a whole could accept the basic idea, as well, since, in general, Basel II promised not to increase, but to maintain the average level of minimum capital while reshaping the capital requirement, making it more adequate to the risk profile of banks (i.e., approximate the economic capital).[3]

Since then, 4 years have passed, and the original 20-page paper has increased to more than a 200-page-long document, several times rewritten, becoming more and more complicated and losing its appealing simplicity. We have arrived at the threshold of acceptance—and nobody cheers anymore.

In this paper, three aspects of Basel II are examined. The first part investigates how the new regulatory framework fits into a civil-law-based legal system (Section 2). In this respect, American and European regulatory philosophy and law are compared. The second part discusses the possible reaction of the average Hungarian bank, emphasizing some basic features of the new framework (Section 3). To do so, the possible options of the average manager are outlined and examined carefully. The third part analyzes the cyclical nature of the Hungarian banking sector's activity and examines the consequences of the pro-cyclical nature of Basel II regulation with respect to economies with less deep financial intermediation (Section 4). Finally, concluding in Section 5, the authors summarize why they have become skeptical about Basel II.

2. DIVERGING REACTIONS: EUROPE VERSUS THE UNITED STATES

The mission of the Basel Committee was to build-up a new Capital Accord that creates a level playing field. On the basis of the Basel II Accord, the European Union determined to work out a new European Capital Directive (CAD3), which would be implemented throughout the EU. In contrast, in July 2003, American banking agencies published the Advanced Notice of Proposed Rulemaking (ANPR) that officially reinforced that the new Basel II regulation will only partially be implemented in the US.

---

3. See BCBS, 1999.

Common law systems tend to use more elastic regulatory policies and practices giving greater role to the discretional right of supervisors. In contrast, civil law systems prefer strict, well-regulated rules that give less autonomy to supervisors. Hungary, as a mixed Franco-Latin/Germanic type civil law country with a short tradition of democratic jurisdiction, also prefers more definitive regulation.

Different Views on Basel II

In 1988 Basel I was aimed at becoming a standard for an internationally active Group of Ten Country (G10) banks, but by now it has become a basic international standard and has been implemented by more than 100 countries worldwide. Basel II aimed at creating an international standard for all the "significant" banks all over the world, but by now, it is clear that the new regulation will not fulfill this function. There is a characteristic difference between European and American approaches with respect to Basel II. It will be a mandatory industrial standard in Europe, but just a part of the capital regulation for the internationally active large banks in the U.S. Since the publication of the first draft of Basel II, Europe's intention has been the full and strict implementation by means of a European Directive, and both the member states of the European Union and the Union level organizations are very active in the debate on the details of the new regulation.

European comments on the earlier versions of Consultative Papers have always focused on solutions, which better suit European characteristics, and which take into consideration the compromises incorporated in earlier EU directives. Remarks made by European countries and EU institutions include, in equal measure, arguments based on economic reasoning that facilitate the approximation of the new regulatory capital to economic capital, and those that, in the case of strategic segments of key importance, are aimed at lowering the capital requirements stipulated in the new regulation below those indicated in the relevant consultation papers. In fact, efforts towards this end are in line with the initial objective of the regulation, i.e., with the fact that banks' overall capital requirements, including those for operational risk, should not be tougher.

A need for more relaxed capital requirements has arisen particularly sharply in household and small-to-medium-sized enterprise (SME) lending, which is crucial to smaller local banks. In order to address this need, the category of "regulatory retail" has been introduced in both standard and Foundation Internal-Ratings-Based (F-IRB) methods. Firm-size-based adjustment granting concession in capital requirements for SMEs has also been adopted. The retail and mortgage credit risk weights have been reduced from 100% to 75%, and 50% to 35%, respectively, under the standard method, and under the Foundation Internal Ratings-Based F-IRBF method, originally uniform retail weights were broken down first into 2, then 3 categories and flattened significantly. Overall, European authorities and professional associations have succeeded in championing their interests that the planned new regulation should pay attention to the European priority concerning the importance of SME and retail business. Thus, from a European perspective, a major obstacle to the application of the Basel II capital requirements to all regulated institutions, including small local banks and investment firms under the European Union's (EU) activity-based regulations, has been removed.

The U.S. has long foregone lobbying for the best possible adaptation of the planned regulation to U.S. markets. As soon as it became obvious that the straightforward methods of the planned regulation, despite their former sophistication, would not represent any serious progress compared to the current U.S. practice of capital regulation and supervision, emphasis was shifted to the achievement of its partial implementation. Such a shift was unmistakable in the comments by the American Bankers' Association (ABA) on the Basel Committee's Consultative Paper 2 (CP2) already in June 2001, "ABA believes that U.S. Agencies must limit the application to the Accord to only the very largest domestic institutions." However, it was approximately one and a half years later that the international professional community fully realised that the U.S. was not going to apply Basel II comprehensively. The first official statement to this effect was made by Roger Ferguson, vice-chairman of the Board of Governors of the Federal Reserve eral Reserve System in an address to the House of Representatives on 27 February 2003.

U.S. banking regulations will have three categories of banks.[4] Large, internationally active banks (approximately 10 banks, the so-called core banks), which reach a certain size or foreign exposure threshold, would be required to implement the Advanced Internal-Ratings-Based (A-IRB) approach and the Advanced Measurement Approach (AMA) for operational risk. Other large

---

4. See ANPR.

banks (about another 10, so called opt-in banks), could choose applying the same methods voluntarily, while the rest of the institutions (general banks) would remain under the existing rules. The top 20 U.S. bank's total assets account for about two-thirds of all banking assets and about 99% of all foreign banking assets. The "bifurcated" capital rules show concern about the competitive equality. This is the reason why the ANPR invites "the commenters' views on the relative pros and cons of a bifurcated regulatory framework versus a single regulatory framework." However, Mr. Ferguson, somewhat prejudging the issue, said, "My perception is that pricing, and thus competition between large and smaller banks today is relatively little influenced by regulatory capital constraints."[5]

Behind the Curtain: Different Regulatory Policy and Practice

Despite the fact that both the American and European regulatory policy and practice for bank capital regulation and supervision are based on Basel I, they differ to a large extent. In the U.S., banks must maintain 3 different capital ratios: two risk-weighted ratios[6] and a minimum leverage ratio. According to the pre-appointed level of these ratios, U.S. banks are classified into four different groups of capitalization (from well-capitalized to critically under-capitalized), and different immediate corrective actions are associated with these levels. Moreover, the supervisory valuation of capital adequacy at organizations with a complex risk profile is even today based not only on these ratios but also on a complex assessment. In the related Supervisory Letter (SR),[7] the Federal Reserve instructed supervisors and examiners "to evaluate the internal capital management process to judge whether they meaningfully tie the identification, monitoring, and evaluation of risk to the determination of the institution's capital needs." Considering that sometimes even high capital ratios do not indicate the real capital position, the SR Letter defines the main areas of sound internal capital adequacy analysis and the types of risks that banks have to cover during internal capital assessment. Accordingly, besides credit and market risk, banks have to consider interest rate risk and operational risk, as well. This approach appears to be very consistent with Basel II regulation. It does not, however, prescribe a direct capital charge

---

5. Ferguson, Basel II: A Realist's Perspective (speech on the conference of Risk Management Association, April 9, 2003).
6. The classic Basel I ratio and the risk-weighted assets to Tier 1 capital ratio.
7. SR 99-18(SUP), July 1, 1999.

against the operational risk, while identifying and controlling forms of this risk are an integral part of the banking capital assessment. The spirit of the comprehensive capital supervision is more or less in line with the second pillar of the Basel II Accord, i.e., one might say, that the essence of the second pillar is based on the current supervisory practice of American authorities. The disclosure rules are also amongst the most comprehensive in the U.S. This is why Federal Reserve Governor Ferguson commented that . . . "U.S. banks have long been subject to comprehensive and thorough supervision that is much less common in most other countries planning to implement Basel II."[8]

In EU member states, banks' capital is regulated by the Capital Adequacy Directive, which is, in practice, the EU codification of the Basel I Capital Accord. Directives, however, only stipulate joint minimum requirements; the relevant rules of the individual member states may well be tighter than those enshrined in the directives. Nevertheless, since European banks hold a Single European Passport, member states complying with fair competition do not, as a rule, adopt tighter national regulations. In terms of capital requirements, the only exception is the United Kingdom (UK), where, in addition to the minimal 8%, an individual capital ratio has also been set, which, depending on the individual banks' risk profile, may well exceed the minimum capital requirement. Though supervisory authorities in a few countries on the Continent have also sought to introduce risk-based capital supervision, such supervision has failed to become an integral part of financial regulatory practice. Compared to the current situation, the introduction of Pillars 2 and 3 of Basel II would be a major step forward in European regulatory practice. Supervisory practice in European countries is still a far cry from risk-based capital analysis as laid down in the U.S. SR letter. The adoption of such supervisory practice would definitely mean significant progress. Furthermore, the adoption of uniform supervisory principles, mandatory in each member state, also complies with the principle of fair market competition in the EU. (Again, the only exception to current practice is the UK, since individual capital ratios can only be set on the basis of the supervisory deliberation of a given institution's risk profile.)

---

8. Ferguson: Basel II—discussion of complex issue (Testimony before the Committee on Banking, Housing and Urban Affairs, U.S. Senate, 18 June 2003).

Comments on and working material for the implementation of the Basel Committee's Consultative Paper 3 (CP3) also reflect differences in regulatory philosophies. While the EU is focused on stability, the U.S. emphasises the importance of further fine-tuning the weights that are more in line with risks. The European Central Bank (ECB) proposes that ". . . once agreed upon and published, the New Accord should not be subject to major revisions until at least the implementation of the rules, envisaged at the end of 2006." In contrast, in ANPR the U.S. authorities wrote that "The Agencies plan to conduct at least one more Quantitative Impact Study (QIS), and potentially other economic impact analyses, to better understand the potential impact of the proposed framework on the capital requirement . . . . This may impact the Agencies' further proposals through recalibrating the A-IRB risk weight formulas and making other modifications to the proposed approaches if the capital requirements do not seem consistent with the overall risk profiles of banking organisations or safe and sound banking practices."

What was discussed above suggests that the most significant difference in regulatory policy approaches to Basel II is that U.S. supervisory authorities' priority is to take full and accurate cognisance of the individual institutions' position, on the basis of which cognisance the simplest possible rules can be drawn up and employed. In contrast, the EU prefers the creation of an enforceable and uniform regulatory regime. As far as smaller and less sophisticated institutions are concerned, the EU prefers the itemised standardised method, or its simplified version, to less highly regulated methods based on comprehensive supervisory deliberation. Like Basel I, such methods, not in the least unaffected by the numerous compromises made along the way, have nothing to do with economic capital. Rather, they stipulate regulatory capital, which may well be substantially different from economic capital, thus amounting to a very detailed and uniformly applicable regulation.

"Common Law" Versus "Civil Law" and the Implementation of Basel II

Legal systems are generally broken down into two main categories: those based on Roman law ("civil law" systems) and Anglo-Saxon legal systems based on precedents ("common law" systems). The key difference between these two types of legal system's is that whilst the first functions almost exclusively by applying statutory provisions stipulated by jurists, the second assures an important role for the judgments of courts in legal disputes, as well, and these judgments continuously affect the law itself.

Within the category of civil law systems, three further sub-groups are differentiated in the professional legal literature. The basis for the most rigid French-type legal system is the jurisprudence applied under Napoleon, where judges do not interpret but simply apply the rules. The German-type legal system is based on the jurisprudence applied by Bismarck in the period following the German unification. The Scandinavian-type system, though also based on civil law, occasionally treats civil law prescriptions less rigidly, and thus to an extent represents a transitional type between the two main groups of legal systems.

A close relationship can be seen between the different legal systems on the one hand, and the development level of the financial sphere on the other. LaPorta et al. (1996) have analyzed the legal system of 49 countries in respect to investor protection. They found that in countries applying the most rigid rules based on French civil law, the legal protection of investors' rights could be classified as weakest, while in countries applying common law, it could be considered as strongest. Countries applying a legal system based on German and Scandinavian-type civil law take a middle position in this respect. The data used by LaPorta et al. for the legal systems was examined by Levine, Loayza and Beck (2000), together with their own database as regards to financial intermediation. They concluded that formal rules, as well as their enforceability, exhibited a close relation with the financial development. In countries where the quality and enforceability of rules protecting investors' rights was better, the operation of financial intermediaries was smoother.

Proceeding from Hayek's (1973) argument for the superiority of English over French legal traditions, Mahoney (2000) found empirical evidence that legal origin plays a causal role in the development of financial systems. In his view, this is mainly due to the fact that Anglo-Saxon-type legal systems support private sector economic activity more strongly, while those based on civil law support state intervention more efficiently. However Beck, Demirgüc-Kunt and Levine (2002), analyzing the channels through which legal origin influences financial development, found this political channel to be of secondary importance. They reached the conclusion that the so-called "adaptability channel" plays the key role. This means that common law jurisdictions have the ability to evolve with changing conditions, as the court judges the cases on individual bases. Giving discretional right to judges, outdated, inefficient rules are automatically replaced by efficient ones. Accordingly, common law countries foster financial development more effectively than the more rigid civil law systems.

Why do we think that legal origin is important not only for financial development but for the regulatory policy and Basel II implementation issues as well? All the arguments mentioned above can also be effectively applied to financial regulation. In common law countries where legal systems promote the active role of judgment of courts, financial regulation can be less rigid, giving more discretional regulatory and supervisory right to the Supervisory Authority. In these countries, market participants are accustomed to operating under circumstances where the regulation is more elastic, and the judgments of the authorities are based more on the real nature of cases and less on the rigid, strict rules. In contrast, civil law countries need more all-comprehensive, strict financial regulation, as they can less effectively absorb the innovations by responding to the unforeseen and changing conditions on the case-by-case basis.

The countries of EU have different legal origins; however, the civil law's system, and especially the most rigid French civil law, is dominant. (See Table 1) Accordingly, the legislation process in the EU can be characterized by the detailed codification, which attempts to cover every possible case. On this point, it seems to be logical that the U.S., as a common law country, and the EU have different approaches to the implementation of Basel II. The EU adheres more to the written rules, laid down in Basel II, or its European version, the CAD3. The U.S. tries to implement a system that builds more on common law tradition.

Table 1. Legal origin of EU countries

ENGLISH	SCANDINAVIAN	GERMAN	FRENCH
UK	Denmark	Austria	Belgium
Ireland	Finland	Germany	France
	Sweden		Greece
			Italy
			Netherlands
			Portugal
			Spain

Source: LaPorta et al. (1996)

As regards her historical traditions, Hungary, a constituent state of the former Austro-Hungarian Monarchy, has a civil law system based on the German model. An already inflexible practice of law enforcement under the traditional legal system became extremely rigid in the forty years of the socialist era. Legislation then was highly regulated administratively. The main instrument of regulation was not acts passed by Parliament. Rather, it was governmental and ministerial decrees and ministerial instructions, all easily enactable and amendable en masse, passed by various agencies of public administration.

Since the regime change, legal regulations have been revised and, as a result, 966 Councils of Ministers and ministerial-level legal regulations as well as 1,250 instructions and legal guidelines have been repealed in the economy alone (Sárközy, 1994). Nevertheless, the absence of different traditions and legitimate legal bodies, legislation and law enforcement have only been able to take the course of itemised law enforcement based on detailed regulation, no matter the regime change. Thus, the legal system of today's Hungary is even more rigid than that of other countries with the same legal origin. For this reason, having analysed Hungarian legal regulations, Wood (1997) included Hungary in the category of countries with a mixed Franco/Germanic legal system. This legal stance is unmistakable in the comments made on Basel CP3 and communicated to the Basel Committee by the Hungarian authorities, which request the Committee to provide further detailed interpretation of the individual rules.[9]

It should be noted that Basel II as such, especially its second and third pillars, is/are deeply rooted in the common law tradition, since in a number of issues it relies on discretionary rulings by supervisory authorities and on the power of the public. The impact of the differences between the various legal systems becomes particularly conspicuous when it comes to the full/partial and detailed implementation of the first pillar. Another moot question to be tackled in the future is, basically, how civil law countries will be able to integrate the far-reaching discretionary powers that the second pillar grants to authorities into their respective legal systems. Provided that this becomes an element of supervision for financial institutions that is supported by both legislation and approved by market participants, international convergence of financial regulation will be achieved.

---

9. See comments on CP3 at *http://www.bis.org-on.*

Even the three pillar architecture of Basel II itself means that problems stemming from differences between characteristics of legal systems have already begun to dissolve due to the globalization of international banking market. Widespread international acceptance of uniform rules and standards governing national financial systems in growing number of countries automatically leads to fewer differences between legal systems. And in the case of financial regulation and especially Basel II, this happens through the shift towards the common law system, which promotes the financial development more effectively.

3. DILEMMAS AND TRADE-OFFS OF THE AVERAGE HUNGARIAN BANK

Basel II will have different effects on individual institutions in different countries. This depends not only on the different banking structure and the different portfolio structure in the individual countries, but on the discretionary decisions to be taken by the local Supervisors. From now on we will concentrate on the "Average Hungarian Bank."[10] The Average Banks' total assets sum up to 334 billion Hungarian Forint (HUF, i.e., Hungarian currency), (approx 1300 million Euro), it is mainly corporate-oriented, but has a growing retail portfolio, as well. However, the corporate portfolio consists in larger part from SMEs, a significant part of which belongs to retail.[11]

No matter which approach the different banks adopt, they face the same alternatives, the decision among which could be lessened by some simple computation and analysis. During the analysis, the deficiencies of the risk management systems, the database and the IT systems come to the surface. In the following sections the Average Hungarian Bank dilemmas will be investigated, while the basic principles of Basel II will be detailed only to the extent that is necessary to understand the trade-offs the Average Banks faces.

---

10. In determining the Average Bank special financial institutions (as e.g., the development bank), those banks, whose reports were not available (represent less than 5% of the market) were left out from consideration. After long discussions we have left out the National Saving Bank, as well, just because its dominance (22% of the market) would distort the picture about the average. Consequently, the Average Hungarian Bank was formed of the statistics of 22 individual banks, "who" represent 73% of total assets in the Hungarian banking sector.

11. Unfortunately, the FSA (Financial Supervisory Authority) Report does not disaggregate the corporate according to big corporate, SME and retail SME. We cannot but do some estimation in this respect based on individual banks studies.

Figure 1. The asset structure of the average Hungarian bank

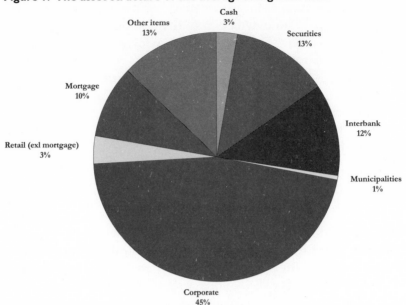

Source: Own calculation based on the database of the Hungarian Bankers Association.

Credit Risk.

As is well known, the first decision point is between the **standard method** and the **IRB method**. Before considering the alternatives offered by the Regulators, the Bank management should realize that without considerable restructuring of data stores, the Bank capital requirement will significantly increase, since, without being able to classify individual claims and assign the right collateral, the bank is required to use 100% or, what makes things worse, 150% risk weight, even in those cases, where a reduced weight could have been applied in Basel I standards (sovereign, banks). That is the basic challenge the Average Bank faces, the first time it gets involved in a Basel II project. The immediate reaction that could already been observed is: "Let's start a data warehouse project immediately "whatever it costs"!

The basic information problems of the Average Bank can be summarized as follows:

* Different exposures are often stored according to different business lines (corporate, retail, treasury) in different— nonintegrated—information technology (IT) subsystems, which may or may not be connected with interfaces. Individual claims could be collected from these different systems. The lack of a unified customer system is one of the most serious deficiencies of the Average Bank.

- Eligible ratings—sovereign, bank—are often stored separately from claims and administered by a different business unit (often called: "International Relationship Management").
- Guarantees and collaterals are not necessarily directly connected to the individual exposures and are not necessarily revaluated from time to time.

These are the problems the Average Bank should solve, no matter which option it chooses.

Standard Method.
Since the basic construction of the standard method is very similar to the actual Basel I—the Average Banks often suppose that if they choose the standard method, it means they should do nothing. In their case, the original message of Basel II—i.e., the new capital adequacy accord should promote more sophisticated risk management—will not get through. The Average Bank may consider the standard method as a "nothing to do" alternative, with the exception that at least one IT project should be launched. Nevertheless, it is true that like in Basel I, the standard method assigns risk weights to the net exposures, where these risk weights do not reflect the bank's inner model and have do nothing with economic capital.

The main differences as compared to the actual regulation are as follows:

1. **Refinement of Scale.** As is well known, the actual scale of weight (0%, 20%, 50%, 100%) has been refined (0%, 20%, 35%, 50%, 75%, 100%, 150%). This will mean a capital ease for SMEs, retail (75%) and mortgage loans (35%), while—generally, only rarely—it may provoke capital increase (150%).
2. **Refinement of customer groups.** This will be the first surprise for the management of the Average Bank. So far, they had to classify the different exposures in 4 groups: "sovereign," "bank," "mortgage" and "rest of the world." Now they need to be able to classify the exposures into 12 different groups (claims on sovereigns, on Public Sector Entities (PSE), on Multilateral Development Banks (MDB), on banks, on security firms, on corporates, included in retail portfolio, secured by residential property, secured by commercial real estate, past due loans, higher risk categories and other assets).

During our consultancy experience it was the first point which caused surprise: most of our clients—the Average Bank—realized that their IT system could not automatically sort exposures according to this classification. The actual credit systems in most cases do not store all the necessary parameters:

- real estate is not necessarily divided into residential properties and commercial real estate, and is not correctly revalued or attached to the claims;
- past due loans can not be easily sorted out and consequently, it cannot be decided whether they are well-covered by reserves or not.

3. **Use of outside credit ratings.** One of the most relevant changes in Basel II is the risk-sensitive classification within the individual customer groups. In the case of the standard method, this means the possible use of the rating of any ECAIs (External Credit Assessment Institutions). As far as the Average Bank is concerned, this will not help a lot. In case of sovereigns and banks, if the Bank registered the rating at all, then it was stored separately, i.e., data warehouses should be reorganized. In case of corporations, the Bank faces the problem of the non-existence of a Hungarian Rating Agency[12] on one hand, and the scarce rating of Hungarian companies by eligible international rating agencies, due to their negligible market size, on the other. The Average Hungarian Bank, like most of its counterparts in Eastern Europe, must face the problem of missing and/or not stored eligible ratings.

4. **Risk mitigation techniques.** In the 1988 Basel Capital Accord (Basel I), a very restricted range of collaterals and guarantees were accepted as risk mitigation techniques (mainly government guarantee and bonds, cash, and residential mortgages). Basel II opens a wider door for risk mitigation—even in the case of the standard method. That is the point, where the Average Bank faces enormous problems: collaterals and guarantees are usually stored separately from the reported credit data. It does not mean that collaterals are not registered, nor that after a tedious work done by credit departments that credit and collateral data cannot be assigned to each other as prescribed in the qualitative requirements of Basel II.

Let us now consider the alternatives the individual Bank faces applying the Standard Method.

---

12. In 1997 with the help of the World Bank the Hungarian Credit Rating Agency was established, but in a 5 year time it went bankrupt, due to lack of business perspectives.

Rated or Nonrated Corporations

According to CP3 (paragraph 42): "At national discretion, supervisory authorities may permit banks to risk weight all corporate claims at 100% without regard to external ratings." This option will be considered by the Hungarian Financial Supervisory Authority (HSFA),[13] and by all probabilities will be accepted as an alternative.

The "nonrating" option will be selected by the Average Hungarian Bank, since most of its customers do not have a rating at all, and developing a new data system for that minor part of a portfolio, which is rated, does not pay out.

SMEs As Potential Retail Customers

The regulatory retail portfolio consists of individuals and SMEs fulfilling the following four requirements:

- **Orientation criterion:** individual or small business. Neither in the CP3, nor in the CAD3 is it clearly defined which business units can be classified as "small business." It is not yet clear whether the definition will be at national discretion or international standards will be given. The question is of great relevance from the point of view of the local Average Bank, since a locally big corporation can easily be classified as small business according to European standards.
- **Product criterion:** the enlisted products—revolving credit, lines of credit, personal term loans and leases, small business facilities—are the standard services provided by the Average Bank for an average customer.
- **Granularity criterion:** A final and definitive decision from the authorities about the granularity criterion is anxiously awaited by the Average Bank. The former criterion (in CP2), which has been mitigated in CP3 to a level of "one possible way," required that none of the exposures can exceed 0.2% of the overall portfolio, which would require minimum 500 retail customers. In the case of a retail bank, it would not cause any problem; however, in case of a corporate bank with a significant SME business line, the granularity criterion is a hot issue. In the Average Bank, the granularity criterion would give rise to IT development, since the "regulatory retail portfolio" can be built only in an iterative way, restructuring the actual data base on customers. However, this IT development "pays out," since the exposure within the regulatory retail portfolio has a 75% risk

---

13.   FSA = Financial Supervisory Authority.

weight—contributing to the reduced capital requirement.

*   **Low value of individual exposures:** The regulatory limit—1 million euro—is significantly above the average maximum size in the Hungarian retail business, consequently, it will not be a bidding constraint for the Average Bank.

All in all, the design and construction of the regulatory retail portfolio will require significant efforts on the part of the Average Bank, which will only undertake these efforts if the possible outcome is a significant reduction in capital requirement. Otherwise, retail portfolio will be determined without SMEs, since individual claims fulfill the above-mentioned criterions without any doubt.

The findings of a recent survey run by the National Bank of Hungary[14] give an idea of the significance of the above problem in the Hungarian banking sector. In the survey, the Senior Loan Officers of the seven leading commercial banks (representing 76.5% of the total market) were interviewed about their SME lending practice. According to the results most of the banks classify a significant part of SME loans as "retail." The maximum annual turnover of an SME is 1.2 M Euro (far below any official limit); consequently, the average exposure is about 0.5 Million Euro (taking into consideration that the average debt of SMEs as compared to total turnover is 40%). This part of the portfolio will fulfill the granularity requirement without doubt.

The average is 0.5 M Euro, however, the bulk of the SME portfolio can be found in the 0.5–1 M Euro range, and the Average Bank does not necessarily treat it as retail lending. Potentially, these claims can be classified as regulatory retail, since scoring methods are widely applied. Whether these exposures will conform to the granularity requirement is not yet clear. If we try to estimate the share of these type of loans within the Average Bank corporate portfolio, the result will be between 20–25%, which means that the regulatory corporate portfolio can be reduced by 20–25%.

Risk Mitigation Technique: Simple or Comprehensive Method

Risk mitigation techniques cover on-balance-sheet netting, guarantees, credit derivatives and collaterals. The basic principle, which is quite different from that determined in Basel I—that the different techniques reduce the original risk to a certain extent, the "zero or nothing" principle—does not prevail any more. So far

---

14. Behlendi, A. – Naszodi, A. (2003).

only those collaterals and guarantees have been accepted which eliminated the risk in 100%; partial risk mitigation was excluded. The New Accord gives place to a more subtle risk mitigation, pushing the institutions toward more thorough registering systems.

While netting, credit derivatives and guarantees are quite straightforward, in case of collaterals the New Accord offers a possible choice: an institute can use the simple or the comprehensive method. While in the list of appropriate collaterals there are minor differences—both methods accept financial collaterals—the applied principle of risk mitigation is quite different:

- According to the simple method, the risk-weighting of the collateral is substituted for the risk-weighting of the counterparty. In other words, if we have a 100 HUF corporate exposure with a risk weight of 100%, and it is covered in 60% by a bank bond, which has a rating of 20%, then we will have 40 HUF corporate exposure with 100% risk weight and 60 HUF bank exposure with a risk weight of 20% (see Figure 2). If the collateral is a government paper, then the 0% risk weight can be applied, however, the value of the government bond should be discounted by 20%.
- According to the comprehensive method, the value of the collateral after it is adjusted by a haircut, can be deducted from the original exposure (which is adjusted, as well):

$$E^* = \max \left(0, \left(E \times (1+H_e) - C \times (1 - H_c - H_{fx})\right)\right)$$

The two methods coincide in the case of a cash (or bank deposit) collateral; in all other cases, the comprehensive method seems to be more preferable for the banks. Let us consider the previous example again. The adjusted value of the collateral—using the supervisory haircut (max 12%), assuming that the bank has at least a BBB credit rating—is $60 \times (1 - 12\%) = 52.8$, i.e., the original exposure can be reduced by this sum to 47.2 HUF (see Figure 2).

For this reason, it seems preferable to use the comprehensive method (even in the case of supervisory haircuts) than the standard method. To our great surprise, in a partial survey run by one of the Hungarian professional periodicals,[15] most interviewed

---

15. Bank és Tőzsde (Bank and Stock Exchange) 2003 June: "Moving Target—Bank Managers say about Basel II."

Figure 2. Standard approach—credit mitigation

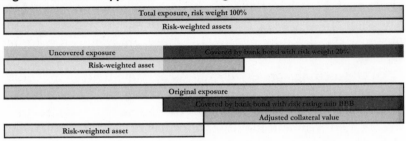

bank managers (all but one of seven) declared that they would apply the simple approach. We are convinced that this declaration is not based on detailed calculation but on the attractiveness of the "simple" method.

These are the options the Average Bank faces when it applies the standard method. All in all, the standard method increases the capital charge for the claims on sovereigns, banks, and some past due claims, while it may reduce the capital charge for the claims on corporate if well-rated or collateralized; and by in any case reduces the capital charge for the claims on the retail portfolio and claims secured by the residential mortgage. The reduction depends on the alternative the institutions choose and the realized and necessary IT development cost. If the IT restructuring is too expensive compared with capital reduction and increased growth potential, the institutions will not necessarily choose the option that is slightly more favorable for them.

This conclusion is supported both by the QIS3 results and our approximation of the effect of the standard method on individual Hungarian Banks. According to QIS3, the effect of the standard method in the case of local (not global, nonmultinational) retail oriented institutions (Group 2) more or less coincides with the results of the country study done by the HFSA. In the QIS3 experiment, eight Hungarian banks took part under the professional control of the HFSA. All the banks selected the standard approach.

Given the individual detailed balance sheets of the Hungarian Banks, we have rerun the QIS3, however, now taking into consideration the mitigation effect of CP3. Our experiment is a constrained one, since due to a lack of all the necessary data we have to apply the following assumptions:

- Off-balance-sheet items are negligible (we have left out from comparison all off-balance-sheet items, both in calculating Basel I and in calculating Basel II).
- Due to lack of data we did not take into consideration credit mitigation techniques (these increase the calculated capital requirement).
- Regulatory retail portfolio does not contain SMEs (i.e., we did not reduce the corporate exposure).
- Corporate exposures are non-rated, i.e., their risk weight is uniformly 100%.
- Claims on sovereigns denominated in foreign currencies have a BBB credit rating and a risk weight of 50%.
- Claims on banks denominated in foreign currencies have a rating BBB and a risk weight of 50%.
- Claims on PSE follow the rating of banks.
- Mortgage is considered only pledged against residential.

The results do not contradict to the QIS3 country results, however, a slight decrease in the overall capital requirement can be observed, due to decreased mortgage risk weights. The approximation accurately reflects the "hot points" of individual banks and nicely illustrates the well-known fact that the standard approach is more advantageous for retail banks. We have run the calculations for four typical corporate and five typical retail banks; the results are as follows:

Table 2. Contribution to change in capital requirement—standard approach

	QIS3 EU BANKS GROUP 2 *	QIS3 HUNGARIAN FSA**
Corporates	−1%	+2,7%
Sovereign	0%	0,5%
Bank	+1%	1,7%
Retail (total)	− 7%	− 2,8%
- mortgage	− 4%	− 0,5%
SME	− 2%	− 0,8%
Other	− 2%	+ 0,2%
Overall Credit Risk	−11%	+ 1,6%

(*) BCBS: QIS 3. Overview of Global Results. 2003 May.
(**) HFSA: A QIS3 eredményei—Magyar országtanulmány. Összefoglaló. (Results of QIS3—Hungarian Survey, Summary, 2003 June)

Table 3. Contribution to capital requirement—individual retail and corporate banks

	Sovereign	Banks	PSEs	Retail (non-mortgage)	Retail - mortgage	Overall credit risk
Retail 1	1,2%	1,0%	0,0%	−3,2%	−0,4%	−1,4%
Corporate 1	3,3%	0,9%	−0,3%	−0,3%	−0,5%	3,1%
Retail 2	3,4%	1,0%	−0,9%	−0,9%	−1,8%	0,8%
Corporate 2	1,8%	1,5%	−0,6%	−0,2%	−0,3%	2,2%
Retail 3	0,7%	3,1%	−4,5%	−2,5%	−2,4%	−5,6%
Corporate 3	3,8%	2,1%	−0,1%	−0,4%	−0,7%	4,7%
Retail 4	0,2%	0,1%	−1,5%	−1,4%	−2,5%	−5,0%
Corporate 4	0,5%	0,7%	−2,2%	−1,3%	−0,7%	−3,1%
Retail 5	2,2%	0,3%	−0,8%	−3,1%	−1,8%	−3,2%
Corporate 1	2,2%	2,6%	−1,3%	−1,3%	−2,2%	0,0%

Source: Own calculation based on the database of the Hungarian Bankers Association.

Figure 3. Contribution to capital requirement—individual retail and corporate banks

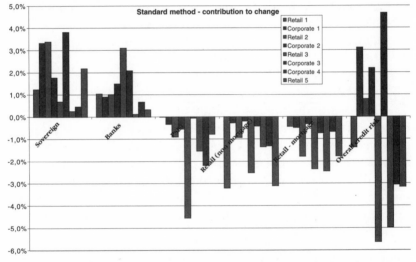

Source: Own calculation based on the database of the Hungarian Bankers Association.

There is one retail bank whose capital requirement increases, mainly due to a huge portfolio of non-HUF denominated government bonds. There is also one corporate bank whose capital requirement decreases due to the significant local authority exposure of the bank. Otherwise, retail banks face capital requirement reduction; corporate banks face a significant increase. This will determine their strategy: retail banks have enough time to roll out to F-IRB, if at all; while corporate banks are pushed to start the F-IRB project as soon as possible.

The IRB Method.
QIS3 results strongly supported the prevailing hypotheses concerning IRB:

1. Small, retail-oriented banks in niche markets will not choose A-IRB because it was elaborated for internationally active global banks. In G10 countries, sixty-five Group 1 banks (internationally active big banks) and 123 Group 2 banks participated. The number of Group 2 banks completing the A-IRB was negligible and was omitted from the results.
2. F-IRB may contribute to significant capital reduction in the case of Group 2 (more local, more retail-oriented-banks), especially through the retail portfolio:

Table 4. Contribution to change in capital—EU Group2 banks, Comparison of Standardised and IRB Foundation Method (*)

	STANDARDISED APPROACH	IRB FOUNDATION
Corporates	− 1%	− 5%
Sovereign	0%	+ 1%
Bank	+1%	− 1%
Retail	− 7%	− 18%
SME	− 2%	− 5%
Other	− 2%	+ 1%
Overall Credit Risk	− 11%	− 27%

(*) BCBS: QIS 3. Overview of Global Results. 2003 May.

The basis of the IRB method is a reliable rating system, and a well-calibrated model, with the help of which Probability of Defaults (PDs) of individual rating classes can be determined. The IRB is more than a simple capital calculation method; it aims at transforming the risk management system of the bank: "Rating systems and estimated designed and implemented exclusively for the purpose of qualifying for the IRB approach and used only to provide IRB inputs are not acceptable" (CP3, paragraph 406). Looking back from the IRB basis to the standardized approach, we have to admit that the latter is really nothing other than a more complicated, and in case of retail banks, more favorable capital calculation method, which will not affect significantly the risk management of the Average Bank.

From this point of view, one can appreciate the U.S. regulators standpoint, according to which the largest ten U.S. internationally active banks will adopt the A-IRB, while all the others can remain under Basel I.

The Average Hungarian Bank is not a participant, but the victim of the debate over who should accept the decision of the EC or, more importantly, who should accept the decision of its mother bank. Since the Average Hungarian Bank is owned by an Austrian, Belgian, Italian or German bank, and since most of these mother banks are generally internationally active globally and will adapt the IRB method, the Average Hungarian Bank will certainly "roll out" into IRB, no matter whether it serves its local interest or not. At present, the Average Hungarian Bank will not adopt IRB, especially because it is far from fulfilling the qualitative requirements. Let us enumerate some of those that would cause serious problems:

1. **The notion of "default."** The actual "default" definition in the Average Bank does not coincide with the Basel II notion. What is more, in the rating system there is no grade for the defaulted exposure.

2. **Design of the rating system.** The actual rating system in the Average Bank consists of five to seven classes; however, none of them is a "default" category. The portfolio is usually over-concentrated.

   In 2000, the Basel Committee Model Task Force prepared a survey on the rating practice of internationally active banks.[16] Almost at the same time the National Bank of Hungary assessed the rating systems of the Hungarian Banks.[17] The results, which endorse the above statement, are summarized in the following table:

---

16. Range of Practice in Bank's Internal Rating Systems—A discussion paper by the BCBS (January, 2000).
17. Lending risk management in the Hungarian banking sector (In: Report on Financial Stability, National Bank of Hungary, February 2001).

Table 5. Comparison of rating practice

	BCBS (2000)*	NBH (2000)**
Scope of the survey	Large internationally active banks	22 Hungarian banks (80% market share in corporate lending)
Number of grades	2–20 for performing loans 0–6 for non-performing loans	3–10 for all loans; no or only one grade for nonperforming loans
Average number of grades	10 plus 3	5
Portfolio distribution among grades	Typically max. 30% of the rated exposures in a single grade	Typically most of the exposures in one or two grades

Sources: *: Range of Practice in Bank's Internal Rating Systems—A discussion paper by the BCBS (January, 2000) ** Lending risk management in the Hungarian banking sector (In: Report on Financial Stability, National Bank of Hungary, February 2001) pp. 68–76.

As can be seen from Table 5, the general rating practice of the Average Bank is quite far from the requirements of Basel II. Introduction of IRB would require the immediate restructuring of the rating systems and the rating practice. So far, little effort has been made in this direction in different banks. That is, PDs, which should be based on long-term averages, are still far from being estimated by statistical models.

As far as retail portfolios are concerned, a somewhat different approach is required. In this respect, the Average Bank is in better position, since it operates a scoring system. These scoring systems were designed using statistical data collected in the past few years. It is possible to use the results of scoring system building in order to create homogeneous groups separated by PDs and loss given default (LGD). This kind of exercise has just started in several banks.

3.   **Operation of rating system.** In the Average Bank, the actual rating usually overwrites the former rating, i.e., historical data has not yet been compiled, and thus the permanent control of the rating database has not yet been solved.

4.   **Corporate governance.** The risk awareness of the Average Bank has significantly developed in the recent past; nevertheless, the integrated risk management unit, required by Basel II, has a long way to cover.

5.   **Application of rating.** According to Basel II, limits and pricing should be based on the rating system used for regulatory purposes. At present, the Average Bank has limit and pricing system, which has some relationship with the rating system, but it would be exaggeration to say that pricing and limits are based on it.

These are the main deficiencies, which make it difficult to apply the IRB approach in the Average Bank. In order to overcome these difficulties, the management of the Average Bank should understand the principles of Basel II in more detail and should decide about the necessary IT developments. The cost of these projects may pay out in some retail banks but not necessarily in all banks.

All in all, Basel II may contribute to a better risk management in the Average Bank but will not necessarily have this effect, while it may reduce the capital requirement of the retail-oriented banks without achieving any crucial change in risk management culture.

Operational Risk

The measurement of operational risk is one of the most controversial parts of the New Accord. There is nobody who would say that either the basic, the standard or the advanced approach is well supported by solid professional reasoning. All approaches are basic approximations in order to measure a risk, where both the theoretical background and the statistical database are actually missing.

For the Average Bank, the capital requirement on operational risk would mean a significant increase in regulatory capital. According to various estimations, this increase will be in the order of 10–13%. There is no chance for these banks to apply the Advanced Measurement Approach, simply because the lack of data will keep the Average Bank from applying any of the advanced methods.

Usual Actions in the Average Bank

In the Hungarian "Average Bank," the immediate reaction to Basel II was the "project effect": "Let's set up a project team to manage the adaptation of Basel II principles." In a recent interview-series,[18] eighty percent of banks announced that they had already set up a project team. Twenty percent of interviewed banks referred to their "mother banks," and said that their Basel II activity will be incorporated into their mother's project. Expectations of the mother bank's contribution are generally high: all in all, ninety percent of the foreign-owned banks expect some kind of support,

---

18. Bank és Tőzsde (Bank and Stock Exchange) 2003 June: "Moving Target—Bank Managers say about Basel II."

be it IT, systems, rules, methods or models, from the mother bank. The immediate winners of this widely spread approach are the IT and consulting firms, who will charge the financial institutions from the very outset and who are not interested in the "increasing risk awareness" at all.

4. PROCYCLICALITY OF THE HUNGARIAN BANKING SYSTEM

The relevant literature reveals that no uniform stance seems to have been adopted on the procyclicality of the capital held by banks. Some studies propose that the new regulations are unlikely to increase the procyclicality of capital significantly. These studies mainly point out the role of buffer capital, i.e., the amount in excess of the minimum capital requirement, as well as the "through the cycle" nature of ratings. [Lidquist (2002), Ayuso et al. (2002), Gambacorta-Mistrulli (2003), Catarineu et al. (2003)].

This proposition has, however, been strongly opposed, for example, by Danielsson and Shin (2002), and Danielsson et al. (2001), who mainly cite the fact that risk is endogenous. The envisaged Basel regulations will create a strong relationship between capital and the risks assumed, simultaneously rendering banks' response increasingly homogeneous. In periods of enhanced business activity, they encourage credit expansion through relaxing capital requirements, whereas in an economic downturn they may restrain lending by imposing more stringent capital requirements. As capital-related incentive spurs the entire sector to engage in uniform lending conduct, any insignificant procyclicality on the level of the individual banks may lead to major procyclical swings.

Though the new capital regulations will link risk with the amount of capital needed to cover against risk, i.e., they will protect deposit holders satisfactorily from a microprudential aspect, it is still to be seen whether systemic risk sensitivity runs counter to this or not. It not only fails to reduce risk but also increases the vulnerability of the banking sector. The uniform reaction by banks to endogenous risks heightens systemic risks and may in turn reinforce the procyclical behaviour of banks, which, though for the time being, are undetectable in terms of capital, definitely exists. If what was outlined above becomes a common feature, the new capital regulations may be cited as a textbook example of the contradiction between micro- and macroprudential stability and between the stability of the individual institutions and systemic stability.

Since the establishment of the two-tier banking system in 1987, the extension of credit by Hungarian banks to the domestic private sector proceeds in tandem with business activity, in keeping with international experience. At the same time, however, Figure 4 reveals that, in the period under review, long-term economic trends have exerted a deeper impact on banking activity than heightened business activity. Lending first declined gradually during the entire period of the transformation crisis and then increased year by year.

Figure 4. The output gap and the private credit to Gross Domestic Product ratio in Hungary

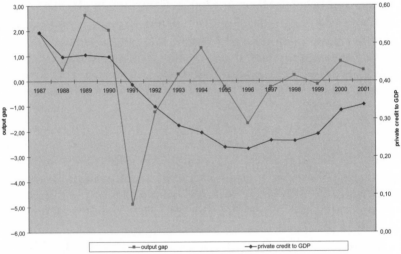

Source of data: National Bank of Hungary database.

The 1987 to 1995 period of the transformation crisis was characterised by a steady reduction in the credit portfolio of the corporate sector, which was being transformed and undergoing a wave of bankruptcies, even in the years when business activity picked up. Such developments were, however, inevitable ramifications of transformation. The pickup in economic activity has contributed to a gradual increase in the credit to gross domestic product (GDP) ratio since 1996. The question of whether the rather procyclical nature of lending suggests cyclical co-movement, or whether it is simply the manifestation of the deepening of financial intermediation (which inevitably occurred after the transformation crisis) is fully justified in connection with the period between 1996 and 2002, as well. In our opinion, although changes in the role of financing the economy of lending were primarily brought about by structural developments, the extent of these changes was also somewhat affected by the prevailing business cycle.

The most general characteristics of procyclical banking behaviour include credit expansion and the fact that provisions for credit are low in the times of heightened business activity and high in economic downturns. Business activity and the extent to which credit is covered by provisions will correlate negatively with each other, irrespective of the place or time. As far as Hungary is concerned, it is only the cyclical variations in provisioning after the consolidation period of the banking system that are worth investigating, since during the period between 1987 and 1995, the size of provisions was determined chiefly by changes in regulations and measures implemented in the course of consolidation. Figure 5 also points to strong negative correlation between provisioning and the business cycle in Hungary.

Figure 5. Provisioning and the output gap in Hungary

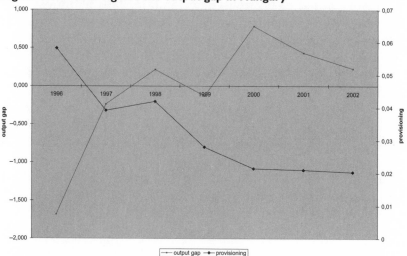

Source of data: National Bank of Hungary database.

The correlation between provisioning and the business cycle is strong even in international comparision.[19]

Table 6. Correlation between provisioning and the output gap

COUNTRY	CORRELATION
Hungary	−0,86
United Kingdom	−0,38
Italy	−0,21
Spain	−0,41
Germany	−0,21

Source: Borio-Furfine-Lowe (2001), and the National Bank of Hungary database.

At the same time, however, there arises the question whether the situation in Hungary suggests excessive procyclicality or stabilization following the consolidation period of the banking system. Figure 5 reveals that, despite the existing strong negative correlation, the latter is more likely to be the case. After the consolidation of the banking sector, the provisioning ratio declined continuously, from an extremely high value to levels characteristic internationally and common in stable banking sectors. The gradual decline in provisioning only came to a halt in 1998, when the Russian crisis led to portfolio deterioration. This halt must have been procyclical in nature, even if it was, on the level of the output gap, overcompensated by the business cycle typical in election years.

Overall, it is still too early to analyse the procyclicity of the operation of the Hungarian banking sector, as no conclusive statement on it can, for the time being, be made. The issue of procyclicity only arose from 1996, when the transformation crisis was over, and the consolidation of banks had been completed. However, the time elapsed, since is still too short for definitive conclusions to be drawn. Moreover, the entire period saw relatively favourable business cycle developments. What *can* be demonstrated, however, is that the banking indicators that are the most suitable for documenting procyclicity are currently more pro-

---

19. The statement should be discounted because of two factors. One is that a longer time series was used to calculate the correlation in the case of the countries included in the table than the one that we applied to calculate the domestic indicator applying to the period between 1996 and 2002 (generally between some year in the 1980s and 1999). The other that foreign indicators compare provisioning to overall portfolio of assets rather than the overall credit portfolio that we deem as more accurate.

foundly shaped by longer-term trends characteristic of structural transformations than by short-term business cycles. The business cycle can only lead to minor departures from such trends. This may also make the analysis of the prospective procyclical effects of the Basel II regulation difficult to perform. At the same time, potential, strongly procyclical capital regulations may be particularly detrimental in Hungary, where credit crunches in economic downturns may become an impediment to the inevitable deepening of lending. However, caution must be exercised when anticyclical regulations are introduced, lest the restraining of cyclical excessive lending in upturns should, overshooting the mark, hamper the deepening of financial intermediation.

It follows that in Hungary, and in transformation economies in general, where financial intermediation should deepen significantly in the near future, the procyclicality of Basel II may turn out to be the source of highly unpredictable risks. It cannot be ruled out that regulatory authorities will be unable to make a clear distinction between a credit boom, a phenomenon invariably concomitant with the deepening of financial intermediation, and procyclical excessive lending. Nor can it be ruled out that tougher capital requirements in downturns will lead to a procyclical credit crunch to a much higher extent than would otherwise be justified by a recession alone. Provided that such influences prevail, Basel II may assist with preventing the gap, measured by the depth of financial intermediation between converging central European countries (CEC) countries, Hungary included, and advanced market economies, from widening more than necessary and justified by economic and financial fundamentals.

CONCLUSIONS OR BASEL SKEPTICISM

Basel II is a natural but not necessarily the most successful answer to the deficiencies of Basel I. It is generally accepted that Basel I was a kind of "rule of thumb," which lacked theoretical underpinning. The New Capital Accord was a simple and brilliant framework in 1999, when the first consultative paper was released by the BCBS. Basel II promised not to increase but to maintain the average level of minimum capital, while reshaping the capital requirement, making it more adequate to the risk profile of the banks (i.e., approximate the economic capital). Since then, 4 years have passed, and nobody cheers anymore.

The authors attempted to underpin the widespread "Basel-skepticism," reconsidering three aspects of Basel II from the view of a small European emerging market, namely, Hungary.

We have compared the American and European approach to Basel II. Different approaches could have been explained by different legal backgrounds: in the EU countries, the most rigid French civil law is dominant, while in the U.S., the common law prevails. Accordingly, legislation process in the EU can be characterized by the detailed codification, which attempts to cover every possible case. The EU adhere more to the written rules, laid down in Basel II or its European version, the CAD3, while the U.S. tries to implement a system that builds more on common-law tradition. The interesting contradiction is that the Basel II basic philosophy is deeply rooted in the common-law tradition, since in a number of issues, it relies on discretionary rulings by supervisory authorities and on the power of the public.

In the Hungarian "Average Bank," the immediate reaction to Basel II is the "project effect": "Let's set up a project team to manage the adaptation of Basel II principles." In a recent interview-series, eighty percent of banks announced that they had already set up a project team, often controlled by a global mother bank. Banks do not investigate the alternatives provided by Basel II; they would apply, e.g., the IRB method, if the mother does so, even in the case when the standard method is more appropriate for the given institute. Expectations of the mother bank's contribution are generally high: all in all, ninety percent of the foreign-owned banks expect some kind of support, be it IT, systems, rules, methods or models, from the mother bank. The immediate winners of this widely spread approach are the IT and the consulting firms, who will charge the financial institutions from the very outset and who are not interested in the "increasing risk awareness" at all.

The third aspect, we have examined, is the Basel effect on the depth of intermediation through procyclicality. We have found that in Hungary, and in transformation economies, in general, where financial intermediation should deepen significantly in the near future, the procyclicality of Basel II may turn out to be the source of highly unpredictable risks. It cannot be ruled out that regulatory authorities will be unable to make a clear distinction between a credit boom, a phenomenon invariably concomitant with the deepening of financial intermediation and procyclical excessive lending. Nor can it be ruled out that tougher capital requirements in downturns will lead to a procyclical credit crunch to a much higher extent than would otherwise be justified by a recession alone. Provided that such influences prevail, Basel II may assist with preventing the gap, measured by the depth of financial intermediation between converging Central European countries, Hungary included, and advanced market economies, from widening more than necessary and justified by economic and financial fundamentals.

Legal rigidity, practical inefficiency and increasing systemic risk—why should we forget out skepticism toward Basel II?

REFERENCES

A QIS3 eredményei—Magyar országtanulmány. Összefoglaló. (Results of QIS3—Hungarian Survey, Summary) (2003), Hungarian Financial Supervisory Authority, June (*http://www.pszaf. hu*).

Advanced Notice of Proposed Rulemaking (ANPR), (2003), Board of Governors of the Federal Reserve System, July.

Ayuso, J., Pérez, D., Saurina, J. (2002), "Are Capital Buffers Procyclical? Evidence from Spanish Panel Data," Banco de Espana, Servicio de Estudios, Documento de Trabajo, No. 0224.

Bank és Tőzsde (Bank and Stock Exchange, a Hungarian Journal) (2003), "Moving Target – Bank Managers say about Basel II," June.

Basel Committee on Banking Supervision (1999), "A New Capital Adequacy Framework," Consultative Paper, June.

Beck, T., Demirguck-Kunt, A., Levine, R. (2002), "Law and Finance—Why Does Legal Origin Matter?" The World Bank Policy Research Working Paper 2904, October.

Behlendi, A-Naszodi, A. (2003), Preferred treatment of SMEs (Studies of the NBH, to be published).

Borio, C., Furfine, C. H., Lowe, P. (2001), "Procyclicality of the financial system and financial stability: issues and policy opinion," BIS Paper, No.1., March, pp. 1–57.

Catarineu-Rabell, E., Jackson, P., Tsomocos, D. P. (2003), "Procyclicality and the new Basel Accord—banks' choice of loan rating system," Bank of England Working Paper, No. 181.

Comments on CP3, *http://www.BIS.org*

Crockett, A. (2003), "International Standard Setting in Financial Supervision," BIS Lectures, February 5.

Danielsson, J., Embrechts, P., Goodhart, C., Keating, F., Renault, O., Shin, H. S. (2001), "An Academic Response to Basel II," Financial Market Group Special Paper, No. 103, May.

Danielsson, J., Shin, H. S., (2002), "Endogeneous Risk," Working Paper, London School of Economics, September 21.

Ferguson, Jr., R. W., (2003), Basel II—discussion of complex issues, *BIS Review*, 28.

Ferguson, Jr., R.W., (2003), Basel II, *BIS Review*, 10.

Gambacorta, L., Mistrulli, P. E. (2003), "Bank Capital and Lending Behavior: Empirical Evidence for Italy," Banca d'Italia Termi di discussione del Servizio Studi, Number 486.

Hayek, Friederich (1973), *Law, Legislation, and Liberty*: Vol. I: Rules and Order, Chicago, University of Chicago Press.

La Porta, R., Lopez-de-Silanes, F., Shleifer, A., Vishny, R. W. (1998), "Law and Finance," *Journal of Political Economy*, 106.

Large, A. (2003), "Basel II and Systemic Stability," *BIS Review*, 14.

Lending risk management in the Hungarian banking sector (In: Report on Financial Stability, National Bank of Hungary, February 2001.) pp. 68–76.

Lindquist, K-G. (2003), "Banks' buffer capital: How important is risk," Lecture on 2nd Nordic Econometric Meeting, Bergen, May 8–10. (*http://www.nhh.no/for/conferences/nordic-econometric/ Lindquist.pdf*)

Mahoney, P. (200), "The Common Law and Economic Growth: Hayek Might be Right," University of Virginia School of Law Legal Studies Working Papers Series, January.

Quantitative Impact Study 3, Overview of Global Results, (2003), BIS, May.

"Range of Practice in Bank's Internal Rating Systems" (2003), A discussion paper by the BCBS, January.

European Commission, (2003), Review of Capital Requirements for Banks and Investment Firms, July.

Rutledge, W. L. (2003), "Implementing the New Basel Accord," *BIS Review*, 15.

Sárközy, T.(1994), Javaslat a piacgazdaságot szolgáló modern kormányzás felépítésére (Recommendation to build up a streamlined governmental structure), published by KJK, pp. 152, (editor—KJK is a Hungarian publisher).

Supervisory Letter SR 99-18(SUP) of the Board of Governors of the Federal Reserve System, July 1, 1999.

The New Basel Capital Accord, Consultative Document, (2003), BIS, July.

Wood, P. R. (1997), *Map of World Financial Law*, London, UK, Allen & Overy Global Law Maps.

16

The New Basel Capital Accord and Its Impact on Japanese Banking: A Qualitative Analysis

Adrian van Rixtel, Ioana Alexopoulou, and Kimie Harada[1]

I. INTRODUCTION

The development and introduction of the new Basel Capital Accord (Basel II) has instigated intensive and heated debates in many countries and industries. Some fear that the accord will be counterproductive; others, and by far the majority, believe that it will establish safer and healthier banking systems in the medium and long run. Discussions have also concentrated on the question: which banks will be among the winners and which among the losers? *Risk* magazine concluded in January 2002 that the Swiss and UK banks were set to win, but the Japanese to lose under Basel II (*Risk*, January 2002).

One does not need much imagination to conclude that over the past 10 years or so, Japanese banks could not be typified as being in a winning position. Saddled with bad loans and eroded capital positions, they had to retreat from international markets and put all their efforts into the resolution of their problems. Taking this into account, some argue that Basel II is not of direct relevance for Japanese banks yet, and that banks in Japan have other things to worry about right now than a new Capital Accord. Or, as it has been put more aptly, it is simply "a question of priorities" (*Risk*, November 2002).

---

1. The views expressed in this chapter do not reflect in any way the official views of the European Central Bank (ECB). Assistance from Mr. Seiichi Tsurumi, Japanese Bankers Association, in organizing interviews and gathering information is gratefully acknowledged.

Although this certainly may be correct, at least to some extent, Japanese banks know that they will be confronted with a new capital regulatory framework in the foreseeable future. Therefore, they need to prepare, and one can simply not believe that Basel II considerations do not play some role in Japanese banks' strategic considerations and operational practices. Thus, this chapter investigates the possible implications for Japanese banks of the development and implementation of the new Basel Capital Accord. To this purpose, we have followed a qualitative research strategy consisting of the following elements. First, a detailed analysis of the relevant academic literature was conducted. Second, this was augmented by a structural investigation of relevant publications by the financial industry. This includes the work of the Basel Committee itself and the various consultation rounds related to that work, and various reports filed by major commercial and investment banks, rating organizations, and international and national policymaking bodies. It also includes investigations of industry-specific publications such as *Risk* magazine. Third, we conducted a day-by-day search of major related daily news publications to identify specific trends that could provide information regarding the short-term (tactical) and long-term (strategic) implications of Basel II for Japanese banking. This approach is based on the well-known trend analysis developed by John Naisbitt (see Naisbitt, 1984). The publications that were investigated were in particular the main Japanese financial daily (*Nihon Keizai Shimbun*) through the Nikkei Net System and the *Financial Times*. Fourth, to fill existing information gaps, we conducted interviews with key individuals active in the Japanese financial system. In total, 21 interviews were conducted with representatives from Japanese commercial banks and national and international rating agencies, policy makers, and banking analysts. All in all, given the inherent uncertainty related to Basel II (i.e., the accord is not in a steady state yet), we felt that this was the most fruitful approach to follow.

The structure of this chapter is as follows. First, a general overview of certain specific elements of Basel II is presented. Second, the characteristics of the Japanese banking system and its main problems are discussed for the major banks in particular. Third, the impact of the original Capital Accord on Japanese banking is investigated. Fourth, the formal reactions of Japanese banks published on the Basel Committee's Web site are analyzed.

Then, the tactical and strategic implications of Basel II for the Japanese banking industry are discussed, merging all the information obtained. Finally, some conclusions are presented.

2. THE MAIN CHARACTERISTICS OF THE NEW BASEL ACCORD

The New Basel Capital Accord basically addresses only the denominator, i.e., risk-weighted assets, of the capital adequacy ratios that were the cornerstone of the first Basel Accord of 1988, and leaves fundamentally the numerator, that is bank capital, alone. In its essence, the New Accord consists of three mutually reinforcing pillars affording better protection to the stability of the national and international banking systems, and can be summarized as follows (see for example: Basel Committee on Banking Supervision (1999), (2001a), (2001b) and (2003b); Credit (2001); Deutsche Bundesbank (2001); ECB (2001); EDS (2003), Jackson (2001); JP Morgan Securities (2001); McDonough (2003); Morgan Stanley (2003a) and (2003b)). Pillar 1 sets out the minimum capital requirements. Compliance with these requirements is measured by using the "capital ratio," which must be no lower than 8%. Pillar 2 concerns the so-called Supervisory Review process. This clarifies the need for qualitative banking supervision and is designed to capture external factors, such as the influence of the business cycle, as well as risk areas which have not been taken into consideration when calculating the minimum capital requirements. The provisions on minimum capital requirements —Pillar 1—and the supervisory review process—Pillar 2—are joined by transparency requirements which form the third pillar of the New Accord. These are designed to allow for a complementary use of market mechanisms for regulatory objectives. This concept is based on the expectation that well-informed market players will reward credit institutions characterized by effective risk-management of their investment and credit decisions on the one hand and penalize riskier behavior on the other hand. This provides credit institutions with additional incentives to control and manage efficiently their risks.

The New Capital Accord allows financial institutions to estimate the probability of default (PD) associated with each borrower according to its business conditions and hold capital based on such estimates (Basel Committee on Banking Supervision (2001)). In the Accord a mechanism is introduced that acknowledges any deterioration in the value of financial institution's loan assets at an early stage and sets requirements for banks to promptly increase their capital relative to the risks associated with a loan project and any other change in the degree of risk. This mechanism, which is called the internal ratings-based approach (IRB), produces a statistical measurement of both the unexpected losses and the expected losses that banks face in relation to their credit risk exposures. Consequently, the measurement of the amount of risk-weighted assets would be based solely on the unexpected loss portion of the IRB calculations. Then banks will compare the IRB measurement of expected losses with the total amount of provisions that they have made. For any bank, this comparison will produce a "shortfall" if the expected loss amount exceeds the total amount of provisions, or an "excess" if the total amount of provisions exceeds the expected loss amount. The shortfall amount will be deducted from Tier 1 capital by 50% and by the same amount from Tier 2 capital (*Risk* Magazine (2003)).

The proposed New Capital Accord gives banks three options for assessing credit risk. First, the standardized approach, tailored for smaller, less sophisticated banks, uses ratings provided by agencies to determine capital requirements. Companies rated BBB or BB would have a risk weighting of 100%, requiring a capital charge of 8%, while a company rated AA would have a risk weighting of 20%, requiring a capital charge of just 1.6%. Second, under the foundation IRB method, banks estimate the probability of default (PD) for their borrowers and then use figures provided by prudential supervisors for loss given default (LGD), exposure at default (EAD) and maturity (M) to calculate capital requirements. Third, under the advanced IRB approach, banks use their own estimates for all the above mentioned variables. To qualify for the advanced approach, banks need to collect several years of data on the performance of their borrowers to demonstrate to supervisors the soundness and reliability of their rating systems (*Institutional Investor* (2003)).

Another major innovation in the New Capital Accord is the explicit inclusion of operational risk, which is defined as ". . . the risk of losses resulting from inadequate or failed internal processes, people or systems, or external events" (Basel Committee on Banking Supervision (2003b)). The Accord gives banks three alternatives for operational risk. The basic indicator and standardized approaches link the operational risk charge to a bank's gross income. The advanced measurement approach allows banks to determine their own operational risk charge if they can meet strict requirements that include having well-tested risk control systems and detailed historical data.

An important impact of the New Capital Accord's capital regulation is the effect on financial pro-cyclicality (see for example ECB (2001)). The minimum capital requirement may become binding in a downturn if banks' capital ratios fall close to the 8% level. The capital shortage may induce banks to reduce lending beyond what would be warranted on the basis of the reduced demand for loans in an economic downturn. The quantitative impact on the actual regulatory capital requirements would depend on the portfolio composition of individual banks. The increase in the minimum required amount of capital under the IRB approach might be substantial in a deteriorating economic environment, on account of the element of volatility of the probability of default measures. Hence, banks could face increasing capital needs in periods when capital is most costly and could choose to reduce assets instead, which might make the downturn more pronounced.

With respect to bank capital, i.e., the numerator of the capital adequacy ratio which as mentioned before remains basically untouched, Basel II follows Basel I and provides a common international definition of bank capital that divides capital into two tiers. Tier 1 capital is common to all of the signatory countries, thus making it useful for cross-country comparisons. It consists of common stock holder equity and disclosed reserves (except for some forms of preferred stock that U.S. bank holding companies take into account). Tier 2 capital, which consists of leeway elements that at least one of the signatory countries considered to be bank capital, can include any combination of the eligible capital elements permitted by the national regulators. Tier 3 capital is short-term subordinated debt (maturity between 2 and 5 years) that can be used to support a bank's capital requirements arising from market risks on trading book activities (see for example JP Morgan Securities (2002)). The amendment to the Capital Accord to incorporate market risks in January 1996 was designed to capture the various market risks borne by financial institutions and introduced capital charges for them (BIS 1996). The amendment permits a bank to divide its business between its term lending and deposit-taking activities, known as the "banking book," and its trading activities, known as the "trading book." Tier 3 capital may not be set against credit risk, only against market risk capital requirements.

In October 2002, the Basel committee initiated a study involving 365 banks across 43 countries, including 66 Japanese banks, to gauge the impact of Pillar 1. The results were released in May 2003 in the Quantitative Impact Study No.3 (QIS 3) and are broadly in line with the objectives of the Accord (Basel Committee on Banking Supervision (2003c)). The minimum capital requirements would be broadly unchanged for large internationally banks taking into account the fact that they are more likely to use the IRB approaches. For smaller, more domestically oriented G10 and EU banks, capital requirements could be substantially lower under the two IRB approaches, largely reflecting the importance of retail business for these banks. Thus banks oriented on retail business will see their credit risk weights fall significantly. For instance, under the standardized approach, risk weights on residential mortgage portfolios fall from 50% to 35% and on retail and SME (small- and medium-sized enterprises) lending from 100% to 75%. Also weights will differ according to the size of the borrowers, with larger risk weights for large corporate borrowers. The discussion of the treatment of small- and medium-sized enterprises (SMEs) under the new Accord has been extremely difficult. The Basel Committee decided in July 2002 to differentiate between risk weights applied to loans to SMEs and loans to larger firms (see Jacobo Rodriguez (2002), p. 24). Another aspect of the proposed weighting scheme is that risk weights will be lower for non-performing loans which are covered by adequate provisions, i.e., generating an incentive for banks to develop and maintain adequate provisioning levels.

After the completion of the consultations on the Third Consultative Paper (CP3), which was published in April 2003, and in interaction with the results of QIS 3, the Basel Committee aims to resolve the outstanding issues by no later than midyear 2004 with the view of full implementation of the rules by the end of 2006 (Basel Committee on Banking Supervision (2003e)). The areas where more work will be done are the following. First, changing the treatment of expected versus unexpected credit losses. Second, simplifying the treatment of asset securitization, including eliminating the so-called Supervisory Formula.[2] Third, reviewing of how to handle loans related to credit card business. Fourth,

---

2. A supervisory formula has been developed for treating retained or purchased exposures in traditional and synthetic securitizations where an external or qualified inferred rating is not available. The applicability of the supervisory formula approach will depend primarily on the requirements for calculating the IRB capital charge for the underlying asset type (Basel Banking Supervision Committee (2001)).

reviewing certain credit risk mitigation techniques. Given the inherent uncertainty at this stage, it is clear that this paper cannot present a final assessment of these areas. According to the Federal Reserve Board (2003) implementation of the rules will happen differently for each bank as it is more important to "do it right" rather than "doing it quickly." So all banks have to submit to the regulators a formal implementation plan by late 2004.

Not surprisingly, similar to the experience with the 1988 Basel Accord, the New Basel Capital Accord has been increasingly the topic of research by major banks, supervisory and monetary authorities, and academics.[3] A full overview of this work is beyond the scope of this paper but in the context of the research objective pursued, the following can be mentioned.

First, a significant number of studies focus on the pro-cyclicality of Basel II. Reisen (2001) argues that speculative-grade borrowers will suffer from a dramatic rise in debt costs and heightened cyclicality of global bank credit as a result of Basel II, if the internal rating approach is implemented. On the same issue of the importance of cyclicality is ECB (2001), where again it is argued that banks estimates of probabilities of default would likely vary over time and depend on economic cycles, and that the New Accord probably could increase pro-cyclicality (see also Danielson et al. (2001)). A comparison of pro-cyclicality effects of both Basel I and Basel II is made in Heid (2003) where it is argued that the feared increase in volatility of actual capital and output did not materialize under Basel I but most likely will occur under Basel II. Corcóstegui et al. (2003) investigate internal rating systems and propose solutions for the pro-cyclical bias in the New Accord. Altman and Saunders (2001) argue that the agency ratings could produce cyclically lagging rather leading capital requirements, resulting to instability in the banking system. Regarding other aspects of Basel II, Mori and Harada (2001) describe a methodology that quantifies risk mitigation effects by insurance in Pillar 1 capital charges. The authors recognize that developing a rigorous methodology to incorporate insurance effects is critical for the purpose of making the regulatory framework risk sensitive. Also according to the New Accord, banks take greater economic risks by diversifying into more risky assets and activities which do not lead

---

3. For academic research regarding the general role of capital and risk-based capital requirements, and impact of these requirements on banks see for example: Lackman (1986); Wall and Peterson (1987); Cooper et al. (1991); Shrieves and Dahl (1992); Berger et al. (1995); Hellmann et al. (2000); Barrios and Blanco (2003); Gup (2003); Ishikawa et al. (2003).

to higher capital requirements. Rodriguez (2002), argues that the "existence of risk categories that create a divergence between economic risks and measures of regulatory capital has led to widespread regulatory capital arbitrage."[4]

To conclude, the banks that most likely will be the winners under Basel II (i.e., banks that will see their risk-weighted assets decrease and thus experience an increase in capital adequacy ratios) will be banks which have substantial retail operations, with high shares of their total lending consisting of consumer loans, residential mortgages and loans to small- and medium-sized enterprises (SME's), banks which have adequate provisioning schemes for nonperforming loans, and banks which have the resources to develop the (costly) internal rating systems (i.e., most likely the largest banks), as the IRB approached will lower capital charges compared with the standardized approach (see also Morgan Stanley, 15 July 2003).

3. THE JAPANESE BANKING SECTOR

Overview

The Japanese banking industry has been extensively discussed in a large number of studies (for some recent examples see: Van Rixtel (2002), Van Rixtel et al. (2003)). In the context of this contribution, only its main characteristics will be described in order to assess the possible impact of the New Basel Capital Accord on the Japanese banking sector.

The structure of the Japanese banking system is characterized, firstly, by the presence of a very small number of very large banking groups and a very large number of very small institutions, and secondly by a sharp decline of the total number of institutions over the past years. The increased concentration in the Japanese banking sector, which is shown in Table 1, has affected in particular the city and Second Tier regional banks among the major banks, and smaller financial institutions such as *shinkin* banks, and credit, agriculture and forestry cooperatives. These institutions perform the following functions. The major banks in Japan are the commercial or ordinary banks, whose activities are set by the Banking Law. These banks consist of the city banks, regional banks, Second Tier regional banks and foreign banks. The city banks are the

---

4. See also D. Jones (2000).

largest of all commercial banks; their funding consists basically of deposits, direct credit from the BoJ and borrowings from the interbank markets. The regional banks have their headquarters predominantly throughout the country in smaller cities, and mostly operate in local areas. The member banks of the Second Association of Regional Banks, or the Second Tier regional banks, are former *sogo* or mutual savings banks, all of which were changed in commercial banks in February 1989. Within the group of the so-called long-term financial institutions, the long-term credit banks or LTCBs have been the most important banks, of which originally three existed (only two left as of end-March 2003). The trust banks are also long-term financial institutions, and were, unlike the LTCBs, permitted to conduct both ordinary banking and trust business. Finally, financial institutions for small businesses exist which comprise three groups, i.e., credit associations or *shinkin* banks, credit cooperatives and the Central Co-operative Bank for Commerce and Industry.

The city banks, one long-term credit bank, most of the trust banks and some regional banks and smaller financial institutions have organized themselves through an intensive merger process in seven bank conglomerates, of which the top four in particular dominate the Japanese market.[5] The most significant merger was the one between Fuji Bank, the Industrial Bank of Japan and Dai-Ichi Kangyo Bank in September 2000, to form a mega bank group called Mizuho Financial Group. This was followed by three other mega mergers involving its main competitors in April 2001. Bank of Tokyo-Mitsubishi, Mitsubishi Trust and Nippon Trust merged to form the Mitsubishi-Tokyo Financial Group. The second merger was between Sakura Bank and Sumitomo Bank which established the Sumitomo Mitsui Banking Corporation (SMBC). The third merger involved Sanwa Bank, Tokai Bank and Toyo Trust to set up the United Financial of Japan (UFJ) group. The most recent consolidation was in December 2001 when Daiwa Bank, Kinki Osaka Bank and Nara Bank merged. In March 2002, Asahi Bank joined them to form another financial group that was tentatively named Resona Holdings in October 2002; its main institution, Resona Bank, was rescued by the government in May 2003 (see Section 2). Table 2 shows that, as of end-March 2003, the

---

5. In official publications, the major banks are often interpreted as the following 11 large banks: Mizuho Bank, Mizuho Corporate, Mizuho Trust, Tokyo-Mitsubishi Bank, Mitsubishi Trust and Banking Co., UFJ Bank, UFJ Trust Bank, Sumitomo Mitsui Banking Corporation, Resona Bank, Chuo Mitsui Trust and Banking, and Sumitomo Trust & Banking Co.

Mizuho Financial Group was the largest banking conglomerate in Japan with (consolidated) total assets of about Yen 131 trillion, deposits of Yen 67 trillion and loans of around Yen 70 trillion. The second largest group was Sumitomo Mitsui Financial Group with total assets amounting to Yen 101.5 trillion, followed by Mitsubishi Tokyo Financial Group, UFJ Group and Resona Holdings. In terms of strategy, Mizuho is focusing on integrating more closely its three main predecessor banks (Dai-ichi Kangyo Bank, Fuji Bank and Industrial Bank of Japan).[6] Mitsubishi Tokyo Financial Group and UFJ Group are paying more attention to their retail business, with the latter having established 24-hour access to ATMs. Finally, Sumitomo Mitsui has the largest nonperforming loan portfolio and consequently gives high priority to solve that problem in particular (Megabanks series Nikkei Net, September 2003).

---

6. Kashyap (2002) describes some integration problems such as the failure of Mizuho's computer systems on the first day of its operation.

Table 1. Financial institutions in Japan in 1991 and 2002

Category	1991			2002			2003
	Number	Share in total deposits (%)	Total assets (in Yen trillion)	Number	Share in total deposits (%)	Total assets (in Yen trillion)	Number
City banks	12	31.1	376.6	7	23.9	363.1	7
Long-term credit banks	3	1.4	76.6	3[1]	1.0	53.1	2
Trust banks	7	2.8	59.3	8	3.4	64.5	27[4]
Regional banks	64	19.5	187.9	64	18.8	205.7	64
Second Tier regional banks	68	7.1	68.8	53	5.8	61.9	51
Shinkin banks	451	10.3	96.0	349	10.7	112.1	326
Credit cooperatives	407	2.8	24.1	247	1.6	18.3	191
Labour cooperatives/banks	47	0.9	7.5	39	1.3	13.4	21
Agricultural cooperatives	3,600	7.0	58.4	1,264	7.6	75.2	944
Securities companies	272[3]		27.0	290[3]		19.4	280
Life insurance companies	26		130.3	42		184.4	42
Nonlife insurance companies	24		26.2	35[2]		33.5	24
Postal life and annuity			51.8	24,778[2]		124.8	
Postal savings		17.1	92.9	24,778[2]	25.9	159.4	
Government institutions	11			11			9

Sources: Van Rixtel et al. (2003), except last column, which is from Japanese Bankers Association (2003).
Note: Figures are as of the end of 1991, March 2002 and March 2003 (the end of the fiscal year).
1. Long-term credit banks include the Industrial Bank of Japan, Shinsei Bank and Aozora Bank.
2. The number is as of March 2001.
3. These figures include 52 and 49 foreign securities companies as of March 1991 and March 2002, respectively.
4. Of which 8 are full members of the Japanese Bankers Association.

Table 2. Japanese financial groups in 2003 (on basis of consolidated accounts; end-March 2003) *(trillion of yen)*

GROUP NAME	ESTABLISHED	MAJOR FINANCIAL INSTITUTIONS IN GROUP	TOTAL ASSETS (% CHANGE LAST YEAR)[7]	LOANS (% CHANGE LAST YEAR)[7]	SECURITIES (INVESTMENT) (% CHANGE LAST YEAR)[7]	DEPOSITS (% CHANGE LAST YEAR)[7]	EQUITY (% CHANGE LAST YEAR)[7]
Mizuho Financial Group[1]	September 29, 2000	Mizuho Bank, Ltd., Mizuho Corporate Bank, Ltd., Mizuho Securities, Mizuho Trust & Banking Co.	130.9 (−11%)	69.9 (−18%)	24.1 (−1%)	67.3 (−14%)	3.9 (−32%)
Sumitomo Mitsui Financial Group[2] (SMFG)	December 2, 2002	Sumitomo Mitsui Banking Corporation	101.5 (−3%)	61.1 (−4%)	24.1 (+17%)	62.9 (−3%)	3.4 (−12%)
Mitsubishi Tokyo Financial Group[3] (MTFG)	April 2, 2001	The Bank of Tokyo – Mitsubishi Ltd., Mitsubishi Trust and Banking Corporation	95.6 (0%)	47.8 (−5%)	24.6 (+4%)	65.0 (+3%)	3.3 (−6%)
UFJ Group[4]	April 2, 2001	UFJ Bank, UFJ Trust Bank, UFJ Tsubasa Securities	78.1 (0%)	45.2 (−5%)	18.1 (+16%)	53.3 (−1%)	2.7 (−18%)
Resona Holdings[5]	December 12, 2001	Resona Bank, Resona Trust & Banking Co., Saitama Resona Bank, Kinki Osaka Bank, Nara Bank	41.0 (−6%)	29.5 (+8%)	6.6 (+7%)	35.5 (+3%)	0.6 (−56%)

Table 2. Japanese financial groups in 2003 (on basis of consolidated accounts; end-March 2003) *(trillion of yen)* **(cont.)**

GROUP NAME	ESTABLISHED	MAJOR FINANCIAL INSTITU-TIONS IN GROUP	TOTAL ASSETS (% CHANGE LAST YEAR)[7]	LOANS (% CHANGE LAST YEAR)[7]	SECURITIES (INVEST-MENT (% CHANGE LAST YEAR)[7]	DEPOSITS (% CHANGE LAST YEAR)[7]	EQUITY (% CHANGE LAST YEAR)[7]
Mitsui Trust Holdings[6]	February 1, 2002	The Chuo Mitsui Trust and Banking Company, Ltd.	14.9 (−6%)	9.7 (−2%)	3.4 (−9%)	12.7 (−1%)	0.3 (−38%)
Sumitomo Trust & Banking Co., Ltd.	1925	Sumitomo Trust & Banking Co., Ltd.	17.3 (−7%)	10.7 (−1%)	3.7 (−30%)	11.8 (−4%)	0.7 (−4%)

1. Established by the merger between Dai-Ichi Kangyo Bank, Fuji Bank and Industrial Bank of Japan. The name of the financial holding company is Mizuho Holdings Inc.
2. Established by the merger between Sumitomo Bank and Sakura Bank.
3. Established by the merger between Bank of Tokyo, Mitsubishi Bank, Mitsubishi Trust & Banking and Nippon Trust & Banking.
4. Established by the merger between Sanwa Bank, Tokai Bank and Toyo Trust & Banking.
5. Established by the merger between Daiwa Bank and Asahi Bank.
6. Established by the merger between Chuo Trust & Banking and Mitsui Trust & Banking.
7. Numbers in brackets are the percentage changes from the figures as of end-March 2002.
Source: Fitch Ratings (2003), Van Rixtel et al. (2003) and own calculations.

Current Situation in the Japanese Banking Sector

The most dominant problems in the Japanese banking sector are the continuing heavy burden of nonperforming loans, other asset problems and low capital adequacy ratios. These problems have been ongoing since the burst of the "Bubble" economy in the early nineties and, although a careful recovery may be observed recently, convinced the IMF to conclude in its Financial System Stability Assessment published in September 2003 that ". . . the financial system remains fragile, and that a more comprehensive and accelerated approach is required to restore the health of the financial system" (IMF (2003), p. 1). It is clear that the actions of Japanese banks in the context of these problems are strongly intertwined with their reaction to the development and implementation of the New Basel Capital Accord, and therefore attention to the specifics of the current problems in the Japanese banking industry will be paid here (see also: Bank of Japan (2003d) and (2003e); Fitch Ratings (2003); Goldman Sachs, 29 May 2003; Hanazaki and Horiuchi (2003); IMF (2003); ING Financial Markets (2003); JP Morgan Securities (2003b), (2003c), and (2003d)). Because of limitations of space, in many instances we will refer largely to the relevant literature regarding the banking problems in Japan. This is also done against the background of providing additional information on the impaired banking system in Japan, which in our view is important to be able to assess fully the possible impact of Basel II on Japanese banking.

The problems in the Japanese banking sector become very clear when looking at the yearly growth rates of various balance sheet items of the seven large financial groups presented in Table 2. Basically all financial groups saw their total assets and loans fall from end-March 2000 to end-March 2003, and in particular their capital base (in terms of equity) was eroded significantly. In addition, five out of seven groups experienced a decrease in the total amount of deposits. Regarding securities' holdings, as registered on their investment accounts, the picture is somewhat mixed, reflecting more bank-specific conditions and policies, as certain banks increased their positions (i.e., Sumitomo Mitsui, Mitsubishi Tokyo, UFJ, and Resona), whereas the remaining banks, in particular Sumitomo Trust & Banking Co., decreased their securities investments. Another indicator for the soundness of a bank is its rating of financial strength such as published by various rating agencies. Such ratings published by Moody's lay in the case of Japanese banks between D– and E+, whereas for the banking systems of the G-7 countries the average ratings lay between A– and C+ (source: IMF (2003), p. 14).

PROBLEM OF NONPERFORMING LOANS. As is shown in Table 3, the absolute amount of nonperforming loans for all banks as published by the Financial Services Agency (FSA) has been reduced significantly from Yen 43.2 trillion as of end-March 2002 to Yen 35.3 trillion as of end-March 2003, a remarkable decline of almost 19% in one year. However, this figure is almost the same as the 2001 figure, thus indicating that basically the net increase or flow in bad loans that developed between March 2001 and 2002 has been eliminated, but that the high stock or level of bad loans reported two years ago still needs to be addressed.[7] Given this situation, Japanese banks will have to continue to take significant loan losses and make adequate provisions. Furthermore, Table 3 shows that the reduction in nonperforming loans was heavily concentrated at the group of the major banks, and that bad loan disposal at regional banks basically did not reduce the stock of bad loans over the past three years. The Bank of Japan recorded in its report on the results of Japanese banks for Fiscal Year 2002, which was released in August 2003, that "... the level of nonperforming loans removed by major banks was historically high, and the pace of removal was faster than that set by the government" (Bank of Japan (2003d), p. 24). Moreover, in October 2003 is observed regarding Japanese banks that "... their lending attitudes seem to be becoming slightly more accommodative in areas such as terms and conditions for loans" and "... the lending attitudes of financial institutions as perceived by firms in general are improving somewhat, although those perceived by small firms remain severe" (Bank of Japan (2003e), p. 16). More optimistic views (and effectively somewhat downplaying the concerns raised by the IMF and certain academic circles in particular) are to find among private sector banking and financial analysts in Tokyo, most of whom have revised their expectations upwards.[8] This optimism is based on

---

7. The total amount of "nonperforming loans" in the Japanese financial was estimated at Yen 237 trillion by Goldman Sachs in 2002 (see The Banker January 2003).
8. According to figures published by Goldman Sachs, Japanese banks resolved more nonperforming loans in the second half of fiscal year 2002 than in the full fiscal year 2001. For other (some somewhat more, others somewhat less) positive views, emphasizing that the resolution of Japan's bad loan problems is entering its final phase, see for example: Nikko Citigroup (2003a); JP Morgan Securities, 20 October 2003, ING Financial Markets (2003), Fitch Ratings (2003), Goldman Sachs, 29 May 2003.

reported declines of new bad loans, increased loan work outs and high growth rates of loan sales in the course of 2003. On the one hand, this development highlights a tougher attitude on behalf of the FSA—in particular regarding the major banks—and increased purchases of bad loans by the Resolution and Collection Corporation (RCC), on the other hand an increased willingness of banks to resolve their bad loan situation and repay public fund injections, partly in order to mitigate dependence on government support and the attached conditions of business restructuring and revitalization programs. The increased pressure of the FSA on banks under minister Takenaka, in combination with a change towards more independent auditing in Japan, have been emphasized as being the main factors behind the bail-out of Resona Bank in May 2003 (see Asian Wall Street Journal, 6 August 2003). The collapse of Resona Bank was effectively initiated by its auditors, who could not accept the amount of deferred tax assets (DTAs) the bank had put on its accounts. As we will see later, these assets are a main part of Japanese banks' Tier 1 capital, and thus the auditors' rejection of Resona's calculated amounts of claimed DTAs forced it into insolvency and de facto nationalization.[9]

Table 3. The status of nonperforming loans for all banks according to the Financial Reconstruction Law[1]
(end of period values; in Yen trillion)

	NONPERFORMING LOANS BASED ON THE FINANCIAL RECONSTRUCTION LAW[1]		
	As of March 2001	As of March 2002	As of March 2003
City banks, long-term credit banks and trust banks[2]	20.0	28.4	20.7
Of which the major 11 banks[2,3]	18.0	26.8	20.2
Regional banks[4]	13.6	14.8	14.7
Total of all banks	33.6	43.2	35.3

9. Resona's collapse and subsequent bail-out have been discussed extensively in for example IMF (2003) and JP Morgan, 28 May 2003, JP Morgan, 11 June 2003, Fitch Ratings (2003), JP Morgan Securities, 15 October 2003, Financial Times, 27 October 2003.

Table 3. The status of nonperforming loans for all banks according to the Financial Reconstruction Law (cont.)[1]
(end of period values; in Yen trillion)

	NONPERFORMING LOANS BASED ON THE FINAN-CIAL RECONSTRUCTION LAW[1]		
Cooperative financial institutions	9.4	9.2	9.2
Total of all deposit-taking financial institutions	43.0	52.4	44.5

1. Financial institutions that are declared bankruptcy are excluded; figures for "non-performing loans based on the Financial Reconstruction Law" are the sum of the assets classified as "bankrupt/de facto bankrupt," "doubtful," and "special attention."
2. Figures of nonperforming loans for UFJ Bank include those transferred to UFJ Strategic Partner Co., Ltd.
3. "Major 11 banks" stand for city banks, long-term credit banks and trust banks, excluding Shinsei Bank and Aozora Bank.
4. "Regional Banks" include Saitama Resona Bank.
Source: Financial Services Agency, various issues of "The Status of Nonperforming Loans as of end-March" (see *http://www.fsa.go.jp/indexe.html*).

Over the past 10 years, many initiatives have been developed by the Japanese authorities in order to solve the bad loans problem.[10] The most recent steps include the following, some of which have been interpreted as a signal of a toughening regulatory policy stance regarding the banks (Japanese Bankers Association (2003b); IMF (2003)). The FSA introduced in October 2002 the so-called "Financial Revitalization Program" (or "Takenaka Plan" named after the minister for financial services) which main objective was to half the bad loan ratio by fiscal year 2004.[11] This program paved the way for the establishment of the Industrial Revitalization Corporation of Japan (IRCJ) in May 2003. Its main aim is to provide assistance to revitalize "revivable" corporations by purchasing the loans made by banks to these corporations. Furthermore, the program introduced a new inspection scheme, addressed provisioning by banks and introduced discounted cash flow (DCF) methodology, and, in order to develop better governance at Japanese banks, proposed the audit of capital levels by external experts from fiscal year 2003 onwards. The adoption of the DCF method by all major banks and some regional and Second

---

10. For an overview, see Van Rixtel (2002), Chapter 6.
11. For more specific details on this plan and the political dimensions, see for example The Banker (2003a) and CSFB, 2002.

Tier regional banks in fiscal year 2002 has been strongly welcomed by the BoJ as a positive step ". . . to build a framework for more appropriate evaluation of loans" (Bank of Japan (2003d), p. 23). In the course of 2003, the FSA conducted so-called "special inspections" which resulted in specific actions being taken by individual banks such as accelerating their bad-loan disposal (see for example CSFB, 2003b). In April of the same year, the FSA announced measures for increased governance at banks receiving public support and set new guidelines for the conversion of preferred stocks (CSFB (2003a)). In September 2003, the FSA announced to expand its budget for injections of public money into undercapitalized banks by Yen 2 trillion (Nikkei Net, 11 September 2003).

Based on the results form the special inspections and subsequent regulatory instructions, banks, which had received public funds in the past, disclosed their revised financial revitalization plans in September 2003 which set targets for profitability, capital adequacy ratios and restructuring until fiscal year 2006 (CSFB (2003c); Morgan Stanley (2003c); FSA (2003b)). Subsequently, 626 regional banks and credit associations submitted business improvement plans to the FSA in October as well. Regarding developments at individual major banks[12], Sumitomo Mitsui Banking Co., which has the largest bad debt burden of the major banks, announced in October 2003 to sell Yen 1 trillion of nonperforming loans to an investment fund established by Goldman Sachs and other firms. UFJ Bank formed a joint venture with Merrill Lynch for the same purpose. The Bank of Tokyo – Mitsubishi reported that it had halved its bad-loan ratio to 4% at the end of September 2003, a year and a half earlier than the end-March 2005 target date set by the government under its financial revitalization program. The bank had announced in February its intention to raise capital through a public share offering, the first one of a Japanese bank in 13 years (The Economist (2003)). Sumitomo Trust and Banking has made it clear to hope to be the second large bank to meet this target, and announced its intention to repay fast the Yen 200 billion capital injection which it received from the government in 1999. One of the two remaining long-term credit banks, Aozora Bank, announced its intention to sell Yen 400 billion in bad loans to the government over three years. The major banks in particular seem to speed up the disposal of bad loans and the return of (not cost-free) government capital injections in order to

---

12. Based on various reports obtained through the Nikkei Net system.

avoid higher interest rate payments and government interference with their business, and many of them have established specialized companies or units to dispose of bad loans.

OTHER ASSET PROBLEMS. Another asset problem of Japanese banks has been their significant exposure to price developments in capital markets, in particular to stock and bond prices, resulting from their substantial holdings of both types of securities. Based on the figures presented in Table 2, it can be calculated that securities holdings (investment account) as a percentage of total assets at end-March 2003 for the four largest financial groups—Mizuho, Sumitomo Mitsui, Mitsubishi Tokyo, and UFJ—were 18.3%, 23.7%, 25.7%, and 23.2%, respectively. According to Table 4, as of end-March 2003, the total amount of stock holdings of major Japanese banks was Yen 18.4 trillion, and their total combined bond portfolios amounted to Yen 62.2 trillion. Compared with end-March 2002, stock holdings were down by 35% and bond-holdings up by almost 20%. A similar development, although less pronounced, can be observed for the regional and Second Tier regional banks. Their stock and bond portfolios were Yen 4.8 trillion and Yen 46.0 trillion, down 20% and up 7% respectively (see Table 5). As the risk weights for stocks are much higher than for bonds, the reduction in stock holdings and increase in bond holdings during FY2002 significantly lowered the total amount of risk-weighted assets of Japanese banks, as is shown in Chart 1.

Due to the adoption of mark-to-market accounting, price changes affecting the valuation of stock and bond portfolios directly affect the banks' capital position (Van Rixtel (2002)). Evidently, this is particularly a problem when stock prices fall and long-term interest rates rise at the same time. And, of course, even when interest rates fall, the gains on bond portfolios may be insufficient to compensate for stock losses. For example, during FY 2002, the net realized stock-related losses of Japanese banks totaled Yen 3.9 trillion yen, whereas net realized bond-related gains due to lower long-term interest rates amounted to Yen 0.8 trillion, a net difference in losses of almost Yen 3 trillion (see Bank of Japan (2003d), pp. 16–17). Furthermore, the amount of unre-alized capital gains on securities holdings is important as well, for example given their relationship to Tier 1 and 2 capital (see Section 4).

Table 4. Assets of major banks

	FY 1998	FY 1999	FY 2000	FY 2001	FY 2002
Loans and bills discounted	324.494 (−8%)	308.465 (−5%)	303.651 (−2%)	285.155 (−6%)	261.355 (−8%)
Investment securities	81.358 (−8%)	91.050 (12%)	122.989 (35%)	101.948 (−17%)	106. 161(4%)
Government bonds	18.328 (−10%)	29.220 (59%)	53.143 (82%)	43.326 (−18%)	53.144 (23%)
Other bonds	8.950 (−11%)	8.378 (−6%)	8.495 (1%)	8.509 (0.2%)	9.018 (6%)
Stocks	38.667 (−2%)	39.203 (1%)	36.974 (−6%)	28.409 (−23%)	18.438 (−35%)
Securities loaned	260 (−59%)	141 (−46%)			

Source: Bank of Japan.
Note: Other bonds include local government bonds and corporate bonds. Figures in brackets are annual percentage changes.

Table 5. Assets of regional banks and Second Tier regional banks

	FY 1998	FY 1999	FY 2000	FY 2001	FY 2002
Loans and bills discounted	191.305 (0.0%)	184.895 (−3.4%)	182.591 (1.3%)	180.633 (−1.1)	178.303 (−1.3%)
Investment securities	44.761 (2.3%)	49.528 (10.7%)	56.008 (13.1%)	57.758 (3.1%)	60.429 (4.6%)
Government bonds	13.910 (8.3%)	16.769 (20.6%)	19.500 (16.3%)	21.928 (12.5%)	23.636 (7.8%)
Other bonds	19.028 (10.0%)	19.951 (4.9%)	20.849 (4.5%)	20.941 (0.4%)	22.323 (6.6%)
Stocks	6.312 (−3.5%)	6.212 (−1.6%)	7.390 (19.0%)	5.974 (−19.2%)	4.753 (−20.4%)
Securities loaned	97 (25.97%)	87 (−10.3%)	2 (−97.7%)		

Source: Bank of Japan.
Note: Other bonds include local government bonds and corporate bonds. Figures in brackets are annual percentage changes.

Regarding the exposure of Japanese banks to developments in the stock market, it has become official government policy to reduce the amount of stock holdings by banks. This mainly for two reasons: firstly, to reduce the effects of stock price fluctuations on banks' capital positions and, secondly, to unwind the extensive

Chart 1. RISK-WEIGHTED ASSETS OF JAPANESE COMMERCIAL BANKS

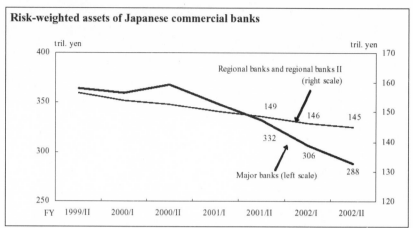

Risk-weighted assets of Japanese commercial banks

cross-shareholdings between banks and nonfinancial corporations that characterized for so long the Japanese economic system.[13] In order to achieve these goals, the following policy measures have been taken (among others: IMF (2003); JBA (2003b)). First, parliament passed a law in November 2001 that restricted stock holdings of banks to no more than their respective Tier 1 capital as of end-September 2004, with a maximum grace period of two years. Second, under the same law, the government established in January 2002 the Banks' Shareholdings Purchase Corporation which main function was to assist banks in meeting the stock holdings restriction in time by buying shares. The Law was amended in July 2003 to make it easier for banks to sell stocks to the Corporation by easing conditions, such as abolishing an 8% contribution (fee) requirement for banks to the stock purchases. These conditions attached to the Corporation's operations had made the scheme not very successful. Third, the Bank of Japan started its own stock-purchasing scheme in November 2002, by acquiring stocks from banks with stock portfolios in excess of their Tier 1 capital (see Chart 2). In September 2003, the Bank announced the extension of its program by one year. As a result of the two share-purchasing programs, the major Japanese banks managed to reduce their stock holdings from Yen 28.4 trillion at end-March 2002 to Yen 18.4 trillion at end-March 2003 (see also

---

13.   See Baba et al. (2002) for a statistical overview of the unwinding of cross-shareholdings in the Japanese economy. The importance of these holdings has been reduced substantially since the early nineties. JP Morgan (2003c) reported that the unwinding of cross-shareholding had passed its peak.

Table 4). The major banks are also reducing their cross-shareholdings with regional banks, which could have strategic implications for the structure of the Japanese banking system. Chart 3 shows that banks had almost met the target of lowering their stock holdings to the amount of Tier I capital already at the end of fiscal year 2002 (end-March 2003). However, it has to be acknowledged, following the IMF, that this target ". . . is still an unusually large exposure for a bank to have to the equity market" (IMF (2003), p.18).

Chart 2. Stock purchases scheme of Bank of Japan
(amounts purchased; billion of Yen)

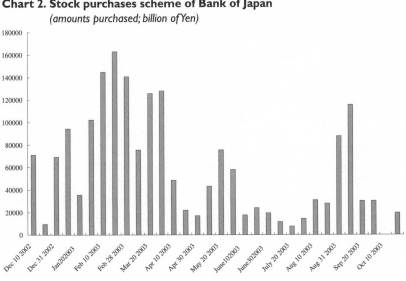

Source: Bank of Japan

The reduction in Japanese banks' exposure to the stock market that has been achieved, however, has not been effectuated for the bond market as well. As has been reported above, bond holdings by Japanese banks have been steadily increasing over the past years (see Tables 4 and 5). Thus, Japanese banks, in particular the major banks, have experienced a significant increase in their interest rate risk exposure. A positive factor in this respect has been the relatively low average duration of Japanese banks' bond portfolios, which has been estimated by various investment banks between 3.5 and 4 years (Goldman Sachs (2003W), 17 June 2003; interview ING Financial Markets, October 2003). Table 6 shows that the duration of the total bond portfolio as estimated by

Chart 3. STOCKHOLDINGS AND TIER I CAPITAL LEVELS OF LARG-EST JAPANESE BANKS

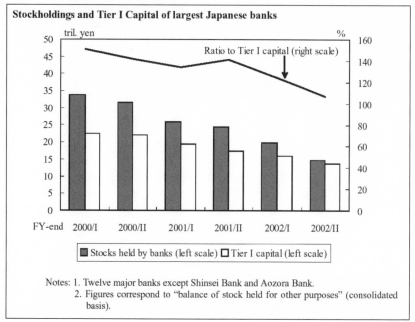

Stockholdings and Tier I Capital of largest Japanese banks

Notes: 1. Twelve major banks except Shinsei Bank and Aozora Bank.
2. Figures correspond to "balance of stock held for other purposes" (consolidated basis).

Goldman Sachs was the highest for Mitsui Trust Holdings with 6.4 years, and the lowest for Resona Holdings with 2.7 years. The average duration of the bond portfolios of the major Japanese banks was estimated at 4 years.

Table 6. Estimated duration of bond portfolios of major Japanese banks (as of end-March 2003; number of years)

	JGBS	LOCAL GOVT. BONDS	CORPO-RATE BONDS	OTHERS	TOTAL
Mizuho Financial Group	3.7	6.1	3.5	5.5	4.3
Sumitomo Mitsui Financial Group	3.4	5.4	3.5	5.4	3.9
Mitsubishi Tokyo Financial Group	3.3	3.4	2.4	4.9	3.9
UFJ Holdings	3.4	6.3	3.9	4.7	3.8
Subtotal	3.5	4.9	3.3	5.1	4
Resona Holdings	2.6	5.3	2.3	2.8	2.7
Sumitomo Trust & Banking	1.7	5	3.4	6	4.5
Mitsui Trust Holdings	6.3	4	3.1	7.6	6.4

Table 6. Estimated duration of bond portfolios of major Japanese banks (as of end-March 2003; number of years) (cont.)

	JGBS	LOCAL GOVT. BONDS	CORPO-RATE BONDS	OTHERS	TOTAL
Mizuho Trust & Banking	3.6	5.4	2.9	3.7	3.7
Subtotal	3.6	5.1	2.7	5.6	4
Total	3.5	4.9	3.2	5.2	4

Source: Goldman Sachs (2003W, 17 June 2003).

Thus, the price sensitivity of bond portfolios of Japanese banks can be interpreted as relatively low, and thus developments in bond markets will have relatively modest valuation effects in terms of unrealized and realized profits and losses. Although this is true, it has been reported by Standard & Poor's that Japanese banks have increased longer-term maturity bonds in their portfolios in order to achieve small improvements in their interest rate margins, given the very low levels of interest rates (see S&P (2003b)). Thus, even if the duration of these portfolios has been low, it may have increased over the past two years compared to historic levels. On the other hand, it has to be acknowledged that bond market dynamics can change rapidly: for example, during April and May 2003, large banks were net sellers of long-term bonds and net buyers of short-term paper, effectively reducing the duration of their portfolios (JP Morgan Securities (2003a)).[14] As the experience of these months showed, the combination of high bond market volatility and high bond holdings can lead to significant increases in risk-levels for Japanese banks, and endanger their capital position, forcing them to reduce their bond holdings rapidly which may result in higher market volatility and interest rates.

The large combined stock and bond holdings of the major Japanese banks have resulted in significant equity and interest rate exposures. Stress testing in the context of the IMF's Financial System Stability Assessment showed that the Japanese banking system is quite sensitive to a combination of specific market developments. The IMF concluded that ". . . measured by the

---

14. During the same period, regional banks and Second Tier regional banks were net buyers of long-term bonds, thus increasing their duration. Thus, between the various sectors of the banking system the degree of interest rate risk exposure may differ significantly, which would seem to offer possibilities of risk-sharing mechanisms.

loss-bearing capacity of shareholders' equity, the Japanese banking system is undercapitalized relative to the interest rate, equity price, and credit risks in the system" (IMF (2003), p. 19).

WEAK CAPITAL BASE BUT STABLE SOLVENCY RATIOS. The burden of nonperforming loans and the related loan losses and provisions, and losses on securities' holdings, in particular stock holdings, have eroded the capital base of Japanese banks (see for example: Hoshi (2001); Kashyap (2002); Van Rixtel (2002); Fitch Ratings (2003); Hanazaki and Horiuchi (2003); IMF (2003)). As is shown in Table 7, the capital levels of internationally active Japanese banks—i.e., the major Japanese banks—decreased from around Yen 47 trillion at the end of March 1999 (FY 1998) to almost Yen 25 trillion at the end of March 2003 (FY 2002), a decline of 47%. However, since their risk-weighted assets decreased by 45% during the same period, their risk-weighted capital adequacy ratios maintained relatively stable and significantly above 8%. The reverse situation can be observed at the smaller, i.e., not internationally active banks, which experienced a steady increase of both regulatory capital and risk-weighted assets. In terms of risk-weighted assets, the 26% decrease for the major (internationally active) banks in FY2002 and the 21% increase for the smaller (i.e., noninternationally active) banks in the same year is remarkable.

Table 7. Risk based capital adequacy ratio—all banks

	FY 1998	FY 1999	FY 2000	FY 2001	FY 2002
Capital adequacy ratios (consolidated risk-based) of internationally active banks	11.02%	11.79%	11.05%	10.63%	10.50%
Regulatory capital	46.617	43.369 (−7%)	40.700 (−6%)	33.677 (−17%)	24.671 (−27%)
Tier I capital	26.352	24.353 (−8%)	23.445 (−4%)	18.378 (−22%)	13.679 (−26%)
Risk-adjusted assets	422.789	367.697 (−13%)	368.125 (0%)	316.735 (−14%)	234.834 (−26%)
Consolidated risk-based capital adequacy ratio of banks not active internationally	6.70%	8.38%	9.57%	9.44%	8.52%
Regulatory capital	7.998	12.878 (61%)	14.625 (14%)	15.557 (6%)	17.033 (9%)

Table 7. Risk based capital adequacy ratio—all banks (cont.)

	FY 1998	FY 1999	FY 2000	FY 2001	FY 2002
Tier I capital	5.934	8.907	10.479	10.966	12.017
		(50%)	(18%)	(5%)	(10%)
Risk-adjusted assets	119.260	153.582	152.818	164.729	199.770
		(29%)	(−0.5%)	(8%)	(21%)

Source: Bank of Japan.
Note: For each period, figures for internally active banks and banks not active internationally at the time of the survey are compiled separately on a consolidated basis. Figures in brackets are annual percentage changes.

An issue that received considerable attention in the course of 2003 was the importance of deferred tax assets (DTA's) in Japanese banks' Tier 1 capital (see for example: FSA (2003a); Fitch Ratings (2003); Goldman Sachs, 31 July 2003 (2003a); Hanazaki and Horiuchi (2003); IMF (2003); Risk (2003a); Standard & Poor's (2003a)). This was not the least because of their role in the fall and subsequent bail-out of Resona Bank and the widespread believe that if Resona's auditors' criteria would be applied to other major banks, most of them would instantaneously turn out to be under-capitalized or even insolvent. This because at the major banks, as is shown in Chart 4, deferred tax assets account for more than half of their Tier 1 capital.

DTA's are basically tax credits against loan-loss provisions made for nonperforming loans, and are based on the future reductions in taxes that banks will receive when the doubtful borrower will actually default. Thus the realization of DTA's depends on two crucial assumptions: first, banks must generate taxable income in the future—i.e., they must generate sufficient profits and thus have sufficiently high earnings projections—and second, the bad loans for which provisions have been made must actually go bad and become irrecoverable. Another structural weakness of DTA's as bank capital is their sensitivity to stock-market developments. As has been reported in Goldman Sachs, 31 July 2003 (2003a), just like unrealized losses on stock holdings result in deferred tax assets, unrealized gains on stock holdings create deferred tax liabilities. In other words, rising stock-market prizes lead to lower net DTA's, and thus erode DTA's in the capital base of Japanese banks. In Japan, the government changed the accounting rules in March 2000 to allow banks to register DTA's on their accounts and to include them in their Tier 1 capital. Thus, as stated by Hanazaki

CHART 4. BREAKDOWN OF TIER I CAPITAL OF JAPANESE COMMERCIAL BANKS

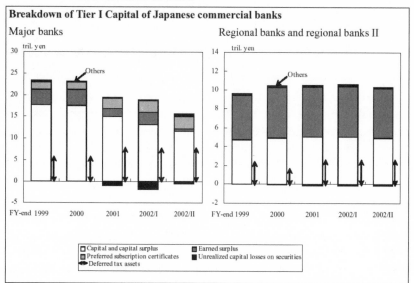

and Horiuchi (2003), p. 323, ". . . as of March 2000, the banks' capital had increased quite abruptly due to this accounting reform." Given the high uncertainty surrounding the economic value of DTA's, their effective use as bank capital has been questioned severely. In certain countries, such as Hong Kong and Korea, banks are not allowed to include DTA's in their capital at all (S&P (2003a), p. 1). In the United States, the use of DTA's in bank capital is restricted to the lower amount of 10% of Tier 1 capital or one year's profits (IMF (2003a)). Under the guidelines of the Japanese Institute of Certified Public Accountants , the amount of DTA's that can be used as Tier 1 capital is limited to expected profits over the next five years, and the extent to which they are actually used must be approved by the banks' auditors. The Institute also requests in its guidelines that deferred tax assets be estimated with caution, thus giving considerable discretion to auditors in estimating a bank's capital, and consequently raising the uncertainty about the amount of Tier 1 capital in the Japanese banking system. In reaction to the DTA discussion, the FSA has required that banks disclose the specific profit assumptions on which their DTA calculations are based. This was based on the conclusions of the Working Group on Regulation of Capital Adequacy Ratio, which focused on the use of DTA's as bank capital in particular and published its findings in July 2003. Its most important conclusion was the ". . . broad agreement over the recognition that the ratio of deferred tax assets against capital should be reduced in the future" (FSA (2003a)).

4. LESSONS FROM THE PAST: BASEL I AND JAPANESE BANKS

The original Basel Capital Accord has been discussed extensively in Japan and some observers have interpreted this framework as a conspiracy of certain Western banks in order to halt the international expansion of the relatively undercapitalized Japanese banks (see for example: editorial Nihon Keizai Shimbun, 9 June 2003). According to the Accord, internationally operating banks would have to meet a capital to weighted assets ratio of eight percent by the end of 1992. The Japanese Ministry of Finance interpreted this date as the end of Fiscal Year 1992 (i.e., the end of March 1993), and that it would be applied to internationally operating banks only (see Hall (1992) and (1993)).[15] For domestic banks, i.e., banks with no international offices, the 8% requirement was later lowered by the MoF to only 4%. In the case of Japan, up to 45% of banks' latent gains on securities holdings were allowed to be counted as Tier 2 capital. According to the Anti-Monopoly Law, Japanese banks could hold up to 5% of the equity of a single firm. Given the rise in share prices during the so-called "Bubble" period, these cross-shareholdings embodied substantial revaluation reserves, and consequently the unrealized gains on these securities holdings were included in Tier II capital (Frankel and Morgan (1992), p. 588). Since banks had acquired the stocks of corporations a long time ago as part of maintaining long-term business relationships, unrealized capital gains were "hidden" from the balance sheet in accordance with Japanese accounting standards. However, the burst of the "Bubble" in the early nineties and the sharp drop in stock prices eroded this part of Japanese banks' Tier II capital rapidly, raising concerns among Japanese and international supervisory authorities. The slump in the Japanese equity market caused equity portfolios increasingly to become a factor of instability for the banks' financial health. From 1991 to 1992, the

---

15. The IMF has stated that all Japanese banks should be subject to the 8% requirement. The claim of Japanese authorities that the Basel Capital Accord applies to internationally active banks only is refuted by the Fund, as it states that this terminology is not defined in the Accord. See IMF (2003), p. 23. Furthermore, the IMF argues that the practice of including provisions made for certain doubtful loans (loans that "need attention" and "need special attention") in Tier 2 capital is not in line with the Basel Capital Accord.

revaluation reserves were halved, resulting in a significant worsening of the solvency position of the Japanese banking sector. In addition, the drop in stock prices made it virtually impossible for Japanese banks to issue new equity (as a matter of fact, not a single Japanese bank has issued new stocks for the past 12 years). Furthermore, the stock market's slide led to soaring unrealized losses on the banks' balance sheets, which have to be deducted fully (100%) from Tier 1 capital. Japanese banks reacted by issuing substantial amounts of subordinated debt that counted as Tier 2 capital, and which were largely absorbed by connected Japanese insurance companies (Hanazaki and Horiuchi (2003)). As we will see later, this process started to exacerbate "double gearing" problems, as banks and insurance companies increasingly provide each other with capital.

Regarding existing research on the effects of Basel I on Japanese banking, Ito and Sasaaki (2002) conclude that the Accord had a significant impact on Japanese banking behavior, because as stock prices decreased, banks with low capital ratios decreased the provision of loans as well. As a result, the market for subordinated debt became increasingly important. Montgomery (2001) argues that the stricter capital adequacy requirements that were introduced caused a contraction in loan growth in the Japanese economy. Using a panel of Japanese banks balance sheets for the fiscal years 1992 to 1999, this study found that the minimum capital requirement of 8% increased the sensitivity of total loan growth to capitalization for international banks operating in Japan. However, this effect was not found for the domestically operating banks that had to comply with the 4% capital adequacy requirement. Horiuchi and Shimizu (1998) reject the capital crunch hypothesis for Japanese banks, as they claim that the issuance of subordinated debt compensated for declines in capital, helped by the existence of long-term relationships inherent to the structure of Japanese banking and economy. Investigating the stock market effects of the adoption of risk-based capital requirements on international banks in different countries, Cooper et al. (1991) found mixed evidence—based on actual developments in banks' stock prices—regarding the perceived effect by financial markets of Basel I on Japanese banks. This result is explained by uncertainty that may have existed among investors regarding the treatment of hidden reserves, and by substantial differences of opinion between market experts on the impact of the Capital Accord on Japanese banks.

Finally, against the background of the banking crisis in Japan over the past 10 years—a period when Basel I was effectively in place—some have questioned the effectiveness of the Basel framework for countries that have banking systems characterized by the existence of long-term relationships (Hanazaki and Horiuchi (2003)). These authors claim that accounting indicators such as capital adequacy requirements are not that useful in relationship banking systems, because information asymmetries between insiders and outsiders make it for the insiders (i.e., the banks) relatively easy to disguise actual bad loan problems, bank loans become "opaque" and stated capital levels become relatively meaningless. They point at the fact that the three major banks that collapsed at the height of the Japanese banking crisis—Hokkaido-Takushoku Bank, Long-Term Credit Bank of Japan and Nippon Credit Bank— had published capital ratios well above 8% just prior to their collapse (9.3%, 10.4% and 8.2% respectively). The same pattern can be observed in the case of Resona Bank, which, as we have seen, was rescued by the Japanese government in May 2003. As a matter of fact, it has been argued by many that the existence of various types of long-term relationships in the Japanese economic system, such as relationship banking ("main bank" system) and the large informally organized industrial conglomerates ("Keiretsu"), made it relatively easy for Japanese banks to hide bad loans in various affiliated companies and promote non-transparency to the maximum extent possible (see Van Rixtel (2003)). In this respect, it should be noted that nontransparency and nondisclose have characterized for many years the banking system and supervisory behavior in Japan, which, at times, reinforced skepticism about the true value of official reported figures of bank health and performance.[16] Again, this pattern can be observed in the case of Resona Bank's failure, as media reports have started to emerge that its actual problems are much larger than previously assumed (see for example Financial Times, 11/12 October 2003, and 27 October 2003).

---

16. See in this respect also the problems the IMF faced in conducting stress tests for its Financial System Stability Assessment of Japan in 2003 (Financial Times, 24 October 2003).

5. THE FORMAL REACTION OF JAPANESE BANKS TO THE NEW BASEL ACCORD

A large number of organizations, including individual banks, banking associations as well as rating agencies from major countries, have expressed publicly the view that the Basel Committee on Banking Supervision's new proposals are very restrictive. In this section, a summarized overview of the major issues that have been raised by the Japanese banking industry and their representative bodies is presented. No attention will be paid to the specific comments on the proposed treatment of securitization under the New Capital Accord, which will be discussed in Subsection 6.2.1. The official reactions of these organizations to the Basel Committee's various consultative papers are listed on their respective homepages and the homepage of the Committee itself. Japanese institutions that provided comments over the past few years have been the following: Japanese Bankers Association, the Regional Banks Association of Japan, The Second Association of Regional Banks, the National Association of Shinkin Banks, the Shinkin Central Bank, the Norinchukin Bank, Sumitomo Mitsui Banking Corporation and the Japan Center for International Finance (see list of references for specific documents). In the overview presented here, the focus will be on their responses to the Committee's Third Consultative Paper (CP3).

Regarding the comments on Pillar 1, one common opinion expressed is that the new framework of the internal rating-based (IRB) approach should be simplified, so that banks can implement the regulatory requirements more efficiently. The Norinchukin Bank expressed that the requirements should be translated into more flexible schemes that can be used to evaluate risk measures taken within the actual operation of banks' internal rating methodologies. The bank mentioned stress testing as one specific effective tool to deal with pro-cyclicality concerns. The Japanese Bankers Association argued in favor of simplifying the credit-risk framework and adopting a more flexible interpretation that takes into account the actual (high) costs of developing computer systems and altering operational procedures. More in general, it has been highlighted that banks have to manage considerable swings in capital requirements due to business cycle developments and will face increased volatility in their capital charges because of certain restrictions which the New Accord imposes upon the use of capital management tools. Thus, the general pro-cyclicality criticism that Basel II does not smooth cyclical effects regarding capital requirements is supported (*Financial Times*, 12 September 2003; The Banker, 1 October 2003). Furthermore, Japanese banks expressed concerns regarding the significant burden imposed by transitional measures and the requirements regarding the stipulations for estimating loan given default (LGD) and exposure at default (EAD) under Pillar 1. The minimum holding periods of seven years for both LGD and EAD related data and five years for probability of default (PD) data are claimed to be excessively long, particularly at the beginning of the implementation of the New Accord.

As regards Pillar 2 of Basel II, Japanese banks argued that the supervisory review process imposes a significant burden on bank capital requirements. In addition, the double standard regarding capital adequacy regulations, as emphasized by Norinchukin Bank, will lead to an increase in overall regulatory capital needs. It is feared that after the proposed measures under Pillar 2 have been implemented, the authorities may raise capital requirements, which could even contradict or invalid calculations of capital needs made under Pillar 1.

Finally, the Japanese banks and their organizations stressed the need for further simplification of Pillar 3. They acknowledged that the scope of the third Pillar has been considerably narrowed in CP3 in comparison with the Second Consultative paper (CP2). However, it is argued that some disclosure requirements continue to be defined vaguely, which constitute important legal and operational uncertainties for the banks involved. Regarding Pillar 3, further simplification, including taking into account the work in this respect of the International Accounting Standards Board (IASB) is proposed. All in all, the position of Japanese banks and their associations regarding CP3 addressed predominantly certain peculiarities with respect to practical and operational issues of the New Capital Accord, and not so much fundamental disagreement with its basic structure. The Basel II draft accord will have to be completed by mid-2004, and Japanese institutions hope to be able to reach a final agreement on the outstanding issues that takes into consideration their specific wishes.

6. THE TACTICAL AND STRATEGIC IMPLICATIONS OF THE NEW BASEL ACCORD FOR JAPANESE BANKING

The section investigates the likely impact of the development and implementation of the New Basel Capital Accord on Japanese banks' business practices and the structure of the Japanese banking system. The main source of information for this analysis is formed by the series of (15+6) interviews conducted during the period September–November 2003, augmented by information from academic and policy-institutions' research, industry reports and media sources.

The analysis distinguishes between so-called *tactical* and *strategic* implications of Basel II on Japanese banking. *Tactical* implications relate to the day-to-day business operations of Japanese banks and how their operational framework may be affected (micro-dimension). The investigation has generated as possible main tactical consequences of the new Capital Accord the adoption of a new business model based on risk management tools, the erosion of the "main bank" system and relationship banking, the reorientation of retail and wholesale banking activities, the acceleration of the disposal of bad loans and the negative impact on the competitiveness of Japanese banks in derivatives business. *Strategic* implications focus on the structure of the banking system as such and the development of financial markets and services. The analysis concludes that Basel II—in its current form—could hamper the development of securitization in Japan, will be a catalyst for the development of the Japanese syndicated loan market, will also function as a catalyst for the further development and use of risk-transfer instruments, could put pressure on smaller financial institutions in the segmented Japanese banking system, might be a catalyst for the emergence of more market-based credit markets and could have important macroeconomic consequences that might have profound consequences for the Japanese banking system. All in all, most interviewees expected that Basel II predominantly will function as an important catalyst and that its main impact will not be so much felt in the short run (1–2 years), due to the priority of tackling the bad loan and undercapitalization problems first, but much more, and significantly so, in the medium run (3–4 years, just before and around implementation of the New Accord) and the long run (after implementation).

It is clear that this analysis is surrounded by a significant degree of uncertainty. First, the definite and steady-state form of the New Basel Capital Accord is—as of November 2003—not clear yet.

Industry reactions to CP3 have been quite numerous and often critical in substance and thus may lead to more or less important changes of the Accord. Second, Basel II allows for a considerable degree of national discretion in defining and applying specific elements of the Accord, and it is not certain yet how Japanese supervisory authorities will use this discretion. Three, it is also not fully clear yet which specific option for assessing credit risk under the New Accord—i.e., the standardized approach or one of the two internal ratings-based (IRB) models—Japanese banks will adopt. Most likely, as expected by market analysts, several major banks will opt for the advanced IRB option, but the majority of Japanese banks will follow the standardized approach.

Regarding the overall impact of the New Basel Capital Accord on Japanese banking, according to the summarized testing results of the 66 Japanese banks participating in QIS3 which have been published by the Financial Services Agency (FSA) and Bank of Japan (BoJ) on their websites, it is not to be expected that the Accord will affect significantly the capital adequacy levels of Japanese banks (see Bank of Japan (2003c) and (2003d)). The results show that under the standardized approach the risk-weighted assets of these 66 banks will likely be reduced by 2% and their capital adequacy ratio will improve by around 0.1% (see: Bank of Japan (2003), BIS Q&A report). This basically because of the mutually offsetting effects of on the one hand higher capital requirements for nonperforming loans and on the other hand lower capital charges for retail activities (i.e., for consumer loans, mortgages and loans to small- and medium-sized enterprises). Furthermore, capital charges stemming from operational risk requirements will be relatively modest for Japanese banks, given their low net operating revenues. These effects estimated by the supervisory authorities are supported by private sector research. Estimates of Morgan Stanley show that for the four large financial groups (Mizuho, MTFG, SMFG and UFJ), risk-weighted assets could decrease between 0.5% and 2.2%, and capital adequacy ratios may improve between 0% and 0.2%.[17] For five large regional banks (Chiba, Fukuoka, Shizuoka, Suruga and Yokohama) the impact may be larger: risk-weighted assets may decrease between 1.8% and 8.4%, and capital ratios could improve between 0.2%

---

17. Preliminary results provided by Mr. Hideyasu Ban, Equity Research Japan (Banks), Morgan Stanley, October 2003.

and 0.9%. So, all in all, these projections show that the direct overall impact of Basel II on risk-weighted assets and (risk-based) capital adequacy ratios of particularly the largest banks may be relatively modest.

Tactical Implications

ADOPTION OF A NEW BUSINESS MODEL. The possible impact of the New Basel Capital Accord on Japanese banking that was mentioned the most frequently by interviewees was that it would function as a very important catalyst for the further introduction of a new business model. This model would be in line with more sophisticated market-conform and incentive compatible business models based on risk-return considerations and incorporating state-of-the-art risk management tools. In this sense, the Accord will function as a catalyst for further reform of day-to-day business operations, particular in the sense of greater emphasis on risk-management considerations, in addition to the guidance from the FSA and BoJ and pressure from financial markets. In the past, specialized credit officers often looked at one specific risk only, but, partly due to Basel II, this is changing now, and a much more integrated approach of the various risks is followed. Thus, the New Accord will accelerate risk management on a consolidated basis. Japanese banks have often been criticized for not paying sufficiently high attention to risk-management aspects, but several interviewees were strongly convinced that this will fundamentally change under the looming introduction of the new Capital Accord. It is clear that under Basel II, banks that will have the most advanced capital and risk-management tools and modeling capabilities will be among the winners, as they will be able to use the advanced IRB approach. However, some interviewees stressed that the large banks in Japan, which are the most likely candidates to adopt the advanced approach, are facing considerable data-problems, particular regarding loss given default (LGD) that is difficult to estimate under Japanese bankruptcy proceedings. Furthermore, under relationship banking and the "main bank" system (see next subsection), also the probability of default (PD) may be difficult to estimate. This could frustrate the adoption of the advanced approach by the major Japanese banks. Nevertheless, several other interviewees were convinced that the four large financial groups would finally adopt the advanced IRB model, given international competitive pressures.[18]

Information on the specific preparations of Japanese banks in their business models for the introduction of the New Accord is relatively scarce and hard to specify. Some interviewees stated that most major Japanese banks have started to hire significant numbers of external, often foreign, consultants to develop risk-management systems, and are spending considerable amounts of resources on this. Others were more skeptical in this respect and pointed at the, in their view, generally relatively worrying state of computer and database systems at Japanese banks. Regarding specific preparations, it was reported in January 2003 that the UFJ Group intended to introduce a leading edge internal rating system in order to benefit from the specific credit risk approaches proposed under Basel II (Nikkei Net, 23 January 2003). With respect to other preparatory actions, some interviewees pointed at investigations currently undertaken by various large financial groups on which specific amount of capital could be saved by further consolidations of business activities of the various groups' subsidiaries. Regarding the operational risk requirements under the new Accord, interviewees stressed that these have become a major consideration for most Japanese banks only during the past few years, mainly because of the development of the Basel II framework.

Regarding day-to-day business, some interviewees expressed the view that Japanese banks may be forced to allow for greater autonomy in credit decisions of local branches, and thus adopt a more decentralized decision-making framework, due to greater emphasis on risk-return considerations .

EXPECTED EROSION OF THE "MAIN BANK" SYSTEM. A clear majority of interviewees expressed their conviction that the introduction of the New Basel Capital Accord will lead to a gradual erosion of the "Main Bank" system in Japan. Under this informally organized system, Japanese banks have been operating as monitors—also on behalf of other lenders—of large numbers of commercial firms. Even firms that do not belong to one of the large industrial groups that dominate the Japanese economy (Keiretsu) normally maintain an informally based relationship with a (large) commercial bank (see Aoki et al. (1994)). In other words, following the

---

18. One interviewee believed that only one financial group would choose the advanced approach, and expressed serious doubts if the three others would be ready in time.

terminology of Diamond (1984), the "Main Bank" system functions as a delegated monitor for the Japanese capital market as a whole. It bas been claimed that this function is especially relevant when borrowers are in situations of severe financial distress (Sheard (1994), p. 86), although more recently the specific importance of the "Main Bank" system has been disputed (see Miwa and Ramseyer (2001)). Basically, the system can be interpreted as a more extreme version of relationship banking (see Boot and Thakor (2000)). Kobayashi et al. (2002) document very clearly that so-called "forbearance lending" took place in Japan after the collapse of the "Bubble" economy, under which banks were very reluctant to write off bad loans as they were concerned about the possible negative effects on long-term customer relationships, even when there was little prospect that the loans could still be recovered. Brewer III et al. (2003) show that (long-term) banking relationships in Japan have apparently been so important that the failure of several banks at the height of the banking crisis not only affected their client firms but the rest of the Japanese economy as well. However, a number of interviewees highlighted that under the "Main Bank" system, maintaining long-term relationships with borrowers—apparently sometimes at high costs—resulted often in inefficient and basically economically unsound lending decisions from the perspective of risk-return considerations. Therefore, this custom will most likely, slowly but steadily, become less significant as a result of Basel II, in combination with other factors such as the decreasing importance of cross-shareholdings in the Japanese economy in general and the reduction of stock-holdings by the major banks in particular, and the advance of new lending models in Japanese banking (for the latter see Subsection 6.2.5). The decreased emphasize on long-term relationships could also reduce the practice of "double gearing" involving mutual capital stakes between banks and (life) insurance companies, effectively hampering the possibility of banks to issue subordinated bonds which count as Tier 2 capital.

The likely impact of the New Basel Capital Accord on "Main Bank" relationships and relationship banking involves also important political economy aspects. In a paper published on its website in March 2003, the FSA strongly emphasized the need to maintain long-term banking relationships for smaller banks with respect to small- and medium-sized enterprises (SME's). On the one hand, this would be a relatively cheap way for the banks involved to obtain important credit-related information that would facilitate estimating credit risk in the more risk-based credit decision-making framework under Basel II. On the other hand, several market analysts argued that it would mitigate political concerns that SME's would be squeezed, in particular when the new Accord would be implemented.

GREATER EMPHASIS ON RETAIL BANKING. Not surprisingly, several interviewees expressed the view that the development and introduction of Basel II will increase the focus on retail banking, given the relatively favorable treatment of this activity under the New Accord. This could lead to a substantial increase in the level of competition in the Japanese banking sector, not only between individual banks, but in particular between the various banking segments as well. As has been discussed in Section 3, still considerable degrees of specialization in Japanese banking exist between various sectors. Some interviewees were convinced that when the bad loan situation is resolved, the major banks will try to capture important market shares of the regional banking business, with its dominance of retail activities in specific geographical regions. A strong winner here could be the Mitsubishi Tokyo Financial Group, given its strong balance sheet and its well-established ties with several regional and Second Tier regional banks. Over the past two years, retail banking activities such as consumer and housing loans have been growing substantially in Japan, whereas wholesale banking such as lending to major corporations has been on a steady downward trend. It has been reported that the combined loans of the around 160 largest banks to individuals were above Yen 100 trillion for the very first time as of 30 September 2002, and that also housing loans have increased quite substantially (Nikkei Net, various reports). Although it is rather difficult to specify to what extent Basel II is playing a role here, some interviewees believed that also here it could be playing the role of catalyst.

ACCELERATION OF THE DISPOSAL OF BAD LOANS. As has been explained in Section 2, the New Basel Capital Accord will have huge implications for the capital adequacy ratios of banks with large amounts of nonperforming loans. That is, the capital ratios of these banks may decline significantly, particularly in cases where insufficient provisions have been made. Dependent on the degree of provisioning, the risk weight for problem loans will increase: the lower the degree of provisioning, the higher the specific risk weight applied. For example, the risk weight of problem loans will increase to 563% when no provisions for these loans have been made at all. The study conducted by the FSA and BoJ for a sample group of 66 banks showed that the average risk weight applied to their problem loans would be 157% (Nikkei Net, 25 August 2003). According to the same study, for some individual banks their overall risk-weighted assets may increase by 10 to 20% as a result of the implementation of Basel II (Nikkei Net, various reports).

This leads to the rather straightforward conclusion that Japanese banks better accelerate the disposal of their bad loans and have them reduced substantially before the implementation of the New Accord. Various interviewees stated that this is exactly what Japanese banks are doing now (as discussed in Section 3), and that Basel II is playing a role. Of course, several other forces play an important role here as well, such as the increased pressure of the FSA on the major banks to resolve their bad loans and the aim of Japanese banks to limit government interference with their business, which was the price they had to pay for receiving public capital injections. In this respect, it should be noted that the BoJ, regarding the results of the study involving 66 banks which showed a very modest impact of Basel II on risk-weighted assets and capital rations, has clearly stated that these results are conditional on the banks' bad loan disposal: "It is expected that Japanese banks will not face any difficulties with respect to the implementation of the New Capital Accord if they are committed to deal with the disposal of their nonperforming loans by the end of fiscal year 2006" (own translation, Bank of Japan Q&A paper, 2003).

NEGATIVE IMPACT ON COMPETITIVENESS OF JAPANESE BANKS IN DERIVATIVES BUSINESS. Finally, the last tactical implication of Basel II on Japanese banks that has been identified was the possible negative impact of the treatment of foreign exposure (counterparty risk) on derivatives business. Credit risk exposures of foreign banks to Japanese banks could be charged with higher risk weights, both under the standardized approach and the IRB approach. This because these weights are related to the ratings of Japanese banks as one option under the former and may be even higher in the internal risk ratings of foreign banks under the latter approach (JP Morgan Securities, 31 January 2001). Given the importance of interbank credit exposures in the derivatives business, this could to some extent affect negatively the competitiveness of Japanese banks in derivatives.

POSSIBLE POSITIVE IMPACT OF THE USE OF RATINGS FROM JAPANESE RATING AGENCIES. One private sector analyst expressed that Japanese banks could have a competitive advantage because of the enhanced importance of ratings from private sector rating agencies under Basel II. Namely, it has been claimed that the ratings of the two main domestic Japanese rating agencies, i.e., JCR and R&I, have been more lenient for Japanese banks then the ratings from the main international operating agencies such as Moody's, Standard & Poor' s and Fitch Ratings (see also JP Morgan Securities, 31 January 2001). Because banks may use the highest rating in case there are two or more ratings available, this could lead to reduced capital needs for Japanese banks.

Strategic Implications

ON THE ONE HAND: IN GENERAL, HAMPER THE DEVELOPMENT OF SECURITIZATION IN JAPAN. The New Basel Capital Accord introduces internationally harmonized regulations regarding the supervisory treatment of securitization activities. These activities have developed enormously since the introduction of the original Capital Accord. Under Basel I, banks often used securitization to lower effective capital requirements, whereas at the same time credit risk was not reduced (Jones (2000); Deutsche Bundesbank (2001); Federal Reserve (2003)). This practice of regulatory arbitrage (see Section 2) will be frustrated severely by Basel II, as in the proposed framework the rules for securitization will become much stricter.[19]

---

19. Of course, it needs to be seen to what extent financial innovations will undermine in practice the goal of Basel II of effectively reducing regulatory arbitrage. Because of the greater use of securitization instruments, such as certain derivatives and asset-backed securities, and the related increase in certain risks, some have argued that capital ratios of 8% are too low to effectively cover for these risks (see Gup (2003)). Regarding the impact of risk-based capital requirements on the development of securitization, Jagtiani et al. (1995) could not find a consistent impact of these requirements on the speed of diffusion across banks' off-balance-sheet activities. See also Donahoo and Shaffer (1991).

As regarding the perceived impact of the New Basel Capital Accord on the securitization market in Japan, a significant majority of interviewees agreed that its development could be hampered by the implementation of Basel II. This, first, because of certain legal and practical peculiarities of securitization in Japan, which in the view of several interviewees are not satisfactory taken into account in the Basel II proposals. Second, interviewees emphasized that the market for securitization in Japan is still in its early stage ("infant industry" argument), and that the necessary catch-up with the major overseas markets may be thwarted by the implementation of the New Accord. Third, the concern was raised that the treatment of securitization under Basel II will provide nonbanks, i.e., foreign nonbanks, a competitive edge vis-à-vis banks in Japan. Finally, interviewees feared that the stipulations concerning securitization may frustrate significantly the development of related new financial instruments and techniques (financial innovations) (see also Jacobo Rodriguez (2002)). To a large extent, the concerns raised by the interviewees, of whom many were not employed by Japanese banks, follow the official comments on securitization of Japanese banking institutions and organizations on the various consultative papers published by the Basel Committee. Therefore, the published reaction of Japanese banks on the securitization proposals will be discussed first. Subsequently, an overview of the Japanese securitization market will be presented. Then, the possible consequences of the Basel II proposals are analyzed for the various segments of the securitization market in Japan.

The Japanese Bankers Association (JBA) and six overseas financial industry groups submitted proposals in August 2003 to the Basel Committee aimed at mitigating concerns about the negative implications of the New Capital Accord for the securitization market. Under the current proposals, banks active in securitization could be faced with a rather substantial increase in their risk-weighted assets and consequently their capital adequacy rules could fall. In addition, separately the JBA discussed securitization aspects in its formal and published reactions on the various consultative papers published by the Basel Committee, which was also done by the Norinchukin Bank and Sumitomo Mitsui Banking Corporation. Their main concern was the "infant industry" argument mentioned above, i.e., the asset securitization market in Japan is still underdeveloped, so that Basel II could adversely impact its future development. The issues raised by these institutions addressed mainly six requests: lowering of the risk weights for securitization instruments, permission to use private ratings, more favorable treatment of liquidity facilities under Asset Backed Commercial Paper Programs (ABCP), less severe treatment of banks that provide so-called "implicit recourse," adoption of a more positive approach towards the securitization of own-bank assets, and the permission of early amortization.[20] The first request entails that the risk weights for securitization instruments need to be reduced, since the risk weights of these instruments that hold the same credit rating as corporate instruments are higher, both under the standardized approach and the internal ratings-based (IRB) approach. Especially the criteria regarding below-investment grade (BB+ or below) securitization instruments differ substantially from those for corporate instruments, and therefore it is requested that these risk weights should be lowered. Regarding the second request, it is argued that private ratings (i.e., non-disclosed ratings) should be permitted in parallel to public ratings, which is against the current proposal of the New Accord that private ratings do not qualify. Although the JBA agreed that there are differences between published and nonpublished ratings, it argued that there is no essential difference in the calculation and monitoring processes of these ratings themselves. This view is supported by Rating & Investment Information (R&I), one of the two leading local rating agencies in Japan (R&I (2003)). This company stated that historically, few individual financial transactions have been published in Japan. Therefore, it proposed that in Japan private ratings and published ratings should be treated equally until further development of financial markets has been established and the general use of public ratings is accepted. As

---

20. The treatment of securitization under Basel II is a highly technical exercise beyond the scope of this paper. A very good overview of the issues is provided in Kothari (2003a). Regarding Japan, only the main issues will be described briefly.

regards the third request, i.e., the more favorable treatment of liquidity facilities under ABCP programs, under the 1988 Basel Capital Accord, a bank that supports ABCP conduits (i.e., Special Purpose Companies (SPC) or Entities (SPE) involved in the securitization process), and of which it has guaranteed the payment of principal by providing liquidity support, does not have to make risk-related provisions. However, this will change under the New Basel Capital Accord, as risk weights applied to liquidity enhancements of ABCP conduits will be generally be set at 100%. Sumitomo Mitsui Banking Corporation (SMBC) requested in its official comments that this application of a uniform risk weight of 100% should not be adopted. The Norinchukin Bank regarded the treatment of liquidity facilities as excessively stringent and asked for a review based on the actual risks related to these facilities. The JBA criticized the treatment of eligible liquidity facilities under the IRB approach, since the assignment of risk weights is different. All in all, the concern of these organizations is that, since in Japan securitization is still in the development stage, Basel II should not hamper the development and market position of the specific securitization instruments and practices which are currently most predominantly used. The other requests are explained briefly. As regards the issue of implicit recourse, applying excessive penalties to banks which are found to have provided implicit recourse would be harmful to the development of the market. From the perspective of being the originator of a securitization product, Japanese banks requested that the securitization of a bank's own assets should at least not increase a bank's regulatory capital requirement. It is also emphasized that under loan participation practices in Japan, the removal of assets from a banks' balance sheet is recognized as an off-balance-sheet item under Japanese accounting standards. Furthermore, Japanese banks criticized the stipulation under Basel II that early amortization in the context of securitization should not be allowed, because they regard this as discriminatory treatment. For example, credit-linked notes and similar products do have provisions for early amortization, for example because of prepayment of the underlying assets (see Kithara (2003a)).

Most requests mentioned above are views related to banks being active in securitization transactions as originators and sponsors. However, requests and questions regarding the treatment of banks being investors in securitization products were also raised by Japanese banking organizations. For example, the Norin-chukin Bank requested that the higher risk weights applied to securitization assets acquired should be brought in line with the treatment of corporate bonds.

Regarding the actual development of the securitization market in Japan, it has been growing quite rapidly during the past several years and is now the third largest market in the world. However, in terms of size, as is shown in Table 8, it is still far behind the U.S. and European Union.

Table 8. Comparison of issuance activity in the securitization and syndicated loan markets in 2002 (in Yen trillion)

	SECURITIZATION MARKET	SYNDICATED LOAN MARKET
Japan	5	15
The United States	334	116
European Union	20	64

Source: Bank of Japan, Market Review, "*Kurejitto Sijyo Kaikaku to Nihon Ginko no Torikumi,*" ("Credit markets reform and the achievement of the Bank of Japan"). Note: ABCP is excluded from the figures for the securitization market.

The differences in size can be explained by the fact that the various more advanced segments of credit markets such as the syndicated loan market, nonrecourse loan market, securitization market and credit derivatives market were until recently not very well developed in Japan. New issuance of securitization products in Japan in 2002 amounted to about Yen 5 trillion, which is much smaller than the Yen 334 trillion in the same year in the United States. However, the size of the Japanese market has been growing steadily during recent years, which is shown in Tables 9, 10, and 11. Residential Mortgage Backed Securities (RMBS) and Collateral-ized Debt Obligations (CDOs), which mainly consist of Collateral-ized Bond Obligations (CBOs) and Collateralized Loan Obliga-tions (CLOs), appear to hold the greatest promise among the various market segments. Furthermore, products related to the real estate sector, such as Commercial Mortgage Backed Securities (CMBS), could also see increased activity as a result of the securi-tization of nonrecourse loans. In addition, government-affiliated financial institutions are expected to make greater use of securiti-zation techniques as well (Deutsche Bank (2003)). Issuance vol-ume in the first half of 2003 has clearly been supported by the CDO sector, mainly by originating banks which have been using them to reduce their risk-weighted assets (Nikkei Net, 23 July 2003). The share of banks' issuance in the total amount of securitized products issued rose to 42% in 2003, from 26% one year earlier (see Table 10). This process will be discussed in more detail in the next subsection.

Table 9. Japanese securitization products (according to underlying assets)
(in percentages)

	EQUIPMENT LEASES	CREDIT RECEIVABLES	CONSUMER LOANS	RMBS	CMBS	CDO	OTHERS
2001 Jan.–Dec.	0.242	0.161	0.153	0.14	0.174	0.068	0.062
2002 Jan.–Dec.	0.187	0.1	0.132	0.206	0.127	0.143	0.104
2003 Jan.–Sep.	0.125	0.111	0.059	0.184	0.088	0.307	0.127

Table 10. Originators of Japanese securitization products (breakdown by industry)
(in percentages)

	CONSUMER CREDIT (SHINPAN)	LEASING	BANKS	LIFE INSURANCE	GOVERN-MENT AFFILIATED	CONSUMER FINANCE	CAPTIVE FINANCE	NONLIFE INSURANCE	OTHERS, N/A
2001 Jan.–Dec.	0.243	0.221	0.113	0.059	0.062	0.042	0.036	-	0.224
2002 Jan.–Dec.	0.169	0.155	0.258	0.097	0.104	0.057	0.036	0.002	0.123
2003 Jan.–Sep.	0.129	0.115	0.42	0.044	0.091	0.022	0.061	-	0.118

Table 11. Asset-backed securities issuance
(Yen billion; products with long-term credit ratings only)

	EQUIPMENT LEASES	CREDIT RECEIV- ABLES	CONSUMER LOANS	MORT- GAGES	REAL ESTATE	CDO	OTHERS	TOTAL
2000 Jan.–Dec.	646	460.1	69.2	438.6	581.3	126.3	447.4	2,768.9
2001 Jan.–Dec.	836.2	557.9	527.9	484	601.5	234.1	96.9	3,338.5
2002 Jan.–Sep.	931.5	499.1	667.6	1,025.6	590.2	712.7	287.8	4,714.6

Source: Deutsche Bank Group.

However, despite its attractiveness as a financing tool and a vehicle to improve balance sheets, securitization is not still widely used in Japan (see for example Deloitte & Touche (2002)). As is stated in Kanda (1998), there are both legal and nonlegal factors inhibiting the securitization market in Japan. As legal obstacles can be mentioned, first, that compliance with the legal requirements for perfecting an asset transfer is costly, and second, that this requires notarial certification of individual loans. Furthermore, the regulatory structure of the securities industry in Japan is complex and rigid, reflecting a long political history in which various ministries had jurisdiction over specific industries. Non-legal obstacles to the further development of the market for securitization in Japan that can be mentioned are specific regulatory characteristics, political factors, interaction among the various ministries involved and fragmentation of financial markets (see for more details: Ogaki (1996); Kanda (1998)). One positive development has been that recently it has become cheaper to set up a Special Purpose Entity (SPE), which now requires a minimum amount of capital of only Yen 100,000.

Given that the securitization could play a much more important role in financing and risk-hedging activities in Japan, the BoJ has started to support actively the development of this market. In order to contribute to smooth corporate financing, the BoJ has recognized ABCP as eligible collateral and has started purchasing ABCP from February 2002 (Bank of Japan (2003)). From July 2003, the BoJ expanded the range of eligible assets and added asset-backed securities (ABS) backed by housing loan credits and real estate to its eligible collateral (see: Ishiga et al. (2003); Sugihara et al. (2003); BoJ (2003)). Although the BoJ's purchases of ABCP and ABS aimed to promote further growth in the use of these instruments as well, it is feared that the New Basel Capital Accord may thwart this attempt. There are serious concerns that the ABCP market might be downsized due to the implementation of Basel II (Nikkei Net, 26 September 2003). This is because under the New Accord, there are some notable changes to the risk-weightings applied to ABCP, which are regulatory securitized products in Japan. Under the New Accord, these assets can have a maximum risk weight of 200%, compared with 0% under Basel I.

One market participant expected that after the envisaged implementation of Basel II at the end of 2006, due to these heavy weights, the ABCP market in Japan could be halved. In its present proposal, the Basel Committee has come to realize that so-called liquidity support to ABCP conduits might actually be serving as a credit enhancement mechanism (Kothari (2003a)). Unless this treatment has been modified, it is to be expected that the Japanese ABCP market will be affected negatively by the implementation of the New Capital Accord.

In reaction to the proposed treatment of ABCP under Basel II, Mizuho Corporate Bank has issued Yen 100 billion in ABCP without back-up lines, and also other banks have started to plan issuing ABCP without repayment guarantees (Nikkei Net, 8 July 2003). This because under the New Capital Accord, some part of the commercial paper issued by banks with repayment guarantees will be considered being risk-weighted assets, and thus lower banks' capital adequacy ratios. Furthermore, the BoJ announced in October 2003 that it would review the specific problems of the Japanese securitization market in order to promote its growth, and to that purpose, it established a study group (so-called "Securitization Forum") in November 2003 (Hirata and Shimizu (2003); Nikkei Net, 26 October 2003). Thus, it seems that not only market participants but also the supervisory authorities are concerned about the negative impact of Basel II on the development of the securitization market in Japan.

All in all, there was widespread concern among both interviewees and the banking institutions that reacted formerly to the Basel Committee's proposals that, given the underdeveloped nature of the securitization market in Japan and, as was discussed above, the existing legal and nonlegal problems that obstruct its rapid development, the introduction of the New Capital Accord could seriously hamper the expansion and deepening of the market for securitization in Japan. Thus, because the relatively underdeveloped nature of securitization in Japan, Basel II could turn out to be a heavy blow to this young market.

The strong growth of the securitization market in Japan in the course of 2003 has been heavily influenced by the use of credit-risk related securitization instruments by banks to reduce their risk-weighted assets and credit-risk exposure in the context of resolving their balance sheet problems (see Table 10 and in more detail Subsection 6.2.2). In this respect, there is a clear and direct connection with the bad loan problems. It has been argued by many that securitization could be an excellent tool to solve or mitigate the nonperforming loan problems in Japan (see for example: Herr and Miyazaki (1999); Deloitte & Touche (2002); Euromoney, 15 May 2002).[21] Thus, if the New Basel Capital Accord would affect negatively the market for securitization in Japan, then the contribution of this instrument to resolving the bad loan problems would be affected negatively as well. Of course, it is difficult to calculate the net effect, as the use of securitization instruments under the proposed framework of Basel II will be more heavily charged with capital. Thus, on the one hand, securitization could mitigate capital needs by reducing bad loans and risk-weighted assets; however, on the other hand, most likely the use of these instruments itself would lead to higher capital charges.

ON THE OTHER HAND: MORE SPECIFIC, CATALYST FOR THE DEVELOPMENT OF RISK-TRANSFER INSTRUMENTS. Contrary to the general negative impact of the New Capital Accord on securitization, in the view of a considerable number of interviewees the use of specific securitization instruments which aim at the transfer of credit risk could actually be promoted by the Accord, because of the greater emphasis on (capital) risk-management and credit risk considerations in Basel II. As expressed by one interviewee, the keyword for Japanese banks in the context of Basel II is risk-transfer, which is now possible due to the introduction of new technologies and

---

21. Specialized securitization products have been developed by (foreign) investment banks, which aimed at contributing to resolving the bad loan situation. An example is the introduction of nonperforming loan-backed commercial mortgage-backed securities (NPL-backed CMBS), see JP Morgan (2001).

financial engineering. This applies in particular to the use of credit derivatives, but also to various kinds of Collateralized Debt Obligations (CDOs) which were discussed in the previous subsection.[22]

Regarding the use of credit derivatives in the Japanese banking sector, the total amount of credit derivatives' contracts increased from USD 13.95 billion at end-December 2002 to USD 22.91 billion at end-June 2003, a staggering increase of 64% in six months (see Table 12). This was fully due to the growth in the use of credit default swaps with 75%, in particular the amount of contracts bought which increased by 87%. Thus, Japanese banks were buying protection against credit risk exposure in particular, in the context of their considerable balance sheet problems. Some market analysts expressed the view that Basel II considerations could have played a role, although minor, as well. Although the use of credit derivatives may be affected negatively by Basel II as well, which is related to the specific definition that will be used in the case of default,[23] the expectation is that the combined impact of the resolution of the bad loan problems in Japan in parallel with the implementation of Basel II will stimulate the further development of these instruments.[24] This particularly so given that credit derivatives could be used as effective buffers to mitigate procyclicality concerns, which may be relevant for Japan (see Subsection 6.2.6).

---

22.   Credit derivatives are swap, forward and option contracts that allow one party (protection buyer or originator) to transfer credit risk of a reference asset, which it may or may not own, to one or more other parties, without actually transferring the ownership of the underlying asset (Kothari (2003b); Kiff and Morrow (2000), p. 3). The three major types of credit derivatives are credit default swaps (CDS), which are the most important category, total return swaps and credit-spread put options. In addition, they can be embedded in credit-linked notes, which are a securitized form of credit derivatives. See also Merrill Lynch (2003) and Barclays Capital (2003). See for Japan: Ito and Harada (2003).
23.   In CP3, the Basel Committee mitigated to a considerable extent these concerns: "The Committee has decided to make a significant change to the credit risk mitigation framework after extensive and fruitful consultation with the industry."
24.   Hiwatashi and Ashida (2003) emphasize the need for more effective risk transfer methods, which are being developed by insurance companies. These new products could be used to cover a wide range of operational risks.

Table 12. Credit Derivatives Contracts (in millions of USD)

Credit Derivatives	Jun-99	Dec-99	Jun-00	Dec-00	Jun-01	Dec-01	Jun-02	Dec-02	Jun-03
Total OTC Contracts	11,159	16,538	14,691	13,281	14,309	17,432	16,363	13,951	22,914 (64%)
Credit Event / Default Swaps (Sold and Bought)	10,230	12,831	12,248	11,698	12,815	15,127	14,442	12,446	21,727 (75%)
Credit Event / Default Swaps (Sold)	5,173	3,388	3,259	3,599	4,275	4,357	6,250	4,557	6,973 (53%)
Credit Event / Default Swaps (Bought)	5,057	9,443	8,989	8,099	8,540	10,770	8,192	7,889	14,754 (87%)
Total Return Swaps (Sold and Bought)	338	2,707	1,630	956	888	1,269	973	443	377
Total Return Swaps (Sold)	65	1,289	459	0	19	175	175	411	0
Total Return Swaps (Bought)	273	1,418	1,171	956	869	1,094	798	32	377
Credit Spread Products (Sold and Bought)	36	16	0	0	0	0	6	15	21
Credit Spread Products (Sold)	36	16	0	0	0	0	3	8	10
Credit Spread Products (Bought)	0	0	0	0	0	0	3	7	11
Credit-Linked Notes (issuance and purchase)	502	921	731	561	550	1,024	887	992	734
Credit-Linked Notes (issuance)	270	629	591	561	144	0	0	0	0
Credit-Linked Notes (purchase)	232	292	140	0	406	1,024	887	992	734
Others (Sold and Bought)	55	55	82	67	55	12	55	55	55
Others (Sold)	55	55	55	55	0	6	0	0	0
Others (Bought)	0	0	27	12	55	6	55	55	55

Source: Bank of Japan. Historical Data Series on "The Results of the Regular Derivatives Market Statistics in Japan (Yoshikuni Statistics)".

Note: Figures for credit derivatives are available from end-June 1999. Credit derivative figures are not collected by the BIS on a global basis as part of the Yoshikuni Statistics. Figures in brackets are annual percentage changes.

Regarding the use of other instruments that may be used to reduce credit risk exposure of Japanese banks, the use of Collateralized Debt Obligations (CDOs) has been discussed in the previous subsection. One interviewee feared that possibly the negative effects of Basel II on this type of securitization instrument would be more severe than for credit derivatives, which could have some impact on the further development of this market segment. In Japan, the use of Collateralized Loan Obligations (CLOs), which are formally a subset of CDO's, has been growing quite substantially in the course of 2003 in Japan as well, parallel to the growth in credit derivatives, as they provided substantial capital relief for Japanese banks (IFR (2003); Nikkei Net various reports).[25] Table 13 shows that the cumulative issuance volume of CLOs during the first half of 2003 was almost 110% higher than during the first half of 2002. The increase use of CLOs started in the fall of 2002 when Mizuho Corporate Bank used this instrument remove Yen 1.3 trillion worth of loans from its balance sheet. This was followed by similar actions by Sumitomo Mitsui Banking Corporation and UFJ, although smaller in size (Nikkei Net, 3 February 2003). Table 13 also shows that CBOs play a very minor role in Japan and that, although small in size, synthetic CBOs increased dramatically by more than 550%.[26]

Table 13. Collateralized debt obligations in Japan

	2002		2003
	Full year	January-July	January-July
CLOs	374,542	143,800	300,888
CBOs	49,200	49,200	14,000
Synthetic CBOs	280,900	20,900	137,000
Nonperforming loans	19,100	9,600	0

Source: Nikko CitiGroup (2003b).

25. CDOs can be classified according to the various kinds of underlying assets in which they invest such as Collateralized Loan Obligations (CLOs), which are CDOs of leveraged bank loans, Collateralized Bond Obligations (CBOs), which are CDOs of high yield and investment grade bonds, and bank balance sheet CLOs, which are CDOs of investment grade bank loans. See Barclays Capital (2003).
26. Synthetic CDOs can be interpreted as credit derivatives, which transfer risk on entire credit portfolios, and thereby have been very useful for Japanese banks to mitigate their balance sheet problems. See Merrill Lynch (2003). Mizuho Bank introduced Yen 14 billion of collateralized bond obligations in March 2003 (Nikkei Net, 31 March 2003).

**CATALYST FOR THE DEVELOPMENT OF THE SYNDICATED LOAN MAR-
KET IN JAPAN.** Several interviewees expressed the view that Basel II
will stimulate the syndicated loan market in Japan because of the
increased attention for so-called concentration risk under the New
Accord. That is, higher risk weights will be applied to large credit
exposures to individual borrowers then for smaller borrowers.
Thus, banks may want to limit their lending to individual corporate
borrowers, which can be very well achieved in the form of syndicated loans, as they allocate various shares in the total loan among
a large number of lenders. Syndicated loans would also be attractive from the view that they allow banks to maintain customer
relationships, which may be squeezed under Basel II, but remove
the related loans largely from their books.

The amount of syndicated loans extended in Japan in the first
half of fiscal 2003 increased by almost 36% from a year earlier to
USD 64.3 billion, which made the Japanese syndicated loan market
the third fastest growing market in the world, behind France and
Germany (Goldman Sachs (2003c)). As is shown in Table 14,
Mizuho Financial Group has been leading the market and its
amount of syndicated loans reached USD 22.4 billion in the first
half of 2003, followed by Sumitomo Mitsui Financial Group with
USD 20.9 billion during the same period. The four major banks
had a combined total amount of syndicated loans of USD 56.7
billion, or 65.9% of the total Japanese market during 2002.

**Table 14. Amount of syndicated loans at the four major Japanese
banks**

					USD MILLION
Amount	2002 IH	2003 IH	Year on year	2002 full year	as % of 2002
Mizuho	18,510	22,412	21.1	36,038	62.2
SMFG	14,090	20,888	48.3	25,592	81.6
MTFG	6,084	9,590	57.6	17,562	54.6
UFJ	3,067	3,785	23.4	6,795	55.7
Total	41,751	56,674	35.7	85,987	65.9

Source: Goldman Sachs (2003c).

The main factors that promoted the syndicated loan market, in
addition to a possible catalyzing role of the New Capital Accord,
have been as follows. First, major banks saw this market as an
interesting opportunity to collects fees, being the arranging bank,

while reducing their loan concentration risk at the same time. According to the Bank of Japan, the major banks reported a significant increase in fees and commissions during FY200, which largely came from loan syndication and commitment lines as well as mutual fund business and some other activities (Bank of Japan (2003a)). The main participants in these syndicated loans organized by the major banks have been the regional banks and institutional investors, who used this opportunity to establish business relations with borrowers who had been difficult to approach on an individual basis, and broaden their profit capability (Hayami (2002b)). The participation of regional banks is an extremely important development, as it established a much needed increase in the amount of risk-sharing between various Japanese banking sectors. As was discussed in Section 3, the situation of regional banks in terms of balance sheet strength generally has been much better than that of the major banks, and so the growth of syndicated loans has established a much more balanced and sound allocation of credit risk in the Japanese financial system. Second, for companies whose credit ratings are at BBB or below, syndicated loans have been a cheaper way to obtain funds rather than issuing corporate bonds, which allowed them to diversify their corporate financing. A possible third factor that can be mentioned is the announcement of the BoJ to consider purchasing syndicated loans as eligible collateral for its lending operations. As syndicated loans to SME's had been increasing, the BoJ has been studying the possibility of accepting syndicated loans as eligible assets in order to enhance corporate financing and to foster the development of the syndicated loan market (Bank of Japan (2002FFF)).

PRESSURE ON THE SEGMENTED STRUCTURE OF THE JAPANESE BANKING SYSTEM. In the view of a considerable number of interviewees, the New Basel Capital Accord may be an important impetus for structural reform in the Japanese financial system, as the Accord is expected to promote further consolidation in the banking sector. As was discussed in Section 3, the Japanese financial system is still characterized by significant degree of market segmentation, with for example specialized financial institutions for small businesses and agriculture financing. Given the likely move towards greater attention for retail banking activities at the large banks, the smaller banks may get squeezed in the process and feel themselves forced to reconsider their activities and strategies. Various market analysts observed considerable concerns at smaller banks in this respect, although the ultimate net impact may be somewhat mitigated because these banks will also benefit from the lowered risk weights for their traditional business areas such as SME financing. Basel II may also inhibit the further diversification of activities by the large financial groups, which currently do not possess major insurance operations, and may put existing informal relations with the insurance sector under pressure. It has been argued by many that the New Accord will frustrate the continuation of the universal banking and bank assurance models, to a considerable extent because of the introduction of capital charges for operational risk (see for example: Morgan Stanley, 4 June 2003, and 15 July 2003; JP Morgan Securities (2001)). As result, the practice of "double gearing", i.e., banks and life insurance companies providing each other with capital, may have to be reduced significantly.[27]

CATALYST FOR MORE MARKET-BASED CREDIT MARKETS. Furthermore, interviewees saw the introduction of the New Basel Capital Accord as a welcome opportunity to promote in Japan the move towards more emphasis on market-based credit pricing and thus ultimately towards a more efficient allocation of credit at the macro-level. This mainly because under Basel II banks will have to differentiate credit risk much more importantly at the level of the individual borrower than was the case under Basel I. Smith (2002) has shown that loan spreads in Japan are substantially lower, on average, then in the US and major European countries. This study also concluded that Japanese banks reflected differences in credit risk much less in their rates than foreign banks in the Japanese market, i.e., they were ". . . willing to offer lower-priced loans to a riskier set of Japanese borrowers," and did not distinguish between good and bad risks. It is difficult to predict to what extent exactly the New Accord will result in credit risk and credit costs being reflected much more accurately in Japanese lending rates. This would also require a better relationship between the pricing (i.e., economic value) of a loan and the value of the underlying collateral, in other words would require an improvement in collateral management by Japanese banks. In this respect, an important question is whether banks can move from collateral-based lending, characterized by insufficient considerations for fundamental economic values, towards lending more based on risk-return

---

27. The important mutual capital links between Japanese banks and life insurance companies have been criticized in Fukao (2002), BIS (2003) and IMF (2003).

considerations. The need for improvement of lending practices in the Japanese market has been identified clearly in various reports published by the Bank of Japan. For example, Miyauchi (2003) discussed the need for the adoption of a new lending model by Japanese banks, as various factors such as a lack of covenants in loan agreements, credit management based on loan continuation, unclear loss-sharing rules and underdeveloped secondary markets for loan assets, in combination with existing provisioning rules, hinder Japanese banks from acting swiftly against deteriorating loans. Bank of Japan (2003) also argued in favor of the need to change the traditional lending practices of Japanese banks and the importance of discounted cash flow (DCF) methods for establishing the economic value of loans, which Japanese banks started to adopt in FY2002. All in all, several interviewees expressed a careful optimism that the introduction of the New Basel Capital Accord will promote this development towards a more market-oriented lending model in the Japanese credit markets.

MACROECONOMIC IMPACT OF THE NEW BASEL CAPITAL ACCORD. Finally, in addition to the effects on the functioning of the Japanese lending markets and the allocation of credit, there could be other macroeconomic implications stemming from the introduction of Basel II by Japanese banks. The impact of risk-based capital adequacy ratios on macroeconomic variables such as aggregate lending and economic activity has been extensively discussed in the academic community, in particular after the development of Basel I in the second half of the eighties.[28] Regarding the possible effects of Basel II in this respect, it has been argued that the IRB approach will lead to increased volatility and cyclical sensitivity of the minimum capital requirements of banks that choose for this methodology, suggesting the need for dynamic provisioning and capital buffers in order to avoid capital constraints during periods of deteriorating economic conditions (see ECB (2001), p. 64ff). This could pose a significant challenge indeed in the case of Japan, given the high degree of concentration in the Japanese banking market in general and the large market share of the Big Four

---

28. For general studies of macroeconomic implications of risk-based capital adequacy requirements and pro-cyclicality concerns, see for example: Blum and Hellwig (1995); Corcóstegui et al. (2003); Heid (2003). For more specific studies that investigate the impact of these requirements on aggregate lending (credit crunch studies) see: Hall (1993); Berger and Udell (1994); Brinkmann and Horvitz (1995); Peek and Rosengren (1995a); Thakor (1996). For investigation of capital crunch studies, see for example Peek and Rosengren (1995b).

financial groups in particular. If the IRB approach were to be adopted by Japanese banks, it will be among the largest banks. Given their dominant position in the lending market, the increased pro-cyclical impact of the New Capital Accord could exacerbate economic downturns, as the increased capital needs of the banks that adopted the IRB approach may force them to reduce their lending even more. Furthermore, it has been argued, for example by Allan Greenspan, that due to the limited capability of Japanese capital markets to provide backup financing when Japanese banks cannot perform their intermediation role, the Japanese financial system is relatively vulnerable to shocks. As has been documented extensively elsewhere, the Japanese financial system is still characterized by a dominance of bank-based financing. Although the published BIS Q&A mimeograph of the Bank of Japan downplayed the risk of credit-crunch type of situations in relation to Basel II, it needs to be seen what the actual impact will be.

7. CONCLUSIONS

This paper has asserted that the New Basel Capital Accord is an important catalyst in shaping the business practices and structure of the Japanese banking industry in the years to come. This in parallel with other factors such as the resolution of the bad loan problems, the economic recovery and related performance of the stock market, the political climate and the proliferation of political interests, the process of financial innovations and the significance of international competitive forces. Generally, Japanese banks seem to be less worried about the effects of the New Accord on their business then they were at the time of the development and implementation of the Original Accord. This could be explained by the fact that the Accord does not have an impact on the definition of capital, as the numerator of the capital adequacy ratio is not changed. As was shown in Section 3, the capital position of Japanese banks is still weak. If Japanese accounting firms were to adopt the same tough stance as Resona Bank's auditors, one would have to fear for the solvency of several major Japanese banks. However, regarding the definition of capital under Basel II, the door seems not to be fully closed yet. In the September 2003 issue of the Federal Reserve Bulletin, it is explicitly stated that ". . . However, the definition of regulatory capital under Basel II remains under consideration by the Basel Committee" (footnote 5, p. 398).

Furthermore, the implementation of the New Capital Accord may increase to some extent financial stability concerns in the Japanese financial system. For example, the "Bubble" economy was to a large extent caused by increased competition between various sectors in the Japanese financial system due to financial liberalization and financial innovations: when certain groups of financial institutions became squeezed as a result, they engaged more and more in excessive risky lending activities. If Basle II were to effectively establish the same pressures, for example due to increased competition in retail banking activities between segmented industries and markets, attention will have to be paid to avoid that history repeats itself. Furthermore, as has been shown in Section 6, the use of securitization and credit derivatives has grown very fast over a very small period of time. Several bodies, including the BIS, have warned for the inherent risks embodied in the use of these instruments for financial stability, in particular for the risks of credit default swaps (BIS (2003)). One may hope that price of short-term mitigation of credit risk exposure and balance sheet restructuring will not be longer-term instability.

It is clear that Basel II will also have important consequences for the specific operation of national supervisors as well. Under the second pillar of the New Capital Accord—i.e., the supervisory review process—their role is enhanced substantially (see ECB (2001)). They will have to monitor closely the credit risk assessments of banks, which in certain cases will undoubtedly become much more complex, and intervene where deemed necessary. The supervisory authorities will be faced with substantially higher demands in terms of expertise and supervisory capacities in order to be able to exercise the role assigned to them under the second pillar. Although the Japanese banking supervisory authorities have enhanced their capabilities enormously over the past years, both in terms of know-how and numbers of staff, it is not fully clear if not more needs to be done.

Along the same line, it is clear that the IRB approach contains significant subjective elements, for example the calculation of the risk weights based on the banks own internal ratings which need to be approved by the regulatory authorities. Given the high degree of subjectivity, the success of Basel II is directly linked to an objective application of the rules that would establish a level-playing field between banks, both nationally and internationally.[29] A study by Price Waterhouse Coopers among 21 large European banks showed that banks fear big differences regarding the implementation of Basel II by national supervisory authorities, with possible detrimental effects on competitive positions. The subjective character of Basel II is generally not favored by Japanese banks as well, which experienced a substantial degree of supervisory discretion during the height of the recent banking crisis, and see it as an important legal risk.

Finally, given the high degree of subjectivity and judgment under Basel II, it is clear why there is the need for the third pillar of market discipline. If the responsibilities and requirements under the first and second pillars are not effectuated in a correct manner, outside market participants such as rating organizations have to discipline both banks and supervisors. This requires adequate disclosure and transparency practices, and the elimination of discrete and informal legal frameworks which constitute considerable legal risks for the banks involved as well. For anyone who has been following Japanese banking, in particular during the past 10 years, the only conclusion can be that disclosure and transparency were often not promoted and not established effectively (Van Rixtel (2002)).[30] In the past years, the Japanese government in general and the FSA in particular have taken important steps in order to mitigate these concerns, but as has been argued quite persuasively by the IMF, there is still room for improvement (IMF (2003)). In this respect, it will be very interesting to see which specific initiatives will be developed in order to further promote compliance with market discipline, such as the frequency and content of disclosure by Japanese banks.

REFERENCES

Altman, E., and Saunders, A. (2001), "An analysis and critique of the BIS proposal on capital adequacy and ratings," *Journal of Banking and Finance*, 25, pp. 25–46.

Aoki, M., Patrick, H., and Sheard, P. (1994), "The Japanese Main

---

29. Jacobo Rodriguez (1999), p. 15, states that ". . . Basel II leaves so much discretion to national regulators that one could make the case that international capital standards have ceased to exist, even if there is still an international agreement on capital standards."
30. For example, Shrieves and Dahl (1998) concluded that during the period 1989–1996, the discretionary accounting behavior of Japanese banks was instrumental in enabling them to comply with the BIS capital adequacy rules.

Bank System: An Introductory Overview," in Aoki, M., and Patrick, H. (eds.) (1994), *The Japanese Main Bank System: Its Relevance for Developing and Transforming Economies*, Oxford: Oxford University Press.

Asian Wall Street Journal, (2003), "Japanese Bailout Shows How Two Men Unraveled Postwar Financial Ties," August 6.

Baba, N., Nishizaki, K., Inamura, Y., and Shimizu, T. (2002), "Changes in Japan's Financial Structure since the Later Half of the 1990's: the Supply of Risk Capital and Major Market Reforms," *Market Review*, Bank of Japan, January.

Bank of Japan (2003a), "Proposal for a new scheme to promote smooth corporate financing by nurturing the asset-backed securities market," April 8.

Bank of Japan (2003b), "Evaluating the Economic Value of Loans and the Implications: Toward Transformation of the Business Model of Banks and Non-Bank Firms," April 28, mimeograph.

Bank of Japan (2003c), "Purchases of Asset-Backed Securities," June 11.

Bank of Japan (2003d), "Review of Japanese Banks' Activities: Profits and Balance Sheets in Fiscal 2002," August.

Bank of Japan (2003e), "Monthly Report of Recent Economic and Financial Developments – October 2003," October 15.

Bank of Japan (2003aKimie), "Kurejitto Sijyo Kaikaku to Nihon Ginko no Torikumi," (Credit Markets Reform and the Achievement of the Bank of Japan), *Market Review*, 2003-J-7.

Bank of Japan (2003cKimie), "Jiko Shihon ni Kansuru Atarasii Basel Goui, Daiji Sichu Kyougi An no Gaiyo," (The New Basel Capital Accord, Outline of the Third Consultative Paper).

Bank of Japan (200dKimie), "BIS Kisei Minaoshi Dai3ji Sichu Kyougi An: Q&A," (The BIS Criteria Amended Third Consultative Paper: Q&A).

Bank of Japan (2003FFF), "Syndicated Loan no Tanpo Ukeire ni tsuite," September 12.

Bank of Japan (2003VVV), "Proposal for a new scheme to promote smooth corporate financing by nurturing the asset-backed securities market," April 8.

Bank of Japan (2003GGG), "Purchases of Asset-Backed Securities," press release, June 11.

The Banker, (2003a), "Bank loan reform plan hits fierce opposition," January.

The Banker, (2003b), "Latest US move sets the pace for the world," August, pp.22–24.

Barclays Capital (2003), "Guide to Cash Flow Collateralized Debt Obligations."

Barrios, V.E., and Blanco, J.M. (2003), "The effectiveness of bank capital adequacy regulation: A theoretical and empirical approach," *Journal of Banking & Finance,* 27, pp. 1935–1958.

Basel Committee on Banking Supervision (1999), "Capital Requirements and Bank Behaviour: The Impact of the Basle Accord," Working Paper, No. 1.

Basel Committee on Banking Supervision (2001a), "Overview of the New Basel Capital Accord," mimeograph.

Basel Committee on Banking Supervision (2001b), "The New Basel Capital Accord: an explanatory note," mimeograph.

Basel Committee on Banking Supervision (2001c), "Working Paper on the Treatment of Asset Securitisation," October.

Basel Committee on Banking Supervision (2003a), "Bank Failures in Mature Economies," mimeograph.

Basel Committee on Banking Supervision (2003b), "Third Consultative Paper," April.

Basel Committee on Banking Supervision (2003c), "Quantitative Impact Study 3 – Overview of Global Results," May.

Basel Committee on Banking Supervision. (2003d), "Bank Failures in Mature Economies," July.

Basel Committee on Banking Supervision. (2003e), "Press release: Basel II: Significant Progress on Major Issues," October.

Berger, A. N., and Udell, G. F. (1994), "Did Risk-Based Capital Allocate Bank Credit and Cause a "Credit Crunch" in the United States?" *Journal of Money, Credit and Banking,* 26, 3, Part 2, pp. 585–628.

Berger, A.N., Herring, R.J., and Szegö, G.P. (1995), "The role of capital in financial institutions," *Journal of Banking & Finance,* 19, pp. 393–430.

BIS (2003), "Annual Report 2002."

Blum, J., and Hellwig, M. (1995), "The macroeconomic implications of capital adequacy requirements for banks," *European Economic Review,* 39, pp. 739–749.

Boot, A.W.A., and Thakor, A.V. (2000), "Can Relationship Banking Survive Competition?" *Journal of Finance,* Vol.LV, No.2, April, pp. 679–713.

Brewer III, E., Genay, H., and Kaufman, G. (2003), "Banking relationships during financial distress: The evidence from Japan," *Economic Perspectives,* Federal Reserve Bank of Chicago, Third Quarter, pp. 2–18.

Brinkmann, E.J., and Horvitz, P.M. (1995), "Risk-Based Capital Standards and the Credit Crunch," *Journal of Money, Credit and Banking,* 27, 3, pp. 848–863.

Brunner, A.D., and Kamin, S.B. (1998), "Bank Lending and Economic Activity in Japan: Did Financial Factors Contribute to the Recent Downturn?" *International Journal of Finance and Economics*, 3, pp. 73–89.

Calomiris, C., and Mason, J.R. (2003), "How to Restructure Failed Banking Systems: Lessons from the US in the 1930's and Japan in the 1990's," NBER, Working Paper, No. 9624.

Claessens, S., and Embrechts, G. (2002), "Basel II, Sovereign Ratings and Transfer Risk External versus Internal Ratings," Discussion note on the seminar "Basel II: An economic assessment."

Cooper, K., Kolari, J., and Wagster, J. (1991), "A note on the stock market effects of the adoption of risk-based capital requirements on international banks in different countries," *Journal of Banking and Finance*, 15, pp. 367–381.

Corcóstegui, C., González-Mosquera, L., Marcelo, A., and Trucharte, C. (2003), "Analysis of procyclical effects on capital requirements derived from a rating system," Banco de España, mimeograph.

Credit (2001), "Basel: the new Accord," March, pp. 39–42.

Credit Suisse First Boston (2002), "Major banks: The 'Takenaka Plan' to end the NPL problem: Where now?" October 25.

Credit Suisse First Boston (2003a), "Major banks: Announcement of new guidelines for the conversion of preferred stock," April 7.

Credit Suisse First Boston (2003b), "Major banks: FSA announces results of special inspections," April 28.

Credit Suisse First Boston (2003c), "Major banks: Revised financial revitalization plans," September 22.

Credit Suisse First Boston (2003d), "Major banks: Growing awareness at FSA of insufficient reserves against large troubled borrowers," October 30.

Danielson, J., Embrechts, P., Goodhart, C., Keating, C., Muennich, F., Renault, O., and Song Shin, H. (2001), "An Academic Response to Basel II," Special Paper No.130, Financial Markets Group, London School of Economics, May.

Deloitte & Touche (2002), "Speaking of Securitization," Issue 1, Volume 7, April 22.

Deutsche Bundesbank (2001), "The new Basel Capital Accord (Basel II)," *Deutsche Bundesbank Monthly Report*, April, pp. 15–41.

Diamond, D.W. (1984), "Financial Intermediation and Delegated Monitoring," *Review of Economic Studies*, LI, 393-414.

Donahoo, K.K., and Shaffer, S. (1991), "Capital Requirements and the Securitization Decision," *Quarterly Review of Economics and*

Business, Vol.31, No.4, pp. 12–23.

The Economist, (2003), "Japanese banks: The great capital scramble," February 15.

European Central Bank (2001), "The new capital adequacy regime – the ECB perspective," *ECB Monthly Bulletin,* May, pp. 59–74.

Federal Reserve Bulletin (2003), "Capital Standards for Banks: The Evolving Basel Accord," September, pp. 395–405.

Financial Services Agency (2003a), "Progress Report: Working Group on Regulation of Capital Adequacy Ratio," July 28.

Financial Services Agency (2003b), "Reviewed business revitalization plans of capital injected banks (FY 2002 ~ FY 2006)," September.

Financial Services Agency, various issues of "The Status of Non Performing Loans as of end-March."

Financial Times, various issues.

Financial Times, (2002), "IMF 'to show that Japanese banks failing capital test.'" December 20.

Financial Times, (2003), "Industry queries Basel moves," August 1.

Financial Times, (2003), "Basel II rules could damage banks' capital market liquidity, warns SIA," August 10.

Financial Times, 20 August 2003, "Financial institute criticises Basel rules on bank capital."

Financial Times, (2003), "Basel II under fire," August 21.

Handelsblatt, (2003), "Widerstand gegen Basel II wächst," August 21.

Financial Times, (2003), "Basel rules 'could cost €10bn,'" August 25.

Financial Times, (2003), "US regulator voices Basel concerns," September 14.

Financial Times, (2003), "US banks say Basel plan is a threat to high-risk lending," September 15.

Financial Times, (2003), "Credit default swaps take off," September 30.

Financial Times, (2003), "Reform – Changing the industry landscape", Special Report, Banking in Europe, October 8.

Financial Times, (2003), "Basel committee vows to stand by timetable," October 15.

Financial Times, (2003), "Resona 'insolvent' at time of rescue, claims DPJ," October 27.

Fitch Ratings (2003), "Japanese Banks: Results for 2002/3 – Where's the Way Out?" 25 June.

Frankel, A.B., and Morgan, P.B. (1992), "Deregulation and Competition in Japanese Banking," *Federal Reserve Bulletin,* August, pp. 579–93.

Fukao, M. (2002), "Financial Sector Profitability and Double-Gearing," NBER , WP 9368.

Goldman Sachs (2003a), "Japan Banks: Deferred Tax Assets Decline Dramatically as the Equity Market Rises," July 31.

Goldman Sachs (2003b), "Japan Banks: Massive Increase in Loan Work Outs and Equity Sales," May 29.

Goldman Sachs (2003c), "Japan Banks: Reacceleration for syndicated loans," July 23.

Gup, B.E. (2003), "The New Basel Capital Accord: Is 8% Adequate?" mimeograph.

Hall, M. J. B. (1992), "Implementation of the BIS Rules on Capital Adequacy Assessment: A Comparative Study of the Approaches Adopted in the UK, the USA and Japan," *BNL Quarterly Review*, 180, pp. 35–57.

Hall, B. J. (1993), "How Has the Basle Accord Affected Bank Portfolios," *Journal of the Japanese and International Economies*, 7, pp. 408–440.

Hammes, W., and Shapiro, M. (2001), "The implications of the new capital adequacy rules for portfolio management of credit assets," *Journal of Banking and Finance*, pp. 97–114.

Hanazaki, M., and Horiuchi, A. (2003), "A review of Japan's bank crisis from the governance perspective," *Pacific-Basin Finance Journal*, 11, pp. 305–325.

Hanazaki, M., Souma, T., and Wiwattanakantang, Y. (2003), "Silent Large Shareholders and Entrenched Bank Management: Evidence from the Banking Crisis in Japan," mimeograph.

Hayami, M. (2002), "The Challenges Facing Japan's Economy," speech given at the Naigai Josei Chousa Kai, July 24.

Hayami M. (2002b), "Shihon Sijyo no Isso no Hatten ni Mukete—Enkatsu na Kigyo Kinyu wo Support surutameni," (Toward Further Development of Capital Markets—To Support Smooth Corporate Finance,), Speech of Governor, Bank of Japan.

Heid, F. (2003), "Is regulatory capital pro-cyclical? A macroeconomic assessment of Basel II," mimeograph, Deutsche Bundesbank.

Herr, K.E., and Miyazaki, G. (1999), "A proposal for the Japanese non-performing loan problem: Securitization as a solution," mimeograph, April.

Hida, N., Fjita, K., Ihara, M., and Baba, N. (2002), "What do we learn about current developments in the bank lending market in Japan from BOJ's Senior Loan Officer Survey?" *Market Review*, Bank of Japan.

Hirata, H., and Shimizu, T. (2003), "Purchase of SME-related ABS by the Bank of Japan: Monetary Policy and SME financing in Japan," Bank of Japan Working Paper Series, No. 03-E-3.

Hiwatashi, J., and Ashida, H. (2003), "Advancing op risk management using Japanese banking experience," *Operational Risk*, March, pp. 18–22.

Horiuchi, A., and Shimizu, K. (1998), "The deterioration of bank balance sheets in Japan: Risk-taking and recapitalization," Pacific-Basin Finance Journal, 6, pp. 1–26.

Ieda, A., and Ohba, T. (1999), "Risk Management for Equity Portfolios of Japanese Banks," Bank of Japan, *Monetary and Economic Studies*.

IFR Special Report (2003), "Big CLOs may be put on hold," pp. 24–25.

Institutional Investor (2003), "Basel under threat," pp. 24–31.

International Monetary Fund (2003), "Japan: Financial System Stability Assessment and Supplementary Information," IMF Country Report No.03/287, September.

International Financing Review (2003), "Big CLOs may be put on hold."

ING Financial Markets (2002), "Banks: What happens to capital if deferred tax assets are excluded?" April 26.

ING Financial Markets (2003), "Japan's Bad Debt Burden – Getting Lighter," October.

Ishiga, K., Okada, Y., and Kato, T. (2003), "The Bank of Japan's Eligible Collateral Framework and Recently," *Market Review*, Bank of Japan.

Ishikawa, T., Yamai, Y., and Ieda, A. (2003), "On the Risk Capital Framework of Financial Institutions," Discussion Paper No. 2003-E-7, Institute for Monetary and Economic Studies, Bank of Japan.

Ito, T., and Michael, M. (1999), "Japan's Big Bang and the Transformation of Financial Markets," NBER, Working Paper, No. 7247.

Ito, T., and Sasaki, Y. (2002), "Impacts of the Basle Capital Standard on Japanese Banks' Behavior," *Journal of the Japanese and International Economies*, 16, pp. 372–397.

Ito, T., and Harada, K. (2003), "Market Evaluations of Banking Fragility in Japan: Japan Premium, Stock Prices, and Credit Derivatives," NBER Working Paper, No. 9589, March.

Jacobo, Rodriguez (2002), "International Banking Regulation: Where's the Market Discipline in Basel II?" *Policy Analysis* (Cato Institute), No. 455, 15 October.

Jagtiani, J., Saunders, A., and Udell, G. (1995), "The effect of bank capital requirements on bank off-balance sheet financial innovations," *Journal of Banking & Finance*, 19, pp. 647–658.

Jackson, P. (2001), "Bank capital standards: the new Basel Accord," *Bank of England Quarterly Bulletin*, Spring 2001, pp. 55–63.

The Japan Center for International Finance (2001), "Comments on The New Basel Capital Accord."

Japanese Bankers Association (2001), "Opinion paper on the New Basel Capital Accord."

Japanese Bankers Association (2002), "Comments on the Second Working Paper on Securitisation."

Japanese Bankers Association (2003a), comments on CP 3.

Japanese Bankers Association (2003b), "Japanese Banks 2003," September.

Jones, D. (2000), "Emerging problems with the Basel Capital Accord: Regulatory Capital Arbitrage and Related Issues," *Journal of Banking and Finance*, 24.

JP Morgan (2001), "Japan Credit Outlook," November 8.

JP Morgan (2003a), "Effective Nationalization of Resona Group: 'Open Bank Assistance' Limits all Creditors' Risk," May 28.

JP Morgan (2003b), "Banking Industry: Government Decides to Inject Capital Into Resona Holdings," June 11.

JP Morgan (2003c), "Banking industry: Unwinding of Cross-Shareholdings Past Its Peak," July 1.

JP Morgan Securities (2001), "Basel 2 and the Japanese banks," JP Morgan Securities Asia Pte. Ltd., January.

JP Morgan Securities (2002), "Tier III: A Review of Short-Dated Subordinated Capital," JP Morgan Securities Ltd., February 14.

JP Morgan Securities (2003a), "Banks' Heavy Selling Destabilizes the Japanese Government Bond Market – But Banks to Come Back to JGBs," July 25.

JP Morgan Securities (2003b), "Final Stage of NPL Disposal for Japanese Banks – Part I: Resona's Credit to Recover upon Bad Bank Separation," October 15.

JP Morgan Securities (2003c), "Final Stage of NPL Disposal for Japanese Banks – Part II: The Reality – New NPLs Still Building in Japan," October 16.

JP Morgan Securities (2003d), "Final Stage of NPL Disposal for Japanese Banks – Part III: Simulation – Heavy Costs Needed to Cut NPLs in Half," October 20.

Kanda, H. (1998), "Securitisation in Japan," *Duke Journal of Comparative & International Law*, 359.

Kashyap, Anil (2002), "Sorting out Japan's Financial Crisis," NBER Working Paper Series, No. 9384, December.

Kiff, J., and Morrow, R. (2000), "Credit Derivatives," *Bank of Canada Review*, Autumn 2000, pp. 3–11.

Kobayashi, K., Saita, Y., and Sekine, T. (2002), "Forbearance Lending: A Case for Japanese Firms," Working Paper 02-2, Research and Statistics Department, Bank of Japan, April.

Kothari, V. (2003a), "New Basel II proposals for Securitisation," mimeograph.

Kothari, V. (2003b), "Credit derivatives: A primer," mimeograph.

Kupiec, P. (2001), "Is the New Basel Accord Incentive Compatible, IMF Working Paper.

Kupiec, P.H. (2001), "The New Basel Capital Accord: The Devil Is in the (Calibration) Details," IMF Working Paper, WP/01/113, August.

Lackman, C.L. (1986), "The impact of capital adequacy constraints on bank portfolios," *Journal of Business Finance & Accounting*, 13, 4, Winter, pp. 587–596.

McDonough, W.J. (2003), "Implementing the New Basel Accord," speech, Global Association of Risk Professionals, New York, February, 11.

Merrill Lynch (2003), *Credit Derivative Handbook 2003: A Guide to Products, Valuation, Strategies and Risks*, April 16.

Miyauchi, A. (2003), "Designing New Infrastructure for a New Lending Model," Working Paper Series, No. 03-E-1, Bank Examination and Surveillance Department, Bank of Japan, January.

Miwa, Y., and Ramseyer, J.M. (2001), "The Myth of the Main Bank: Japan and Comparative Corporate Governance," Discussion Paper, University of Tokyo, CIRJE-F-131, September.

Montgomery, H. (2001), "The Effect of the Basel Accord on Bank Lending in Japan," mimeograph, The Asian Development Bank Institute, September.

Morgan Stanley (2003a), "Basel 2: the Final Frontier," European Banks, June 4.

Morgan Stanley (2003b), "Basel 2 – Changing the Rules of the Game," *Asia/Pacific Financial Services*, July 15.

Morgan Stanley/Ban (2003c), "Major Banks: Evaluating Revised Financial Revitalization Plans," September 22.

Mori, T., Hiwatashi, J., and Koukichi, I. (2000), "Challenges and Possible Solutions in Enhancing Operational Risk Measurement," Financial and Payment System Office Working Paper, No. 3, Bank of Japan.

Mori, T., and Harada, E. (2001), "Internal Measurement Approach to Operational Risk Capital Charge," Discussion Paper, Bank of Japan.

Mori, T., and Harada, E. (2000), "Internal Risk Based Approach – Evolutionary Approaches to Regulatory Capital Charge for Operational Risk," Financial and Payment System Office Working Paper, No. 2, Bank of Japan.

Myer, N. (2001), "The Basel Capital Reforms: Will More Detail Deliver the Results?" JP Morgan Securities Ltd., August 24.

The National Association of Shinkin Banks (2001), "Comments on the New Basel Capital Accord."

Naisbitt, J. (1984), "Megatrends: Ten new directions transforming our lives," Warner Books.

Neue Zürcher Zeitung (2003), "Basel II – Bedenken sind erlaubt," July 29.

Nihon Keizal Shimbun (2003), "New regulations expected to light fire under banks to eliminate soured loans," August 25.

Nihon Keizai Shimbun, "Megabanks Series," September (Mizuho, September 25; Sumitomo Mitsui, September 26; UFJ, September 27; Mitsubishi Tokyo Financial Group, September 30).

Nihon Keizai Shimbun, Nikkei Net Interactive, Nikkei Weekly, various issues.

Nikkei Net (2003), "Syndicated loans gain appeal amid crunch," April 7.

Nikkei Net (2003), "Increased joint loans reflect banks' need to spread risk," June 2.

Nikkei Net (2003), "Big Banks Strive To Hasten Bad-Loan Disposals," October 27.

Nikko CitiGroup (2003a), "Yen Bond Market Monthly," August 19.

Nikko Citigroup (2003b), "Rethinking the Risk Factors of Major Banks," September 26.

The Norinchukin Bank (2001), "Response to the New Basel Capital Accord."

The Norinchukin Bank (2002), "Comment on the Second Working Paper on Securitisation released by the Basel Committee on Banking Supervision."

The Norinchukin Bank (2003), "The third consultative paper for commercial banks released by the Basel Committee on Banking Supervision (Comment)."

Ohgaki, H. (1997), "Structured Finance Nyumon," (Lectures on Structured Finance), Nihon Keizai Shimbunsha.

Oyama, T., and Shiratori, T. (2001), "Insights into Low Profitability of Japanese Banks: Some Lessons from the Analysis of Trends in Banks' Margins," Discussion Paper Series, No. 01-E-1, Bank of Japan.

Peek, J., and Rosengren, E. (1995a), "Bank regulation and the credit crunch," *Journal of Banking & Finance*, 19, pp. 679–692.

Peek, J., and Rosengren, E. (1995b), "The Capital Crunch: Neither a Borrower nor a Lender Be," *Journal of Money, Credit, and Banking*, 27, 3, pp. 625–638.

Peterson, M. (2001), "Basel gives banks the whip hand," *Euromoney*, March.

Pettway, R.H., Kaneko, T., and Young, M.T. (1991) "International bank capital standards and the costs of issuing capital securities by Japanese banks," *Journal of Banking and Finance*, 15, pp. 559–580.

R&I (2003), "BIS Kisei Minaoshi Daisanji Sichu Gian ni taisuru Comments (Japanese version)," (Comment on the Third Consultative Paper (CP3) of the New Basel Capital Accord (Basel 2)).

Regional Banks Association of Japan (2001), "Comments on the consultative document, The New Basel Capital Accord, of the Basel Committee on Banking Supervision."

Reisen, H. (2001), "Will Basel II Contribute to Convergence in International Capital Flows?" Oesterreichische Nationalbank, 29th Economics Conference.

Risk (2001a), "Basel acts on private equity losses," September.

Risk (2001b), "Basel inflicts collateral damage," October.

Risk (2001c), "Wrestling with Basel II," November.

Risk (2001d), "Balancing belief and science," November.

Risk (2002a), "Swiss and UK banks set to win as Japanese lose in Basel II," January.

Risk (2002b), (2002), "A question of priorities," November.

Risk (2003a), "Japanese banks: Turning up the heat," April.

Risk (2003b), "Japanese banks need to improve op risk management, says BoJ," May.

Risk (2003c), "Basel II: A continental rift," May.

Risk (2003d), "Flies in the ointment," May.

Risk (2003e), "We need a better Basel Accord," May.

Risk (2003f), "Is 8% for all seasons?" May.

Risk (2003g), "A race to the finish," June

The Second Association of Regional Banks (2001), "Comments on a New Basel Capital Accord of Second Consultative Documents issued by the Basel Committee on Banking Supervision."

Sheard, P. (1994), "Bank Executives on Japanese Corporate Boards," Bank of Japan, *Monetary and Economic Studies*, 12, 2, pp. 85–121.

Shimizu, T., Inamura, Y., and Nishizaki, K. (2002), "Recent Efforts for Developing the ABCP Market: Improving Financing Conditions for Small to Medium-sized Enterprises and Exploiting Opportunities for Securitization," *Market Review*, No. 2002-E-2, Financial Markets Department, Bank of Japan, June.

Shinkin Central Bank (2001), "Consultative Document Comments on the New Basel Capital Accord."

Shrieves, E.E., and Dahl, D. (1992), "The relationship between risk and capital in commercial banks," *Journal of Banking and Finance*, 16, pp. 439–457.

Standard & Poor's (2003a), "Banking on the Unknown: Japanese Lenders' Reliance on Deferred tax Assets," July 22.

Standard & Poor's (2003b), "Japanese Banks' Risk Exposure to Rising Interest Rates," August 29.

Sugihara, Y., Hosoya, M., Baba, N., and Nakata, K. (2003), "Shinyo Risk Iten Shijyo no Aratana Tenkai," (New Development on Credit Risk Transfer's Market), Market Review, Bank of Japan.

Sumitomo Mitsui Banking Corporation (2001), "Comments on the second consultative document the New Basel Capital Accord."

Van Rixtel, A.A.R.J.M. (2002), *Informality and Monetary Policy in Japan: The Political Economy of Bank Performance*, Cambridge University Press.

Van Rixtel, A.A.R.J.M., Wiwattanakantang, Y., Souma, T., and Suzuki, K. (2003), "Banking in Japan: Will "Too Big To Fail" Prevail?" in B. Gup (ed.), *Too Big to Fail: Policies and Practices in Government Bailouts*, Praeger, Westport, CT, 2004.

Rodríguez, L.J. (2002), "International Banking Regulation – Where's the Market Discipline in Basel II?" *Policy Analysis*, No. 455.

Shimizu, T., Inamura Y., and Nishizaki, K. (2002), "Recent Efforts for Developing the ABCP Market: Improving Financing Conditions for Small to Medium-sized Enterprises and Exploiting Opportunities for Securitization," *Market Review*, Bank of Japan.

Shinkin Central Bank (2001), "Consultative document – Comments on the New Basel Capital Accord."

Smith, D.C. (2002), "Loans to Japanese borrowers," Pacific Basin Working Paper Series, No. PB02-11, Center for Pacific Basin Monetary and Economic Studies, Federal Reserve Bank of San Francisco, December.

Standard and Poor's (2001), "Standard and Poor's Response to the New Basel Capital Accord."

Spiegel, M. M. (2002), "The Disposition of Failed Japanese Bank Assets: Lessons from the U. S. Savings and Loan Crisis," *FRBSF Economic Review*, 1–15.

Sumitomo Mitsui Banking Corporation (2001), "Comments on the second consultative document: The New Basel Capital Accord."

Thakor, A.V. (1996), "Capital Requirements, Monetary Policy, and Aggregate Bank Lending: Theory and Empirical Evidence," *The Journal of Finance*, 51, 1, March, pp. 279–324.

Wagster, J.D. (1996), "Impact of the 1988 Basle Accord on International Banks," *Journal of Finance*, Vol. 51, 4, 1321–1346.

Wall, L.D., and Peterson, D.R. (1987), "The effect of capital adequacy guidelines on large bank holding companies," *Journal of Banking and Finance*, 11, pp. 581–600.

Yanagisawa, M.P. (2001), "Japan's Financial Sector Reform: Progress and Challenges," Speech at People's University.

ABOUT THE AUTHORS

Ioana Alexopoulou is an economist statistician at the European Central Bank. Her research includes work on implied volatility, credit risk, and the corporate bond market. She is a graduate of Birkbeck College, University of London. Her current work involves the investigation of what information can be extracted from different volatility measures.

Ben Branch is a professor of finance at the Isenberg School of Management of the University of Massachusetts. Since 1991, he has served as the Chapter 7 bankruptcy trustee for the Bank of New England. Since 2001, he has also served as manager of VFB, the limited liability corporation for the estate of Vlasic Pickle International. Prof. Branch is the author or co-author of numerous articles and books, including *Bankruptcy Investing*.

Christine Brown is an associate professor in the Department of Finance at the University of Melbourne (Australia). Originally trained as a mathematician, she teaches in the areas of risk management, corporate finance, and financial institutions management. Her current research interests include pricing of derivative securities and the efficiency of the markets in which they trade, financial institutions management, dividends and option pricing, and real options. She is co-author of *Management of Financial Institutions*.

Kevin Davis is the Commonwealth Bank Group Chair of Finance in the Department of Finance, Faculty of Economics and Commerce, at the University of Melbourne (Australia). He was head of the Department of Accounting and Finance from January 1997 to February 2000 and was responsible for the introduction of the Masters of Applied Finance degree in 1994. His research interests include financial markets and instruments, financial institutions management, financial engineering, corporate finance, and valuation. He is the author or co-author of numerous books and journal articles. In 2003, he was appointed by the treasurer of Australia to lead a study of financial system guarantees. Prof. Davis will be supported by a study team comprising officials from the Department of the Treasury, the Reserve Bank of Australia, and the Australian Prudential Regulation Authority.

Peter Docherty is a lecturer at the University of Technology, Sydney. He holds master's and Ph.D. degrees in monetary economics and the history of economic thought from the University of Sydney. He has taught at the University of Sydney and the University of New South Wales, and currently teaches at the University of Technology, Sydney. His research interests include monetary economics, banking, and the history of economics, and he is currently completing a book on endogenous money macro models.

Benton E. Gup holds the Robert Hunt Cochrane-Alabama Bankers Association Chair of Banking at the University of Alabama. He also has held banking chairs at the University of Tulsa and the University of Virginia. Dr. Gup is the author or editor of 22 books and more than 90 articles about banking and financial topics. He has served as a consultant to government and industry, and he has a Ph.D. from the University of Cincinnati.

Kimie Harada is a professor at Daito Bunka University, Tokyo. Her research interests are the Japanese economy, particularly banking, corporate governance, and financial crisis. She obtained her doctorate from the University of Tokyo in 2003. Her papers, with Takatoshi Ito, include "Market Evaluations of Banking Fragility in Japan: Japan Premium, Stock Prices and Credit Derivatives," (NBER Working Paper No. 9589), and "Japan Premium and Stock Prices: Two Mirrors of Japanese Banking Crises," (NBER Working Paper No. 7997).

Kevin T. Jacques is a senior financial economist in the Office of Financial Institutions Policy at the U.S. Treasury Department. He is responsible for advising senior Treasury and Administration officials on issues including the revised Basel Accord. In addition, he is an adjunct professor of finance at Georgetown University. His research has appeared in numerous journals. Prior to joining the Treasury Department, he was an assistant professor of economics at John Carroll University and a senior financial economist at the Office of the Comptroller of the Currency. Dr. Jacques received his Ph.D. in economics from Michigan State University and his B.B.A. and M.A. in economics from Kent State University.

George G. Kaufman is the John J. Smith Professor of Finance and Economics at Loyola University in Chicago, co-chair of the Shadow Financial Regulatory Committee, and a consultant to the Federal Reserve Bank of Chicago. He also serves as a consultant to various government agencies and to industry. Dr. Kaufman has an extensive list of textbooks, monographs, and articles dealing with financial economics, institutions, markets, and regulation.

Júlia Király received her Ph.D. in economics from the Budapest University of Economics, where she is a Fellow Lecturer. She is the academic director and CEO of the International Training Center for Bankers (Hungary), a private consulting/training company. In 2002, she was appointed president of Postabank in Budapest (the second largest Hungarian retail bank) and prepared the bank for privatization (Postabank was sold this September for 400M Euro, 2.7 book value to the Erstebank ÖAG). Dr. Király has several textbooks published for the International Training Center for Bankers and the Budapest University of Economics, and has published extensively in academic professional journals, including those of the World Bank.

Paul H. Kupiec is the Associate Director of FDIC's Division of Insurance and Research and Co-Director of FDIC Center for Financial Research. His former positions include Deputy Chief of the Banking Supervision and Regulation Division in the Monetary and Exchange Affairs Department of the International Monetary Fund, director in financial research at Freddie Mac, Vice President at J.P. Morgan, and Senior Economist at the Federal Reserve Board. He has also served as a visiting Economist at the Bank for International Settlements. His published works appear primarily in professional risk management and academic finance journals. Dr. Kupiec received a Ph.D. in Economics from the University of Pennsylvania.

Katalin Mérő is deputy head of the Banking Department, National Bank of Hungary. She is responsible for analyzing the systemic risk in the Hungarian financial intermediary system and editing the semi-annual report on financial stability of the NBH. Previously, she was director of strategy and economic analysis at K&H, a large Hungarian commercial bank. Prior to her banking career, she worked as a researcher at the Economic Research Institute and the Research Institute for Labour.

Pipat Luengnaruemitchai is a graduate student researcher in the Department of Economics, University of California, Berkley. His fields of specialization include international finance, money and banking, and macroeconomics. The title of his dissertation is "Essays in International Finance."

Marc R. Saidenberg is an assistant vice president at the Federal Reserve Bank of New York in the Risk Management Function in Bank Supervision. He represents the Federal Reserve Bank of New York on the Basel Committee's Models Task Force and other working groups. These groups have developed the internal ratings-based approaches for credit risk and other aspects of the proposed new Basel Capital Accord. He has published articles on bank regulation, credit risk modeling, and agency problems in banking. Dr. Saidenberg joined the bank in September 1995 and received his Ph.D. in economics from the University of California at Berkeley.

David C. Schrim is chairperson, Department of Economics and Finance at John Carroll University. He has broad interest in teaching and research in financial economics. His research has been published in leading academic journals. He is also co-editor of *Global Portfolio Diversification*, Academic Press, 1995. Dr. Schrim received his Ph.D. from Penn State University, M.A. from Duke University, and B.A. from Thiel College.

Til Schuermann is a senior economist at the Federal Reserve Bank of New York's Research Department, where he focuses on risk measurement and management in financial institutions and capital markets. He is also a Sloan Research Fellow at the Wharton Financial Institution Center. Prior to joining the New York Fed in May 2001, he spent five years at the management consulting firm Oliver, Wyman & Company, where he was a director and head of research. Dr. Schuermann has numerous publications in the area of risk modeling and applied econometrics and has edited the book, *Simulation-Based Inference in Econometrics*. He received his Ph.D. in economics in 1993 from the University of Pennsylvania.

Chris Terry is an associate professor and head of the School of Finance and Economics at the University of Technology, Sydney. He was awarded his doctorate from New York University in 1975, the year in which he joined the New South Wales Institute of Technology, which became the University of Technology, Sydney. He was head of the Economics Department from 1983 to 1986, head of the School of Finance and Economics from 1987 to 1989, and associate dean (postgraduate programs and research) in 1994 and 1995.

Rowan Trayler is a senior lecturer in the School of Finance and Economics at the University of Technology, Sydney. Prior to joining the faculty at the University of Technology in1987, he worked for 16 years in the finance industry, including 11 years at Barclays Bank Australia Ltd. Since joining the University of Technology, he has been involved in the development of the master of business in finance program, lecturing at both the postgraduate and undergraduate level in banking and finance.

Adrian van Rixtel is a senior economist in the Directorate Monetary Policy of the European Central Bank. From September to November 2003, he was a visiting associate professor, Center for Economic Institutions, Institute of Economic Research, Hitotsubashi University, Tokyo. Previously, he held positions at the Monetary and Economic Policy Department of De Nederlandsche Bank (Netherlands Central Bank) and private financial institutions both in London and Amsterdam. Dr. van Rixtel earned his Ph.D. at the Tinbergen Institute, Free University Amsterdam, the Netherlands. He has extensive experience covering Asian economies, in particular the Japanese economy, and held visiting scholar positions at the Bank of Japan and Ministry of Finance. His research on Japan has been published in various articles and books and discussed in publications such as *The Economist* and *The Wall Street Journal.*

James A. Wilcox is the Kruttschnitt Professor of Financial Institutions at the Haas School of Business at the University of California, Berkeley. His articles have been published in the *American Economic Review*, the *Journal of Finance*, the *Journal of Economic Perspectives*, the *Journal of Money, Credit and Banking*, the *Journal of Banking and Finance*, the *Journal of Housing Economics*, the *Review of Economics and Statistics*, and elsewhere. From 1999 to 2001, he was the chief economist at the Office of the Comptroller of the Currency. He has also served as the senior economist for monetary policy and macroeconomics for the President's Council of Economic Advisers and as an economist for the Board of Governors of the Federal Reserve System.

INDEX